Plate I: *Frontispiece — see details of cover photograph*

Bonsai

Its Art, Science, History and Philosophy

Written and Illustrated by
Deborah R. Koreshoff

First published in 1984
by Boolarong Publications, Brisbane, Australia.
Reprinted in 1985.
Reprinted in 1986.
Reprinted in 1987.

American edition:
by Timber Press, Portland, Oregon.

English edition:
by Croom Helm, London.

M   South African edition:
Macmillan South Africa, Johannesburg.

Copyright © Deborah Koreshoff *4-88 Publ 4000*

Cataloguing-in-Publication data:
National Library of Australia

Koreshoff, Deborah R.
  Bonsai, its art, science, history and philosopy.

  Simultaneously published: London: Croom Helm; Portland, Oregon:
  Timber Press; Johannesburg: Macmillan South Africa Pty Ltd.

  Includes index.
  ISBN 908175 75 2
  1. Bonsai. I. Title
635.9'772

British Library
Koreshoff, Deborah
  Bonsai — its art, science, history and philosophy.
  1. Bonsai
  I. Title
  635.9'77 SB 433.5

ISBN 0-7099-1556-X

American Library
ISBN 0-917304-68-3

South African Library
ISBN 0 86954 200 1

Boolarong Publications
24 Little Edward Street, Spring Hill, Brisbane. Qld.

Design, colour reproduction and photo-typesetting by
Press Etching Pty. Ltd., Brisbane.

Printed by James Ferguson Pty. Ltd., Brisbane.

Bound by Podlich Enterprises Pty. Ltd., Brisbane.

Cover and Frontispiece:

"Dragon Flying through the Clouds"
Japanese Black Pine, *Pinus thunbergii*
Height: 49 cm, Japanese Handmade Pot
Grown by my father from seed in 1951, trained since 1951
Photograph taken in 1982

Although all the Bonsai photographed in the text of this book are from my own collection and have been shaped by me, I have chosen one of my father's pines for the cover photo and the frontispiece.

The idea of using the same tree for both photos was suggested by my father with the view of displaying Bonsai both in its usual containerized form and as we see the tree in the landscape of our imagination.

This Japanese Black Pine, grown from seed in 1951 and planted on the rock in 1956 typifies the subtlety and suggestiveness of Bonsai Art. The more we look into the beautiful form the more the tree has to tell us.

My parents have called this pine "Dragon Flying Through The Clouds" for in the scaly bark and the twisting and turning trunk we see the dragon as he flies through the swirling clouds of mist. There is a beautiful passage written by Okakura Kakuzo that describes the dragon as he is seen in nature for brief moments . . .

Hidden in the caverns of inaccessible mountains, the dragon awaits the time when he slowly rouses himself to activity. He unfolds himself in the storm clouds; he washes his mane in the blackness of the seething whirlpools. His claws are in the forks of the lightning, his scales begin to glisten in the bark of rain-swept pine trees. His voice is heard in the hurricane which, scattering the withered leaves of the forest, quickens the new spring.
The dragon reveals himself, only to vanish.

PHOTOGRAPHY BY PENNY WRIGHT
I wish to thank Penny Wright very much for the beautiful photography in this book. Just as Bonsai is an Art, so does it take an Artist in Photography to capture a tree's beauty and its mood.

This book is dedicated with respect
and very much love to my parents
Vitaliy and Dorothy Koreshoff.

My father, being born in Manchuria in 1909
learnt bonsai, as a young boy, from an old
Chinese gardener. His wisdom, artistry and
quiet love for trees was later passed on to my
mother.
I can't express how valuable their guidance has
been, and continues to be . . .
Most of all they have taught me to recognize
the signs of Nature and to respect the wisdom
embodied there and in our own hearts.

To see a world in a grain of sand
And a heaven in a wild flower,
Hold infinity in the palm of your hand
And eternity in an hour.

William Blake.

Foreword

This book is intended to give you correct and practical information of the Art of Bonsai. It aims to look at the subject of bonsai from many viewpoints. The horticultural and artistic sides take up the greater portion of the book, however, the reader is also presented with some knowledge of the historical and philosophical aspects of the art.

The practice of growing bonsai has evolved gradually through the centuries, and as the years go by more and more people are turning their leisure hours to the creation, care and appreciation of these living works of art. It is unique in the gardening world as in no other garden hobby does the grower become so fond of his plants or put so much of himself into them. They very soon become like additional members of the family to the dedicated enthusiast. Bonsai has been described — and rightly so — as horticulture in its highest and most refined form. Likewise, bonsai is unique in the world of Art. It is an artform in which the work is never completed due to the fact that the medium is alive and growing constantly. Bonsai growers do not endeavour to stop the growth of trees but to direct their growth in much the same way as Western gardeners direct the growth of trees and bushes to form hedges. This fact makes bonsai the only art form to use four dimensions instead of two or three. To the bonsai grower, time can be a friend, as year by year our artistic creations become more refined and signs of age bring added beauty to our tree's design.

Also, in this age of synthetic materials, mass production, disposable goods and speed, most people long for some closer contact with Nature. With bonsai we can lose ourselves in a dense forest, or woodland glade, feel exhilarated at the sight of a tree cascading gracefully over a sheer ravine or appreciate a single aged tree with individual beauty . . . all in an area of one or two feet square . . .

In short, it would be hard to find a hobby as fascinating as this ancient Art of Bonsai.

Contents

List of Photographic Plates

List of Figures

All sketches by the author

Plate II: *Topiary garden in Bangkok, Thailand.*

Plate III: *Trees shaped in a formal oriental garden. Garden of Mr. S. Tanaka, Kyoto. In* Gardening The Japanese Way, *by Sima Eliovson, A.H. & A.W. Reed Ltd. 1970*

CHAPTER ONE

"An Introduction to the Art of Bonsai"

Historical Background of Bonsai

If a man could say nothing . . . but what he can prove,
history could not be written.
Dr. Johnson

Nowdays the hobby of bonsai is fairly well known and practiced in many countries throughout the world. Yet, as it becomes more widespread, its true origins are tending to be forgotten. It is a hobby that has been introduced to the Western World through Japan and it is for this reason that many people consider it to be originally a Japanese Art. This is not so. Bonsai is a relatively recent Art in Japan and did, in fact, originate in China.

There is no single date existing where we can say conclusively — "this is when bonsai began". Like most art forms and most things generally, it evolved slowly but steadily into its present form. The beginnings are hazy but nevertheless it is interesting to look back at what we do know about the thoughts and practices of mankind in times past.

As mentioned above, bonsai originated in China, probably as an amalgamation of various interests. Firstly, considering the horticultural side of bonsai, man found long ago that he could more easily transport container-grown plants as well as the fact that he could obtain more perfect control over the production of flowers and fruit. In China these purely functional reasons for growing container plants were highly important as different plants were associated with various ceremonies and customs throughout the Chinese year. At the Lunar New Year, for example, it was proper to display a flowering apricot in your home. Having the plants easily transportable and making sure that the flowers coincided with the desired date was thus of extreme importance.

Other civilizations besides the Chinese have grown container plants since antiquity for similarly functional (rather than aesthetic) reasons. Records indicate that the Ancient Greeks and Romans did, as well as the Babylonians, Persians, Hindus, Egyptians and men of ancient Europe. The idea of keeping plants in containers may have originated when man had to move his home for one reason or another. Gradually, it was found that with good soil and fertilizing, trees could be kept for quite a long time under such conditions.

In Egypt we have pictorial records showing us that trees were grown in "pots" cut into rock, about 4000 years ago. Interesting examples are seen in the temples of Neb-hepet Rē' Mentu-hotpe (2061–2010 B.C.) and Hatshepsūt (1520–1479 B.C.) at Deir el-Bahri near Thebes. In one temple illustration, we see Frankincense trees being transported in pots from Punt on the Somali Coast to Egypt for Queen Hatshepsūt's formal garden villa[1]. The fact that this undertaking was recorded in art indicates that men of antiquity thought of this project as one of great importance.

Records also tell us that Pharoah Rameses III donated 514 gardens to temples. These gardens were made up of potted olives, date palms, lotus, rushes, lilies and grasses[2]. While the growing of these container plants is partly ornamental, it is only in the sense that an indoor plant is ornamental. They were, in fact, largely functional as they were grown for fruit, herbs and medicine.

Another example of early container growing of trees for similarly functional reasons is found in India. Following is an excerpt from an article by a past president of India[3]:

The Japanese claim to be the originators but thousands of years before the art-loving Japanese stumbled upon their bonsai, the Science of Dwarfing Trees for an altogether different purpose was known in ancient India as "Vaamantanu Vrikshaadi Vidya" (Vaaman-dwarfed, tanu-body, Vrikshaadi-of trees and Vidya-science), the science of dwarfing trees. Whilst the Japanese look upon bonsai as only a decorative art, the science of dwarfing giant trees was a very important part not only of ancient Hindu botany, but also of ancient Hindu science of healing the sick. The Ayurvedic Physicians of ancient India used hundreds of jungle trees like the Banyan, the Peepul, the Tamarind, the Neem, the Acacia, etc. for the purpose of curing human ailments. Five parts of these trees (Panchaanga) viz. root, flower, bark, leaf and fruit, were extensively used in Ayervedic medication.

The Ancient Hindus, who had an empire covering the globe, lived in different climatic conditions varying from arid and sandy deserts to luxuriant and evergreen forests. Under such varying conditions of life it was not possible for the Ayervedic physicians, particularly for those living away from natural forests, to obtain the panchaangas (i.e. the five parts) of giant trees situated hundreds of miles away, at a minute's notice. For medical emergencies, they had to have the forest giants in their backyards! It was this medical necessity which made the ancient Hindu botanists tame nature to suit the mood and the need of man. They had to grow the Banyan and the Peepul, the Babul and the Neem and a hundred other giants of the jungle in their backyards to get the five medicinal parts fresh and when required. The giant had to bend down and be a dwarf to meet the eye and the need of man. Thousands of giant trees were therefore dwarfed and taught to live a hundred years in little pots filled with the soil each tree needed to thrive. They were healthy and vigorous trees consistently under training to remain miniature in stature and mighty in other respects.

The writer of the above article suggests that this is, in fact, the beginnings of bonsai. However, while practices such as those related may have influenced the starting of the art of bonsai, the main reasons for the growing of such container plants seem to be associated with medicine and food rather than for any appreciation of form and beauty.

Returning to the development of bonsai in China, we find similarly functional and purely horticultural developments in the art of growing containerized plants. One day, though, in the distant past, a naturally stunted and aged tree was spotted growing in a narrow crevice high up on the side of a cliff. The tree that had been designed by Nature had so much character and beauty that the person wished to have it close by so that he could view it whenever he desired. Using the techniques already learned for keeping trees healthy in containers, the tree was uprooted and replanted in an attractive ceramic pot and placed in his garden courtyard. At this point the small tree in the pot was being appreciated for something other than its ceremonial value or functional value (for food etc.). It was now appreciated for its form and aesthetic quality.

Another idea regarding the development of bonsai in China is that it was an extension of the Art of Garden Planning[4]. Garden planning, we are told, was a well developed art many centuries ago — as early as the dynasties of Hsia, Shang and Chou (c.a. 2205 B.C.–255 B.C.) (N.B. See Chronological Table of Dynasties at end of Historical Section). Documented examples of work accomplished in those dynasties are: the Yow Terrace, built by King Jiek of Hsia, the Luk Terrace, of King Jow of Shang and the Ling Terrace and Ling Pond of King Wen of Chou. The plants in these gardens were not left to grow wildly but were trimmed to conform with the artistic layout of the garden.

This practice can be compared to the Western Art of "Topiary" — that is, the trimming of garden plants into formal geometrical shapes or realistic sculptural forms, such as chessmen or animals (see Plate II). As far as we know, topiary was invented in ancient times by a friend of the Roman Emperor Augustus and there are definite records that it was practiced in the first century A.D. In the writings of Pliny the Younger a terrace of topiary is described as being *embellished with various figures and bounded with a box hedge, from whence you descend by an easy slope, adorned with the representation of divers animals in box, answering alternately to each other.* Cypress and boxwood were the main tree materials used for topiary in ancient Rome[5].

In England, topiary reached its highest and most elaborate forms in the 16th and 17th centuries, the favoured tree being the Yew. The oldest garden of topiary still existing is "Levin's Hall" in Westmorland, North England. This garden was begun in approximately 1730. The art of topiary, however, fell out of fashion in the 18th century with the preference for "Naturalism". Alexander Pope satirically describes a gardener who put up for sale, *Noah's Ark in holly, the ribs a little damaged for want of water*[6].

It is interesting to compare Western Topiary with the Chinese way of trimming garden trees. It can be argued that both practices produce artificial results, yet the style and general feeling of a Chinese garden is entirely different (see Plate III).

When we view an example of topiary, what we see first is a mass of foliage — foliage is the form. When we view the Chinese style shaped tree, we see first the shape and design of trunk and branches. Foliage is only there to accentuate this design. Also, topiary is more likely to be symmetrical in form and Chinese shaping assymmetrical.

Such cultural differences extend throughout the arts. Comparing the landscape paintings of both Western and Oriental artists can be an interesting exercise, as it points out many of the reasons why some Western bonsai enthusiasts find it difficult to create bonsai styles and tend to prefer the bushy potted tree (see Plates IV and V).

In the Western landscape, first of all, the artist tends to fill in as much detail as possible onto the canvas, while the Oriental landscape is characterized by a large proportion of empty space and economy of expression. With just a few brushstrokes a tree and a cliff may be portrayed, while the rest of the area is left empty. The Oriental art forms are typified by understatement. The viewer is not shown everything and consequently must participate by using his own imagination.

Another difference between the paintings of the two cultures may be seen in their use of colour. The Western artist, in the majority of cases, uses rich and varied colours, giving the viewer a feeling of opulence and idyllic serenity. The Oriental artist, on the other hand, frequently works in monochrome and the pictures give one a feeling of frugality and with the economy of calligraphy the essentials of life are conveyed.

Yet another difference, as suggested above in reference to topiary, is in the Western preference for symmetry, uniformity and order. Trees are usually serene field-grown trees with masses of foliage. The Oriental artist works with assymmetrical balance and with simplicity in tree design. There is far less foliage than in the Western counterpart, in fact, it is only highlighting trunk and branches.

As time passed, rocks were brought into the gardens to supplement the arrangement and the effect was that of a large mountain or rocky landscape brought down to the scale of a backyard garden. In the ancient writings of the Han dynasty (206 B.C.–221 A.D.), many such gardens are mentioned. Some of these gardens, however, were not so small as we may think. In the garden of Yuen Kwang-han, for example, there were artificial rock hills of 200 feet high[7].

Related to the idea of creating natural settings on a small scale, we find that there is an interesting legend during the East Han dynasty (25–221 A.D.) of a magician called Fei Jiang-feng, who could collect within an urn, mountains and trees as well as buildings and living creatures[8]. If we consider that legend is usually based on some material fact, it certainly seems possible that this magician could have been the first cultivator of miniature trees. Also, the fact that he was considered a magician is not surprising, since it is only recently, in the past four decades or so, that the concept of bonsai as a secretive, half magical and "unnatural" art, has been dispelled.

In the Tang dynasty (618–907) we find that the idea is developed of rock landscapes being brought further down in scale from garden size to container size. In the corridor of the tomb of the Tang Prince Chang Huai in Chien Ling, Shensi, there is a wall painting depicting two maid servants holding artistic pot plants. In one poem by Tu Fu (an important poet of the Tang dynasty) a rock landscape is described which has been reduced to the size of one cubic foot. Another poet of the same dynasty, Pee Yat-yau, also describes a miniature rock landscape.

In the writings of the Sung dynasty (960–1280) (e.g. So Suen, Chao Hsi-kok) further mention is made of artificial and miniaturized rock and tree landscapes and from this we can gather that the interest is becoming more widespread. It was, however, an interest that only the wealthy could indulge in.

The name used to refer to miniature trees and landscapes has undergone many changes. During the Tsin dynasty (265–420), the name "pun-sai" or "pen-sai" was used to refer to pot plants. In that same dynasty, pot plant cultivation was becoming a popular hobby as we read that Tou Yuen-ming (365–427), a government official as well as a poet and essayist, resigned from office to lead a quiet life on the land and grow chrysanthemums in pots.

Just as the miniature rock landscapes fascinated the people of the Tang dynasty, so did potted trees become more popular in this period. Wang Wei (699–759), a gifted poet and painter of the time grew orchids in a yellow pot — decorating the soil surface with white pebbles. Wang Wei is regarded as the founder of the Southern School of Landscape painting (called "Nanga" in Japan). Such paintings were made by literati or scholarly men and were characterized by subtle monochromatic designs and the poignant simplicity of calligraphy.

Paintings of the Tang and Sung dynasties also feature plants cultivated in pots. The varieties that seem to have been popular are the pine, cypress, plum, orchid, chrysanthemum and bamboo. Pot plants are also mentioned often in the poetry and prose of this period. During the Tang and Sung dynasties, pot plants were called "pun-wan" and in the following Yuan dynasty (1280–1368) they were called "shea tzu ching". In these developments of potted tree culture, figurines and landscape were often added to the arrangement.

Finally, in the late Ming (1368–1644) and early Ching (1644–1911) dynasties, "pun-ching" was used to refer to pot plants with landscape. Many books were written about "artistic pot plants" in the Sung, Ming and Ching dynasties.

In the periods "Kang-Hsi" to "Chia-ching" (1662–1821) in the Ching dynasty, China was prosperous and peaceful. Consequently, many people from all areas practiced the art of growing miniature trees[9]. In 1688 the hobby was called pen-tsuai (that is, the Chinese characters for "bon-sai") in a book on general botany: "Pi-chuan Hua-ching". The word was used as a verb meaning "to plant into pot"[10].

From this growth of interest, many different styles emerged from various geographical locations. There was the "Pagoda Style" from Yangchow, the "Earthworm Style" from Szechuen, the "Dancing Dragon Style" of Anhwei, the "Three-winding Style" of the North, the "Flat-top Style" of Hunan and Hupeh, and the "Five-tree Style" of Kwang-tung. Also, at the end of the Ching dynasty the vogue was to train trees into auspicious Chinese characters[11]. (see Figure 1)

Figure 1: *Tree trained in form of auspicious Chinese character*

Figure 2: *Map of China*

These unusual styles, however, gradually died out.

All these developments just related are the "roots" of what we now refer to as "bonsai" (and which the Chinese call "punsai" or "pensai" to refer to trees without landscape). But the plants were, for the most part, just trees planted in pots and not bonsai (bonsai must be "shaped" to represent an aged tree with character).

The final development took place toward the end of the Ching dynasty and the beginning of the Republic of China, that is, about 1900. It was at this time that cultivation of potted trees in a monastery in the Kwang-tung province began to use the "Clip and Grow" method of training — a method that produces effects similar to the Chinese brush paintings (see Plates VI and VII).

This practice, which came to be known as the "Lingan School", consequently turned pot-plants into works of art[12].

Figure 3: *Example of tree trained by Lingnan "Clip and Grow" Method*

There are some interesting reports of bonsai practice in mainland China in present times[13]. Quite definite differences exist between the north and the south. In the south, around Canton, many rockeries may be seen and landscape settings in containers are a common sight. The rocks are mainly formations chosen from limestone areas and are called "karst". They are mostly silexite or stalactite that has been sawn and then glued together to form interesting arrangements. The climate in the south of China is fairly humid and therefore suitable for rock plantings. In the north, around Peking, more of the species suitable for colder climates, such as pines, maples and junipers are used and the foliage is often trimmed in a style similar to a "poodle-cut".

Today, the centres for bonsai are around Canton and Shanghai. "East Park" Canton is a commercial bonsai area and it is in surrounding areas that bonsai are produced and exhibited on a wide scale. The Shanghai Botanical Garden is also a very important bonsai area as the surviving bonsai that were given to China as a gift from Japan in 1928 are displayed here as well as those made in China.

An interesting variation to the usual type of bonsai may be seen in the Long Hua Botanic Garden that is located on the outskirts of Shanghai. As well as a large collection of bonsai planted in ceramic and stone containers, the west-facing gable wall of a building is adorned with "bonsai plaques". They are described in the "Journal of The British Royal Horticultural Society" thus[14]:

> The plaques *had been made by painting shallow trays or dishes and then affixing to them, with cement, several pieces of rock to form miniature landscapes. Pockets and crevices in the rocks were then filled with soil and planted with seedling trees and shrubs etc. The plaques I was shown were three years planted and contained, amongst other plants, Serissa serissoides, Ulmus parvifolia, Pinus thunbergii, Podocarpus macrophylla var. nakii and a tiny Sedum sp., like S. dasyphyllum.*

The bonsai gardener, Mr Wang, believed these plaques were the only examples of this type of cultivation in China.

In May 1978, the Yuk Sui Yuen Bonsai Exhibition was held in Canton — the first public show for ten years. Apparently the "Gang of Four" had stopped the displaying of bonsai in the recent past, but now the exhibit is planned to be an annual event. The show in 1978 included about 250 trees from private collections.

Now, for the moment, we will leave the subject of bonsai in China and turn our attention to its development in Japan. One of the major influences on Japanese bonsai is the bonsai of China. In fact, Chinese culture and art has always had a strong influence on the Japanese. Even as early as the Chin dynasty (221–206 B.C.), Japan was having contact with China, as we read that a Chinese magician Hsu Fu was sent by the meglomaniac emperor to Japan in a quest for the Elixir of Life. A little later, in the Han dynasty, the emperor Kwang Wu conferred an honour upon the Japanese King and Japanese ministers consequently visited China to pay tributes to the Emperor[15].

Also, in the Southern dynasties (420–585), the Sui dynasty (589–618) and the Tang, Japan sent envoys to China specifically to learn Chinese culture[16].

In the sixth century, Buddhism was brought to Japan. It was first introduced from China via Korea and then later influences came direct from China in the form of Ch'an Buddhism. As many of the buddhist priests were also bonsai or miniature potted plant enthusiasts, it is conceivable that word about bonsai would have been filtering into Japan at this time.

One writer[17], mentions that by the tenth century, bonsai was mentioned in Japanese history and that other writings of the time describe the collecting of dwarfed trees in nature. The writer also says that illustrations exist of an even earlier period. These statements, however, are not documented and most references agree that one of the first authentic records of bonsai or miniature potted trees in Japan is seen in the "Saigyō Monogatari Emaki", a picture scroll dated 1195. The scroll depicts the life of Saigyō, a priest who was also a member of the higher class. A potted plant is pictured in the scroll and we are told that Saigyō considered the hobby as a status symbol. The scroll is also supposed to be strongly influenced by contemporary techniques in China[18].

Other writers consider that the introduction of potted tree culture in Japan was during the Yuan dynasty, when Japanese ministers, merchants and students visited China and learned much of Chinese culture. Many writers document that the first record of miniature potted trees in Japan is in the "Kasuga-gongen-genki", a picture scroll by Takashina Takakane (1309). The "Kasuga-gongen-genki" illustrates the miracles after prayers were offered at the Kasuga Shrine at Nara and also the main events in the life of the Buddhist priest Honen Shonin (1133–1212) — founder of the Jodo sect of Buddhism and a keen bonsai enthusiast. It is interesting to note that while the scroll was completed in 1309, it illustrates life in the Heian period (794–1191) and this suggests that bonsai may have existed before the time of the scroll.

Another early reference is found in the famous "Tsurezure-gusa" or "Gleanings from my Leisure Hours" — a two volume collection of essays by Kenko Yoshida (1283–1351) and written in 1331. He writes, *To appreciate and find pleasure in curiously curved potted trees is to love deformity.* Other writers, close to this time, apparently held similar views. This suggests that the styles mostly favoured by the upper classes in the Kamakura period (1180–1333) were grotesque and unnatural. It may be noted that before and during the Kamakura period, the ideas and techniques associated with the Art of the Japanese Garden were quite advanced, however, the training of trees was largely in grotesque styles.

In the Muromachi period (1338–1573), bonsai or potted trees are mentioned in the famous Noh play "Hachi-no-ki" or "The Potted Trees" by Seam (1363–1443). In the play, a poor samurai burns his potted trees to warm his guest Tokiyori — who is a shogun travelling incognito. While the play was written in the Muromachi period, it concerns the life of Tokiyori Hojo who lived in the years 1227–1263. The play thus indicates the potted tree culture from the Kamakura period and also tells us that the pine was one of the trees appreciated at that time. This is interesting for it shows that form was valued, not just the beauty of flowers or coloured foliage. The value of the pine, however, could also be due to the fact that it is a symbol of longevity in the Orient.

In the Muromachi period that followed the Kamakura, much progress was made in different arts and crafts, despite the fact that it was an unsettled time of wars and rival warlords. Perhaps one of the reasons why advancements in the arts were made was that the populace needed some form of relaxation. The Tea Ceremony style was then developed and much progress was being made in the fields of ceramics, painting, architecture, landscaping and floral art.

In the early Muromachi period, dwarf trees were collected and potted, but training techniques had not progressed far. The so-called "Tako" or "Octopus" style was fashionable — in fact, this styling technique was popular right up to the beginning of the 20th century (the style was called "Horai" in China). In this style the trunk and branches are excessively curved in a tortuous-looking way. The curves are usually too regular and too exaggerated. As far as size was concerned, the potted trees of the Muromachi period were generally large[19].

Another direct influence from China can be traced back to the end of the Chinese Ming dynasty, when a government official called Chu Shu-sui, objecting to serve under the Manchu rulers of the Ching dynasty, escaped to Japan and introduced there many Chinese arts as well as the growing of potted trees[20]. Such direct influences from China would have affected the techniques and styles in Japan, considerably.

Following this turbulent era was the Tokugawa or Edo period (1603–1867), a long and peaceful time under feudal government, in which all forms of art and craft developed greatly and became popularized. It is also in this time, in the latter half of the 17th and early 18th centuries, that gardening and landscape gardening reached its greatest stage of development — many wonderful garden varieties of plants being developed or improved and new techniques and skills learned.

In a certain print produced in the Tokugawa era, we see a contemporary bonsai nursery. The artist is Kiyoharu — a noted Ukiyoe artist and the nursery depicted belongs to Ibei Ito (the print is owned by Kan Yashiroda)[21]. The interesting point here, is the fact that the print depicts bonsai varied in both species and style and also the fact that no Tako-trained bonsai are illustrated. All the trees, however, are planted in deep containers.

According to Yoshimura[22], in the early 1800's, a group of Japanese scholars of the Chinese classics as well as poets and artists, met in Itami City (near Osaka), to discuss the recent styles in potted trees. It is also thought that at this time they decided to call artistic potted trees "bon-sai".

At this same time, many nurseries were set up in the Azakusa Park suburb of Tokyo. This was a strong influence in the growth of popularity of the hobby, but in the many garden shops that existed there in the second quarter of the 19th century (particularly around 1829), the main style was Tako-tsukuri, so it did not do much to improve potted tree styling.

In the Temo period (1830–1844), even more of the common public were becoming interested in bonsai, coupled with the fact that Japanese of many different classes and occupations were travelling and/or studying in China.

Shinobu Nozaki (who wrote the first book on bonsai in the English language), tells us that in the years 1829–1853 the study of shaping bonsai is still in a rudimentary stage. The main varieties used are the silver-needled goyo-matsu (Japanese Five-needle Pine), the Japanese Apricot (both young and old trees), the Flowering Cherry, Kaido (Aronia) and Oranges of various kinds[23].

In 1854–1867 there was not much improvement in styling as it was essentially a period of political unrest and internal strife. The main varieties are the silver-needled goyo-matsu and the Camellia[24].

Many books on trees and gardening were published during the Tokugawa period. One of the oldest books on the subject of horticulture was published about 280 years ago. It is called the "Kadan Komuku" or "An Outline of Flower Gardens" and lists flowers, grasses and flowering trees suitable for the four seasons of the year. Other books specializing in certain types of trees indicate that in the Tokugawa period the prime interest was in flowering trees and plants. It is also of interest that books of the Tokugawa period use the word "Hachi-ue", not "bon-sai", to refer to miniature potted trees. In fact, the word "bon-sai" is not in the common usage of the people at this time.

In the "Kinsei-jufu", published in 1830, containers of various shapes and depths are illustrated. Other gardening books published in the 20's and 30's show that the main feature of the age is the growing of dwarf conifers and variegated or fancy-leaved varieties of trees and shrubs — all in bright containers. In the Bunka and Bunsei eras (1804–1829), the interest changed from flowering trees to fancy-leaved trees. For most enthusiasts, the shape of the plant was not so important. The vogue was for anything unusual or novel and such plants commanded a high price. At this time, the styling of trees as seen in "Modern" bonsai, was practiced more in landscape gardening than in containers.

A small group of growers, as indicated by the group that met at Itami City and Ibei Ito (as seen in the print mentioned above), grew more refined and simple bonsai — so while the ceramic industry flourished through the production of brightly painted containers, they still made a few containers that were elegant and simple, with quiet colours and beautiful shapes.

At the end of the Tokugawa period there was a heightened interest in Southern Sung style painting and the popularity of literati art generally, was growing. Also, bonsai was being used more and more as the subject for paintings and poetry. However, on the whole, up to 1870, little progress was made in bonsai styling technique and the common trend was for overly gnarled and grotesque trees.

In the year 1867, the feudal government fell and the "Modern" period began. The 1870's and 1880's mark a period of "Occidentalism" and overseas trade was set up. As more foreigners came to Japan, they began to take a fancy to the artificial styles of miniature trees, such as the Tako style. The visitors to Japan thought these trees were typical of Japanese bonsai and began to purchase them. As they became increasingly popular, more were made and an export trade was set up. The main centre producing Tako style trees was Edo (modern day Tokyo) and it was largely for these commercial reasons.

Kyoto and Osaka, on the other hand, kept to the more literati-type tree designs and as transport within Japan improved, growers from the Kyoto-Osaka area were disgusted at the styles being produced in Edo and gradually the trend in Edo changed toward the more elegant styling.

There was a high interest in bonsai in the last years of the 19th century and the first decade of the 20th century, with the development of a wealthy merchant class. There was more demand for bonsai within Japan as well as for export purposes. Techniques and styles improved and this marked the beginnings of "Modern Bonsai".

Professional collectors were working from this time on, digging naturally stunted trees out from the cliffs and mountains. Gradually, however, material became scarce with the growing popularity of bonsai. This led to the need for propagation of bonsai material and nursery raising and training therefore became a booming industry. The work of the nurseries had a lot to do with the rapid improvement of propagation techniques, growing methods and the development of various styles. While records indicate that the nursery business is at least 200 years old, it was now a far more extensive practice.

Another early reference to "bonsai" is found in the "Seiwanmoen-Zushi", published in Osaka in 1875. A special effort was made in this publication to call the hobby "bonsai" and this shows a change in attitude toward the art of growing miniature trees.

The Meiji Era (1868–1912) marks the beginning of Modern Bonsai. The Emperor Meiji, who was himself a gifted poet, encouraged bonsai as a national art and the name "bonsai" was made official in this era. The literati group was the main influence in the adoption of the term "bonsai" at this time.

Another group of bonsai growers, however, thought that the term "bonsai" was being used too loosely and so in the mid-Meiji period, the term "Bijuku Bonsai" or "Art Bonsai" was coined to set their work apart from ordinary potted trees. Periodicals published at the time used the term as well[25]. Exchanges and monthly auctions were held at Dangozaka in Hongo, Tokyo and special bonsai magazines appeared[26].

As mentioned above, more foreigners were coming to Japan as the National Seclusion Policy was ended with the Meiji Revolution. As well as this, more people generally were coming to appreciate the form of the potted trees and not just flowers or coloured foliage. Nozaki[27], mentions that some of the varieties in vogue at the time were: Aka-matsu (Japanese Red Pine), Kuro-matsu (Japanese Black Pine), Bushu-kan, roses, etc.

Before this period, the trend was for large flowering trees or goyo-matsu, shaped into the artificial octopus style. Now came a movement toward smaller trees. In 1880, one grower in Asakusa grew very small Red Pines and for a while the public began to equate bonsai simply with the idea of smallness. The shape, temporarily, became less important than the size. Then, about ten years later, there was a movement toward medium-size bonsai and this trend has continued to the present day, with the majority of growers aiming for trees that can be easily carried in two hands.

Another important development in the Meiji era is found in the related art of Ceramics, where potters were beginning to produce more shallow trays that could be used by growers to create landscaped effects.

The literati influence was also becoming stronger. These growers lived mainly in the Kansai district of Kyoto and in Osaka and their influence spread out from this centre slowly but steadily. The influence of late Edo literary figures such as Sanyo Rai and Nanga (Southern School) or Literati painting of artists such as Chikuden, Tanomura and Taiga Ike, had a strong effect on the styling of bonsai in the early Meiji era — firstly within the group of literati growers and then spreading to the general populace.

"Modern Bonsai" in Japan is characterized by naturalistic beauty and from the Meiji era on, the trend was becoming progressively stronger. In 1892, an exhibition of the best bonsai from throughout Japan was held and this gave bonsai more exposure. As Nozaki states, after the turn of the century bonsai was becoming less of a wealthy person's hobby and more accessible as a popular hobby for the general public. After about 1902, a greater variety of plants were used, including the Japanese Black Pine, Sugi (Japanese Cedar), Tama-sugi (a variety of Japanese Cedar), Hinoki (Japanese Cypress), Ibuki, Momi (Japanese Fir), Keyaki, Pomegranite, Maple, Wax Tree, Mulberry, Japanese Apricot and Tree Peony.

In the Taisho era (1912–1926), the great advancements that were being made in bonsai were suddenly brought to a standstill due to the destructive flood that swept through the Tokyo area. The magazines that had begun publication in the mid-Meiji era gradually stopped. However, it didn't take long for the wheels to start turning again and in 1914 a nationwide bonsai exhibition was held in Tokyo[28]. Then in June 1921, the Bonsai Promotion Group organized by Seian Shimuzu and others was formed and they held monthly exhibitions and published a magazine called "Bonsai".

The next problem came in 1923 with the Kanto Earthquake and the group subsequently disbanded. After this, many of the Tokyo growers moved to Omiya in Saitama Prefecture,

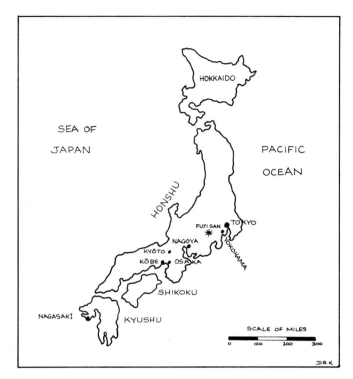

Figure 4: *Map of Japan*

North of the Metropolis and established the Bonsai Village which has today become the centre of bonsai.

Nozaki[29], calls the period 1914 to the present day (i.e. 1940, when the book was published), the "golden age" of bonsai, with an even wider range of varieties being used than before. Among them he lists: Japanese Black Pine, Nishiki-matsu (a variety of Japanese Black Pine with corky bark), Hon-goyo-matsu (the true or genuine goyo-matsu), Japanese Cedar, Japanese Juniper, Ezo-matsu (Yezo Fir), Japanese Apricot, Pomegranite, Boke (Heath rose), Yamakaido, Fuji (Japanese Wisteria), Ume-modoki and Satsuki (a species of the Japanese Azalea). In fact, the late Taisho, early Showa (1926 to present) periods, mark the beginning of widespread use of the azalea for bonsai.

It is within this present century that the first great public exhibitions of bonsai were held. In October 1927, an exhibition of the masterpieces of the Taisho and Showa eras — sponsored by the Bonsai Magazine — was held at the Asahi Newspaper Hall in Tokyo[30].

This encouraged the setting up of a larger show the following year at Hibiya Park. This particular show was held at the request of Mayor Nagata of Tokyo, to honour the emperor's accession to the throne. This show was of importance in the history of bonsai as it was the first time bonsai was used at a public ceremony. Trees were brought in for the show from all over Japan, and even the Imperial Household put some of their trees on display. Following the success of this show, several similar events were held.

March 1934, however, marks an event of considerable importance. It was the first Kokufu-kai bonsai exhibition held at Ueno Park, Tokyo, in the grounds of the Art Gallery — and, since the gallery has always been extremely selective in the types of shows it allows there, this gave bonsai a new status. It was now unquestionable that bonsai was an accepted and respected art form.

Two exhibitions were held that year at Ueno Park — one in spring and one in autumn. These shows became annual events — being suspended only during the Pacific War and being resumed in 1947[31].

In 1964, the Japan Bonsai Association was established and a bonsai exhibition was held in Hibiya Park to mark the Tokyo Olympics. Another show of importance was held in 1970 at the Ōsaka World Exhibition (Expo 70), and similar exhibitions have been held annually since 1980.

One other event that expresses the importance of bonsai in present times is Japan's gift of a bonsai collection to the U.S.A. in 1976 for their Bicentennial celebration. The trees, some 350 years old, are now kept in the National Arboretum, Washington D.C.

Thus we see that in Japan, the art as it originated in China, was developed and it soon acquired characteristics peculiarly Japanese. Generally speaking, Japanese bonsai are soft in feeling and form. Also, the Japanese favour "Naturalistic" bonsai and have devised styles to represent trees growing in many different natural locations, such as the "broom style" for field-grown deciduous trees or the "windswept style" for a pine on the seacoast.

Chinese bonsai, on the other hand, is more dramatic and rugged in feeling. Usually there are fewer branches and the trees are extreme in stylization — being almost surrealistic at times. Favouring the more extreme forms we find that the Chinese have a special love for cascade and literati styles, yet even the Chinese version of an upright "field-grown" tree would have a different flavour. Being mostly trained by the "clip and grow" method would encourage more acute angles, denoting that the tree has gone through some hardship to reach its present stature. Such trees have immense character and are peculiarly impressive.

Japan, in effect, became the connecting link between the origins of bonsai in China and the interest of bonsai in the Western World. However, in recent times, Mr Wu Yee-sun, a prominent banker and bonsai enthusiast from Hong Kong, has done much to spread the word about Chinese bonsai in the Western World through the distribution of his book[32]. The publication includes much of the history of Chinese bonsai, as well as illustrations of some of the masterpieces from his collection.

Until the turn of the century, bonsai was little heard of outside the Orient — France, in one account, being regarded as the first foreign country to recognize the art[33]. The opening of Japan to the Western World by Commodore Matthew Perry in 1854[34], however, exposed some occidentals to bonsai and even as early as 1826, Von Siebold and others described bonsai as horticultural curiosities[35]. In 1901, however, a talk by Mr Toichi Tsumura, M.F.S, who described the beauty of bonsai before the 11th Session of the Japan Society, London, was recorded. In his talk he mentioned a collection of bonsai kept in England. There is record of this collection existing in 1907 and probably in Windsor Castle[36].

"Cassell's Encyclopaedia of Gardening"[37], (1905), describes bonsai as monstrosities and in many English Journals of the same time there were accounts describing the cruelty that was thought to be practiced on the trees[38].

In 1909, an exhibit was held in London — the first bonsai exhibition outside the Orient — and the miniature trees amazed all who laid eyes on them. In those early years, however, all bonsai exported from the Orient failed to survive in the hands of Westerners. This fed fuel to the notion that the Orientals had some secret method of growing these miniature trees.

After World War 2, bonsai culture spread even more widely throughout the world — particularly in the U.S.A. due, to a great extent, to the American forces that were stationed in Japan. Because of the fast growth of interest in bonsai in the Western World, it became evident that some form of instruction was necessary and two bonsai masters of the present day: Yuji Yoshimura and Toshio Kawamoto realized this fact.

Previously, in the Orient, the art of bonsai had been passed on to the next generation by the younger enthusiasts observing the masters at work. Only a few who watched really understood what the masters did and out of those few an even smaller proportion had artistic ability and feeling. In this way a small group of masters of great ability was maintained. When the hobby reached the Western World, a different teaching method had to be devised, as Westerners, for a start, wanted to be shown and to be given explanations rather than to merely observe. Also, being from a different cultural background, even the artistic among the group had less of a chance to develop a feeling for the bonsai designs.

To reduce this difference, Mr Yoshimura with the assistance of one of his English pupils, published the first really comprehensive and practical book on bonsai. To explain the difference between container-grown trees and bonsai, he analysed the examples of famous old specimens, renowned throughout Japan and divided them into a few groups according to the general shape of the trunk and the distribution of the main branches. It is from this work that the "rules" of bonsai emerged that were intended initially to point out the difference between a potted tree and a bonsai.

This classification of styles has, over the years, helped Western growers immeasurably in the production of bonsai rather than bushy pot-plants but, at the same time, to those who consider them as being rigid and unbendable rules, the trees either lack character or the grower becomes disheartened when he finds that most trees do not grow according to the rule book.

The ''rules'', in effect, should only be regarded as guidelines. They indicate the ''ideal'' form that will give direction to your efforts. However, if every tree followed the ''rules'' exactly, art would disappear. To be successful in the shaping of bonsai, the grower must learn to make an artistic compromise between the ''rules'' or ''perfect'' form on the one hand, and the individual characteristics of the tree in front of him, on the other. No two trees in nature are alike and it is this difference and the way you make the compromise that will give the tree character and be a mark of your artistic ability and imagination.

Yet the guidelines for styling are very important to learn and they will be discussed fully in Chapter 7. One writer[39], has described the rules thus: *They may possess and hold the subjectivity of all the past Oriental bonsai gardeners . . . their subjectivity being the subjectivity of MANY becomes more objective and not so strict.* If one has really thought about the ''rules'' and put them into practice it would be found that this description is quite correct.

While Mr Yoshimura worked in the U.S.A, Mr Kawamoto, working in Japan, realized that radical changes had been made after World War 2 and that there were few of the wealthy bonsai enthusiasts of pre-war times. Therefore, the only way for bonsai to survive was to introduce it to the masses. Money was scarce, however, and the traditional (aged) bonsai material was beyond the price range of the average person.

Mr Kawamoto's idea was to turn toward the use of younger, cheaper plants. However, even though Japan had changed considerably, a young plant in a pot could in no way be called a ''bonsai''. At the same time, most enthusiasts would lose interest waiting for the plant to mature. The answer was found in Mr Kawamoto's idea of Saikei (i.e. ''Living Landscapes'' — a sister Art to Bonsai, and discussed in Chapter 8).

By the artistic arrangement of these young plants and rocks, in shallow trays, the effect of a miniature landscape can be instantly produced and give immediate pleasure while waiting for the stock to mature. Later, when the plants are more developed, they can be separated and trained into bonsai. In order to teach this art form, the Nippon Bonsai-Saikei Art Institute was formed, with the only branch outside Japan located in Sydney, Australia. Today, however, many people are creating Saikei for its own sake, so that it has, in fact, become an art form in its own right.

To follow the path of bonsai's development from its earliest influences and examples to its present form, is a fascinating journey. As we go along, the differences at each stage are interesting as are the similarities. It is in the differences, firstly, that we see how man at various stages reacted to the individual influences of his particular environment; while the similarities show us the things that don't change as time goes on.

It is interesting to look back — to rethink the thoughts of old and imagine how it used to be. It is also of interest to look ahead and wonder . . . Bonsai, it is true, has changed considerably as it has developed through the centuries, but the change has come slowly and has occurred where it has been necessary.

One thing that we can say for certain about the future is that it will not stay quite the same as it is now or as it has been in the past. New artists will come along, horticulturalists will be born with fresh new thoughts and so new advancements will be made. Yet there is much to be said for the hobby as it is practiced today. Fresh and new ideas must merge — not clash — with the conservative ones, for it is in this evolutionary way that the good practices of old are preserved alongside with the best of the new thoughts.

Trees are essentially the same — yet each one is an individual and has characteristics all its own. Such a statement works just as well when applied to bonsai hobbyists. Use the proven knowledge and guidelines of the past as they represent the distillation of the collective thoughts of past artists. But, at the same time, let your own personal artistic feelings and love for trees show through. With these two influences to guide you, you can't help but follow the right path.

CHRONOLOGICAL TABLE OF CHINESE DYNASTIES

HSIA	
SHANG	
WESTERN CHOU	
SPRING AND AUTUMN PERIOD	approx. 2205 B.C.–255 B.C.
CHIN	221 B.C.–206 B.C.
HAN	206 B.C.–221 A.D.
TSIN	265–420
SOUTHERN DYNASTIES	420–585
SUI	589–618
TANG	618–907
SUNG	960–1280
YUAN	1280–1368
MING	1368–1644
CHING	1644–1911

* * * * * * * * * *

CHRONOLOGICAL TABLE OF JAPANESE PERIODS AND ERAS

HEIAN PERIOD	794–1191 A.D.
KAMAKURA PERIOD	1180–1333
MUROMACHI PERIOD	1338–1573
TOKUGAWA OR EDO PERIOD	1603–1867
Genroku era	1688–1704
Temo era	1830–1844
MEIJI PERIOD	1868–1912
TAISHŌ PERIOD	1912–1926
SHŌWA PERIOD	1926 to present.

* * * * * * * * * *

What Keeps a Bonsai Small?

One aspect of bonsai that frequently amazes onlookers is the reasonably small size of the tree in conjunction with its great age. To many, this feat is looked upon as nothing short of a miracle.

The opinion of a great number of people is that the tree stays small because of "something" that is done to the rootsystem — more specifically — rootpruning. Yet this idea is not entirely correct, as can be seen by the increase of vigour and growth after rootpruning and the renewal of soil. It is, in fact, nature that keeps the balance. If the roots can't continue to spread due to the confines of a narrow crevice in a cliff-face or a bonsai pot, then the above ground portion grows at an extremely slow rate to balance the small increase of the rootsystem.

The tree is thus miniaturized due to the restricted size of the root ball. However, if the tree is left in a pot for many years it grows slowly as the roots fill the container to its capacity and then when all space and nutriment in the soil have been used, the tree actually stops growing, weakens and eventually dies.

You may well ask how the dwarfed tree growing in a small crevice on the side of a cliff may continue to live and grow slowly for many years. In Nature, there are more opportunities for the tree to obtain additional food in the form of decaying leaves and soil that are deposited around the roots after rainfall as well as bird droppings and minerals from the actual rock. The rootsystem atrophies in places but regenerates in others, the result being that the tree lives frugally and manages to survive for many years.

To keep a container-grown tree in good health the tree should be taken out of the pot and the roots cut back periodically. Some trees should be rootpruned yearly, some every two years and some can live quite happily for about five years undisturbed, (the reasons are discussed in depth in Chapter 4). This cutting of the roots stimulates new root growth and consequently the top sends out new shoots which need to be trimmed. The tree, therefore, is continually being refined and is never really a "finished" work of art.

It is interesting to note that potted trees were kept in Babylon, Persia, Egypt and Europe even before China. The reason why the former didn't stay small, however, was due to the fact that each time the plants became pot-bound they were planted into a larger container rather than having their roots trimmed and the plants returned to the same pot with new soil.

Providing rootpruning and repotting are done at the correct time of the year, it is, in fact, quite an easy procedure for the tree to go through. When a tree is growing naturally in the ground, it is usually the case that the top part roughly balances the below ground portion. This is because the rain-water dripping off the leaves and branches forms a ring of moist soil and, consequently, this is where the feeder roots are located.

As the tree grows more and more in height and width, so do the roots grow in width and depth. Yet, as the tree develops, it is only the newly formed roots on the outside of the entire rootsystem that are acting to feed the tree. The older portion of the rootsystem is merely transporting the food and moisture that has been collected and providing an anchor for the tree. Therefore, when we rootprune and when we trim the top, the balance above ground and below is maintained and the rootsystem is kept perpetually young and active.

In summary then, the reason why a bonsai stays small is because of the size of the container, as well as top pruning or trimming. The periodic rootpruning is only to keep the tree in a healthy condition.

Methods of Obtaining Tree Material for Bonsai

COLLECTED FROM NATURE

Many centuries ago, a man was walking through the mountainous terrain of China and as he looked up to marvel at the almost perpendicular cliff-face towering above him, he saw an old and beautiful tree, clinging precariously to the rock, in only a handful of soil. The man straightaway fell in love with the plant and, knowing a little about container-growing, he decided to attempt the dangerous climb up to the tree and try to pull it out with as much root-system as possible.

The attempt was successful and the man took the beautiful old plant home and potted it into an ornamental container that his family had owned for many years. It now stood in his courtyard, where he tended it daily and admired it when he sat quietly in the cool evenings. As the man grew older, sometimes his grandchildren would play in the courtyard and many times he would describe the perils of collecting his prize. The cliff-face, he would say, was like a perpendicular sheet of glass and its head was hidden in a shroud of swirling mist.

The tree regained much of its vigour with the extra care and attention and grew more beautiful every year. This was the start of bonsai from naturally dwarfed trees and some of the most beautiful trees we see in Chinese and Japanese photo albums of bonsai were begun in this way. The wind twists and polishes the silvery wood — fantastically exposed — and years of living on frugal amounts of food and water has kept growth miniature and compact. It is not every old, weatherbeaten tree that will turn out to be a masterpiece — perhaps one in a hundred trees collected will be considered truly beautiful. Yet the character in such a tree will surpass anything that is shaped wholly by man.

This is the oldest way of obtaining bonsai stock and it can be the most exciting method as we can instantly obtain a thick old trunk and other characteristics of age. Admittedly this is not

Figure 5: *Ancient tree with driftwood*

enough to make a good bonsai. Beauty, style and character are, perhaps, the most important qualities but if they are present, they are greatly enhanced by age.

Long ago, in China and Japan, such trees could be found in small crevices on mountains, on the poor dry soil of hillsides and seacoasts, on inhospitable bogs and swamps and on the cliffs of tiny islands jutting out of a treacherous ocean. Nowdays, however, there are not many more to be found. When bonsai became more popular, around the end of the nineteenth century, professional collectors set themselves up to supply the growing demand for old, attractive stock.

The job of the professional collector of olde was difficult, dangerous and deeply imbued with superstition and ritual. For days the collector may wander amidst sheer cliffs and gorges, scanning the crevices, with keenly trained eyes, for a likely specimen. When a tree has been spotted high up and perched between rocks, a place is made at the foot of the cliff where he will sleep for the night. One writer describes the ritual thus[40]:

> . . . *he draws a circle some 6 feet in diameter, and stands on the edge of it. He takes off his upper cloth, or working coat and places it within the circle, facing toward him. The coat is a substitute for his Deity, and he places grains of rice before it as an offering. Then he prays solemnly, "I am a dwarf tree collector by profession. Please let me rent the spot for the night".*

Having prayed, the dwarf tree collector settles down for the night feeling secure that no horrific monsters or goblins with long noses and fiery eyes will creep up and attack him.

At daybreak, work begins. A rope is thrown up and with a grapple-hook, caught to a tree trunk high up on the cliff, the collector then hangs, spider-like, as he works his way, gradually, toward the tree he wishes to collect. Finally he reaches the spot and commences the long and arduous task of prizing the tree loose from the crevice. Many of the trees thus collected are really glorified cuttings and will need two or three growing seasons to fully recover and send out new roots and foliage.

Such work takes patience and courage, as well as faith. These old collectors firmly believed that if they omitted just one part of the ritual, or if they didn't make an offering or pray to the Deity beforehand, an evil and mischievous goblin could sneak up and untie the supporting rope.

As time went on, such trees were found less frequently and collectors such as the old man described above, ceased to exist. Eventually, in most of the areas that may have some suitable stock, collection of plant material became prohibited to protect the National Flora and Fauna. After World War 2, bonsai was even more a hobby of the masses and so stock had to be available in larger quantities. Propagation techniques had to be developed and improved and nurseries were consequently set up to meet the growing demand.

The main methods for propagating bonsai stock will be discussed in a moment. However, before moving on, a few more details about collecting trees from the wild will be considered.

While such stock may be becoming scarce in Japan and China, other countries where bonsai is a more recent hobby, may still have areas rich in suitable trees. One point to keep in mind is that if the tree is of a variety that will shoot back easily from old wood, it need not be a naturally stunted tree. It can be cut down drastically and subsequent growth can be developed when it has been transplanted into better soil (the varieties that can be treated this way and the techniques involved, are discussed in Chapter 2, in the section on Pruning and Trimming).

When choosing a tree to collect, look for the following qualities: Firstly, the tree should be small and compact in size and, if not, should have the ability to send out new branches when cut back hard. Secondly, the rootsystem should be compact and fibrous so that there will be sufficient feeder roots left when the tree is cut out of the ground. As with the top section, though, some trees will regenerate these roots easily when cut back, while others will not.

If the tree cannot be safely removed from the ground in one go, remove the tree over a period of a year. First of all, just prior to the growing season of the tree, dig a circular trench around the plant, with a radius of about ⅓ of the tree's ultimate height. The trench is then filled in with new fresh soil, to encourage feeder roots to develop in the following season. After twelve months, the tree should have sufficient roots developed close to the trunk and the tree can be completely removed by cutting a radius a little larger than the first trench and shortening back any tap-root that may be there. For two to three years, the tree will be in a training container — firstly, perhaps, in a large tub or box and then transferred into a large planter. Eventually, however, it can be transferred into an attractive bonsai pot of the proper dimensions.

If the plant is particularly difficult to remove from the earth, the process described above can be extended over a period of two years or more, by first cutting a trench only ½ or ⅓ of the circumference and year by year gradually working to complete the circle.

In Australia, we have a special problem associated with naturally collected stock. It is not that all the good stock has already been collected, but that many of the Australian Native trees are extremely difficult to transplant and, even if successful, often do not lend themselves to classical bonsai styling. Because of the dry, harsh climate in much of the Australian bushland, many of the small trees have such a long, sparse rootsystem that they seldom survive the cutting back process. All the fine feeder roots are usually quite a distance away from the actual tree.

A few varieties, however, are quite adaptable. The Port Jackson (Ficus rubiginosa), Moreton Bay (Ficus macrophylla) and Queensland Small-leaf (Ficus eugenoides) figs can be cut back right into hard wood. They can also be wired without branches dying back. The River Sheoak (Casuarina cunninghamiana) is another excellent subject. It can stand hard cutting but since it grows right on the edge of the river, the rootsystem seldom needs much shortening, as it is compact and fibrous. In violent storms, or when the river floods, many of the trees actually come loose and float down the river till the torrent subsides and they, once more, take root. The foliage and bark are somewhat like a pine and many can assume weird and fantastic shapes from the many hardships they must go through.

The Banksia, particularly the "Old Man Banksia" (Banksia serrata), as well as some other Australian Natives such as the Eucalypts, are also excellent for bonsai since they have a growth in between the branches and the rootsystem, called a ligno-tuber. Many times in the hot, dry Australian summer, the whole top of a tree may be burned away in raging bushfires, while the entire rootsystem shrivels up from severe drought. Often these two conditions occur simultaneously and the tree recovers by sending out new top and root growth from the ligno-tuber. This means that when collected from the wild, new growth will regenerate when the tree is cut severely.

Apart from naturally growing trees, old gardens can provide suitable material in the form of old privet hedges and azalea bushes — varieties that will shoot easily from old wood. Abandoned orchards or vineyards may also be good places to search.

Plate IV: *Example of Western Art. "Birch and Beech"* in The Magazine of Art, *Vol.8, 1885, Cassell and Company Limited.*

Plate V: *Example of Eastern Art. "Scholar Contemplating the Moon" by Ma Yuan, in* Classical Chinese Painting, *Abbey Library, Murrays Sales & Service Co. 1976*

For the bonsai grower who is just beginning this fascinating hobby, digging trees from the ground can be most exciting, for providing hardy varieties are collected and at the correct time of the year, a good-sized trunk with many of the characteristics of age, can be obtained immediately.

Methods of Propagating Tree Material for Bonsai

The following sections will be concerned with different methods of propagating bonsai stock. Each method will be discussed in reasonable detail, however, it should be realized that an entire book may be written on the subject and consequently, if more information is required, the reader is directed to the bibliography of suggested reading at the end of the Propagation section.

All propagation techniques are imitations of processes that occur in Nature — whether they occur frequently, under reasonably common conditions or occasionally, under unique or unusual conditions. Throughout history, man has observed such workings of nature and attempted to duplicate them and perhaps adapt them to his particular needs. The processes involved are natural, yet, as time passes, refinements have been made to provide optimum conditions for success.

GROWING FROM SEED

The method of growing bonsai material from seed has certain advantages. Firstly, of all the methods of propagation, growing from seed gives one the most perfect control over the styling process. As the tree develops, buds that emerge in the required positions are allowed to grow and elongate while the awkward ones are rubbed off. If the training is attended to right from the start and if the tree is not left unattended for long periods of time, it may never be necessary to make large or heavy cuts. The resultant miniature tree will have a natural tapering effect on the trunk and branches, as well as a fine ramification of branching.

Also, for small-sized bonsai, propagation by seed is the best method as it develops a taper and fine branching on a minute scale, providing the seedlings are grown in small or shallow containers.

Another advantage is that many varieties exhibit favourable qualities when grown from seed. Zelkovas, from seedlings — particularly if grown for the so-called "broom" style (see Chapter 7) — produce finer, more symmetrical branching, as well as a nice taper and spreading rootsystem. Also, fig varieties develop a thick, buttress base if grown from seed, whereas a cutting does not always do so, and may need some extra techniques applied to develop such a base.

Finally, seed is sometimes the only method of propagating a certain variety. Also, unusual varieties may often be obtained this way.

The disadvantage of this method is that it is slow and most beginners (particularly if not too young) would become disheartened and lose interest if this was the only way of creating a bonsai. As we have already discussed in this chapter, the size of the pot plays a large part in determining the tree's rate of growth and its ultimate size. Consequently, even though this method is slow, it is possible to hasten the process considerably. First of all, determine what size of bonsai you want. If you wish to finish with a small bonsai, grow the seed in individual, small containers. If you are aiming for a tree that is 30 cm to 45 cm (12 to 18 inches) high, then grow your seedling in a 9.5 litre (approximately two gallon capacity) container. For a tree with a trunk at least 5 cm (two inches) in diameter and about 60 cm (24 inches) high, the open ground would be the best training area. Open ground cultivation saves a lot of time in achieving size but the shape and finer branching will be lost unless one continuously trims and selects branches as they develop. Once the tree is neglected during the growing season, the main branches will elongate and thicken — destroying the shape — and the necessary cuts will be heavy and fairly obvious.

Seeds vary considerably in the time they take to germinate and the conditions they require for germination. Some germinate in a matter of days (for example, citrus, maples, elms, figs) and some may take up to two years (for example, holly). Generally, trees that tend to live for a reasonably long length of time, require more exact conditions for germination to occur.

In all seeds there is a built-in timing device that, in many types, has the ability of delaying germination till a favourable season arrives. One of these delaying processes is the fact that many seeds need the freezing temperatures of winter before germination can take place. This is a natural safeguard for the tree, for if the seedling began to grow in late autumn after the seed was dropped, it would probably die with the onset of winter. This effect is called vernalization of seeds. It is also often referred to as stratification. This name originates from the fact that the original process was to place seeds between layers of damp sand and the container then kept in a chilled area.

The effectiveness of the vernalization process depends upon certain factors[41]: There must, firstly, be a sufficient imbibition of water. It should be low enough to hinder growth but high enough for vernalization to occur (according to Lysenko's method). The approximate water content in the seed should be about 45% to 50% of its dry weight, for example 30 parts of water to 100 parts of air-dried seeds.

Secondly, vernalization cannot begin before a period of activation — that is, the time necessary to induce the first apparent respiratory exchange in the recently imbibed seed. Ten to twenty-four hours at 15 to 18 degrees centigrade (60°–65°F) after the beginning of soaking is required.

Thirdly, oxygen is needed by the seed, both chemically and biologically.

Finally, the duration and temperature of chilling is a significant factor. The optimum temperature for vernalization is from one to six or seven degrees centigrade (33°–42°F). The vernalizing effect decreases from zero to minus four degrees centigrade (32°–26°F) and disappears completely below minus six degrees C (21°F). It also decreases above seven degrees centigrade (44°F) and disappears from twelve to fourteen degrees centigrade (54°–57°F). Above fifteen or seventeen degrees (59° or 63°F) devernalization occurs. As far as time is concerned, 40 to 45 days is sufficient and if vernalization occurs for more than three or four months, it becomes less effective.

Some varieties that require vernalization are roseaceous varieties (flowering cherries, peaches, plums, apricots, quinces, crabapples, cotoneasters, pyracanthas, hawthorns), beeches, lime trees (i.e. linden tree), dogwoods, maidenhair trees (i.e. ginkgo biloba), yews and junipers. The roseaceous varieties should be kept moist till planting occurs.

Some varieties, on the other hand, do not require vernalization and furthermore, should be stored dry till spring, e.g. larches, spruces, pines, hemlocks, cryptomerias.

Oily seeds, such as magnolias and camellias, do not stay viable for long and must not be stored in a warm place for any length of time. Once the oil dries and the seeds shrivel, they fail to germinate.

Many tropical and subtropical varieties or hardy trees whose seeds mature well before the cold weather, do not require pre-treatment and will germinate readily if fresh seeds are sown immediately, for example, maples, elms, citrus (the first two are only viable for a short period after ripening, often only for a few days).

Some seeds, in nature, germinate more easily if they are eaten by a bird. Through this process, the seed coating, that inhibits germination, is removed and the hard outer surface is softened through the effects of warmth, moisture and stomach acids. Generally, the types that would respond from this treatment have hard coatings to the seeds and a colourful or tasty surrounding fruit or berry. These types should be soaked and depulped and sometimes treated with acid. Remember, when soaking, that viable seeds sink.

With other types of seeds, scarification is necessary — that is, they are nicked with a knife or file or sanded down. In Nature, the ones that are slightly damaged — perhaps by a bird partially cracking the seed — germinate easier. When scarification is being done, be careful that it is on the opposite side of the seed's "eye" (that is, where the seed was originally attached to the plant or pod).

Another point that may be of interest, is that it has been found that gibberellins (a group of hormones that promote plant growth, and are found abundantly in seeds), play an important part in the breaking of seed dormancy, especially with those kinds that respond to vernalization or exposure to long-day photoperiodism. In seeds that germinate easily, the effect of Gibberellic Acid may be slight. However, with seeds that require a longer period for germination, its effect can be quite pronounced[42].

If you are using old seed and don't want to plant large quantities that may or may not germinate, fluid sowing of pre-germinated seed may be the answer — particularly if the seeds are small in size. The method is this: In a plastic container, place a couple of sheets of absorbent tissue paper and a sheet of paper towelling. Moisten the paper but don't keep it sopping wet. Sprinkle the small seeds evenly over the paper and when they have sprouted the small seedlings are mixed with a fluid gel (either specially prepared agricultural gel or a substitute made of two heaped teaspoons of cornflour to two cups of water. Mix the cornflour in a couple of tablespoons of water first and then mix into the rest of the water when it is near the boil. Boil for about half a minute and use when cold). The gel and seedlings in suspension are sown in the seedbed through something like a cake icing decorator funnel or plastic bag with one corner cut off.

Using this method, small seeds are easy to plant with fairly even spacing, germination is often faster and seeds are not planted that are not viable — thus saving time and space.

After the seed has been collected and pre-treated, they should be planted. Generally, a sandy loam that is kept evenly moist but with good drainage, is the best medium. If "damping-off" (i.e. "collar-rot", a fungus disease that may occur in young seedlings at soil level) is a problem, then seeds should be sown between layers of milled sphagnum moss (a sterile substance).

Most seeds should be planted to a depth once or twice their diameter and remember to firm the soil down at the time of planting so that it won't settle later and leave the seeds without enough soil covering. In the case of very small seeds, such as fig seeds, spread sphagnum on top of the soil before sowing and sprinkle the seeds onto it. Don't cover the seeds as they germinate better when exposed to light.

Multiple or composite seeds, such as cotoneasters, hollies and hawthorns, should be sown thinly. However, it is generally a good idea not to plant too many or plant too closely as it will be hard to separate the plants when they start to grow.

Initially, it is best to water by allowing the water to soak up through the drainage holes, as this won't disturb the seeds or the soil surface. Later though, as the plants begin to grow, overhead watering may be practiced. When potting then, leave a space between the soil level and pot rim to catch the water and allow it to soak into the soil.

After planting the seeds, the seedling box should be covered with a sheet of glass (or polythene) to keep the inside moist and warm. After germination occurs, the glass should be opened slightly for ventilation and then after a week or so, opened entirely. Air and light are essential for seedlings and if additional light is given in the first three or four weeks of life, the young plants improve more than 100% in terms of size and quality.

It is only with trees grown from seed that a tap-root results — vigorous taproots being found particularly on large tree varieties such as the oak. Seedlings should be grown in shallow containers as this encourages the formation of a lateral fibrous rootsystem and, also, the actual tap-root should be cut at an early age (four to six weeks after germination, depending on the size of the seedling for ease of handling). The young tree will then develop an easily managed fibrous rootsystem and can be transplanted into individual containers when the stems are woody.

Following, are a few additional points that may help your development of good bonsai material from seed. As was mentioned earlier, if your young plant is grown in the ground, it will develop in size and maturity far more quickly. The most time-saving way of all is to trim the top of the tree reasonably hard when first planting it into the ground and then trimming very little (in fact only if really necessary) until next winter. When finally removing the tree from the ground, however, it must be treated as if you were digging a tree from the wild (see previous section on bonsai material collected from nature).

A second method is to trim the top of the tree constantly while the tree is in the ground but not cut the roots. This will not be as fast as the first method, but more refinement of style may be attained.

Lastly, the slowest method of developing stock in the ground (but much faster than stock grown in a container) is to rootprune the tree yearly and trim the top whenever necessary.

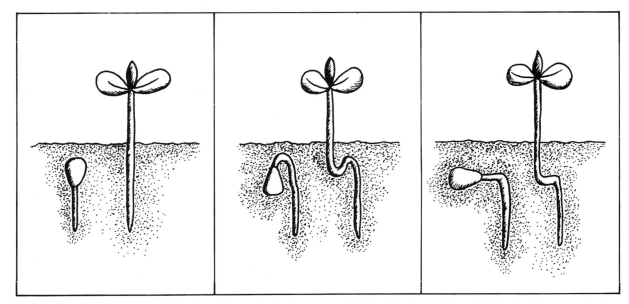

Figure 6: *Placement of seed as a determinant of ultimate trunk shape*

The first two methods are best for slower growing varieties, while the second and third methods are suitable for deciduous trees or fast growing varieties. The third method should be used for trees that are difficult to transplant, such as pines and oaks.

Another additional point to consider is the actual placement of the seed. If you intend to develop an upright style — particularly formal upright or broom style — plant the seed the right way so that the root goes straight down and the top upwards, when germination occurs (the end of the seed that was attached to plant or pod should face upwards). If it is planted sideways or upside down, there will be a curve at the trunk base (see Figure 6)[43].

For informal styles, on the other hand, where a more curved basal section would be desirable, obstacles can be made for the seedlings so that they have to curve to reach the light. After germination, the top layer of soil can be removed by gently washing it out with water and it can then be filled with gravel or pebbles. The young stem and surface roots are thus curved slightly at this very early stage. A sandy loam may be added and, when watered, it will move into the crevices between the pebbles. After a few months, the pebbles may be removed so that sunlight may promote the formation of bark[44].

Growing bonsai stock by seed is a slow method but for many reasons it is a very desirable method. For beginners it may seem like an eternity to wait for results but, generally, as one begins to acquire a collection through the more time-saving ways, and, as the bonsai "bug" begins to bite a little harder, one may begin to think of particular designs to create or dream of having a certain more unusual variety . . . and, thus, the seed is sown. Also, as we wait eagerly for the seed to germinate and for the young plant to develop, the fascination of seeing life develop from a small, dry seed overcomes our impatience and Time, all at once, becomes less of a critical factor.

GROWING FROM CUTTINGS

With every cutting that lives and grows, the Easter story is reborn.
Just as the bread is blessed and broken and the wine shared,
So is the body of the tree broken and the sap shared for the giving of Life . . .

There are many advantages in growing bonsai material from cuttings. First of all, a fairly large number of trees can be propagated in a reasonably short period of time and for very little cost and expenditure of time and effort.

Also, the propagated material, in most cases, has the same characteristics as the parent tree, whereas many seedlings are unreliable in this regard — exhibiting quite marked variations in terms of leaf size, autumn colour, colour of foliage during the growing season etc. If the parent tree is at flowering and fruiting age, the cutting will also flower straightaway, whereas with a seedling, many years may elapse before flowering begins. Make sure that the cutting is taken from a branch that flowers well or has other desirable characteristics, as these will be transmitted to the propagated material.

Another advantage of this method is that a good fibrous rootsystem will be formed. Such a plant will be easy to rootprune and transplant because of the abundance of fine feeder roots. A tap-root is only found on seedlings that have not yet been rootpruned.

With cuttings, as with most methods of propagation, there are a few disadvantages that should be considered. For production of bonsai, it must be realized that unless one starts with reasonably large cuttings, this method is still reasonably slow — though not as slow as growing from seed.

Another disadvantage is that it is difficult for a cutting to produce a good taper and spreading surface roots, unless the grower practices some more specialized techniques for artificially producing these characteristics. (These methods will be discussed in the section on Hardwood cuttings and also in Chapter 2 in the section on Specialized techniques).

While many different tree varieties may be obtained by taking cuttings, some are more difficult or even impossible to propagate this way. Many conifers, for example, are difficult because of their high resin content. Also, cuttings taken from some conifer trees should be obtained from the top branches of vigorous growth. If taken from the side branches, the resultant tree will be asymmetrical and will tend to remain a branch, i.e. the leader tends to grow horizontally and will require support. For semi-cascade or cascade styles, such cuttings may prove desirable[45]. Many nut trees are also difficult, as well as maples, oaks, birches, linden trees and beech trees.

The actual time when the cutting is taken is fairly important with most tree varieties and with professional propagators a difference of thirty days can, quite noticeably, effect the results[46]. However, for the bonsai hobbyist, the quality of a bonsai is more important than the quantity of trees produced, so that too much care about exact timing is not necessary. If you are trimming a bonsai and you would like to have some more trees of that variety, try the cuttings no matter when they are taken. You may be successful, even though a book on propagation tells us it is not the ideal time.

There are a few different types of cuttings, depending on what part of the parent plant has been used. These are generally classified as:

Stem cuttings: softwood, semi-hardwood and hardwood
Leaf cuttings
Leaf-bud cuttings
Root cuttings.

In this section we will be discussing stem cuttings and root cuttings as these would be the most common types used for propagation of bonsai stock.

STEM CUTTINGS

1. Softwood Cuttings

These are cut from the parent tree in spring and are the new, young shoots of the season that are still reasonably soft and sappy. Some deciduous ornamentals, such as maples, that are more difficult to grow from cuttings, may be successfully propagated this way.

Of all types of stem cuttings, this type will generally send out roots more quickly and easily, but there is the difficulty of keeping the cutting turgid. Softwood cuttings, therefore, will greatly benefit from additional propagation equipment, such as a misting system, to cut down on water loss through transpiration. The leaves on the top part of the cutting should not be cut off, as it is an advantage to leave the greatest area that is possible without wilting taking place. One simple way of reducing water loss through the leaves, is to put a plastic bag over the pot of cuttings, in order to keep the atmosphere humid.

Additional heating would also be beneficial for best results. The ideal temperatures for most varieties are 23 degrees to 27 degrees centigrade (73°–81°F) for the base of the cutting and 21 degrees centigrade (70°F) for the top[47]. Roots generally form in two to four or five weeks.

The best type of material for softwood cuttings are twigs that are still flexible but, if sharply bent, would snap. It is best to collect cuttings from growth of average vigour and from sections growing in the sun. They are generally cut 7.5 cm to 12.5 cm (three to five inches) in length and should include two or more nodes.

Remember that if the cutting is made just below a leaf node, the cutting will more easily take in moisture and will also send out roots more easily. Remove the leaves from the lower half of the cutting and if the leaves on the top are excessively large, these may be reduced in size a little, so that the cuttings may be planted closer together and not experience so much moisture loss through transpiration. Note that a better proportion of cuttings will strike if they are planted close together. If flowers or flower buds are present on the cutting, remove these entirely, however, cuttings taken at flowering time are generally less successful.

Another point that may be of help is that cuttings generally strike more easily if they are severed from the parent tree in the early part of the day, when the branchlets are more likely to be in a turgid state. The cuttings should then be planted immediately or kept moist and cool until planting takes place. It is preferable to keep the cuttings moist by keeping the cut ends in water. Recently, it has been found that the sooner the cutting reaches water after it has been severed from the parent plant, the better will be its chances of sending out roots. Any intake of air through the newly cut end acts as an inhibitor to root development and some propagators are actually making the cut underwater.

Softwood cuttings may be struck in pure sand that is kept evenly moist. Some growers, however, like to add some peatmoss to the sand to help the medium stay damp longer.

2. Semi-Hardwood Cuttings

These cuttings are taken in summer and are firmer than softwood cuttings. Some of the varieties that propagate easily from this type of cutting are azaleas, some conifers, cotoneasters, pyracanthas, jasmine, pieris japonica, false cypress, barberry, daphne, pittosporum, euonymous, holly, citrus and olive.

The cuttings are generally 7.5 to 15 cm (three to six inches) in length and the leaves are retained on the upper half and removed on the lower half. Just as with softwood cuttings, if the leaf-size is large it can be reduced in area to allow cuttings to be planted closer together and cut down on the moisture loss through transpiration.

Semi-hardwood cuttings should be severed from the parent tree with a slanting cut, just below a leaf-node and preferably cut in the morning when stems are likely to be turgid. If the cutting is not planted immediately it should be kept moist and cool till planting occurs.

Misting and bottom-heat would also probably help, but a plastic bag over the cuttings will serve the purpose of creating a humid atmosphere fairly well. The rooting medium can be pure sand, sand and peatmoss or a very sandy soil. If pure sand is not used as the medium, a small amount of sand in the hole for the base of the cutting to rest on, will facilitate rooting and make sure that water doesn't collect at the base of the cutting and cause rotting. Care must also be taken not to have air spaces under the cuttings — they must sit firmly on the medium and the medium should be packed down firmly around the cuttings. They should then be watered in. Don't press down on the soil or sand after watering, however, as it may become too closely packed and delay or even prevent rooting.

The medium should then be kept in an evenly moist condition. An interesting method of striking cuttings was apparently first used in Victorian times. A small pot was placed inside a larger one and the space in between was filled with the rooting medium and the cuttings. Watering was done by pouring into the inner pot and letting the moisture seep gradually into the planting medium. For less hardy cuttings a glass bell could be placed over the entire set-up, to reduce loss of moisture in the cuttings through transpiration. The extra oxygen supplied to the cuttings by the closeness of the pot rims stimulates the development of roots and it is easy to make a check on root development by temporarily removing the inside pot.

3. Hardwood Cuttings

This type of cutting takes longer than the two previous methods to develop roots, but they do not perish as easily as the other types and it is less essential to have special equipment, such as a misting system.

Hardwood cuttings are of particular interest to bonsai growers, as it affords the opportunity of achieving a reasonably thick trunk and characteristics of age in a fairly short period of time.

These cuttings are severed from the parent tree in autumn when the current year's growth has hardened. The wood must be mature at this time, otherwise it probably would not survive through the winter months. Some varieties will even strike from older wood at this time, for example, willow, crepe myrtle, pomegranite, chinese quince, fig, olive and wisteria. Hardwood cuttings are particularly successful with a lot of deciduous varieties.

For best results, cut from wood that is moderate in size and vigour and sections that have been growing in full sun. The cutting should have ample food within its stem to keep it alive and turgid until it develops its own roots. Note, however, that cuttings should never be fertilized until it is certain that roots have developed.

The cuttings should generally be from 10 cm to 75 cm (four inches to thirty inches) in length, with a diameter of 0.5 cm to 2.5 cm or 5 cm (¼ inch to one or two inches). The ones that send out roots very easily, however, can be of an even thicker diameter. At least two nodes should be included in the cut length, with the bottom cut made just below a node and the top cut 1 to 2.5 cm (½ to one inch) above a node.

There are a few different ways of making hardwood cuttings. The first way, called the "straight" method, is the most common way and works well for many types. Make the cut on a slant to expose more of the cambium layer and preferably plant the cutting on a slant with the cut surface down (see Figure 7).

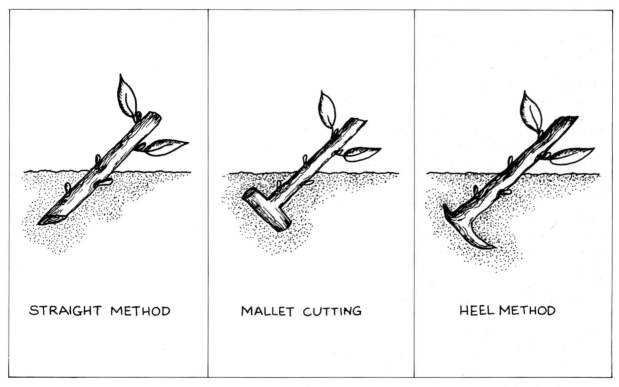

STRAIGHT METHOD   MALLET CUTTING   HEEL METHOD

Figure 7: *Hardwood cuttings, 1. Straight Method, 2. Mallet cutting, 3. Heel method*

The second way is called a "mallet" cutting. Here a section of older wood on the parent tree is included (see Figure 7 above).

Thirdly, there is the "heel" method, where a portion of the older wood is also left on the cutting. The heel should never be left ragged as this will encourage rot to set in, so trim it neatly if necessary (see Figure 7 above). The last two methods increase the water intake of the cutting and expose a greater area of the cambium to facilitate rooting.

Yet another method of making hardwood cuttings is the so-called "tapering" method[48]. This is similar to the "straight" method mentioned above however, two cuts on a slant are made instead of one (see Figure 8).

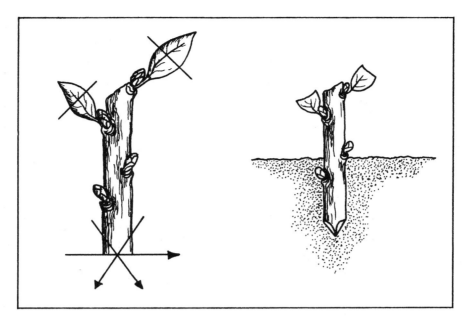

Figure 8: *Tapering method*

The advantage here, is that there is more area exposed that is capable of sending out roots.
   A slightly better method for bonsai growers is the following "Notch" method[49], (see Figure 9).

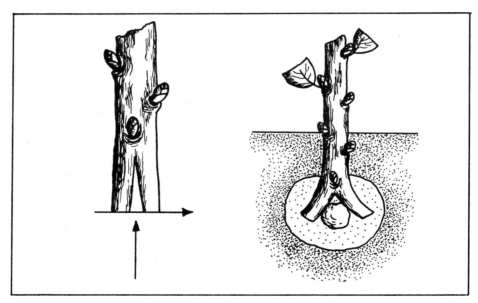

Figure 9: *Notch method*

After the cutting has been severed from the tree, a wedge shaped notch is cut out from the base, as shown in the diagram. The bottom is then flared out, a pebble or piece of wood being inserted in the cut to keep it open. The clay ball surrounding the base retains water and keeps the edge of the cutting in a slightly moist condition that makes rooting easier. The advantage of the "Notch" method is that the cutting will develop with a tapering trunk and well-developed surface roots that continue the line of the man-made buttress.
   Another method for preparing hardwood cuttings produces an even better distribution of the rootsystem. With this method, flaps of the outer bark are lifted away from the inner wood section and kept open with bits of stone or wood. Roots are thus encouraged to develop right around the cutting and not just on one side (see Figure 10).

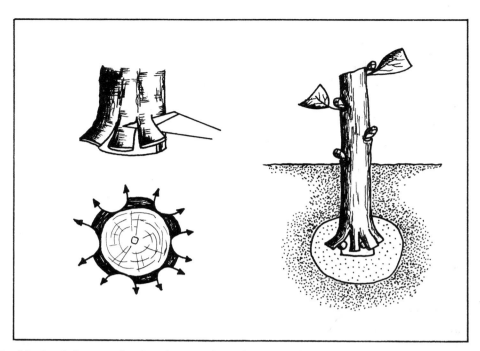

Figure 10: *Method for producing better distribution of rootsystem*

Hardwood cuttings of needled evergreens take even longer than deciduous varieties to send out roots, so the growing medium, while still being mainly sand, should include some soil to supply some nourishment. As with semi-hardwood cuttings, some sand on the base of the cutting hole would help the cutting to send out roots.

If winters are extremely cold, the hardwood cuttings may be taken in autumn and then stored in a moist, cool condition (perhaps a covered box of damp sand) till spring. During the winter months, the callusing that precedes root growth should begin. Watch, however, that the top buds don't swell too much during this period, as this will encourage the top to sprout before the roots begin to grow. If the buds do begin to swell, lower the storage temperatures, or else plant out the cuttings.

If the winters are not too severe, that is, if temperatures do not fall below freezing, then hardwood cuttings, even with a fair amount of sub-branching, can be struck if planted straight out into the rooting medium in autumn. They can be planted in sand in autumn and then in spring a mulch of humus or extra soil can be added on top. The following autumn or spring the cuttings can be transplanted. The pot of cuttings can sit in a shallow tray of water, as this will keep it evenly moist.

If the variety you are attempting to strike is a difficult one, there are a couple of methods that may help, however, special heating equipment would be necessary. The first way is to store the cuttings at temperatures of 18 to 21 degrees centigrade (64°–70°F) for three to five weeks and then, if the winter temperatures are mild, plant them out. If the winters are cold, however, store them in temperatures of 2 to 4.5 degrees centigrade (34°–40°F) till spring[50].

The second way is to place the cuttings upright for three weeks over bottom heat of 21 to 23 degrees centigrade (70°–73°F), while the tops are in temperatures of 7 to 10 degrees centigrade (45°–50°F). The combination of cool temperatures surrounding the top buds and warm root temperatures stimulates roots to grow. The cuttings should be planted as soon as roots begin to develop, providing winter temperatures are mild. If it is too cold to plant out, shut off the bottom heat and leave the cuttings undisturbed in the bed till spring[51].

For varieties such as willows, pomegranites and crepe myrtles, that strike from very large, thick cuttings, the cutting can be split longitudinally and the cut surface placed on the rooting medium (note, however that the cambium must be covered with the sand or soil), (see Figure 11).

A "raft" style (see Chapter 7 on "Styles"), where all the trunks are connected at the roots, may be formed in this way.

Figure 11: *Large, thick cutting split longitudinally*

ROOT CUTTINGS

This type of cutting is taken in late winter or early spring for most varieties, that is, just prior to the main growth period. Varieties that have the characteristic of sending out suckers easily, will generally grow well from root cuttings.

For bonsai growers, root cuttings pose some problems. Firstly, with most, the taper is in the wrong direction and they will not grow if planted upside down (the willow, being an exception). Also, if surface roots do not naturally develop evenly around the trunk, one of the root inducing methods, already mentioned, should be applied.

Root cuttings may be planted vertically in the sand leaving about ⅓ exposed, or else they can be planted horizontally, about 2.5 to 5 cm (one or two inches) deep. This last method can also produce a "raft" style. If planted vertically, new shoots will grow around the cut surface from the cambium layer. These shoots become the branches and the root above the ground becomes the trunk.

If the root cutting is planted vertically and entirely underground with the proximal (top) end just beneath the soil surface, many shoots will emerge from the one place and a "clump" style may be formed. Flowering Quince (Chaenomeles lagenaria) is a good variety to grow this way.

All cuttings should be given good light, but not necessarily direct sunlight.

"Damping-off" (a fungal disease) may pose a problem — particularly with softwood cuttings. In this case, milled sphagnum moss can be sprinkled over the soil surface to prevent its occurrence. Another way to counteract the problem is to spray the bed with a Permanganate of Potash solution. 30 grams (one ounce) of Permanganate of Potash is mixed with 568 mls (one pint) of water. It is then kept in a bottle and used at the rate of 85.5 mls (three liquid ounces) to just over 1 litre (one quart) of water. This is a strong solution but prevents "damping-off" and other fungal diseases from making an appearance[52].

A few additional points concerning cuttings:

Firstly, when the cuttings have been collected from the parent tree, soak them in a weak solution of water and sugar (that is, about two teaspoons to a cup of water). Three or four minutes in this solution should be enough. This is a practice of old Chinese propagators and seems to facilitate the cutting's ability to strike.

Another point is that old propagators used to add a weak vinegar solution to cutting beds (two teaspoons to just over a litre (a quart) of water) as it is believed that cuttings grow better in an acid, rather than a neutral or alkaline medium.

Finally, here is a method for striking difficult-to-root cuttings, such as pines. The technique is sometimes called "girdling". At the approximate position where you wish to sever the cutting, wrap wire tightly around the tree. This wire torniquet is left on through about three months of active growth for pines and about three or four weeks for easier to root varieties. The effect of this girdling is that an accumulation of carbohydrates and nutriments is formed above the wire. Water and dissolved minerals go up from the roots through the inner sapwood or xylem. The carbohydrates are then formed in the leaves through photosynthesis and the food produced is distributed throughout the tree as it travels downward through the inner bark or phloem (see Figure 12).

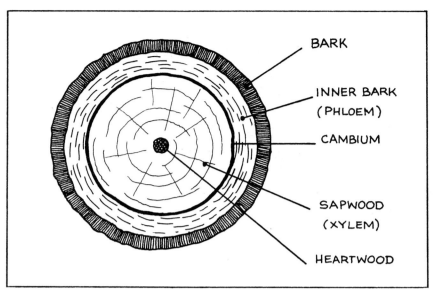

Figure 12: *Cross-section of tree's trunk*

After the necessary time has elapsed, the cutting is made immediately above the wire and roots will form readily (usually, in about three or four weeks) because of the accumulation of energy at that point. Sometimes even before the cutting is severed from the tree, callus tissue and root primordia (in the form of small bumps) begin to form above the wire girdle.

DIVISION OR SEPARATION FROM ROOTS

This technique of propagation is used for plants that have the characteristic of sending up suckers around the base of the original plant or from roots that run just under or on the surface of the soil. Conifers do not usually propagate themselves in this fashion but some deciduous trees and many shrubs and perennials grow this way.

Just as with cuttings, plants that have been propagated by division have the same characteristics as the parent plant. Another advantage is that it may be possible to obtain reasonably old or large stock through this method of propagation.

One disadvantage with stock produced this way is that with some varieties, notably crepe myrtles and wisterias, true root suckers may never flower.

Division, or separation from the roots should be done in late winter to very early spring for most varieties, that is, just prior to the main growth period for the tree. Use sharp cutting tools and don't leave any rough parts that would encourage rotting to occur. The cut edges can be dusted with sulphur powder to help prevent rot or fungal diseases from making an appearance. A reasonable proportion of sand in the soil mix (at least ⅓ to ½ by volume) will help promote more root growth if it is needed. It would also be a good idea to cut back some of the top growth to compensate for the smaller rootsystem now supporting the newly separated tree.

LAYERING

There are many advantages of layering as a method for propagation of bonsai stock. First of all, layers often succeed where cuttings fail. The reason for this is that cuttings depend on their ability to take in moisture from the sand or soil they are planted in, so that they may remain turgid till they develop their own roots. Layers, however, receive moisture directly from the original plant, so that the layered section is more likely to remain in good condition right up to the formation of roots.

Another advantage for bonsai growers is that a section may be chosen that already has many desirable characteristics as far as shape is concerned. It may also be a timesaving method for producing a thick trunk and a good branching arrangement. Also, some of the more specialized bonsai styles — such as clump style (see chapter 7) — may be formed by taking the layer under a group of whorled branches (i.e. many branches extending from the same point).

As with cuttings, layers perpetuate the characteristics of the parent plant. Occasionally, as we walk in gardens or forests, we see a particular branch or branchlet on a tree that has developed unusual characteristics due to a genetic mutation called a "sport". The leaf colour or shape may be different or it may be very small in size. The bark may also be unusual — perhaps being rough or corky. Many varieties of trees were originated by layerings being made from such "sports".

As far as the rootsystem is concerned, layers produce an easily managed, fibrous rootsystem that is usually well balanced and radiating out from the base of the new "trunk".

The technique can also be used to improve the shape of a bonsai, for example, if the tree has no good lower branches or if the lower branches have died (and the trunk does not lend itself to literati style) a layer can be made of the top section so that a smaller but better proportioned bonsai may be so-formed.

The technique may also be used to remedy the problem of a one-sided rootsytem (by "layering" the side deficient in roots) or even to produce an entirely new rootsystem for either better surface roots or in the case of a plant having one long tap-root and very few fibrous roots, in order to increase the finer roots to make the removal of the tap-root a safe process.

Finally, layering is an economical way of producing stock for bonsai as two or more trees may be obtained from one.

The main disadvantage of the method is that not all tree varieties may be propagated this way and with some, like pines, even though it is possible, it is a long process — usually two to five years.

There are two main types of layering: Ground layering and air layering.

1. GROUND LAYERING

With this method, a branch is bent down to the ground. Consequently, it must be reasonably low and supple. If you are layering a plant in the open ground it may be necessary to lighten the texture of the soil by adding more sand and forking it thoroughly to allow for easier access of rootage as it develops. Some growers, however, like to layer straight into a pot, so that there will be less disturbance of the rootage later on, when it is required to be planted in a container.

There are many ways of going about making a ground layering:

1. One way is to bend the branch in a sharp "V" at the point where roots are desired (see Figure 13, no. 1).

2. Another method is that the branch may be cut or broken on its lower side. This would generally speed up the process. The cut or notch may be kept open with a pebble or piece of wood (see Figure 13, no. 2).

3. The following method of cutting places the section to be layered in a more vertical position. The branch is cut on the underside, as seen in the diagram and it is then twisted into an upright position (see Figure 13, no. 3).

4. The part to be layered may be girdled by removing a strip of bark around the trunk. Remember that it must be scraped right down to the beginning of the sapwood. If any of the cambium layer is left, the tree may heal over the wound. The advantage of this method is that it would produce a more balanced rootsystem around the entire base of the new "trunk" (see Figure 13, no. 4).

5. Another method of girdling would be to wire tightly, just below the point where roots are desired. This is slower than the previous technique but is more sure. It also tends to produce a balanced rootsystem around the "trunk" (see Figure 13, no. 5).

6. Trench Layering is yet another method that is particularly used by bonsai growers for the production of raft or sinuous styles (see Chapter 7). The whole length of the branch is layered — not just one point (see Figure 13, no. 6).

With any layering technique, the cut in the branch is more effective in producing roots if it is made just below a leaf node. All layers should be pegged firmly into the soil at the point where it has been bent and the new tree section should be staked to keep it vertical, if so desired, or to stop it from moving about too much. Excessive movement would retard root growth.

Layering is best done in spring to early summer and with many varieties they may be severed from the parent plant the following spring and potted up the autumn after, if they were layered in the ground. Some very quick to root varieties may even be severed from the

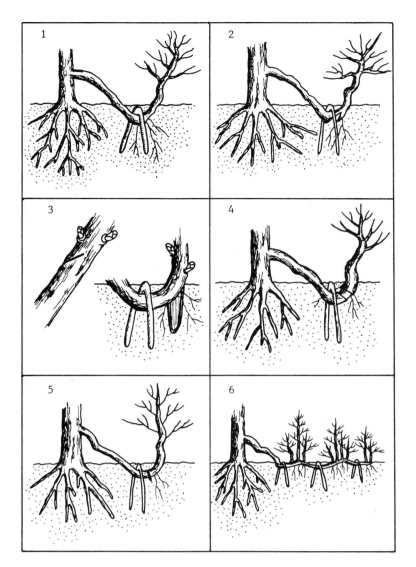

Figure 13: *Ground layering*

parent plant the autumn after the layer has been made. Winters should be mild, however, and care must be taken that sufficient roots have been formed.

2. AIR LAYERING

This technique of layering is known by many different names. Some call it "Chinese Layering" after the country of its origin, while others, in various countries, call it "pot-layering", "marcottage", "circumposition" or "gootee".

Whatever one calls it, it is a very old method of propagation that is believed to have originated in China more than 1000 years ago. The technique is supposed to have been made known to the Western World over two centuries ago.

When air layering was originally practiced in China, the clay and moss-packed wound was probably covered with a section of large bamboo that had been split in half and then secured around the wounded area much in the same way as we would use a split flower pot today. If the weather was dry, a container of water was suspended over the plant and string leading out of the container was directed to the layered part to keep it moist. Later on, special metal or wooden boxes were used to surround the moss-packed section and also to cut down on moisture loss; then split flower pots, paper cones or rubber sheeting was used. If the country had high humidity, perhaps only sphagnum or peat moss covered the wound and the section watered frequently.

The invention of polyethylene brought renewed interest in this ancient method of propagation. Polyethelene sheeting is the best material to use, being much better than vynol, due to the fact that it is porous and has a high permeability to the gases Carbon dioxide (CO_2) and Oxygen (O_2), while water vapour does not pass through easily. It is also a durable material and can stay out in all kinds of weather for a reasonable length of time. With the use of polyethelene, moist conditions may be easily maintained at the point of layering and because it is clear, progress of the root formation can be easily checked. If the plant being layered is shy to send out roots unless the surrounding area is dark, a sheet of black plastic may be wrapped over the clear.

The main advantage of air layering over ground layering is that many branches are too high or too rigid to reach the ground. Layerings are generally made in spring to early summer on wood of the previous year's growth. Larger or older sections, however, may be layered on tree varieties that send out roots fairly easily.

There are a few different methods of making aerial layers. One method is to make two circular cuts around the trunk or branch with a width of 1 to 4 cm (½″ to 1½″), depending on the thickness of the section. The outer bark and cambium should be removed completely. If the cambium is not removed or if the ring-barked section is not wide enough, the bark may heal over and prevent rooting.

Some Japanese propagators believe that the section directly below a fork in either trunk or branch, develops roots more easily than a straight section[53]. Making a layer directly below a leaf-node also helps. If the branch is fairly thin, it may be a good idea to tie a splint to the branch in order to stop it breaking from too much movement in the wind.

After the branch or trunk has been ring-barked, coat the section with a ball of red clay, if you like, and then surround the clay with damp sphagnum moss or peat moss. If the variety will send out roots reasonably easily, this ring-barking method is a good technique to use and both ends of the plastic may be secured tightly to keep the moss-packed wound moist. If the variety is one that will probably take longer to root, the top end of the plastic should be made easy to re-open in order to add moisture if the moss begins to dry out. Access for drainage is important, however, as excess water will prevent root growth for most varieties. The best conditions for root growth is continuous moisture, good aeration and moderate temperatures (i.e. about 18 degrees centigrade (64°F)), in the root area. If the variety takes a long time to root (say 4 years), new sphagnum moss may have to be added yearly (see Figure 14, no. 1).

A variation on the above method is that many deciduous or quick-to-root varieties send out roots more quickly if the upper border of the ring-barked area is made with a serrated cut[54], (see Figure 14, no. 2).

These methods that involve the cutting of a complete ring from the bark generally produce results fairly quickly and have the added advantage of sending out roots evenly around the trunk.

For quick-to-root species, such as willow or cryptomeria, success has been reported with the use of window screening instead of polyethylene covering the moss. The extra air circulation increases the speed of root growth, however the chance of too rapid drying out poses a problem. This would, consequently, be a method to use only if much time can be spent to keep the layer moist, or, if the surrounding atmosphere is very humid[55].

Another way of making an aerial layer is to simply make a slanting cut about 5 cm (2 inches) long and to the centre of the branch or trunk, and keep the cut open with a pebble or piece of wood. It would then be covered as was discussed with the previous method (see Figure 14, no. 3).

Following, are a couple of methods for varieties that are not so inclined to send out roots. One way, is to cut two half-rings instead of completely ring-barking the section. Make the half-rings on opposite sides and approximately 1 cm to 2 cm (½ or ¾″) apart on the trunk (see Figure 14, no. 4).

Another method is to cut and peel-off bark in squares like windows[56] (see Figure 14, no. 5). Alternatively, flaps may be cut that are kept open by pebbles or small pieces of wood (see Figure 14, no. 6).

These methods leave some of the outer bark and cambium intact so that the tree may continue its normal functions for the longer period of time that the layer takes to send out roots.

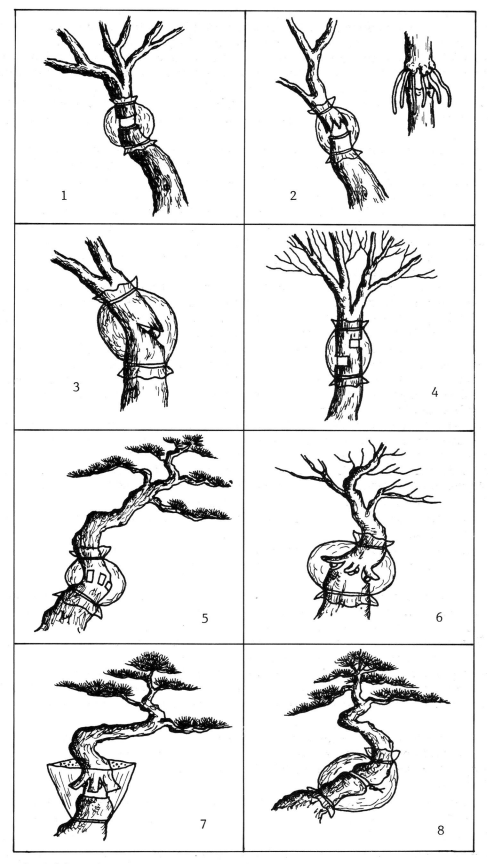

Figure 14: *Aerial layering*

There is yet another technique for aerial layering difficult to root varieties, such as pines. In fact, this method has produced roots in three months instead of the usual three to five years. The procedure is this: In spring, the section to be layered is cut right around with a single cut and then vertical cuts are made above (see Figure 14, no. 7).

The flaps that have been formed are lifted up and bits of clay or other material is placed under the flaps to keep them from closing and healing over. A funnel of heavy plastic is then fastened at the bottom end, below the cut section. The seal need not be made too firm as good drainage facilitates rooting. The funnel is then filled with vermiculite and watered well. The only drawback with this method is that because drainage is so good and because the top is not sealed to retard moisture loss, the layer will have to be watered daily (perhaps two or three times a day in heat-wave conditions). It should never be allowed to become bone dry. While this is a method that requires the grower to spend more time with the plant's care, it certainly speeds up the development of rooting in difficult varieties[57]. Note that the shape of the flaps may be modified. Some growers like to cut them into triangles — points down — as this provides a desirable direction for root development.

Another method of air layering is the so-called torniquet method. With this method, the point where roots are required is bound tightly with thick wire. The area should then be covered with clay and moss as usual (see Figure 14, no. 8). As the wire cuts into the bark a ringbarking effect occurs and roots are formed above the wire. It is a good method as it is fairly safe and sure as well as the fact that it forms roots right around the trunk. It is, however, a fairly slow method. The ring-barking by cutting method is best used for deciduous or quick-rooting varieties, while the torniquet method is mostly used for conifers or those that are slower to send out roots.

As mentioned above, different varieties take different lengths of time to send out roots. Some may take two or more years — these are mainly pines, and some hardwood shrubs — while most softwood layers will root relatively easily — usually between three or six weeks.

When severing the layer from the parent plant, more care may be used by cutting through half-way, leaving the layer for a week and then cutting through the rest of the way (a splint may be necessary if this technique is used). Also, don't separate the layer from the parent plant too early, as the roots are still fairly young and brittle at this stage. It may be a good idea not to remove all of the sphagnum as too many roots may be broken. If the root growth is not too prolific, a prop may be needed when the layer is put into a container. Also, excessive branches and foliage should be cut off to make it proportionate with the root system.

The time between the removal of the layer from the parent tree and its establishment on its own roots is fairly critical. Top pruning helps at this time and additional humidity to the top would also be of benefit. For the first few weeks, give the new plant the normal aftercare for newly rootpruned trees (see chapter 4).

THE TECHNIQUE OF GRAFTING

1. HISTORICAL BACKGROUND

The technique of grafting is a very ancient practice — perhaps one of the oldest arts of plant craft. Evidence exists that shows the Chinese had used it as a method of propagation around 1000 B.C.[58]. Aristotle's discussion of grafting in his literary work also shows a fair degree of understanding of the technique[59].

During the years of the Roman Empire it was much practiced and also discussed in various writings. Pliny the Elder (23–79 A.D.) describes a cleft-graft in the classic "Historia naturalis". The stock must be *that of a tree suitable for the purpose* and the graft must be *taken from one that is proper for grafting; the incision or cleft must not be made in a knot;* the graft must be from a tree *that is a good bearer; and from a young shoot,* the graft must not be sharpened or pointed *while the wind is blowing; . . . a graft should not be used that is too full of sap, no, by Hercules! no more than one that is dry and parched; . . . it is a point most religiously observed, to insert the graft during the moon's increase*[60].

While many writers of ancient times show a real understanding of grafting, other writers seem to have only a sketchy knowledge of its workings and its limitations. It seems possible, then, that grafting was held as a professional or class secret in ancient times. Virgil, for example, wrote: *But thou shalt lend grafts of rude arbute unto the walnut tree, shalt bid the*

Plate VI: *Chinese brush painting of trees with abrupt changes of line and angle — reminiscent of calligraphy. "Listening to the Wind in the Pines" by Ma Lin, in* Classical Chinese Painting, *Abbey Library, Murrays Sales & Service Co. 1976.*

Plate VII: *Chinese brush painting of trees with abrupt changes of line and angle — reminiscent of calligraphy.*

unfruitful plane sound apples bear, chestnuts the beech, the ash blow white with the pear, and under the elm, the sow on acorns fare (Preston's translation)[61]. A popular misconception was that any plant could be successfully grafted onto any other. Another ancient idea that is impossible to achieve was that a tree may be formed with each branch providing a different fruit or vegetable.

Over the years, grafting has prompted many exaggerated and false stories. A New York newspaper once even related that a perfect tree had been propagated for small gardens. This so-called "table d'hote" tree was supposed to provide tomatoes, cucumbers, apples, potatoes and other crops on the one plant[62].

Another early reference to grafting is found in the Apostle Paul's Epistle to the Romans. The grafting between "good" and "wild" olive trees is used as a metaphor (Romans 11: 17–24).

The Renaissance period (1300–1500) brought a widespread interest in grafting, as many new plants were imported from foreign countries and were adapted to new soil and climatic conditions through grafting. In England, "cleft" and "whip" grafts were used extensively by the 16th century and definite realization came that success depended upon the joining of the cambium layers. It was, however, still a mystery as to what the cambium layer was and how it acted to join the graft. At that time there was no good grafting wax to seal the join and wet clay kneaded with manure was used in its stead[63].

During the seventeenth century in England, many orchards were planted, the trees of which had been propagated through budding and grafting. It was in this century that Robert Sharrock wrote about grafting under the heading of "Ubsutuibs". In this work he describes the procedures in great detail. The method of "inarching" or "approach grafting" is called "ablactation" (i.e. suckling or weaning) — a very descriptive title for the technique (see Plate VIII).

In the early eighteenth century, studies on the circulation of sap were made by Stephen Hales. In one of his experiments he approach grafted three trees together and found that the middle one stayed alive even when all of its roots were cut off. Duhamel, who was working around the same time, investigated how wounds healed and how grafts joined together. At this time, it was thought that the graft union was like a filter that changed the sap composition as it flowed through from one plant to the other.

Then, a little later, Thouin wrote the "Monographie des Greffes" 1821, where 119 different methods of grafting are discussed, as well as the changes observed after grafting has taken place.

Another important experimenter in the history of grafting was Vochting who, in the late nineteenth century, continued Duhamel's work on what actually occurred as the graft union healed.

2. ADVANTAGES AS A BONSAI TECHNIQUE

It is true that bonsai stock that has been grown from seed or has naturally grown in the countryside, has many advantages over trees produced by other methods. They generally have a natural grace and beauty that, it may be argued, is missing in material that has been grafted. In Japan, at least up to 1928, grafting of bonsai stock was kept to a minimum. The notable trees that are almost invariably the product of grafting are the Japanese Five-needle Pine and the Nishiki Black Pine (Corky Bark Pine).

The Five-needle Pine is greatly loved by Japanese bonsai growers, but varieties of the best clones are hard to obtain by seed. It is also a weak variety on its own rootsystem. When grafted onto Black Pine roots, the tree grows vigorously, while retaining its small needle size and attractive foliage colour[64]. One of the main advantages of grafting then, is that the desirable qualities of the understock and scion may be combined, while the difficult characteristics are eliminated. It is also used to hasten flowering and fruiting.

Yet another use is to adapt plants to grow in a certain type of soil or climate. In Russia, apple trees were grafted onto the roots of the Siberian Crab Apple to make it more able to withstand extreme weather conditions, while still bearing fruit of reasonable size and flavour[65].

Sometimes grafting must be employed to continue the existence of plants that do not produce seeds, whose seedlings rarely develop characteristics of the parent, or whose seeds are difficult to germinate, as well as being difficult to propagate by cuttings and layerings.

Another use for grafting is for reparative purposes[66]. Following, is an excerpt from a journal describing "bridge grafting" — a reparative technique:

Wounds or girdles may be bridged by scion (see Plate IX), for the purpose of supplying new tissue to connect the parts. The edges of the girdle are trimmed to the fresh firm tissue, scions whittled wedge-shape at each end are inserted, bandages are applied around the trunk to hold the free edges of the bark and the ends of the scions, and grafting wax is applied over the work.

The operation is performed in spring, with dormant scions. The buds on the scions **should not be allowed** *to throw out shoots. If scions are placed close together, they will soon unite along their sides and make a continuous covering of the wound.*

Writing of bridge grafting, Hendrick says (N.Y. Sta. Circ. No. 17): "Its most important use is to preserve trees injured or girdled by rodents or disease. Any ragged or diseased edges should be cleanly cut away, a longitudinal slit should be made in the bark, both below and above the wound, and the edges at the slits loosened slightly. A scion should then be cut two or three inches longer than the space to be bridged, one side bevelled off at both ends and inserted in the slits, its bevelled face against the wood of the trunk.

In order to guard against any accidental displacement, it would be well to drive a small tack or nail through each end of the scion, which, however, must not be split in the operation.

Other scions in a like manner may be inserted at intervals of about 2" over the entire injured surface. The ends of the scions should be covered with grafting wax but it is not necessary to cover all the bridged portion of the trunk.

Scions are sometimes inserted freely in the stub left by a large broken limb, for the double purpose of providing other shoots to take the place of the branch and of facilitating the healing of the wound".

If the techniques of grafting are learned by the bonsai enthusiast, there is the advantage of being able to perhaps improve the styling of trees. A branch, for example, may be added just at the ideal point. It may be particularly useful with varieties that do not shoot readily from old wood. Some of these more specialized techniques are mentioned further on.

3. DISADVANTAGES AS A BONSAI TECHNIQUE

There are some disadvantages with grafting as a bonsai technqiue. Firstly, unlike the previous methods of seed growing, cuttings and layerings, grafting usually takes some practice before a pleasing result, both horticulturally and artistically, is achieved. Even when the workmanship is excellent, scars are often left.

It is for this previous reason that the Japanese, in the past, rarely used grafting as a bonsai technique. Since about 1917, however, much work was done in the field of grafting, so that with scientific developments and the gradual improvement of techniques (such as the making of smaller cuts and making the join at a very early age) the results today are far more pleasing[67].

If you practice grafting and personally prepare the material for your bonsai use, many advantages may be gained as far as the improvement of stock is concerned. Grafted trees obtained from general nurseries, however, are usually of little use to bonsai growers, as grafts are quite noticeable and fairly high up from ground level. There is, therefore, a lack of lower branches and an unattractive trunk that may not be made into "literati" style (a style that has a long, thin trunk with character and fairly short branches starting about ⅔rds of the way up the trunk — see Chapter 7).

4. A FEW POINTS TO OBSERVE[68]

1. There are certain limits as to what may be grafted with what. The limits are sometimes within the species and usually within the genus. Occasionally, plants from different genera may be grafted — some cacti are examples of this — it would, however, be the exception rather than the rule. Grafts are usually more successful if understock and scion are similar.

Certain grafts between species will take one way but not the other. Another point to watch is that if there is an interstock (i.e. a middle section) it must be compatible with both understock and scion.

2. The contact between the cambium layers of understock and scion must be perfect.

3. The understock and scion must be joined together with the right polarity — watch that the scion is not upside down.

4. There should be no movement at the join.

5. There must not be excessive moisture loss at the point of grafting.

6. There must be a temperature suitable for the formation of callus tissue — around 24° to 27°C (75 to 80 degrees F).

7. The understock should be active, while the scion is still in a dormant state (scions may be collected earlier and stored in damp newspaper in the refrigerator till the understocks are at the right stage).

5. DIFFERENT TYPES OF GRAFTS

The three places where the scion may be placed on the understock is the root, crown or upper portion of the plant.

Root Grafts — The scion is placed directly on the rootsystem or roots grafted directly onto the top of the tree to reduce the trunk length. This latter technique works well with deciduous varieties. Tie the grafted roots firmly in place and surround it with a mixture of 50% river sand and 50% peat or sphagnum moss. A plastic bag keeps this mixture around the grafted portion and also retains moisture. A torniquet below will encourage the root development and if small branches are growing from the grafted roots, these may be left on until it is sure the roots have joined to the trunk.

Crown Grafts — The scion is placed in the lower trunk and surface root area.

Grafting in the Top Region of the Tree — Used by bonsai growers to add new branches where desired[69].

Inarching or Approach Grafting is an interesting technique that has many applications for bonsai use. It is also reasonably easy to do as all parts remain on their own roots till the graft is successful. Inarching occurs in nature fairly frequently as trees or branches growing very close together eventually may merge. It takes about one year for conifers to graft properly however, deciduous varieties are often quicker. Following are some ways inarching may be used for bonsai;

1. A branch from a tree can be repositioned on the same tree (see Figure 15).

Using this technique, the position of a branch may be improved or foliage brought closer to the trunk. Slice off from the branch and trunk, similar shapes and tie together securely.

2. A branch from another tree may be grafted to shorten the trunk or simply to produce lower branches (see Figures 16 & 17).

3. Many trees may be grafted together to produce a thicker trunk and more branches. The trees may be spiralled or plaited.

After they graft together it will appear as a gnarled, aged trunk, while the twisted trunk may appear to have been sculptured and twisted around by years of exposure to the wind and other

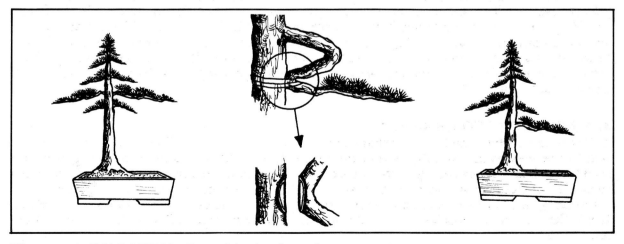

Figure 15: *INARCHING: Repositioning branch on same tree*

Figure 16: *INARCHING: Another tree grafted on in order to shorten trunk*

Figure 17: *INARCHING: Another tree grafted on in order to produce a lower branch*

elements of nature, (see Chapter 2 for further discussion of this process). A multiple trunk style (see Chapter 7) can also be produced this way.

If you wish to thicken a trunk at the base to produce a better taper, the best way is to allow a lower branch to grow without trimming for a while (the reasons for this are described in Chapter 2). A temporary use of grafting is that if a tree does not shoot from old wood, a branch may be grafted at the back and low down on the trunk. It is then left on, without trimming, till sufficient thickening has taken place in the lower trunk region. The branch is then removed and having been grafted at the back, no unsightly scar is visible.

FURTHER SUGGESTED READING ON PROPAGATION

Browse, P.M., *Plant Propagation*, New York: Mitchell Beazley Publishers Ltd., 1979.

Hartmann, H.T. & Kester, D.E., *Plant Propagation: Principles and Practices*, New Jersey: Prentice-Hall, Inc., 1968.

Hull, G.F., *Bonsai for Americans*, New York: Doubleday & Company, 1964, pp78–89.

Murata, K., *Practical Bonsai for Beginners*, New York & Tokyo: Japan Publications Trading Company, 1964, pp34–63.

Plumridge, J., *How to Propagate Plants*, Melbourne: Lothian Publishing Company Pty Ltd., 1976.

Walker, L.M., *Bonsai*, London: John Gifford Ltd., 1970, pp31–50.

Yashiroda, K., *Bonsai — Japanese Miniature Trees*, London: Faber & Faber, 1960, pp82–95.

Starting Bonsai from Nursery Stock: ''The Sculptural Technique''

> *To break the marble spell*
> *is all the hand that serves the brain can do*
> *— Michelangelo —*

This method of starting a bonsai is sometimes referred to as ''instant bonsai''. By this, we mean that in a few hours we can have quite an attractive ''bonsai-in-training'', depending, of course, on the artistic ability of its maker. What is being produced is what the Chinese call the "skeleton" of the design and later, as the seasons pass, the tree will become more beautiful as the foliage fills out this basic form.

When choosing a tree from the nursery, there are a few points that should be kept in mind concerning your choice of variety. Firstly, choose a hardy plant and, also, one that has qualities that will help make it into a presentable bonsai sooner. Choose, for example, a variety that has either short needles or small sized leaves, as well as short internodes (that is, the distance from one leaf-node to the next). If these are not small in size, find out if they will reduce after having been subjected to trimming for a period of time (many of the figs, for example, have very large leaves initially but grow smaller ones after they have been trimmed for a while). Also, try to avoid varieties with compound leaves (i.e. the leaf being made up of subleaves) as they seldom look in proportion. Exceptions are made when the tree has other desirable qualities, such as the beautiful flowering habit of the Wisteria.

Some varieties also produce quite a mature-looking trunk and sometimes bark, at quite an early age. This is a further good point to look for.

Another advantage of nursery stock is that the rootsystem is usually quite fibrous and already used to growing in the confined space of a nursery container. This will make rootpruning reasonably easy.

Many juniper varieties are particularly good trees to work with for the above reasons. An added advantage lies in the pliable nature of their trunks and branches. This makes shaping easier and gives the beginner scope to try many different styles.

A list of some of the suitable tree varieties for bonsai is included here. Remember, though, choose a variety that appeals to you. Everyone's taste is different and if you're not fond of a particular type of tree, you probably won't be so keen to give it all the attention and care it needs to become a first-class bonsai.

SOME VARIETIES SUITABLE FOR BONSAI

CONIFERS:
Pines: Japanese Black Pine (Pinus thunbergii), Jap. Red Pine (P. densiflora), Five-needle Pine (P. parviflora), Monterey Pine (P. radiata)

Chamaecyparis varieties: Hinoki Cypress (Cham. obtusa nana), Cham. ericoides, Cham. squarrosa, Cham. Boulevard.

Cedars: Atlas cedar (Cedrus atlantica), Deodar (Cedrus deodara)

Spruces: (Picea varieties)

Cryptomeria varieties: (Crypt. japonica and Crypt. bandi-sugi)

Podocarpus varieties

Junipers: J. procumbens, J. procumbens nana, J. squamata meyeri, Chinese juniper (J. chinesis), J. chinesis japonica, Sargent Juniper (J. chinensis sargentii), Blue Rug (J. horizontalis glauca), Juniperus hornibrooki (this juniper is a little touchy, so repot only prior to the opening of the new buds in spring).

Larch (Larix varieties)

Swamp Cypress (Taxodium varieties), Dawn Redwood (Metasequoia var.)

Maidenhair Tree (Ginkgo biloba)

DECIDUOUS TREES:
Elms: Chinese elm (Ulmus parvifolia), Japanese Grey Bark Elm (Zelkova serrata), Chinese Hackberry (Celtis sinensis), English Elm (U. procera)

Hornbeams (Carpinus varieties)

Alders (Alnus)

Wisterias

Stone Fruits (Prunus varieties): Plum, Peach, Apricot, Cherry, Japanese Flowering plum-apricot "Ume" (P. mume)

Chinese Quince (Chaenomeles sinensis), Flowering Japanese Quince "japonica" (Chaenomeles japonica)

Apples, crabapples (Malus varieties), Pears (Pyrus varieties)

Roses (Rosa varieties), Hawthorn (Crataegus var.)
Beech (Fagus var.), Oak (Quercus var.)
Grape (Vitis vinifera), Boston Ivy or Virginia Creeper (Parthenocissus)
Japanese Ivy or Jap. Creeper (Ampelopsis var.)
Mulberry (Morus), Persimmon (Diospyros kaki)
Maples: Japanese maple (Acer palmatum), Trident maple (A. buergeranum) Taiwan maple
    (A. buergeranum formosanum), Manchurian maple (A. ginala), English Hedgerow maple
    (A. campestre).
Crepe myrtle (Lagerstoemia indica), Willow (Salix babylonica)
Liquidambar varieties.

BROADLEAF EVERGREENS OR SEMI-DECIDUOUS TREES:

Bougainvillea, Barberry (Berberis varieties), Jasmine (Jasminum var.)
Honeysuckle (Lonicera var.), Ivy (Hedera var.),
Citrus varieties (particularly cumquat and calamondin),
Lilly of the Valley Tree (Pieris japonica), Cotoneaster, Pyracantha,
Serissa, Azalea, Dwarf Rhododendron,
Gardenia (Particularly G. radicans),
Lantana, Indian Hawthorn (Rhaphiolepis var.),
Camellia, Dwarf Pomegranite (Punica granatum nana)
Privet (Ligustrum), Osmanthus, Holly (Ilex var.)
Box (Buxus microphylla),
Olives (particularly African Olive (Olea africana))

SOME AUSTRALIAN NATIVES:

Figs (Ficus varieties): Port Jackson Fig (F. rubiginosa), Moreton Bay Fig (F. macrophylla),
    Queensland small-leaf fig (F. eugenoides)
Sheoaks (Casuarinas): particularly the River Sheoak (C. cunninghamiana)
Banksias: particularly the "Old Man Banksia" (B. serrata)
Lilly Pilly (Eugenia and Syzigium varieties), Pittosporum varieties
Paperbarks (Melaleucas), Bottlebrushes (Callistemon),
Tea trees (Leptospermum).

Once you have decided on a variety, the task remains of hunting for your particular tree. At this point there are further qualities that should be kept in mind when making a final choice of which tree from the batch you are going to purchase.

1. For your first tree, it is best to choose a size that will produce a bonsai about 15–30 cm (6 to 12 inches) high, so choose a stock plant that is about 30–45 cm (12 to 18 inches) tall initially. This will give you enough scope to work with, without being large and unmanageable.

2. Try to find a tree with a spreading surface rootsystem. This may be difficult to find in modern nurseries, where most stock is produced from cuttings. Some faults in the rootsystem, however, may be corrected, as mentioned previously in the sections on layering and grafting (a discussion of these techniques may also be found in Chapter 2).

3. The trunk should be reasonably tapered — being wider at the base to give the impression of sturdiness and stability.

4. It should have an apex. A few varieties tend to produce a "flat top" that is hard to correct.

5. The branching system is probably the most important factor for the beginner to consider when choosing a tree. It is important to choose a tree that has a profusion of branches. When you look into the tree more closely, it would also be an advantage to have a thicker, heavier branch about one-third of the distance up the intended height of the trunk and branches that gradually get thinner as they reach the top (the reasons for this will be discussed fully in the chapter on styling, Chapter 7). Branches should also extend in all directions.

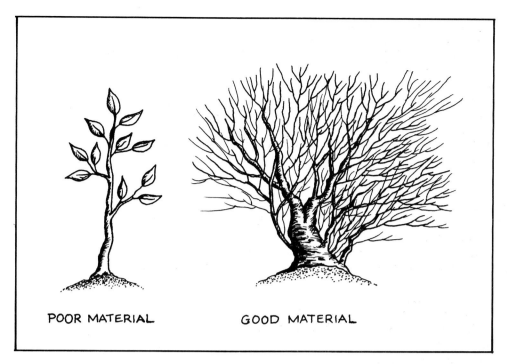

POOR MATERIAL   GOOD MATERIAL

Figure 18: *Poor material vs. good material*

One must approach the making of bonsai from nursery stock, in a similar way as the sculptor approaches his task of chipping away the stone to release the work of art within. At the end of the shaping process, it is quite possible that most of your tree will be lying on the floor, but what remains is the skeleton or framework of your bonsai. Therefore, by choosing a tree with as many branches as possible, the chances of finding a branch in the position you want, are far greater.

It is true that if you are artistic, the final result will probably be more pleasing, however, with practice, even if you feel that you are not so artistically inclined, Bonsai is an artform whereby most people can make an attractive looking tree.

Michelangelo once wrote:

The best of artists hath no thought to show
Which the rough stone in its superfluous shell
Doth not include: to break the marble spell
Is all the hand that serves the brain can do.

This is, perhaps, truer with the making of bonsai from nursery stock than it is with making a sculpture in stone. The tree is there to help the bonsai artist and to suggest ideas that may be unusual while still being perfectly "natural". After all, you were probably attracted to the tree initially because of some inherent quality such as a beautifully spreading lower branch or an attractive curve in the lower trunk region. Such qualities set the character of the tree and, quite often, all that is needed is some modification by the artist to, perhaps, make these characteristics even more of a feature. The extent to which you actually change the tree is limited only by your imagination, but remember that all imagination starts from an examination of Nature herself.

In Chapter 7, the guidelines to styling will be fully discussed. They are, perhaps, the most useful starting point for the beginner, but regard them as guidelines rather than rigid rules. Trees don't grow according to a definite rule book and, just as a particular tree shows similarities to others of the same variety as well as individuality, so should your styling be a compromise between the actual tree you are working with and the guidelines that represent the ideal.

The Art of the Potter

It is with fire that blacksmiths iron subdue
Unto fair form, the image of their thought:
Nor without fire hath any artist wrought
Gold to its utmost purity of hue.
Nay, nor the unmatched phoenix lives anew,
Unless she burn.
Michelangelo, Sonnet 59.

THE POTTER'S APPRENTICE

I sat watching the old potter draw the almost fluid clay into the shape of an elegant cascade pot as his foot rhythmically worked the pedal of the kickwheel. He was perhaps one of the last of the old potters who used the traditional methods of the Chinese pottery makers of ancient times — working without exact knowledge of chemistry but having a feeling for the clay as if it were alive . . .

He would tell me many stories. Sometimes he would describe the dragon kilns that crouched low over the hillsides during the day as if asleep. As soon as the sun dropped behind the hills in the evening, however, they would come alive and with their fiery breath — sometimes light and airy, other times smoke-filled and mysteriously dark — they would begin the alchemical transformation of dull clay and water into jewels of subtle and refined beauty.

The old potter was a maker of beautiful Chinese bonsai pots and one of the stories I like best was when he told me of the very beginnings of his ancient practice[70]:

From the beginning of time, he told me, *man was created from clay. And so it is no wonder that clay, from the Dawn of Civilization plays such an important part in man's life.*

We are interested, however, in the clay form, which are pots for bonsai. Even before Bonsai was grown, pots were made in China for cultivation of different plants . . . A lotus dish . . . bulbs, such as Hyacinth, lilies etc., were grown in a deeper pot. Later on, fruiting and flowering trees were cultivated in differently shaped containers.

The Chinese potter by patient experiment and constant observation and without knowledge of chemistry, made pots and general ceramics of such quality that even modern technology of today cannot compete with their excellence.

Japan borrowed many arts from China — writing, pottery, painting and other crafts as well as Bonsai cultivation. Most of these were modified by the influence of the Japanese way of life.

The old potter told me that the bonsai pots that were made in Japan, particularly in the past, were used for medium quality bonsai, however, if someone owned a very old and beautiful tree, he would try to acquire an old Chinese pot in which to plant it.

The reason for this preference lies in a peculiar "something" that Chinese pottery has. It gives a tactile pleasure when one handles the pot, it makes one to look deep into the translucency of the glaze which has hidden depth in it. One falls in love with the refinement of subdued colour and the individuality of each pot.

Such pots would be over refined and opulent for a small or young tree, in fact a young tree will not be able to stand the competition. On the other hand, if the bonsai is of the first quality, the pot will enhance the tree without detracting from it in any way.

From the Genroku Era (1688–1704) to the middle of the Meiji Era (1868–1912), most of the bonsai pots being used in Japan were originally from China. Many came from Yi-hsing in Kiang-su Province[71] and some from around Canton particularly during the Ming dynasty[72].

*See **Figure 2** for map of pottery centres in China*

These pots (made between 1465 and 1800 in the Ming and early Ching dynasties) are referred to as KOWATARI (which means "old crossing") and are valued today as antique bonsai containers.

From the middle of the Meiji era to the end, more pots were imported into Japan from China and these are referred to as Chūwatari or Nakawatari, that is "middle crossing" pots. While these are not "antique" as the previous pots, they are still regarded as being old.

In the Taisho era (1912–1926) even larger quantities of bonsai pots were made in Yi-hsing and exported to Japan. These are referred to as Shinto or Shinwatari (i.e. "new crossing"), being made fairly recently. They were mass produced in large quantities from 1911 to 1940 due to the increase in numbers of bonsai enthusiasts in Japan. Those pots imported after World War 2 and up to today are called Shin-shin-to or "new-new crossing".

Another area in China — Sek-wan, near Canton in Kwang-tung province — is well known for its production of beautiful bonsai containers. Some growers consider that the clay used for these containers is better than any other as it does not absorb as much heat as other types and therefore keeps the rootsystem of the trees at a far more even temperature[73].

Later the Japanese started to make more of their own pottery and as Kyoto was the centre of art and culture in Japan as well as a place of activity in the bonsai world, many of the potters set up their potteries there. In Kyoto, however, there were no large deposits of clay so that it had to be brought in from other various prefectures. One mark of Kyoto made pottery, then, is the fact that the clay is made up from many different types. There are numerous kilns in the Kyoto area and the potters here were among the first in Japan to sign their work with signature or seal[74].

The Japanese pottery gradually improved in quality and today there are four main areas where bonsai pots are made. These are all within 100 miles of Nagoya[75].

1. Tokoname — produces about 60% of the pots with very good quality clay. The surfaces of the pot are polished when the clay is "leather-hard" which gives the unglazed pots a smooth, refined texture. The unglazed pots are fired to about 1100 degrees centigrade and the glazed pots to 1200 degrees.

2. Shigaraki — produces about 25% of pots. The clay used for these pots does not have as smooth a texture as the Tokoname clay. Very small stones are present in it and the pots tend to be hard and brittle. They are fired to about 1200 degrees centigrade and are mostly glazed. Many of the glazes are made with wood ash.

3. Seto and 4. Yokkaichi — together produce 15% of the pots (note that many potteries exist in one location: Fuji and Hotoku Seito, for example, are in Yokkaichi). The pots are fired to about 1150 degrees centigrade and are characteristically hard and brittle.

These differences just outlined, however, are tending to become less distinct as the various localities are exchanging and mixing their clays[76].

Returning to the subject of pottery in China, the old potter continued: *Why are Chinese pots . . . different to the Japanese pots? . . .*

First, because of the way of manufacture. The Japanese pots, although still made by hand, are produced in a complete mould which means that the clay is pressed into it and the inside of the pot as well as the outside are made to conform to the shape of the mould.

The Chinese use only the inside mould, which gives them the base on which to hold the clay, but the outside is fashioned by hand thus giving infinite scope for variation of shape, design and ornament.

They use glazes which are made of ores of metals for colouring, and ashes of trees as a flux to control the temperature. Cobaltous ore for blues, copper for green, which if in an oxidizing atmosphere of the kiln produces green or in a reducing atmosphere creates a transmutation colour of wonderful red. Iron ores give colours from buff to almost black though browns, but in a reducing atmosphere the famous celadon colour is obtained.

The clay is washed and levigated to the 9th degree and matured in pits for a long time to give it required plasicity. In the old days, the father would prepare enough clay to last him his life and to provide enough for his son to start him off in the Art of Pottery.

Pottery can be divided into three classes — terracotta, stoneware and porcelain. The difference lies in the ability of different clays to withstand temperature. Terracotta is fired from 950 degrees to 1100 degrees C, stoneware from 1100 to 1350 degrees C, porcelain from 1350 to 1400 degrees C and occasionally above that. Clay has to melt a little to become strong and coherent. Terracotta has a very short range and usually is not brought to vitrification point. Stoneware is brought to vitrification point and water absorption is almost nil. Porcelain as we know, is fully vitrified and is a form of glass.

From the bonsai grower's or horticulturalist's point of view, the terracotta pot is ideal. It is porous, lets in air to permeate the soil more easily, thus supplying roots through the porous walls of the pot with needed oxygen. Dries out quickly giving a headache to the gardener, but health to the plant. Its drawback — its fragility and garishness of the glazes.

Stoneware, as the name implies, is stone hard pottery. The glazes are beautiful. The gardener has to be careful when watering plants as the evaporation is proceeding from the surface of soil, and therefore, the soil itself should have as near perfect draining properties as possible.

Porcelain pots are seldom used for bonsai because most of them have overglaze enamel decoration. Occasionally they are used for flowering plants.

The stoneware glazed pot is usually accepted as standard for bonsai hobby. Some are unglazed, made smooth by polishing very refined clay when in "leather-hard" state before firing. This type of pot is usually good looking provided there are no painted designs drawn in a contrasting colour.

Glazed pots are used too, especially of Chinese origin. Cobaltous blue, modified by impurities in the unrefined ore, such as manganese, give a soft and mysterious depth to the glaze. Western usage of refined oxides produces harsh blues and one gets tired of the colour quickly. Greens are from azurite or malachite ore which means copper oxide is good at high temperature and does not give that bright grassy green of terracotta. Here again, the impurities in the ore are responsible for subduing and enhancing the hue. Copper is interesting from another point of view. If the kiln's atmosphere fluctuates between oxidizing and reducing atmospheres (i.e. between clear and smokey flame) the green of the copper becomes red. The beautiful red, which present day chemists can explain and prove the reactions occurring in the transmutation glaze, but cannot reproduce . . .

There is an amusing story in China about copper-red. One day a potter found a vase in a kiln, which instead of being green as it should have been — was of beautiful red. The emperor, being the protector of arts, had first claim on it. When the vase arrived at court, it was admired so much that the emperor ordered it to be cut and used for jewellery; ordering another twelve vases in the meantime. Months passed, the emperor was getting impatient, but the potter, try as he would, was unsuccessful in reproducing red colour. At last the emperor decreed that the potter either produce red vases or be executed. In desperation, the potter jumped into the burning kiln. When the kiln was opened, all of the vases were beautiful copper red. Since then, the Chinese potter, quite logically concluded, that the smoke produced by the burning potter's body was responsible for red. Not wishing to emulate the method of his now famous father, the son started to use pigs. The story itself may be a myth, but the operating principle is correct.

Similarly, the iron glaze, which in oxidation produces buffs, browns and almost black colours, if reduced gives the famous celadon colour. The word celadon is derived from the French describing the pottery of Chinese origin obtained during crusader wars from Saladin's court.

The old potter told me many such romantic stories and while they perhaps give little practical information in terms of bonsai growing and choice of container, they may impart some of the feeling that potters and bonsai cultivators of olde had for these beautiful clay forms.

SOME PRACTICAL INFORMATION ABOUT POTS

THE NEW POT

When using a new pot, there are a few points that should be checked. Firstly, while not essential, it is a good idea to soak a new earthenware (i.e. terracotta) pot, or one that has been sitting in a dry storage area for a while, for about 30 minutes in water. The reason for this is that a very dry or new earthenware pot is likely to draw too much water into itself before roots can take in the moisture for the newly planted tree.

Secondly, check that the drainage holes in the pot allow the water to drain out completely — if there is a raised ridge around the holes, this should be ground down so that water may escape easily.

Also, when choosing the front of the pot, check which side has the better colour and shape. Choose the side that has no warp or scratch marks and make sure that all the legs of the pot touch the table or floor. If they don't, one leg may be supported with some material like plastic cement and this leg placed at the back.

CHOOSING A POT

The following sections will be concerned with how to choose the right pot for a certain tree. However, if ten people were asked to choose a pot for a particular bonsai it is quite possible that each would return with ten different containers — and, each would probably be quite suitable. It must be remembered that the following are only guidelines to direct the grower in making his choice.

The Art of Bonsai is not just the styling of a tree, it is the composite picture of a tree in a pot. Neither element should greatly overpower the other, however, if one errs, it is better to err on the side of a more subdued pot.

If you are in doubt, a more understated style of container would be an oval or a rectangular pot with slightly rounded edges, with plain sides and legs that do not stand out too much from the basic design of the container. When it comes to colour, a simple brown unglazed container would draw less attention to itself, rather than one with a glaze or an unusual finish or texture.

It is generally easier to choose and style the tree before making a decision as to what pot you are going to use. The general feeling of the tree should be considered, that is, whether it is strong and powerful in design or more quiet or delicate. The height and the spread and design of the branches are important as well as the thickness of the trunk. Colour of flowers, fruit, foliage and bark also affect the final choice of pot.

Apart from such artistic considerations, one should also think about the horticultural side of bonsai, for instance, will the size or depth of the container be adequate to keep the tree in a healthy and vigorous state. Many trees use up the moisture in the soil at a far greater rate and therefore they need a deepish container (e.g. willows, crepe myrtles, alders, wisterias, swamp cypress). Others need a deeper pot in order to produce good flowers and fruit (e.g. cherries, pomegranites, wisterias, gardenias, camellias).

In the following sections, some more specific qualities of bonsai pots will be discussed.

Figure 19: *Choosing length of pot according to height or spread of tree*

THE DIMENSIONS OF THE POT

The approximate length of the container can be determined in one of two ways. Firstly, if the main feature of a tree is its height, the pot is often chosen to be about two-thirds to three-quarters of this height. If, on the other hand, the main feature is the horizontal spread of the branches, the pot is chosen to be approximately two-thirds to three-quarters of this length.

The depth of the pot is sometimes chosen to be the same as the thickness of the base of the trunk. However, this last dimension is often difficult to apply exactly and is obviously not used in the cascade styles where the greater depth of the pot is needed to balance the mass of foliage. As a rough guide, a pot depth that is ½ to 2½ times the thickness of the trunk would be suitable. With full-cascade, the depth of the pot should never be the same as the length of the cascade.

SHAPES AND DESIGNS OF BONSAI CONTAINERS

The following table outlines some of the features that influence the visual strength and formality of a pot. A strong tree would have a large, heavy trunk, branches that are angular and heavy, roughly textured bark and heavy surface roots.

	STRONG	LIGHT
FORMAL	Rectangular or square Straight, perpendicular sides Straight line at top of container and at bottom Picture-frame sides (particularly suitable for driftwood style) Wide conspicuous lip Rolled rim Reversed or rolled corners Conspicuous leg e.g. cloud legs or conspicuous straight legs	Oval or round Straight sides slanting out at top Inconspicuous leg
INFORMAL	Rectangular, square, petal or flower, hexagonal, octagonal, round, oval Convex sides — slanting in at top and bottom Straight sides slanting out slightly at top Concave sides — slanting out, top and bottom Flaired out lip Rolled rim Conspicuous leg e.g. cloud legs or very ornamental.	Oval, round, free-form Concave sides slanting out at top only Flaired out lip — narrow base Inconspicuous leg Legs slanting out with or without light design. Narrow, pointed feet — light, lyrical and humorous.

Pots may also be active or passive in feeling. This is a slightly different feature to the visual strength of the pot as it is possible for a pot to be light and delicate while also being active in design.

Generally, the more conspicuous the rim and legs are, and the more ornamental the shape of the container is (e.g. flower shape or greatly flared), the more active the pot will be. Containers that are passive in feeling are usually more self-contained having the rim and feet included in the basic design of the pot.

The following table lists some of the pot shapes that may be used for particular styles (see Chapter 7 for a discussion of the tree styles)[77].

Style	Pot Shape often used	Pot Shape occasionally used
FORMAL UPRIGHT	Shallow to medium rect. Shallow to medium oval	Shallow round, square, irreg. round Shallow irregular oval
INFORMAL UPRIGHT	Shallow to medium, rect., oval Shallow irregular oval	Very shallow round, irreg. round Hexagonal, octagonal, square.
SLANTING	Shallow to medium oval, rect, Irregular oval Shallow round Irregular round	Shallow octagonal, hexagonal or square.
SEMI CASCADE	Semi-deep round, square, octagonal, hexagonal.	Semi-deep irregular round, deep round, octag, hexag., square shallow to medium rect., oval or free-form.
FULL CASCADE	Deep round, hexagonal, octagonal or square.	Semi-deep round, hexagonal, octagonal, square.
WINDSWEPT	Slab of rock, shallow free-form. Shallow oval or rect.	Shallow round, square, hexagonal, octagonal.
LITERATI	Shallow to medium round or free-form, hexagonal, octagonal square.	Shallow oval or rect.
TWIN TRUNK	Shallow to medium oval or rectangular Slab of rock, Free-form	Shallow to medium round or square.
CLUMP STYLE	Shallow to medium round, square, hex., oct., petal, free-form, slab of rock, shallow rect or oval	Semi-deep round, square, hex. octagonal.
RAFT & SINUOUS	Shallow oval, rect., free-form, Slab of rock.	
TWO-TREE SETTING	Shallow to medium oval, rectangular, freeform, Slab of rock.	
GROUP SETTING	Shallow oval, rect., Free-form, Slab of rock	
ROOT OVER ROCK & CLINGING TO A ROCK	Shallow rectangular or oval (Tray with holes or a suiban)	
SAIKEI	Shallow oval or rect.	

A horticultural note: A pot that is much wider at the top than it is at the base is more frost resistant than a pot with perpendicular sides or incurved sides. Incurved pots are also more difficult when it comes to repotting. The rootsystem would have to be sliced around the edges with a sharp knife in order to lift it out of the container.

COLOURS AND TEXTURES OF POTS

Unglazed containers are most often used for the conifer family of trees, however, being more subdued than most glazed containers, they are suitable for many different varieties of trees. Glazed containers may be used for many deciduous trees or flowering and fruiting varieties. Unless the tree is placed in a different container each season, the pot would be chosen to look well with the major colour in the favourite season.

The following table outlines some of the pot colours suitable for certain flower, fruit, foliage or bark colourations:

Colour of Tree Feature	Pot Colours
WHITE	Light yellow, green, celadon, dull red Light to dark blue, white or very dark colours occasionally suitable
YELLOW	Dark green, dark unglazed, blue, celadon Off-white.
ORANGE	Dark brown or purplish unglazed, green (glazed or unglazed)
RED	Light blue, dark blue, green (light or dark) Dull antique white
PINK	Blue, green, white or off-white
BLUE	Dull red, dull yellow, white, off-white, steel grey
PURPLE	Light green (dark green if light purple), celadon, yellowish white, pale brown
VARIEGATED FOLIAGE OR WHITE BERRY	Black, dark green
EVERGREEN CONIFERS	Brown, reddish, purplish or grey unglazed Black or dull white may be suitable
JUNIPERS (Particularly bright green foliage, reddish tint in bark & perhaps driftwood)	Terracotta unglazed
DECIDUOUS WITH LIGHT DELICATE FEELING & SILVERY BARK	Soft grey (glazed or unglazed)
WILLOW	White or off-white — particularly in summer.

N.B. Think carefully before using pots with very bright or harsh colours.

Bonsai Tools

For the beginner, here is a list of the materials and basic tool requirements for starting the hobby (see Plate X):
1. Sharp scissors for top and root pruning
2. Small, sharp knife
3. Wire cutters
4. A potting hook (to remove soil from rootsystem — can be a horse's hoof-pick or sawn-off screwdriver that is slightly pointed and turned over)
5. A potting stick (slightly pointed dowel is good)
6. A piece of fibreglass insect screening (to cover the drainage holes in the pot)

7. Some assorted copper, aluminium or galvanized wire from 22 to about 12 or 10 gauge (8 gauge if a very thick trunk is to be wired). These gauges refer to copper wire. Below is a table showing equivalent sizes of copper and aluminium wire:

Copper Wire	Aluminium Wire
22 gauge	1.0 mm
20 gauge	1.5 mm
18 gauge	2.0 mm
16 gauge	2.5 mm
14 gauge	3.0 mm
12 gauge	3.5 mm
10 gauge	4.0 mm
8 gauge	4.5 mm
6 gauge	5.0 mm

The beginner need not obtain special bonsai tools when starting the hobby. Providing the cutting tools are sharp, you can make do with tools found around the house or yard. Later, if your interest in bonsai continues, you may decide to invest in specially made bonsai tools (see Plate XI). The most important tools are:—

1. SIDE CUTTERS — These are excellent for removing branches from trees. They make a slightly concave cut which facilitates healing and branches are removed entirely without leaving any stub at the base
2. SCISSORS — mainly for trimming and rootpruning (there are many sizes and types)
3. WIRE CUTTERS

ADDITIONAL TOOLS:
4. JIN STRIPPERS — like pliers, to crush the bark when making driftwood styles
5. WIRE BENDERS
6. SAW
7. CARVING TOOLS
8. TWEEZERS/ SPATULA
9. WHISK
10. TROWEL
11. ADVANCED BENDING TOOLS, JACKS AND LEVERS — see Figures 73 to 82

New cutting tools should be broken-in before they are used for bonsai. The special, precision bonsai tools made nowdays have extremely thin cutting edges that may be easily damaged if not worn-in first. Breaking-in tools before proper use is also important to align the blades correctly.

The best method to break-in cutting tools is to make about 50 gentle cuts through about 8 thicknesses of newspaper or some grass-stalks.

Also, tools will last longer if a few precautions are taken with their use.
1. All tools have limitations, therefore don't strain them by cutting a branch or trunk that is too thick (the branch should never be thicker than the blade width). Take care, as well, with very dry, hard wood. Use a saw in these cases and neaten the cut afterwards with cutters or knife.
2. Never cut with the tip of the blade.
3. Try not to cut through roots or branches that are coated with mud and gravel or branches that have wire on them.
4. After use, wipe off dirt and grit with a soft cloth and then remove stains and sap with alcohol or some volatile spirit. Finally, oil the blades and pivot joint with a rust-preventing oil.
5. Store the tools in a dry place when not in use and keep each tool separately so that the blades won't get damaged.

Following the above precautions, tools should last for about 3 years of regular use, without sharpening. When they are beginning to become a little blunt, however, they may be improved by being correctly sharpened. The scissor-type tools are sharpened on the outside bevel and then burrs removed from the inside face of the cutting blade and the mandible-type cutting tools (e.g. side-cutters), are sharpened on the outside curved edge[78].

REFERENCES
Chapter 1

1. Baker, K.F. (editor), *The U.C. System for Producing Healthy Container-Grown Plants*. University of California College of Agriculture. 1957, p. 91.
2. Valavanis, W.N., "A Short History of Container Grown Plants", in *Bonsai Bulletin*, 13.4.7.
3. Davis, M., "Ancient Hindu Bonsai" in *Bonsai Society of Australia Newsletter*. June 1970, pp. 6 & 8.
4. Wu Yee-sun, *Man Lung Garden Artistic Pot Plants*. Hong Kong: Wing Lung Bank Ltd., 1969. pp. 62–64.
5. Allen, O.E. *Pruning and Grafting*, Alexandria, Virginia: Time-Life Books Inc., 1978. p. 75.
6. As Above p. 90.
7. Wu Yee-sun, *Man Lung Garden Artistic Pot Plants*. Hong Kong: Wing Lung Bank Ltd., 1969 pp. 62–64.
8. As Above.
9. As Above.
10. Yoshimura, Yuji, "Miniature Bonsai — Part 1 — Display" in *Bonsai Bulletin*, 9.2.3.
11. Wu Yee-sun, *Man Lung Garden Artistic Pot Plants*. Hong Kong: Wing Lung Bank Ltd., 1969, pp. 62–64.
12. As Above.
13. Lem, D., "A Summer of Chinese Bonsai" in *The Journal of the American Bonsai Society*, 13.3.51–6.
14. *The Garden* vol. 105. Feb. 1980 p. 80.
15. Wu Yee-sun, *Man Lung Garden Artistic Pot Plants*. Hong Kong: Wing Lung Bank Ltd., 1969, pp. 62–64.
16. Masakuni, Kawasumi, "The History of Bonsai — Part 1" in *Bonsai International Magazine*, 18. 52.
17. Walker, L.M., *Bonsai*, London: John Gifford Ltd., 1970. p. 2.
18. Masakuni, Kawasumi, "The History of Bonsai — Part 1" in *Bonsai International Magazine*, 18.52.
19. Yashiroda, K., *Bonsai — Japanese Miniature Trees*, London: Faber & Faber, 1960, pp. 19–23.
20. Wu Yee-sun, *Man Lung Garden Artistic Pot Plants*. Hong Kong: Wing Lung Bank Ltd., 1969. pp. 62–64.
21. Yashiroda, K., *Bonsai– Japanese Miniature Trees*, London: Faber & Faber, 1960, pp. 19–23.
22. Yoshimura, Yuji, "Miniature Bonsai — Part 1" in *Bonsai Bulletin*, 9.2.3.
23. Nozaki, Shinobu, *Dwarf Trees (Bonsai)*, Tokyo & Osaka: The San Seido Co. Ltd., 1940.
24. As Above.
25. Kobayashi, Norio, "History of Bonsai" — excerpted and translated from a series of articles appearing in "Bonsai-Tsu", in *Western Suburbs Bonsai Journal*, Oct. 1972, p. 10.
26. As Above.
27. Nozaki, Shinobu, *Dwarf Trees (Bonsai)*, Tokyo & Osaka: The San Seido Co. Ltd., 1940.
28. Koide, N., Katō, S., Takeyama, F., (directors of the Japan Bonsai Association), *The Masters' Book of Bonsai*, Tokyo, Japan & Palo Alto, Calif. U.S.A.: Kodansha Int. Ltd., 1967, p. 10.
29. Nozaki, Shinobu, *Dwarf Trees (Bonsai)*, Tokyo & Osaka: The San Seido Co. Ltd., 1940.
30. Kobayashi, Norio, "History of Bonsai" — excerpted and translated from a series of articles appearing in "Bonsai-Tsu", in *Western Suburbs Bonsai Journal*, Oct. 1972, p. 10.
31. As Above.
32. Wu Yee-sun, *Man Lung Garden Artistic Pot Plants*. Hong Kong: Wing Lung Bank Ltd., 1969, pp. 62–64.
33. Kobayashi, Norio, "History of Bonsai" — excerpted and translated from a series of articles appearing in "Bonsai-Tsu", in *Western Suburbs Bonsai Journal*, Oct. 1972, p. 10.
34. As Above.
35. Hull, G.F., *Bonsai for Americans*, Garden City, New York: Doubleday and Co., Inc., 1964, p. 26.
36. Tsumura, Toichi, M.F.S., "Japanese Dwarf Trees — Part 1" Lecture given before the 11th Session of the Japan Society, London. Nov. 13th, 1901, in *Bonsai International Magazine*, 16. 220.
37. *Cassell's Encyclopaedia of Gardening*, 1905, 1.220–221.
38. Vining, D.M., "Strange Legacy" in *The Journal of the American Bonsai Society*, 6.1.7–12.
39. Koreshoff, V.A., "Expressions of a Bonsai Purist", in *Bonsai International Magazine*, 10.6.11.
40. Yashiroda, K., "Dwarfed Potted Trees or Bonsai" in *Brooklyn Botanic Garden: Handbook on Dwarfed Potted Trees — vol. 1*, p. 5.
41. Koreshoff, V.A., "Vernalization of Seed to Break Dormancy" in *Bonsai in Australia*, January 1972, p. 24.
42. Koreshoff, V.A., "Discovery of Gibberellins", in *Bonsai in Australia*, September 1971, p. 35.
43. Valavanis, W.N., *Encyclopaedia of Bonsai Art vol. 1 — Bonsai Creation and Design using Propagation Techniques*, Atlanta, Georgia: Symmes Systems, 1975, p. 10.
44. As Above, p. 11.
45. Koreshoff, V.A., "Notes on Propagation of Conifers" in *Bonsai in Australia*, January 1972, p. 23.

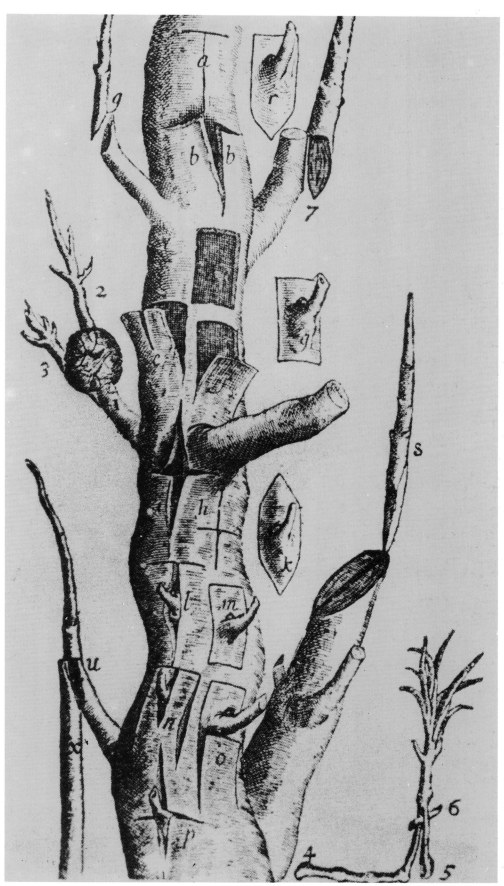

Plate VIII: *The illustration here is reproduced from Robert Sharrock's* History of the Propagation and Improvement of Vegetables, *1672, and shows different types of grafting.*

Plate IX: *Bridge Grafting (after Hendrick). From New York State Circ. No.17.*

46. Hull, G.F., *Bonsai for Americans*, Garden City, New York: Doubleday and Co., Inc., 1964, p. 81.
47. Hartmann, H.T. & Kester, D.E., *Plant Propagation: Principles and Practices*, New Jersey: Prentice-Hall, Inc., 1968, p. 294.
48. Yoshimura, Yuji, *The Japanese Art of Miniature Trees and Landscapes*, Rutland, Vermont & Tokyo, Japan: Charles E. Tuttle Co., 1957, p. 28.
49. As Above, p. 28.
50. Hartmann, H.T. & Kester, D.E., *Plant Propagation: Principles and Practices*, New Jersey: Prentice-Hall, Inc. 1968, p. 291.
51. As Above, p. 291.
52. Koreshoff, V.A., "Notes on Propagation of Conifers" in *Bonsai in Australia*, January 1972, p. 22.
53. Valavanis, W.N., *Encyclopaedia of Bonsai Art vol. 1. — Bonsai Creation and Design using Propagation Techniques*, Atlanta, Georgia: Symmes Systems, 1975, p. 31.
54. Murata, K., & Takeuchi, T., *Bonsai for Pleasure*, Tokyo, Japan: Japan Publications, Inc., 1969, p. 46.
55. Valavanis, W.N., *Encyclopaedia of Bonsai Art vol. 1. — Bonsai Creation and Design using Propagation Techniques*, Atlanta, Georgia: Symmes Systems, 1975, p. 30.
56. Kawamoto, T. & Kurihara, J.Y., *Bonsai-Saikei: The Art of Japanese Miniature Trees, Gardens and Landscapes*. Tokyo, Japan: Nippon Saikei Co. (printers) 1963, p. 31.
57. "A New Technique for Air-layering Pines" in *Bonsai International Magazine*, 13.4. 24–25.
58. Hartmann, H.T. & Kester, D.E., *Plant Propagation: Principles and Practices*, New Jersey: Prentice-Hall, Inc., 1968, p. 394.
59. As Above, p. 394.
60. "Reparative Grafting" in *Bonsai in Australia*, Oct. 1970, p. 26–27.
61. As Above.
62. Allen, O.E., *Pruning and Grafting*, Alexandria, Virginia; Time-Life Books Inc., 1978, p. 60.
63. Hartmann, H.T. & Kester, D.E., *Plant Propagation: Principles and Practices*, New Jersey: Prentice-Hall, Inc., 1968, p. 394.
64. "Reparative Grafting" in *Bonsai in Australia*, Oct. 1970, p. 26–27.
65. As Above.
66. As Above.
67. Valavanis, W.N., *Encyclopaedia of Bonsai Art vol. 1. — Bonsai Creation and Design using Propagation Techniques*, Atlanta, Georgia: Symmes Systems, 1975, p. 20.
68. Cohen, C., "Propagation by Grafting" in *Western Suburbs Bonsai Journal*, April 1972, p. 5.
69. Valavanis, W.N., *Encyclopaedia of Bonsai Art vol. 1 — Bonsai Creation and Design using Propagation Techniques*, Atlanta, Georgia: Symmes Systems, 1975, p. 20.
70. Koreshoff, Dorothy, "The Potter's Apprentice" in *Bonsai Society of Australia Newsletter*, July 1968, pp. 6–8.
71. Masakuni, Kawasumi, "The History of Bonsai — Part 2" in *Bonsai International Magazine*, 18.78.
72. Kawamoto, T. & Kurihara, J.Y., *Bonsai-Saikei: The Art of Japanese Miniature Trees, Gardens and Landscapes*. Tokyo, Japan: Nippon Saikei Co. (printers) 1963, p. 136.
73. Wu Yee-sun, *Man Lung Garden Artistic Pot Plants*, Hong Kong: Wing Lung Bank Ltd., 1969, p. 66.
74. Groszkiewicz, A., "Japanese Pottery and Ceramics" in *Bonsai International Magazine*, 16.254.
75. Young, D.S., "Japanese Bonsai Potteries" in *The Journal of the American Bonsai Society*. 13.3.59.
76. As Above.
77. Yoshimura, Yuji, "Notes on Bonsai Containers" in *Bonsai Bulletin*, 5.1.6.
78. References for section on Tools:
    Coetzee, B. "Bonsai Tools" in *Bonsai International Magazine*, 19.128.
    van der Westhuizen, E., "Care of Bonsai Tools" in *Bonsai International Magazine*, 18.301.
    Patrick, J., "Care of Bonsai Tools" in *Florida Bonsai*, 9.4.9–14.

CHAPTER TWO

''Shaping Techniques''

Pruning and Trimming

INTRODUCTION

The oldest method of controlling or changing a tree's habit of growth is the Art of Pruning and Trimming and it is a technique that was perhaps first used by man after watching Nature herself at work. Nature's pruning may be accomplished haphazardly but it is a continual process that occurs in many different ways. Branches are constantly struggling and competing with others for light, space and air to grow and it is only the better placed ones that manage to survive.

An observant person may learn many of the basic guidelines for good pruning practice by watching Nature prune her trees. Branches that are weak or crossing another limb, for example, often fail to live very long and as the wind blows through a forest, dead boughs and twigs are removed. As a tree or bush increases in size, some growth must be eliminated, for no plant can support all of the foliage and branches it ever produces. In the forest tree, for example, as the top reaches toward the heavens, the lower branches often die through lack of light. Similarly, as a bush grows outward, creating a shape of ever increasing diameter, the inside branchlets and foliage die-back and eventually fall off. Infrequent natural occurrences, such as lightening, fires or avalanches, also may prune a tree and redirect its growth.

The way a tree prunes itself or is pruned by the forces of Nature, imparts the characteristics of age and gives each tree individuality. Seedlings and young trees are very much the same in appearance and have a symmetrical pattern of growth. As the tree ages, however, time and environment leave their marks and the tree generally assumes an assymmetrical design. An example of this process may be observed in the pine tree. When young, the distribution of branches is symmetrical and in definite whorled layers around the trunk. As time goes on, though, some die through disease, lack of light or other natural tribulations, and, consequently, the old tree is left with one or two branches at each level.

Pruning, therefore, is a natural occurrence and the bonsai grower that prunes with regard to the health and beauty of a tree is not doing anything that is harmful or unnatural.

Mankind prunes trees for various reasons and bonsai culture cannot be claimed as being more unnatural than these. Rather, the pruning of trees for bonsai may even be considered as more natural since the trimming is directed toward the production of a tree that suggests the beautiful sculpting that Nature may achieve.

One definition describes pruning as *the methodical removal of parts of a plant with the object to improve it in some respect for the purpose of the cultivator*[1]. Thus we can see that under the general heading, there exists many different reasons for pruning. Some of these are:

1. To assist or speed up the processes of Nature by removing dead, diseased or weak branches.
2. To rejuvenate old plants and thus extend their length of life.
3. To selectively remove parts of a plant in order to improve flowering or fruiting on the remaining part — or, simply to improve the character of the tree and produce a good disposition of branches.
4. The shaping of garden plants — such as can be seen in topiary (see Chapter 1) or hedges. It is interesting to note that many people who condemn bonsai are professed ''garden lovers'' — yet no garden can be entirely without artificial effects — even if it only entails the cutting of lawns.

5. Also, we have the pruning of trees for the culture of bonsai and it is this particular reason and the techniques involved, that concerns us here.

Just as there are many reasons for pruning in general, so too do we find that the bonsai grower prunes for many different reasons. First of all, pruning and trimming is a major factor in the actual process of keeping a tree small (see Chapter 1). Secondly, it is used to remove unattractive and superfluous branches, in order to create a more artistic shape. Thirdly, consistent trimming of a bonsai increases the amount of fine branching in a tree, so that at the end of one growing season, if a tree has been trimmed three times, eight finer branches should have replaced each single branch. The internodes, or distances from one bud to the next, should gradually become shorter and the leaves or needles on most varieties also become smaller, the longer a tree has been trimmed. Fourthly, by using different techniques of trimming, it is possible to regulate the vigour distribution of a tree to a small but effective degree. This aspect will be discussed at the end of the pruning and trimming section.

CUTTING TECHNIQUES

THE SCULPTURAL TECHNIQUE — Usually involves quite drastic pruning as you expose the hidden artistic form.
THE MODELLING TECHNIQUE — 1. The Clip and Grow Technique
2. Pinching and trimming.
With these techniques, the material for the next stage is added onto the existing form. With bonsai, it quite literally "grows" out of that form.

THE SCULPTURAL TECHNIQUE

The so-called "sculptural technique" in bonsai can be likened in many ways to the procedure used by the sculptor who works in wood or stone. Superfluous parts are gradually removed to expose the form seen by the artist and the original material is generally much larger in volume or size than the finished article. With bonsai, this means that, quite often, drastic pruning is involved.

Unlike the sculptor who works with wood or stone, the bonsai sculptor's material is alive and, therefore, artistic cutting must always be done with regard to the continuing health of the tree.

Figure 20: *Sculptural technique*

WHEN TO CUT BACK

Firstly, any drastic top pruning of a tree should be done at the time of rootpruning. As was mentioned in chapter 1, there is a balance between top growth and rootgrowth that should be maintained as closely as possible. If severe rootpruning is attempted without any cutting back of foliage or branches, the tree will suffer because the now diminished rootsystem cannot supply enough moisture and dissolved minerals to the top. Likewise, if the top is cut back very drastically without any trimming of the roots, excessive "bleeding" of sap may occur and the tree suffers from a condition similar to high blood pressure.

ADVANTAGES AND DISADVANTAGES OF PRUNING IN THE VARIOUS SEASONS

Spring Pruning - If you live in an area that has experienced a very cold winter, "winterkill" or "die-back" caused by freezing or an early thaw becomes evident in spring and can be removed from the tree, but heavy pruning is not advisable. The loss of sap is often too severe and "suckers" or "water sprouts" that drain the parent tree of energy are encouraged to develop. Furthermore, the excess sap around the wound may attract bacteria and decay and rotting could be the result.

In mid-spring, however, new vegetative growth may be trimmed back to develop a finer ramification of branchlets or to encourage flowers and fruit on some tree varieties. Alternatively, flowering wood can be trimmed if more foliar growth is desired.

Pruning in late-spring has the effect of retarding early summer growth.

Summer Pruning - If heavy pruning is done in early summer, "sucker" growth is not so likely to result — the reason being that the "growth curve" determined by the flow of sap in the tree, is now on the downgrade. With some fruiting varieties, trimming at this time tends to encourage fruiting growth rather than foliage.

An advantage of doing hard pruning toward the end of summer is that the healing capacity of the wood is fairly high at this time and wounds should heal well before the onset of cool weather. However, a disadvantage that may result is the fact that young growth that is encouraged by such cutting may not have enough time to mature before winter and may suffer die-back if there is a cold snap.

Mid to late summer pruning can have a dwarfing effect, as the leaves that are the food manufacturers, are removed and the tree must rely on stored nutriments to further its growth. Also, since growth early in the season was made at the expense of food stored the previous autumn, most of the reserves have been used and regrowth, therefore, cannot be overly vigorous. Furthermore, because of the reduction in foliage at this time, a limited supply is stored the following autumn and this causes new growth to be held in check the following spring.

Another effect of late summer pruning can be observed in the rootsystem. With most trees, there is a period of active rootgrowth in late summer and autumn and the nourishment for this is supplied from the food manufactured by the top growth that growing season. Because less food was made, the rootgrowth is also less and consequently top growth is limited the following spring.

Autumn Pruning - Any dieback that has occurred through summer can be cut out at this time. However, because winter dieback cannot be anticipated it is sometimes better to leave excess growth through the cold months to compensate. The buds that are left will mature by using the stored food in the tree and will experience a vigorous start in spring.

One caution, if you do intend to prune in autumn. With some trees, immediately after leaf-fall, there is a movement of stored food downward from the branchlets to the heavier branches, trunk and rootsystem. Consequently, if pruning is done before this downward flow, there will be an unnecessary loss of stored food.

Winter Pruning - Just as in autumn, winter dieback cannot be anticipated. Severe pruning in early winter is not so good as healing is not rapid during the dormant months. However, pruning in late winter encourages much vegetative growth and stimulates dormant and adventitious buds to open in spring. If the terminal bud on a tree is trimmed in late winter, the tree doesn't have time to re-establish the concentration of auxin (see further on for explanation) in the new terminal bud before spring and the result is that the growing strength is more evenly distributed throughout the tree. Another advantage of late winter pruning is that the food stored in the heavy wood and roots of the tree may be used for growth in spring.

If pruning was done in spring, after this stored food had moved upward into the growing areas, there would be an unnecessary loss of nutriments.

EFFECTS OF PRUNING DIFFERENT TREE VARIETIES

Another point that should be kept in mind is the fact that with some varieties more care should be taken when cutting them back. Some trees lack what are called "adventitious buds", which means that they either do not send out growth from old wood or they do so unpredictably. Most conifers would be in this category — particularly long-needled types, such as pines. Some deciduous trees such as beech, also do not have the ability to shoot readily when cut back hard.

These effects are especially evident in old trees. They often cannot stand drastic pruning and so it should, first, be considered if an attractive shape can be achieved simply through wiring and trimming. If it is decided that more drastic pruning is necessary, it should be done in stages — that is, gradually reducing the size over two or three repotting seasons. Another method of gradual reduction of size is to saw through the tree half-way at the desired point and saw through the second half the following year. Again, the process should be coupled with rootpruning. Using the latter technique, the side that was sawn in the first year would die, while the side still connected to the bottom part will continue to live and grow.

It is a seeming contradiction that it often takes an old tree longer to achieve the appearance of beauty and age than it does a younger one. The older tree may have only one burst of new growth per year, while a younger plant may grow fairly continuously throughout the growing season — thereby maturing more quickly. In the same sense it often takes longer to develop naturally dwarfed varieties as bonsai. Because they are dwarfed, they grow more slowly and take longer to develop characteristics of age, such as a thick trunk and mature bark.

Most deciduous trees, such as maples, elms and liquidambars, as well as other vigorous leafy evergreens, such as privet, figs and azaleas, can be cut back right into bare wood, providing it is done before new leaf buds open and in conjunction with rootpruning. Some fine-foliaged conifers, such as hemlocks, yews, arborvitae, taxodium, metasequoia and junipers, will also stand quite drastic cutting back — especially when they are young. One difference between deciduous trees and many evergreens is that the latter do not store large quantities of food. Consequently when they are pruned in late winter, there is usually not so much encouragement for the plant to send out vigorous new growth to the extent that a deciduous tree might, and, likewise, in summer, pruning does not have as much of a dwarfing effect as it does with deciduous types. Also, the effect of less food is felt more immediately in many evergreen varieties and the balance between top and bottom growth re-establishes itself sooner in most evergreens than in deciduous varieties.

HOW TO CUT BACK THICK BRANCHES

With deciduous trees and varieties with active cambium layers, such as azaleas, figs and privet, it is better to leave a slightly concave cut when removing branches. Such a cut will heal flat, rather than form an unsightly bulge and will also promote more rapid healing. If side-cutters or a similar tool is used for removing the branch, the wound will naturally be slightly concave. However, if heavy branches are sawn-off, it may be necessary to carve or gouge out the wound. It is the exposed wood that should be hollowed — not the cambium — as it is this area that produces the new cells that will cover the wound. By hollowing the exposed wood it is making it easier for the cambium to cover the wound and because the scar tissue tends to bulge out, the initial hollowing of the wound encourages it to heal flat. If there are branches surrounding the wound, the scar will also be flatter and less obtrusive — particularly if there is a branch above the wound. The reason for this is that the branch would be creating sugars which would then pass downward to the wounded area to assist healing.

Callusing over a very large wound often takes quite a long time, however, if the healing process seems to have stopped, reinjuring the wound will stimulate the callus formation to continue and this procedure can also encourage a flat-looking scar.

With regard to the shape of the wound, it is better to make a long cut rather than a wide one, and, preferably, tapered toward the bottom (see Figure 21).

Figure 21: *Shape of cut made when heavy branch removed*

A large cut in this shape will tend to heal more quickly than a smaller one in a circular shape. The reason for this is that sap tends to travel in an up-and-down direction and a long, tapered cut will provide less interruption to the sap flow, thereby allowing nutriments to reach all areas of the wound and consequently making healing more rapid. Generally, though, the top of the wound is the first to heal.

If the variety contains a lot of sap (e.g. a pine or spruce) it is better to leave a small stub when removing a thick branch. About three months later, when the stub is cut off, a natural bypass will have formed and sap will not run out over the bark of the tree (N.B. "Bleeding" of the milky resin of figs can be stopped immediately by putting water on the wound).

Varieties that do not easily send out buds from old, bare wood, do heal over better if a stub is left when removing a heavy branch. Because the tree does not attempt to grow shoots at the end of the stub a natural internal "wall" is created at the join between branch and trunk. When the stub is removed about three months later, the wound is quite small.

With trees that grow from bare wood, a stub is not left as the tree often attempts to send out shoots from it and in this case an internal "wall" is not created. With such varieties, however, even though the branch is cut reasonably flush with the trunk and slightly concave, as described above, it is an advantage to leave the slightly swollen bulge or wrinkled area at the base of the branch as decay seems less likely and healing proceeds more easily if the tree is pruned in this way.

How to Saw Branches: Always begin sawing from the underside of the branch first. Then saw from the top and the branch will be removed without splitting the trunk or tearing the bark away from the area below the branch. This procedure is also best used when using cutting or carving tools. Always use sharp tools when cutting trees, as a neat, clean cut will definitely facilitate the healing process. A rough cut where a branch has been "chewed" by the cutting tool, or torn away from the trunk, traps moisture that encourages rotting and is an attractive place for disease microorganisms to lodge in.

If the cut is large, it is a good idea to seal the wound. The reasons why this is considered as good horticultural practice are:
1. The cells are sealed, thus stopping excessive loss of sap.
2. The tree is protected from infection caused by fungi lodging in the freshly cut cells.
3. Die-back is discouraged, as the cells close to the cut don't dry out and the sap is able to circulate right up to the edge of the wound without being lost.
4. Callusing of the bark is more rapid.

In recent times there has been much controversy concerning the value of wound dressings and many plant pathologists have reached the conclusion that while some dressings are useless, others may even be harmful. The main argument of these scientists seems to be that trees have in-built systems to cope with the healing of wounds and that wound dressings are merely cosmetic.

This may be true, but a parallel situation can be seen with human beings. We also have in-built systems to heal wounds and when we receive small cuts we rarely bother too much and simply allow our bodies to take care of the situation. If we are very severely wounded, however, we give our body assistance, for example, by having stitches. Thus, with trees, small cuts are more than capable of taking care of themselves, while larger cuts may need a little help so that rotting doesn't set in.

One finding concerning wound dressings, however, may be helpful. That is that thick coatings — particularly of asphalt or tar-based dressings — can assist the disease process, as decay causing organisms may live and reproduce themselves in air bubbles that are formed when the dressing is applied.

One of the best treatments for cuts made on trees is to rub the wound immediately after it is made, with clay and spit. Many people do this, without thinking, after cutting a tree and the Chinese were using this technique of sealing cuts for centuries. Aesthetically, it makes the cut less noticeable, but it also has a couple of practical advantages. If the clay is rubbed into the wound, the abrasive action brings the ''wound hormone'' to the surface — thus assisting the healing process. Also, it was recently found that there is a soil fungus that acts as a parasite on decay-causing micro-organisms.

Some other methods for sealing large cuts on trees are: grafting compounds, water-based plastic glue, egg-white, acrylic paints (some people have tried to match the paint with the colour of the bark), face creams, aluminum duct-tape (recently found to facilitate healing because of its properties of reflecting heat from the wound and holding in the tree's own moisture).

(N.B. Another interesting discovery is the finding that if some of the freshly cut tree is pulverized and the mixture applied to the wound, healing is more rapid. Apparently the wound hormone — ''traumatic acid'' is thus in a concentrated state. Also, if the fresh wound is rinsed with water, the cell-division that promotes healing, is slowed down).

Also be aware that different trees have their own individual characteristics as far as wood is concerned and will react differently to being cut. Conifers, generally, take longer to heal from cuts but the wood doesn't rot easily. Deciduous trees, on the other hand, heal from wounds more rapidly, but the wood tends to rot fairly easily. Consequently, with the latter type, when cutting back or carving out, be careful not to leave any depressions that may hold moisture as this will encourage rotting to begin. If there is any exposed dead wood left as part of the design (see section on Jin, Shari, sabamiki and driftwood) it should be painted with concentrated lime-sulphur which acts as a preservative.

Thus we see that drastic pruning of a tree is safe if: it is not carried to excess, that is, with the wrong variety or at the wrong time; if wounds heal and disease doesn't set in; and, finally, if the tree is in a healthy condition.

Another interesting point is the fact that trees react differently to different types of cutting. Occasional hard pruning has the effect of stimulating growth, whereas continued pinching and trimming arrests overall growth. The reason for this is that the terminal bud of a tree or branch has a high concentration of the hormone known as auxin and this has the effect of inhibiting the side-growth below the bud. When the terminal bud is cut-off then, the latent side-shoots are given a short period of time in which to grow vigorously before the hormone imbalance is rectified with the re-establishment of another terminal bud.

Continued pinching and trimming of a tree, on the other hand, has the reverse effect because the leaves of a tree are the ''factories'' where sugars are manufactured. The constant removal of a proportion of the leaves decreases the food production and therefore slows down the plant's overall growth rate.

STYLISTIC CONSIDERATIONS

Choosing the Correct Front: When shaping by pruning, it is important to be sure of the front of the tree, as random pruning could spoil its eventual balance and style.

Firstly, as a good portion of the trunk will be visible, look to see from what angle the trunk line is most interesting and check that the taper is good. Also, occasionally, the trunk will appear to be larger from one side.

Secondly, do the branches extend all around the tree to create depth? Check to see if there is a suitable limb for the first side branch. If there is, this will help in the selection of the front, but remember that for most styles the first side branch looks well if it is about one third of the way up the proposed height of the tree.

Next, check any heavy, exposed roots that may exist. Like the main branches, they should be situated on the sides of the tree and definitely not straight forward toward the viewer.

Small branches and leaves change with the seasons, and, as defects in these are easily rectified, they should not be major considerations in your choice of front. The trunk, large branches and large surface roots, on the other hand, are difficult to change and should be your main concern.

Points to Note When Shaping by Pruning: Trim to a basically triangular shape (see Figure 22).

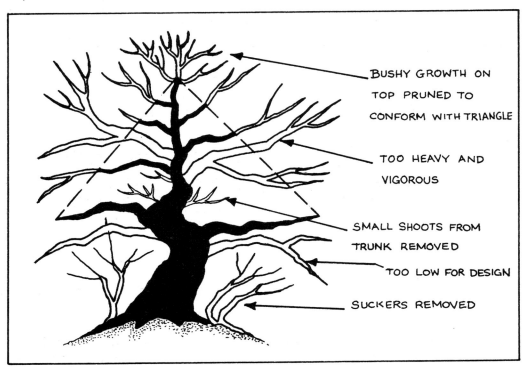

Figure 22: *Prune to basic triangular design*

Some branches should be eliminated because they either suggest that the tree is young or they are in unattractive positions (see Figure 23).

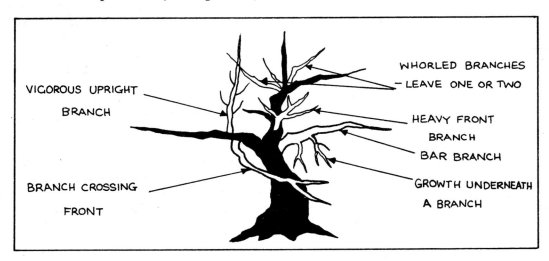

Figure 23: *Some branches to remove*

SOME PROBLEMS THAT MAY BE ENCOUNTERED WHEN USING THE SCULPTURAL TECHNIQUE FOR SHAPING

As mentioned above, if you are using this technique of styling, older trees are generally being used and, consequently, the basic structure provided by heavy surface roots, trunk line and the heavy branches, is already formed and difficult to change. In many instances, there will be deficiencies or problems in one or two of these aspects, that are difficult to rectify.

The Roots: Often, nursery stock has been propagated by cuttings and reasonably frequently, sturdy surface roots develop only on one side. Roots may be encouraged to grow on the side that is lacking, by a technique similar to the layering technique discussed in Chapter 1. The bark must be wounded at the places where roots are required and then planted deeper or covered with soil and moss or sphagnum moss, so that the wound doesn't dry out.

A couple of methods that work well are illustrated in the following diagram.

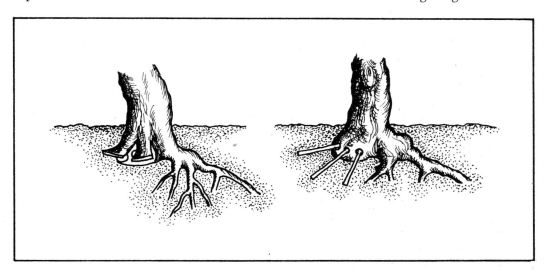

Figure 24: *Two Methods for forming new surface roots*

The first method is similar to one of the methods for taking thick cuttings (see Chapter 1) or making layers (see Chapter 1). The second method of root inducing is to drill holes in the places where roots are desired. Just drill to the beginning of hard wood, then insert matches or toothpicks into the holes, and plant the tree so that the matches are covered with soil. The surface roots develop more quickly in diameter if they are covered with soil and in a moist condition. When the tree tries to callus over the wound, it sends out roots along the toothpick. These methods of root inducing are better done in spring.

Another alternative for the creation of a more balanced root system is to graft attractive surface roots in the places required. Skill is required for this, particularly in order to make the job artistically pleasing and natural in appearance. The advantages, however, are that mature roots can be gained almost immediately and they can be placed in ideal positions.

Following, is an interesting article concerning the development of attractive surface roots on deciduous trees:

HOW TO PRODUCE WELL-FORMED SURFACE ROOTS ON DECIDUOUS TREES[2] —

Prepare a "plate" — it could be of fibro-cement or hardwood board — a couple of inches smaller than the size of the pot and of a similar shape to the intended pot for the tree when it has been styled.

In spring, when most trees can stand rougher treatment and survive — select a tree i.e. a young seedling 2 to 4 years of age, which has good distribution of roots around the trunk. If the tree was raised from a cutting there won't be any tap root to consider. Bareroot the tree and gently force the roots into horizontal position without breaking them. It might be that the junction between trunk and the main roots will not be perfect at first, but with time it will even out.

Place the tree in the correct position on the board (e.g. if Formal Upright — towards the centre; informal, slanted etc., according to the required position). Place the roots in the most attractive position, trying to lay them as flat as possible and tying them tightly to the board with string, but being careful not to damage the bark.

The tree may then be planted in the ground, with addition of good soil, or in a large pot for one or two years with the rootsystem covered with soil.

One year later, you will find the horizontal portion of roots to be much thicker and more even and where they reach the end of the board they turn down and develop branching. Trim the roots 1″ longer than the board and place the tree back in the ground or training pot if you want a more effective rootsystem in a shorter amount of time. When you are satisfied with the results, place the tree in the final container. N.B. If the roots are uncovered and exposed to the air, the bark hardens and increase in diameter is much slower. The roots that develop underground and in moist soil increase in diameter faster.

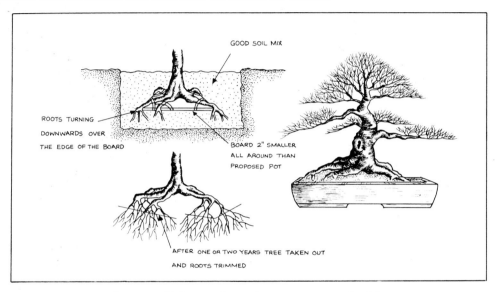

Figure 25: *How to produce well-formed surface roots on deciduous trees*

The Trunk: The most important thing to remember when using the sculptural technique for shaping is that the trunk must taper from a thick base to a delicate apex so that the finished product does not simply look "chopped off". Below are some ways of ensuring that a taper will be formed.

1. For informal styles, cut to a front or side branch.

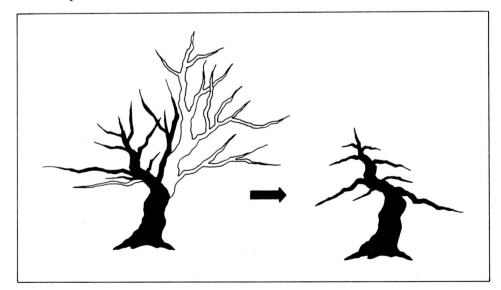

Figure 26: *Cut to front or side branch to form taper*

If the branch needs to be raised a little to give a better angle for the continuation of the trunk line, the original main trunk may be cut a little above the side branch and the branch tied to the stub. After sufficient time when the branch has set permanently at that angle, the stub may be removed. This technique is used often by the Chinese in preference to wiring.

Figure 27: *Tying up new apex to stub*

2. For a straight trunk, a variation on the latter technique of changing the apex is used. This time, the branch chosen to continue the trunk line should come from the front and is tied up as close as possible to the original leader.

3. Another technique[3] of raising a side branch into a vertical position to continue the line of a straight trunked bonsai is to gouge out the wood below the side branch till it reaches a

FRONT

Figure 28: *Tying up new apex for formal upright style*

thickness less than that of the branch. Normally, if we cut to a side branch and attempt to wire it into a vertical position, a break is likely to form on the side where there is tension (see Figure 29) and with the opposite side cut where the main trunk was removed, a "girdling" or "ring-barking" effect is likely to occur.

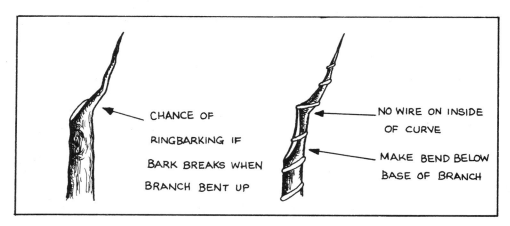

Figure 29: *Gouging out below new apex*

If the trunk is gouged out below the side branch (as seen in the diagram) and the gouged section is made long enough, a bend can be made below the branch section, such that the new leader assumes a vertical direction. As the force of the wire is on the actual curves, be careful not to wire a turn around the base of the side branch as this will encourage cracking in the region.

4. For many deciduous trees or trees that shoot back from old wood: As may be seen in Figure 30, after the initial cut has been made and the tree has sent out numerous shoots, carving may be done in the dormant season so that the branches appear to arise naturally out from the thick trunk. As may be seen in the illustration below, the carving is done in the form of clefts between the branches. A soft tree design is the result from using this shaping technique.

5. The Technique of Jin: This technique should be used for rugged trees with the appearance that they have lived in a severe environment. It is particularly suitable for use with conifers (see section of Jinning further on).

Figure 30: *Carving to form gradual taper into branches*

SOME METHODS FOR IMPROVING THE QUALITY OF THE TRUNK AND ENHANCING THE ILLUSION OF AGE.

1. For a trunk that lacks taper or is too narrow at the base, take advantage of the fact that the high concentration of the hormone auxin in the terminal bud causes a more rapid division of cells in the cambium layer of all sections of the tree below the bud and consequently these parts will thicken more quickly than the parts above the bud (providing the terminal buds on the top part are trimmed back). Therefore, if a lower branch is left to grow without trimming at the back of the tree, that branch will thicken as well as the section of the trunk below it. When the trunk has reached the desired thickness, the branch may be removed and the scar will be at the back of the tree. If a branch for this purpose doesn't exist or won't develop in the correct position, one may be grafted on for the purpose.

2. If there is an overly vigorous section of the tree (usually it is the top section) partial or full defoliation (see section on defoliation further on) may be done on that part to slow down its growth. Parts that have not been defoliated will grow at their normal rate.

3. If the bark on the lower portion of the trunk is cut longitudinally and just to the beginning of hard wood, the cambium will expand freely, forming scar tissue and a more rapid thickening of the trunk will result.

4. The trunk may be girdled with a piece of wire or string — just below soil level. The base of the trunk — just above this point will bulge and thicken due to the accumulation of sap that has been blocked in the downward passage by the girdling wire. One point to watch, however, particularly if wire is used, is that the girdling doesn't cut into the tree and ringbark it. Also, from the artistic point of view, the bulge should be right on soil level and not above it with the thinner section visible.

5. The bottom section of the trunk can be wired with fine wire. When it begins to get a little tight, the trunk thickens a little due to the process described in method 4 above. Before the wire cuts in too much, it should be removed and spirals made in the reverse direction. This can be done as many times as is desired.

6. The base of the trunk can be split into three or more sections by cutting up through the bottom of the rootball with a very sharp knife.

The sections can be eased out to form the effect of a buttressed base and a wooden plug or some such device is placed in the centre to keep the sections in the flared-out position. The technique is particularly suitable for trees that grow rapidly and have pliable wood.

7. Three or more trees may be grafted together (either twisted, plaited or just tied) to produce a more interesting and thicker gnarled trunk, and more branches lower down on the tree (see Figure 166).

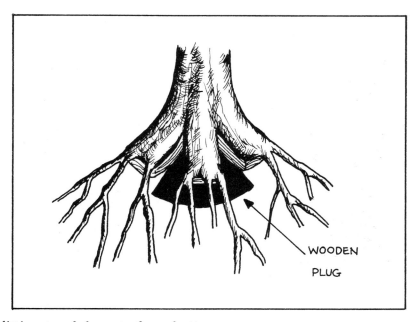

WOODEN PLUG

Figure 31: *Splitting trunk base to form buttress*

This technique, as well as plaiting of the roots, is used often by Chinese bonsai growers. If roots are plaited they must be covered with soil and kept moist until they graft together and thicken. When thickening is sufficient they may be exposed and the plaited or twisted roots become part of the trunk and give the tree an ancient, gnarled appearance (see Figure 164).
8. Careful flexing of the trunk or branches may be done to increase their diameter. This process tends to break the cambium layer loose and the resultant healing process increases the girth. The procedure must be used with caution and may not be possible to use on brittle varieties. (N.B. An experiment was recently conducted where three trees were subjected to different degrees of trunk movement. The first was staked firmly so that it could not move, the second was allowed to move freely in the wind, while the third was artificially vibrated at regular intervals. The trunks of the three trees thickened at different rates. After a period of time, number one was the thinnest, number two was a little thicker and number three was the thickest. A tree that has its trunk free to move as it is developing also grows less in height, has a better taper, a larger rootsystem and can withstand natural elements better than a tree that has been "staked").

The Branches: 1. Very often, one finds an old tree with potential for bonsai styling due to its attractive trunk line and perhaps such qualities as a thick trunk and attractive surface roots. However, to gain such qualities, the tree often has very thick awkward branches that are unattractive and difficult to change. If one is confronted with such a situation, there are a couple of courses of action that may be pursued.

Firstly, if the variety will shoot back from old wood, the best decision would be to cut off all the thick, awkward branches and let new ones develop that sprout in the correct positions (N.B. The tree should be in a larger sized container or in the ground to encourage buds to develop freely). These younger branches, being thinner and more pliable, will be easier to train into directions that complement the line of the trunk and also will be more in proportion — actually making the trunk appear thicker. If you desire the lower branches to be thicker than those higher up, they may be allowed to grow for a while without trimming the terminal bud. When sufficient thickness is achieved, the branches should be trimmed back to the correct length.

An alternative for varieties that will shoot back from old wood, would be to use the Lingnan "grow and clip" technique (see further on). Using this technique, the branch need not be cut off flush with the trunk, but a small section could be left, from which side-buds would develop. One of the side buds would then be chosen to continue the line of the branch. Wherever such cuts are made, a change of line would result that would give an aged, gnarled appearance to the tree.

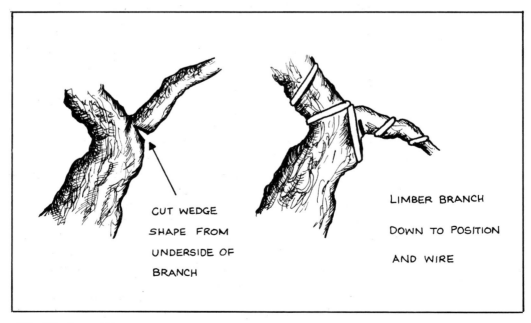

CUT WEDGE
SHAPE FROM
UNDERSIDE OF
BRANCH

LIMBER BRANCH
DOWN TO POSITION
AND WIRE

Figure 32: *Undercutting*

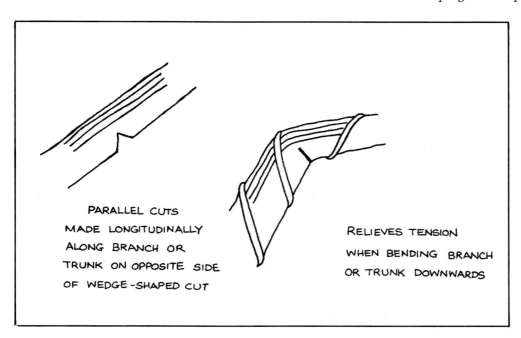

PARALLEL CUTS MADE LONGITUDINALLY ALONG BRANCH OR TRUNK ON OPPOSITE SIDE OF WEDGE-SHAPED CUT

RELIEVES TENSION WHEN BENDING BRANCH OR TRUNK DOWNWARDS

Figure 33: *Undercutting midway along trunk or branch*

If the variety will not shoot back easily or at all, the above courses of action may not be taken. If the thick, awkward branches could be modified so that they had a more attractive line and angle, they would not be so displeasing. Unfortunately, though, such branches are often too thick or brittle to wire into attractive positions. If this is the case, the technique of "undercutting" may be used.

One of the most unattractive aspects of a heavy branch is its initial upward direction that is difficult to modify and which forms an unsightly "bow" if the middle and end sections of the branch are styled into a more downward direction.

If a wedge-shaped section is cut out from the underside of the branch, just at the join of branch and trunk, the branch may be eased down to the desired angle and wired or tied into position (see Figure 32).

If it is desired to make a sharp bend midway along the branch, a wedge is similarly cut on the inside of the desired curve. However, with this procedure there is excessive tension on the outside curve side and snapping of the branch is often the result. To alleviate the tension and make it less likely for breakages to occur, the outside curve of the branch should have a few parallel cuts made longitudinally along it. The cuts should be made down to the beginning of hard wood and the effect of this is that there is a little movement of the bark sideways that relieves the tensile forces stretching the bark along the line of the branch (see Figure 33).

Another alternative for thick, awkward branches on trees that don't shoot back easily from old wood, is to graft smaller ones onto the tree at the appropriate places.

2. A new branch can be encouraged by not trimming it till it reaches the stage of development you are satisfied with. We are again taking advantage of the auxins and gibberellins in the terminal bud that promote the more rapid thickening of the section below it.

3. If there is a weak branch on a tree that you wish to develop but which doesn't seem inclined to grow quickly, or if there is a bud that you wish to develop into a branch but which seems determined to remain latent, it is often possible to increase their vigour by making a horizontal cut in the bark just below the bud or branch. What happens is that as the sugars produced in the leaves of the tree are moving downward toward the rootsystem through the outside layer of the tree (known as the phloem) the flow of sap is interrupted by the cut. The excess sugars then accumulate above the cut and are used by the branch or bud, thereby forcing them into action. This imbalance, however, is not permanent and as soon as the tree heals over the cut, the sap flow will continue down the tree as usual. If you wish to create this imbalance for a longer period of time, the knife may be dipped into grafting solution just prior to making the cut. The healing process will then take a little longer.

LINGNAN — GROW AND CLIP TECHNIQUE

The "Grow and Clip" technique is a method of shaping trees that is akin to modelling, as the work of art is made from a "building up" rather than a "chipping away" process.

The technique originated at the end of the nineteenth century in a monastery in Kwangtung Province, Southern China. In China, before the Cultural Revolution, the monks were somewhat like those of medieval England. They were the learned few of the community and consequently they would be the ones that worked to perpetuate the country's culture. Apart from being well-read in the classics of history, philosophy and poetry, they would also be the poets, painters and calligraphers that created the culture for future generations. As these men practiced their calligraphy, their hands developed a certain characteristic movement associated with the use of the brush. An appreciation for abstract beauty developed as well as for dramatic and abrupt changes of angle.

When these same men turned their hands to landscape painting, the materials also were the same: brush, ink, silk or paper, and, not surprisingly, we find the same characteristics as were displayed in the calligraphy. The trees had an abstract beauty and were rugged and poetic with sudden, dramatic angle changes.

In the courtyards of these monasteries, the monks had cultivated pot plants for many centuries. Some were simply for appreciation of foliage, flowers or fruit, while others were rugged, old trees collected from the mountains. Some of them were modified in design by pulling branches down with string or weights — methods that tend to produce soft curves. As the monks in the monastery at Lingnan painted their landscapes and looked at the spectacular mountains that surrounded their village, they longed to create such designs in their potted trees. The method for achieving these angular and dramatic styles was finally learned by observing Nature at work. As a tree grows, the main line from base to apex naturally pursues a vertical and straight direction. However, if the tree has germinated in a rough environment — many natural hazards may destroy the apex and a side branch is then forced to become the new head of the tree, while changing the line of the trunk as it develops. The technique is, perhaps, the most natural method of shaping trees and it is conceivable that a whole tree may be designed without the use of any means other than pruning. It is a relatively slow method of styling but it is the only effective way of producing sharp angle changes and a rugged and gnarled appearance.

For bonsai growers, the technique is divided into two parts: firstly, drastic pruning, and secondly, a necessary period of growth. An important fact to remember is that the terminal bud stimulates the cells of the cambium layer to divide and multiply rapidly through the action of two hormone groups: auxins and gibberellins, so the first cut should be made only after the trunk or branch has reached the desired diameter. The first cut is then made above a side

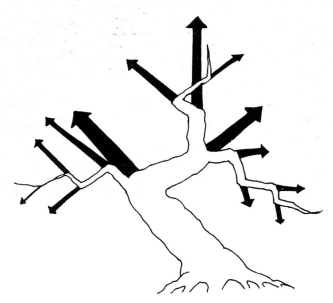

Figure 34: *Lingnan "clip and grow" technique*

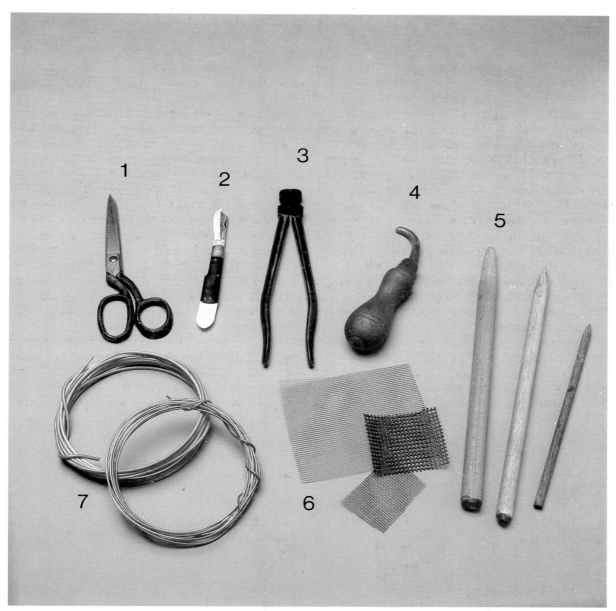

Plate X: *Materials and basic tool requirements*

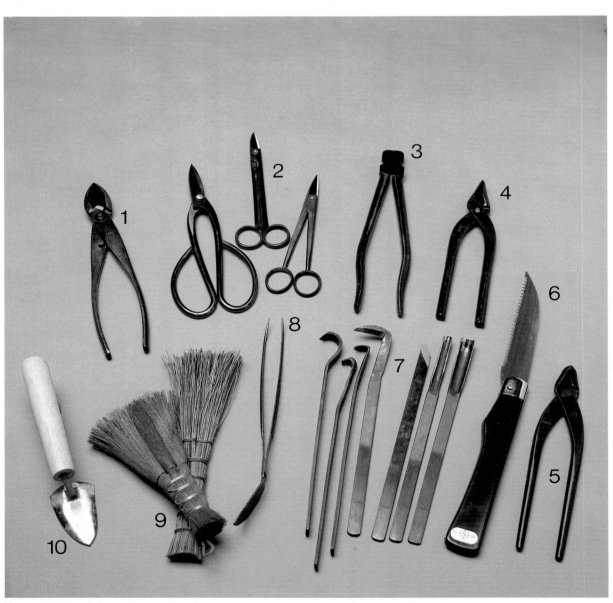

Plate XI: *Bonsai tools*

branch or bud and its location and position changes the line of the trunk or branch as it develops. This replacement section, however, should then be allowed a period of growth without trimming, until its diameter is just a little thinner than the section below. In this way, a taper is gradually developed. During the period of growth, the replacement section grows well beyond the outline of the tree shape and it is often tempting to trim it back. However, if you resist the temptation, thickening of the section will be far more rapid.

The "grow and clip" technique is a method of shaping that is indeed slower than most, yet it can be variable depending on the diameter of trunk you are satisfied with, the variety of the tree and its vigour and growing conditions. If the tree is grown in a large container, or in the ground and if the soil drains well and has adequate nutrition, the tree will thicken and develop far more rapidly. With the increase in the size of the rootsystem, the trunk thickens to cope with the need for increased transport of water and dissolved minerals.

The trees designed by this technique of shaping have a "natural" appearance as they are styled by a method used by Nature herself. However, they also have the poetic quality of the trees in Chinese landscape paintings and the abstract beauty of calligraphy — and, as with these latter two art forms, the aim is not so much to reproduce but to "suggest" reality and to capture the character or essence of a tree or landscape.

Figure 35: *Tree shaped by Lingnan "clip and grow" technique*

TRIMMING TECHNIQUES

When a tree grows in the ground without any trimming by man and without any drastic natural forms of pruning — such as being struck by lightning — an interesting situation arises where the tree has to make compromises as it ages. A tree in youth characteristically grows quickly. Because leaves are few in the early stages, they are reasonably large so that adequate food will be manufactured for the tree to continue developing. Internodes are long and leggy, as the tree works to establish its position and anchor itself in the ground as quickly as possible.

As a tree approaches middle age, however, this rapid rate of growth begins to slow down and in old age the tree does not seem to grow at all. Like all living things, trees have a limit to their growth. Of course some trees naturally grow larger than others and some trees have specialized modifications which allow them to seemingly grow rapidly for an indefinite period of time (The banyans, for example, grow in height, but mainly in width, so aerial roots come down to form props for the ever lengthening branches. With time, it is difficult to determine where the original trunk was. The swamp cypress is another interesting example, where the widening of the buttressed base, with its reinforcing webs, acts as a support for the tree's great height). Generally, though, a tree cannot continue increasing in size forever, yet to remain healthy all plants must grow. The compromise comes with the trees expanding more slowly and characteristically producing smaller leaves and shorter internodes. This is one of the elements that indicates to us that a tree is old and for this reason we try to produce small leaves and short internodes in our bonsai — particularly at the extremities of the branches and at the apex.

To induce the formation of smaller leaves, short internodes and finer, more numerous branchlets forming dense clusters, trimming must be attended to regularly. If trimming is done consistently, the terminal buds, that inhibit side growth, are removed and consequently lateral or axillary buds become more active. The growth of the tree is not stopped, but it is repositioned and the vigour is divided into many leaves and branches, consequently making them smaller.

There is another group of hormones called Cytokinins acting in trees that supposedly work in opposition to auxin i.e. they promote side-branching. Auxin, however, is the more dominant hormone and the effect of the cytokinins can be seen only as we travel further away from the growing tip. Consequently, when the terminal growth is removed, the cytokinins can be seen at work as the tree responds by sending out more side growth.

Another interesting fact is that apical dominance is strongest when minerals and light are inadequate so that position and food elements may also be significant factors in the formation of good side-branching and ramification. As well as this, root and top growth are usually closely related and trimming of roots with repotting and their consequential branching, promotes the development of branches on the top.

Also, as mentioned previously, repeated pinching arrests overall growth due to the fact that a proportion of the leaves are repeatedly being removed, thus cutting down on the amount of sugars being formed by the plant.

Yet another reason why trimming helps to produce smaller leaves and shorter internodes is that if done after the initial spring flush of growth, the secondary growth occurs later in the growth cycle, when sap flow and vigour is not so great. If you desire a lot of side shoot development, but do not mind more active growth in the form of larger leaves and longer internodes, however, it would be better to trim earlier in the growing season.

As trimming is attended to and as more and more fine growth develops, thinning may become necessary to prevent overcrowding.

Another point to consider is that if a tree is to be trimmed, it should be in a healthy condition. If it is not in peak condition, it would be better, in most cases, to leave more foliage on the tree and allow it to recuperate.

Figure 36: *Renewal pruning*

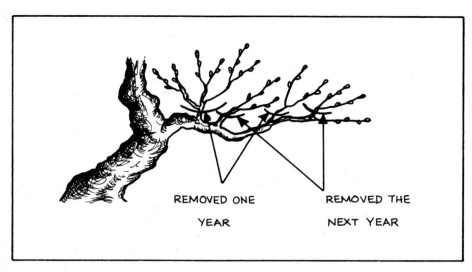

Figure 37: *Renewal pruning on flowering and fruiting trees*

When a bonsai becomes established in design and proportion, the shape is retained by trimming. However, as mentioned before, every tree must grow to remain healthy and to check the expansion of a tree merely by nipping the buds, is impossible. How the proportions of a bonsai are maintained differs with the type of tree it is, its age and the intentions of the cultivator.

With plants that do not produce new buds on old wood, or do so unpredictably, or slowly, trimming can only really limit the size and quantity of new growth produced. Such trees gradually become larger as time goes on. It should be stressed, however, that growth can be severely slowed down so that the expansion in size is not greatly noticeable.

Other tree varieties that will shoot back from old wood may be kept about the same size through the technique of renewal pruning. This can be undertaken in a couple of different ways. First of all, the tree can periodically experience more drastic pruning and then gradually return to the desired dimension (see Figure 36).

The other alternative is to encourage new branches from the trunk or new branchlets to take the place of those becoming too long to fit with the tree's design.

This last technique can also be used to remove old wood that can no longer produce flowers and fruit or can produce them only at the branch ends. It can also be used on conifers and varieties that do not easily shoot back from old wood, providing there are side shoots or buds already existent at the point of cutting (see Figures 37 & 38).

Figure 38: *Renewal pruning on trees that don't develop buds on old wood*

METHODS OF TRIMMING DIFFERENT VARIETIES:

Some varieties are very easy to keep in shape (e.g. pines, spruces, firs, beeches) as they only have one major sprouting of buds per year. Others, however, grow throughout the year (e.g. junipers, maples) and may need trimming quite a few times throughout their active period of growth.

With trees that normally grow upright, particularly with many of the conifers, where apical dominance is especially noticeable, the top will develop far more rapidly and produce more buds than the lower section. Therefore, more attention to trimming the top will be necessary. With many dwarf, prostrate, shrub or creeping varieties, on the other hand, the lower branches tend to be more vigorous and consequently will need to be checked more frequently.

Broadleaf Varieties:

e.g. Maples, elms. These are pruned back to the first or second node after the new soft growth has matured. The reason for this is that the buds at the leaf bases are then ready to develop. Some trees have opposite or paired buds (e.g. maples, serissas, jasmine, privet) and others are alternate (e.g. elms, beeches, hornbeams). If it is the latter, cut to the leaf facing in the direction you wish the branch to develop. If the tree has opposite buds, cut at the length you want and rub off the bud on the wrong side, if you don't want it to develop. If a horizontal line is desired and you only have buds on the upper or lower side of the branch, cut to the lower one. The reason for this is that the growth tends to develop in an upward direction and this characteristic will help you train the branch horizontally.

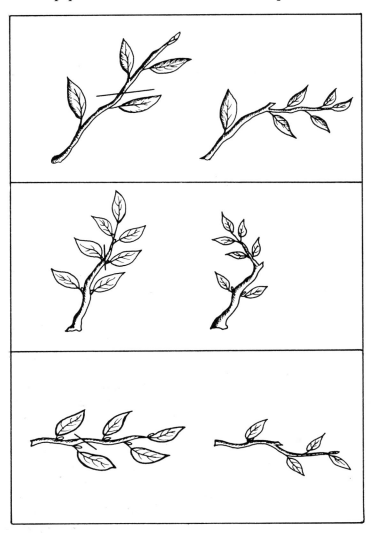

Figure 39: *Cutting to correct bud for certain direction of growth*

Another point here is that if you are wishing to strengthen a certain branch, cut to the upper bud. If on the other hand, you wish the branch to be not quite so vigorous, cut to the lower bud.

Also, when cutting back broadleaf varieties, it is better to make the cut a little above the desired bud and slanting up toward it. If you try and make the cut too close, the bud may be damaged, or the exposed cut so near to the bud, may encourage die-back. Likewise, too long a stub is not good, as the stub is subject to drying up and decaying and may injure the bud. After the bud has begun to grow, the little bit of die-back may be removed with safety. If the growth is soft when trimming is done, fingers may be used to pinch back the tree. However, scissors will be necessary if the growth has hardened.

FIGS: These are extremely vigorous broadleaf evergreens. For normal trimming and training purposes, the procedure as outlined above for broadleaf varieties, may be followed. However, a couple of extra points may be of interest. Firstly, when the tree has reached the desired shape and size, the best method for trimming is to remove the sheath of leaves entirely before it opens and extends into a shoot (see Figure 40).

REMOVE SHEATH OF NEW LEAVES

Figure 40: *Trimming back a fig by removing the sheath*

Secondly, if you wish to let the tree develop a little in size but do not want large leaves or long internodes, the procedure is to remove the outer sheath by twisting it. The first leaf that would develop on the shoot is then exposed. Continue the twisting motion, removing all the leaves until one or two in the centre of the bud are left. These are the immature leaves that would have sprouted at the very end of the shoot if the sheath of leaves had been allowed to open and develop. Because these small leaves are now exposed, they immediately begin to grow, yet they develop with characteristically small leaves and short internodes because they are not fully developed.

WILLOWS: Willow branches develop better and have less die-back if they are not trimmed throughout the growing season, so cut back secondary branches hard in autumn or in late winter prior to spring growth and then allow shoots to develop throughout spring and summer. Willow branches naturally grow in an upward direction but may be flexed down to assume a weeping manner, without the use of wire. In fact, branches are inclined to die back if wire is applied. As they develop long shoots and do not like trimming in the growing season, weeping or cascading designs are the best choices for style.

Figure 42: *Willow trimmed at end of growing season*

Figure 41: *Willow bonsai*

Flowering and Fruiting Varieties:

When determining the best time to trim flowering and fruiting trees, two things should be kept in mind. Firstly, the season of flowering and whether the flowers develop on old or new wood.

VARIETIES THAT PRODUCE FLOWERS ON NEW SPRING GROWTH: (e.g. cotoneaster, pyracantha, citrus, gardenia, jasmine, bougainvillea, crepe myrtle, roses, pomegranite, privet, indian hawthorn). Do hard pruning after flowering and/or fruiting is over, or immediately prior to the growing season (this is usually late winter to early spring). Some produce flower buds laterally and at the base of the new growth, so that after the flowers have developed, the new growth at the end of the shoot may be trimmed to keep the bonsai in shape without affecting the flowering. Others, however, (crepe myrtle, jasmine, pomegranite) produce flowers only terminally — at the tips of the new shoots — and, consequently, the bonsai is usually out of shape for a period of time if flowers are desired. Some, though, flower early, on the end of a short shoot, while the later flowering examples bloom at the end of a long shoot.

VARIETIES THAT PRODUCE FLOWERS ON OLDER WOOD: Many varieties produce flowers on the previous years growth and, as a general rule, it is safe to say that any drastic pruning or heavy trimming should be attended to immediately after flowering or fruiting. Some produce flowers mainly on the tips of last year's growth (e.g. camellias and azaleas) so that after cutting back hard after flowering (usually flowering is in winter through to spring) the tree may be trimmed till mid-summer. All trimming should then cease, as the flower buds for the following season of flowering will then start to develop.

If the flower bud develops on the tip of last year's growth and the bud begins to develop early in the previous growing season, then pruning back to shape will have to be done every second year if flowers and fruit are desired.

Other varieties develop flower buds on the lower nodes of last year's growth (e.g. wisterias). With this type, pinching back of the shoots can be attended to throughout the growing season, providing the first few nodes are not removed. Any heavy pruning, however, should be done immediately after flowering.

Fruit trees differ with regard to whether they form flowers on a. last year's lateral branches or b. terminally, on spurs or short stub branches. In the first group are peaches, most almonds, some apricots, filbert and hazelnut. In the second group are apples, pears, cherries, most plums, most apricots and some almonds.

With all flowering and fruiting bonsai, even though it is a pleasure to observe their seasonal variations, do not sacrifice their shape and style. Especially in the early stages of training it is better to concentrate on developing the basic structure of trunk line and branches and then in building up a dense system of branchlets and twigs. In order to do this, pruning may be necessary at times when buds or flowers would be removed and also, vegetative growth will be far more rapid if the tree doesn't produce the flowers. Another point to keep in mind is that to produce fruit and flowers, a tree must use an exceptional amount of "food" and expend a great deal of energy and a few varieties (particularly when in containers) are seriously weakened by the effort. Pomegranite is a notable example and sometimes branches can be lost if too many flowers and fruit are produced. If the shape of the tree is its main attraction, it would be better to sacrifice flowers and/or fruit if it is seen to have an ill-effect on the plant.

Corded and Scale-Like Growth:
Examples of corded growth may be seen in the so-called "mature" foliage of junipers and scale growth is seen in the "mature" foliage of false cypress varieties (chamaecyparis). The new, light-coloured growth at the tips is pinched out with the fingertips.

   The Australian native "Sheoak" (Casuarina) is an interesting example that is trimmed in a similar way but which has a type of growth quite unlike any other type of tree. The needle-like foliage is made up of a whole series of interlocking segments and these are "fingertip pruned" by pulling them apart at the desired point. This "needle-like" foliage, however, is, botanically, not foliage at all, but are actually the stems of the tree and at each point of division there is a whorl of microscopic leaves.

Tufted Growth:
Seen in the juvenile foliage of junipers and chamaecyparis and in cedars, firs, spruces, larches, cryptomerias, swamp cypress, metasequoia, yew, hemlock. The junipers and chamaecyparis varieties produce new buds frequently throughout the growing season, while the cedars, firs and spruces tend to have one group of buds developing per year. The procedure is to pinch out most of the tuft by gripping the top of the central section with the fingertips and pulling it out. The timing is important, as pinching too early will remove all of the bud and if pinched too late — after the bud has begun to elongate — not enough will be trimmed and growth will tend to become straggly. If "finger-tip" pruning is done on these varieties, there will be no browning back and foliage will become smaller in size and more compact.

Pines:
These grow in a "whorled" pattern of growth and the buds are in the form of so-called "candles". By trimming these candles at different times and in different ways, various effects may be obtained.

   When a tree is established in shape and proportion, the middle, vigorous candle is trimmed out entirely and one or two of the secondary subsidiary candles are left and then pinched in half. If the middle candle is not removed until late in the season — just as it begins to open into needles, the side candles will develop with shorter needles. The reason for this is that if the centre candle is removed early in the growing season, when the natural vigour of the tree is high — the subsidiary candles begin to compete for the apical position and, consequently, grow quickly and with relatively long needles. If, on the other hand, the centre candle is left till later in the season, the development of the subsidiary candles is held back by its dominance. Afterwards, when the centre candle is removed, the side candles are suddenly called upon to grow in order to continue the line of growth. However, because the vigorous growth period has already passed and because the buds have been retarded by the main candle, the subsidiary candles develop more slowly and, as a consequence, have shorter needles. This method of trimming, practiced usually in late spring or early summer, is good for older pines that have a good basic design and where it is desired that new growth be kept minimal.

   If trimming of the centre candle is done in **late** summer, leaving just a few needles at the base, the growth that develops around this cut produces a different type of compact tuft of needles, usually quite reduced in size. If the cut was made too late for growth to extend before winter, the compact tufted form of growth will be latent through the dormant season and emerge the following spring.

A pine in a healthy condition may have all its new buds removed completely, early in spring as the candles are about to grow, in order to force buds to develop further back on the tree. That season, small buds should develop at the terminal ends of branches, perhaps at the bases of needles and even sometimes on older wood. If a branch is required at a particular point, cut back all buds and remove needles except for a few near the required position. Complete removal of candles should not be done every year, as the health of the tree will be jeopardized.

If more trunk and/or branch thickening is required, candles can be left to grow without cutting till autumn. Next spring, numerous buds will develop further back in the tree and they should be fairly small in size.

REGULATING THE VIGOUR DISTRIBUTION

Different trees grow and develop in a variety of ways. The growth habit and ultimate design of a tree — unless affected by outside influences such as being broken in a storm — will be largely determined by the areas of the tree that are most vigorous. Often, in bonsai work, parts of the tree that we wish to be delicate will be overly strong and vice versa. Therefore, it is good to know the natural tendency of the tree you are working with as well as the techniques necessary to regulate the vigour distribution.

Most trees display apical dominance — particularly when young. This type of growth produces a single trunk style. Trees with less apical dominance (mainly angiosperms) produce a more "branched-out" effect with a soft crown made up of many branches. The type of growth characteristic of a certain tree may be determined by the pattern of bud growth and development at the start of the growing season. Pines, for example, exhibit more vigorous bud development at the top of the tree. Often, candles at the top can be 7.5–10 cm (three to four inches) long, while those at the bottom are about 2.5 cm (1 inch). Most trees that display apical dominance through their life, however, change to a more "diffuse" pattern of growth in old age, so that one way of differentiating an old pine from a young pine, is the fact that the older one has probably lost its definite pointed top and has developed a slightly softer crown.

A few trees, on the other hand, develop stronger buds toward the bottom of the tree, while others display even development throughout the tree.

VERTICAL HORIZONTALIS AND VICE VERSA:

In the bonsai world one often hears or reads of the idea that a tree should be styled in a way that is "natural" for the particular variety. The argument is given that if the tree is "forced" into a type or direction of growth that it would not normally have, the result would be "unnatural", "grotesque", and not in line with good horticultural practice.

Whether or not one is influenced by arguments such as these, it is more than likely that when we come across a prostrate or creeping variety we immediately think of shaping the plant into either the cascade or semi-cascade style. This may be a good choice of style for the tree, but we should be aware that there are other possibilities — possibilities that are opposite to the tree's natural habit but which will ultimately lead to a better styled bonsai.

The tree should be thought of as an art medium, for a bonsai is not an exact replica in miniature of a full grown tree in nature, but a stylized model — suggesting the essence of a particular scene rather than presenting a reproduction to scale of the scene itself.

One can make an analogy with other arts. All artists use their medium to recreate a certain vision or idea. If we go to a paint store, we can see colour charts where paint specimens are set out. These have not been "shaped" by an artist's brush and consequently do not suggest anything beyond that which they are. When the artist uses paint, however, he no longer wants paint to look like paint — he mixes it and changes it so that it calls to mind a scene he has observed or imagined.

Similarly, a prostrate plant such as Juniperus procumbens or Juniperus horizontalis glauca, may successfully be made to look like a towering spruce or redwood; or a garden shrub such as azalea or gardenia, may be used to represent a massive aged tree.

Making a "vertical" hoizontalis presents no problem. It is when we tackle the opposite (i.e. a vertical growing tree taken horizontally or down) that we may run into difficulties. The problem here, however, is not aesthetic but horticultural. Trees and plants have a natural tendency to grow upward toward the light. Even when the structure (i.e. trunk and branches) are prostrate, the foliage turns upward to obtain light for photosynthesis. Thus, when we train the horizontal structure into a vertical direction, the tree is healthy and LOOKS natural because of the upward growth of foliage. The opposite effect, however, is harder to achieve since the tree wants to grow up and we are training it into a downward direction.

Some naturally upright trees can be trained into cascades without any setback to the plant. Examples of a few successful trees in this category are: Californian Redwood, pines and cedars. Others, however, are more difficult. Some varieties of spruce, for example, even object to severe training of branches on an upright tree.

The advantage of using prostrate trees for cascades, is that there is no competition between the "head" and "tail" of the cascade. In most vertical growing trees we find a progressive lack of vigour as we move down the "tail" of the cascade. There are, however, ways of overcoming or lessening this problem.

One method of regulating the vigour distribution of the tree is by selective trimming, (this method can be applied to upright trees as well, where there is more vigour in the top-most parts and less in the lower branches). When the time for trimming arrives — early in the growing season — trim the lowest third of the tree first (i.e. the bottom branchlets on the tail of the cascade). A week or two later trim the middle third and two weeks after that trim the top third.

This method may seem to be contrary to what we would normally do, yet the reasons for this procedure are based on the natural growth pattern of plants. Trees do not simply start growing in spring, continue to grow evenly through the growing season and then stop as the cool weather approaches. Rather, they observe a definite growth curve where the sap flow reaches a peak — usually early in summer — and then begins to decline (with perhaps a smaller rise in autumn before it slows down for winter).

If we relate this to the training practice just mentioned, we see that the trimming of the weaker portion early in the growth curve, takes advantage of the excess sap and this stimulates the tree to send out more buds. The second and third trimmings occur progressively later in the season, when the sap flow is not so strong and therefore the tree is not as eager to send out so much new growth. However, since the natural vigour of the tree is strongest at the top — the effect is that all parts of the tree send out equalized growth.

It is also a horticultural fact that the more leaves there are on a branch or branchlet, the greater will be the vigour of that portion of the tree. This fact can be used in conjunction with the above method of trimming. Once the lower third has been trimmed early in the season, it should be left to grow without further cutting that year. The top section, however, after it is cut later in the season, can be further trimmed or have some of its foliage removed as it seems necessary.

Another method of increasing vigour of the lower branches of a cascade, is to place the pot on its side so that the cascade tail is growing in a more upright direction. It is also possible to spray the lower part of the cascade's tail with a foliage fertilizer to help equalize the tree's growth.

As mentioned above, these problems of vigour distribution are not applicable when we attempt to make a "vertical horizontalis". We may, however, encounter stylistic problems, particularly if we are using old nursery stock. In old horizontal-growing trees, there may be a curve close to the ground that seems impossible to modify by wiring. If we really want to straighten or partially straighten this curve, we can do so with advanced bending tools such as jacks, but this takes a long period of time. Quite often this curve can be used in the style of the tree by altering the angle of viewing (see Figures 43 & 44), and either wiring the top part to conform with the first curve or using the Lingnan "grow and clip" method by cutting to a branch growing in the required angle.

At this stage you may be asking the questions: "Why go to all this trouble? Why not work with what Nature has provided, instead of making a tree look like something it is not?" Are we, in fact, merely being fickle by asking a horizontalis to grow vertically and vice versa?

Firstly, I would like to stress that I am not advocating that we consistently make a tree grow opposite to its natural growing habit, but that when, for example, a tree will make a mediocre cascade easily, it might — with a little extra thought — make an outstanding upright.

Secondly, as mentioned above, Bonsai is an Art and all artists use, change and extend the possibilities of the medium they are working with. Again, you may say that our Art is a little different to most, since we are working with a LIVING medium — not simply inert paint or

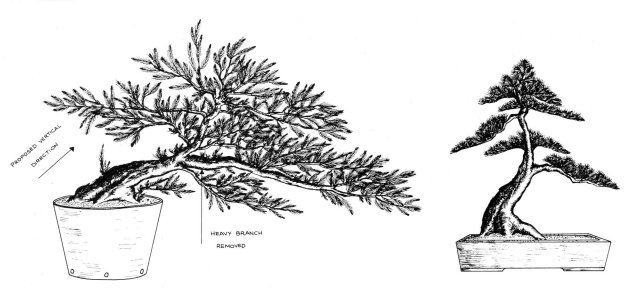

PROPOSED VERTICAL DIRECTION

HEAVY BRANCH
REMOVED

Figures 43 & 44: *Altering angle of viewing*

stone. This is quite true and it would be of no use to artistically change the habit of a tree and in so doing end up with a dead one.

This is where it is essential to know the variety we are working with and work within its limitations. The health of the tree is, in fact, our guide as to whether or not our shaping is natural or not (this, however, does not mean "artistically pleasing" — Nature, herself, can be quite grotesque at times).

There is an idea in philosophy that anything the human mind can imagine exists somewhere at some time — be it past, present or future. Thus we can similarly say that if a bonsai is growing in a particular style and is healthy, then at some place and some time it could occur in nature and is therefore "natural". If a hundred seeds of a single species germinated in a hundred different environments, nature would sculpt each in a different way, and the ones that couldn't adapt would become non-existent.

We may say that a pine is "naturally" an upright tree — not seeking to grow towards the ground but to be majestically tall and spreading. This might be true of the seed that germinates in a position with ideal conditions, yet a pine on the sea-shore might be "shaped" into a windswept style, while the pine in the craggy mountain-side might be a rugged cascade. Which one can we call "natural" or "unnatural"? — we can only say that if it will grow in a healthy manner in that style it is possible that it will occur in nature somewhere, even if we have never observed that particular variety growing in such a way.

DEFOLIATION:

"Defoliation" refers to the removal of leaves from a tree other than the natural leaf-fall on deciduous varieties. The technique is practiced for many reasons;

1. To induce a new crop of leaves that are smaller in size.

2. To get rid of leaves damaged by wind, dryness or excessively hot weather and replace them with a crop of new, fresh foliage.

3. If defoliation is done early enough (i.e. as soon as leaves harden in spring), the second lot of leaves might encourage the new buds of future branchlets to start developing. Thus, ramification may be increased twice in one season.

4. Better autumn colouring may result in deciduous trees.

5. The tree actually "ages" twice in one season.

6. If transplanting has to be done out of season, defoliation of the tree acts as a safety precaution.

7. Partial defoliation of vigorous areas of the tree can be practiced to regulate the vigour distribution.

8. Partial defoliation may be done for grooming purposes, i.e. to remove leaves where they fall outside the line of the design or clutter the view.

Complete defoliation, generally, should not be practiced on conifers and as a general rule, it is best practiced on varieties that branch easily, as these are usually the ones most ready to send out a second crop of leaves. Quite often these will be "thin-leaved" deciduous or broadleaf evergreens, however, certain "thick-leaved" varieties, such as figs, respond well to defoliation.

Method: If defoliation is done early in the season, during the peak of the sap flow, it is better to defoliate over two sessions, so that the tree doesn't suffer a kind of "high blood pressure" effect. The first cutting may involve the removal of three-quarters of every leaf, or cutting off half the number of leaves (either from one side or scattered over the entire tree). A week or two later, the remainder may be removed.

If defoliation is done later in the season, all the leaves may be removed in one session. The procedure is not to tear the leaves off (or else the new bud at the base of the stalk will be destroyed), but to cut them off, leaving a little of the stalk. If the stalk is thick or very long, make sure at least half to three quarters of the stalk is removed. This is important, as it has been found that enough photosynthesis (i.e. the manufacture of sugars) may be carried out in the stalk so as to inhibit the regrowth of leaves.

A tree that is to be defoliated must be in a healthy condition. Also, defoliation should not be done every year unless the tree is young and/or vigorous. The year of rootpruning is probably the best time to defoliate as this is the year when the tree is likely to have larger leaves. It would also have a little extra vigour with which to cope with the removal of leaves.

Another point of caution is that after defoliation has taken place, no water will be lost through the leaves and the tree will probably not be drying out as rapidly as before. If watering is continued at a similar rate as before the leaves were removed, then the soil will become stale and root-rot will probably occur. Frequent light spraying of the branches with water, however, definitely encourages bud development and regrowth of leaves.

The timing of defoliation is important: If it is done too early — when the sap flow is high in the tree — 100% of the leaves will be replaced and they will regrow very quickly but they will probably be as large or larger than the ones removed. If defoliation is carried out too late, on the other hand, leaves will be small but very few leaf buds will sprout — perhaps only 2 or 3 per cent. The graph below shows an experiment done by the U.S.S.R. Academy of Science and illustrates the point that defoliation should be done at the time when smallness of leaves and adequate regrowth will be the result. Generally, early to mid-summer is the best time.

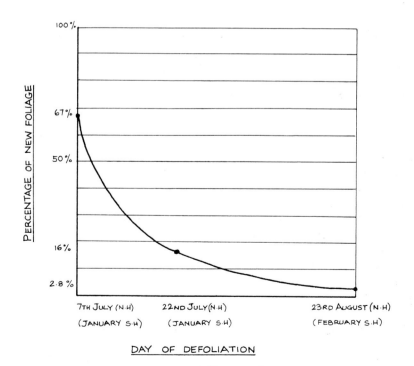

Figure 45: *Graph of effects of defoliation at different times*

Figure 46: *Bonsai with Jins*

Figure 47: *Bonsai with Jins*

TECHNIQUES OF CREATING JIN, SHARI, SABAMIKI AND DRIFTWOOD

IKARIJIN:

Ikarijin — literally means "anchor of God" and in the first book of bonsai in the English language, written in 1940 by Sinobu Nozaki, it is described thus: *Ikarijin, the anchor of God style . . . An old dead branch or part of a trunk of any tree of pine family often turns a silvery grey, giving the tree a beautiful, aged look. This kind of dead branch is regarded as sacred and is called Ikarijin, or "anchor of God" because it resembles in shape the arm of an anchor; a bonsai with an anchor God is greatly prized . . .*

Artistically, a jin can enhance the total design and have a very striking effect. It can also impart the illusion of age and realism while telling us the story of the tree's life. Beyond these meanings, as is suggested by Nozaki, it seems to reveal to us the soul of the tree — as well as the "bones" and "sinew", made visible through a life of hardship.

A jin can be a dead section on the topmost portion of the trunk or it can be at the end of a branch, or, alternatively, a whole branch or branchlet may be "jinned".

Again, as mentioned by Nozaki, above, jins are mostly used on conifers as these trees are more likely to be the ones living in an environment harsh enough to produce such effects. Also, the style of the tree should be suitable. On a tree styled to have a lush head of foliage, for example, a jin would tend to look out of place. The styling should be reasonably extreme and suggest the effects of age and a rough environment. A practical reason why it is better to make jins on conifers is that they generally have a hard type of wood that doesn't rot easily. Jins also look out of place on young or very thin-trunked trees that do not possess much character of their own. On trees like this, a jin tends to look ridiculous and artificially produced.

TOP JIN:

This is, perhaps, the easiest of all the stripped bark styles to create but, nevertheless, it is not so easy to make it appear natural and in character.

Horticulturally, it will not endanger the health of the tree. In fact, as the apical dominance is removed by eliminating the terminal bud, extra vigour is temporarily transferred to the branches immediately below, which begin to fight for dominance — each branch trying to become the new apex of the tree. By pinching these top branches back, however, the extra sap is transferred even lower down, to the bottom branches. This is good, stylistically, as the bottom branches look well if they are the thickest and strongest on the tree and, usually, they have the least vigour.

As mentioned previously, the top jin on a tree can be used to create the effect of a natural taper on a tree that has been cut down drastically. If, for example, very tall nursery stock is used and the top cut off to obtain good proportions of height and trunk thickness, the large cut in the main trunk is hard to disguise. By cutting the tree a little longer, one can create a "jin" and by tapering it, improve the tapering shape of the trunk as a whole.

Artistically, there are two styles of top-jin: smooth or rough. Also, with these two styles there are a few different effects that can be created.

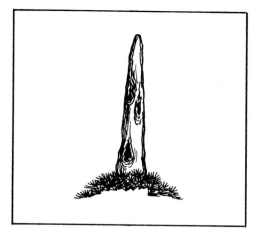

Figure 48: *Example of smooth jin*

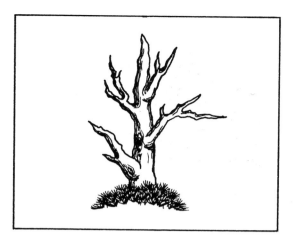

Figure 49: *Example of smooth jin with side stubs and branches*

Smooth Jin: 1. The first type is gradually tapering to a point with any side branches that may be there, smoothly removed. The point of the jin, however, should not be a narrow conical shape like a sharpened pencil, but come to the point in a slightly curved line, somewhat like a large darning needle.

If the section you wish to jin is alive, the procedure for removing the bark is this: first of all, make a cut right around the trunk at the point where you wish the jin to end, otherwise, when pulling the bark off, it may proceed down the trunk, further than you intended. This cut should be made to the beginning of hard wood. After this has been done, press the bark with a pair of pliars or a similar tool, as this separates the cambium and outer bark sections from the hard wood. The bark will separate particularly easily in mid-spring to summer, when the outer bark is almost floating on a layer of sap. After this, remove the bark, if it has not already come apart from the wood. If it is the dormant period, or if the branch is dead, soaking the section in hot water or wrapping it in a hot, damp towel, may assist the process, but a knife or file may be necessary to help remove the bark in these cases. One advantage of making jins out of live sections of a tree is that immediately after the bark has been peeled off, the jin can be wired and repositioned. When the sap has receded, the wire can be removed and the jinned section will stay permanently in that position. If the jin is made of a section that is already dead, a change of position is not so easy to achieve. Some growers, however, have reported success by steaming the wood and repositioning it in much the same way as furniture is sometimes bent. The easiest method would be to wire the jin and then apply a hot towel to the jin for a few minutes, after which it should become pliable enough to reposition. If the jin was made from a live section of the tree, it should then be left to dry out completely (usually two to three weeks is sufficient) and the jin can subsequently be finished with sandpaper or broken window glass, as the Chinese do. After two to three months, concentrated lime sulphur may be painted on the jin. This has two effects. First of all, it acts as a preservative and stops rotting and, secondly, it stops the jin from turning an old brown colour and changes it to a silvery grey. Concentrated lime-sulphur, however, will burn trees and care should be taken not to let any get on the roots, bark, foliage or soil. The lime-sulphur should be applied twice a year for the first couple of years and then once a year in the warmer months as this is when the fungus that would cause rotting is most active. After the lime-sulphur is applied, the colour turns to a stark white that appears artificial. After a couple of days, however, it fades to a more natural colour. To speed this process, paint with lime-sulphur — leave the tree in the sun for about half an hour and then wash the jin with a sharp jet of water. Another way of achieving a not so **stark** white appearance is to mix in black ink or black water paint with the concentrated lime-sulphur. The result is a subdued antique grey colour. An alternative to lime-sulphur would be a wood bleach or wood colour as used by the furniture trade or a mixture of lemon juice and water.

2. Another type of smooth jin is where any side branches are left as part of the design and perhaps trimmed to uneven lengths to appear natural and to fit the overall design.

Figure 50: *Example of sculptured smooth jin*

3. A third type is where an extremely large tree has been cut down and the section to be jinned is of a very wide diameter. Such a section can be carved and sculptured to indicate a large tree that has been snapped off many years ago and where the initial break that was rough and splintered, has now been smoothed. This latter type, however, requires more artistic skill to make it appear natural.

Some other ways of finishing the jins discussed above are:

1. Use a red-hot poker or a small braising burner to create the effect of a charred jin caused by a forest fire. This type is hard to make natural-looking, but time mellows the effect as some parts are bleached and others are blackened with charcoal.

2. Another way of finishing a jin is to attach lichen to the wood. It is often difficult to keep the lichen alive, however, as conditions may be different to the place where it was originally growing. If the lichen successfully grows there, though, the appearance will be of an old man's beard.

Rough Jin: All three variations on the smooth jin, described above, are applicable here. With the wide jin (the third type described), the break would give the appearance of being more recent than the smooth type. The procedure for making a rough jin is this:— First of all, the trunk is cut or sawn about half way through from the back. It is then grabbed with the hands or pliars and roughly torn downwards and toward the front. If you are concerned that

Figure 51: *Example of rough jin*

the jin doesn't extend too far down the trunk, a circular cut may be made, as was described in the section on smooth jins. The rough jin, however, has more sponteneity and relies a lot on chance effects so that the bottom cut is not always made. After the top section has been torn down, the remaining part, which usually has a flat top, should be worked into a roughly pointed shape by gradually tearing away splinters of wood with a pair of pliars.

JINNED BRANCHES:

Just as with jinned tops of trees, the jin may be made rough or smooth and they may be the ends of branches or entire branches or branchlets. Also, the jins may be long or just short stubs.

Artistically, jinned branches can be quite useful in certain designs. Occasionally, a certain tree may have too many branches and the effect may be too cluttered, or the masses of foliage may be wrongly distributed. However, at the same time, if branches are removed the proportion may be lost and the resultant design too sparse. Yet, by jinning some of the branches, the cluttered effect is relieved, while the hint of mass, created by the grey outline of the jin, stops the effect of emptiness.

SPLIT JINS:

In some cases a jin, either at the top of the tree or as a branch, may be too thick and heavy for the overall design. One alternative to merely whittling it away is to split it longitudinally to make it into two or more smaller jins. This works particularly well if using a live part of the tree as the split sections can be spread out and shaped into attractive positions (by wiring or pushing them apart with spacers) which become permanent when the sap has receded.

SHARI:

This is sometimes also referred to as "Shari-kan" or "Uro", and literally means something like "Buddha's bones" or "Saint's relics" (N.B. from the Sanskrit "Shari-ra" meaning bones after the cremation of Buddha).

A shari is where the bark is peeled longitudinally down a section of the trunk, a branch or on any exposed roots. It is definitely easier to create in the active growing season, when the cambium is loose and the outer bark separates easily from the wood. After making shari, it is often a good safety procedure to seal the join between shari and live bark with a tree-sealing compound or plastic glue. This will prevent further dying-back than was intended. Sometimes a shari can look good if it continues down from a jinned branch. One point of caution, however. If a shari is made between two branches, it is advisable to finish it a reasonable distance from the lower branch, and not immediately above a branch. If there isn't enough live bark above a branch there will be little or no sap reaching it and the branch will weaken and possibly even die, while the branch above the shari will receive extra sap and become more vigorous.

Figures 52 & 53: *Bonsai with shari*

Another precaution is to finish the shari in a "V" shape above the soil level. This will avoid the problem of rotting due to moisture in the soil.

An interesting variation is to make a coiled trunk shari style. The procedure is this: A tree is wired and the wire left on until it begins to cut into the bark. Bulges will form above the coils of wire as the sap is inhibited in its downward flow. When the bulging effect is sufficient, the wire is removed and a strip of bark running parallel and below the wire is peeled off. For an artistically pleasing effect, however, the coils should not be made too uniformly. Junipers are a good variety to use for this technique of styling, particularly since it is believed that they have the ability for sap to move in a horizontal as well as a vertical direction[4].

ARTIFICIALLY PRODUCING A DRIFTWOOD STYLE BONSAI:

In the photo albums of Chinese and Japanese bonsai, we often see beautiful old trees that are a windswept jumble of turning and twirling driftwood. These are trees that have been collected from the windy slopes of mountains and hills and the fantastic effects have been sculpted by Nature. When we see such trees, it is natural for us to want something similar, yet we are not all so lucky to have trees like that in the countryside that may be collected. Even in the Orient, such trees are becoming scarce.

The effect may be produced artificially but it would take at least ten years for it to begin to look realistic and natural. The procedure is this: A young tree is pinched back consistently so that many side branches develop — particularly on the bottom sections of the trunk. The tree is then left for four or five years, so that these branches can thicken and develop. After this period of time, the branches have matured somewhat and they are then trained by bending and twisting them in such a way that it appears as if they have been swept around by a strong wind. A year or two later, the branches are ring-barked and jinned. When they are dry, they can be carved or shortened as desired. The top portion of the tree can then be trained and jins or shari may be incorporated in the design.

If a jin is required where no branch exists it is possible to "graft" in a ready made jin at that point. The procedure is to make a deep cut into the tree with a chisel or grafting knife and then whittling away the end of the jin that will be inserted, so that it won't push the cambium layers out of alignment when it is placed in position. The area should be bound with something like grafting tape to secure the jin and keep the bark tightly closed prior to healing. As the tree grows, the cambium produces callus tissue which bulges out, engulfing the base of the jin, and holding it firmly in place.

Figure 54: *Example of driftwood style*

Plate XII: *Chinese Wisteria in bloom*, Wistaria sinensis.
Semi-cascade style, height (From Base to Apex): 59 cm, Chinese pot, grown from cutting struck in 1960, trained since 1971, photograph taken in 1982

Plate XIII: *Japanese grey-bark Elm in Autumn, Zelkova serrata, broom style, height: 45 cm, Japanese handmade pot, grown from seed in 1951, trained since 1966, photograph taken in 1980*

SABAMIKI:

— literally means "hollowed trunk". This effect can be used on its own or it may be in conjunction with jin or shari. Furthermore, it can look equally effective on conifers, deciduous or broadleaf evergreens. With deciduous varieties, or trees with an active cambium layer, the effects of shari or sabamiki may be lost if the tree attempts to heal the wound. It is, thus, advantageous to apply lime-sulphur to the driftwood parts, as soon as the wood dries out, as this will stop the tree from closing the wound. It will also act as a preservative as most of these varieties that heal quickly, also tend to rot easily. When making a hollowed out trunk effect, take care that a run-off for water is provided. If there are any depressions in which water is held, rotting will more than likely result.

One stylistic advantage, is that if a heavy branch has to be removed from the front of the trunk, a hollowed trunk effect may appear more natural than the scar left from the removed branch. The hollowed trunk is usually chiselled out and it may be shallow or deep and whatever shape best complements the style of the tree. With sabamiki, the tree doesn't necessarily have to be rugged in styling, as the hollowed trunk effect can be formed in many different types of tree and environment and with all types it helps to create the illusion of age and mystery.

Figure 55: *Bonsai with sabamiki*

Shaping with Mechanical Aids

INTRODUCTION AND HISTORICAL SURVEY OF DIFFERENT TECHNIQUES

As was mentioned in the historical section in chapter one, originally trees in containers had very little shaping except for an occasional trimming. However, as time passed, and as more styling was being done to the pot plants, it was realized that some additional means of shaping — other than pruning — was becoming necessary.

At the end of the eighteenth century, some Chinese bonsai growers stumbled on the idea of using strips of lead to make a kind of tube around the branch or trunk and then bending the tube to the desired position. Certain disadvantages were seen to exist, however, and the method was supplanted by other techniques. As far as styling is concerned, only one internode can be shaped with each strip of lead — so that a "disjointed" design is the result. Also, bleaching of the bark results as well as the problem of insects lodging under the lead.

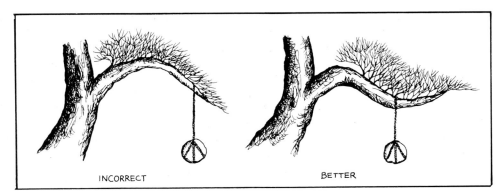

INCORRECT   BETTER

Figure 56: *Using weights for shaping*

Weights (usually a suspended piece of lead) were also used in China, yet this styling technique also has attendant problems. Artistically, the bend can be made only in one vertical plane and the actual curve is governed by the decrease in branch thickness. Variations of design are not possible and usually not enough of a bend is made at the base of the branch and too much at the tip. A slightly more interesting curve may be made if the weight is placed about two thirds of the way along the branch (see illustration), yet variation is still limited. Practically speaking, however, it is hard to determine the actual weight necessary for the particular job. Sometimes a certain weight is adequate for the job in winter, but when the vigour of the tree returns in spring, the branch grows back towards its original position. On the other hand, sometimes a weight may seem to be achieving the desired curve, without being too heavy, but, in a couple of weeks, the branch snaps off unexpectedly.

The method of shaping trees by weights was particularly popular in Japan during the Meiji Era (1867–1912) with those who preferred not to wire trees.

The simple string tie was another method of shaping. Artistically, the designs were similar to those achieved by weights but without the attendant problem of snapping branches. The use of string is still very useful as an auxiliary method of shaping. Sometimes it is good to employ for the first stages or rough shaping of a tree, often in combination with wiring, until the resistance of the tree is lessened. It is also easier to shape springy, brittle or soft-barked trees with string, while those with rough, aged bark will be damaged less if string is used. Another advantage is that if the grower has a large collection or if trees are being grown in the ground where they are thickening quickly, string is less likely to leave scars, as it usually rots before cutting in (N.B. Uncoated natural fibre string should be used).

String, as a shaping technique was used expertly in China and in combination with stakes and sticks (see Figure 57).

Figure 57: *String and stick technique*

By using the string and stick technique, three-dimensional curves may be produced with designs limited only by the imagination of the artist. When using this method, sticks are embedded in the soil at desired positions and the strings can be attached at various positions on both tree and stick. Consequently, quite elaborate curves may be devised, with the only drawbacks being the need for dexterity and the fact that the finished job looks more like the rigging on a sailing boat than a bonsai-in-training. The technique is still an excellent one to use, particularly taking into consideration the cost of copper wire today — however, while being trained by string and stick, trees obviously cannot be exhibited at shows. Trees can also be shaped by tying them to and around stakes, for producing twisted and curved trunked trees (see "Horai Style" Chapter 7), or, for straight-trunked styles, young trees can be tied to a perfectly straight stake to develop an even and undeviating trunk line.

A similar technique would be to shape a piece of heavy wire to the desired curve and tie the tree to it as it grows.

Figure 58: *Tying tree to pre-shaped wire*

As methods for shaping, pruning, string and stick, and weights were all used extensively up to the end of the nineteenth century, (c.a. 1890). At the beginning of the nineteenth century in China, however, the use of wire for the styling of trees, was devised. The technique was then introduced into Japan in the early Meiji era (1868–1912). The method soon became extremely popular and it gradually supplanted the traditional methods of shaping by bamboo sticks and hemp palm ropes and by the beginning of the twentieth century, wiring was used extensively in Japan and became the fundamental technique for the styling of bonsai.

WIRING TECHNIQUES
The sole purpose of wiring bonsai is to change the direction and shape of the branches and trunks and make them conform with the artist's design. Pruning, then, may be seen to bring the tree into the desired proportions and wiring emphasizes and refines the form thus sculpted.

The methods for correct wiring, outlined below, are extremely important and, with practice, they will become easy to apply and be almost second nature to you. These techniques of wiring, all produce "neat" results and this is desirable, firstly from an aesthetic point of view and, secondly, because the best results, strength-wise, will be attained. Messy wiring may do the job, but it does it less efficiently and less economically.

First of all, a little about the type of wire to use. When wiring became the most frequently used method of shaping trees in Japan, copper wire was used. The advantages of copper are these:

If it is annealed, it will become soft and easy to handle and, as it is being wired onto the tree, it hardens to keep the limb in place. To anneal the wire, it should be placed in a low-heat fire and left till it reaches a cherry-red colour. In China and Japan a rice-straw fire is usually used because it isn't too hot. Paper or cardboard is a reasonable substitute. It is important not to put the wire into too hot a fire, or to leave it in the fire too long, or else it will become brittle. The wire should then be allowed to cool slowly and without movement. After annealing, any work or stress, such as bending the wire onto the tree, will make it hard.

What actually happens when the copper is annealed is that when the temperature is raised to a certain point, the atoms move a microscopic distance that effectively relieves the strains within the metal that exist due to imperfections and stress. Because of the internal ordering, the metal becomes easy to bend, however, the action of bending again produces internal imperfections and, consequently, hardness.

It is possible to buy both pre-annealed or non-annealed copper wire and both types will probably be bright and shiny when purchased. If it is not annealed, the act of annealing will straightaway colour it to a dull brown that is unobtrusive on the tree. If it is pre-annealed, it will discolour in a week or two, out in the weather. However, if an instantaneous result is desired, the wire may be rubbed with concentrated lime-sulphur just prior to use, or, if the tree has already been wired, trays of sulphur powder or lime-sulphur (if it won't be knocked over onto the soil) may be placed under the tree and the fumes will discolour the wire more quickly than the natural effects of weather.

As with most things, there are disadvantages, as well as good points and the use of copper wire is no exception. Firstly, copper occasionally develops verdigris (a green patina caused by oxidation) and this is harmful to some trees (particularly stone fruits). Secondly, it is very costly to use — particularly if one simply cuts the wire off the tree when it is time for it to be removed. In Japan, the copper wire is usually unwound from the branches and re-used. It takes a steady hand, patience and adequate time to do the job properly, as it must be remembered that the act of winding the wire onto the tree has hardened it. If you want to unwind the wire from a tree, after it has done its job, some preparation is necessary before it can be reused for another tree. The first step — particularly if the wire is thick — is to re-anneal it. Then, all the irregularities in the wire should be eliminated, as these will cause uneven pressure on the trunk and branches and certain points will cut in very quickly, thus marking and perhaps scarring the bark. The best technique for straightening the wire is to hold it firmly at both ends with pliars and to give a short, sharp, jerk. After this, the act of jerking the wire has made more imperfections in the metal and it will again be in a hardened state. Thus, reannealing will be necessary to soften the wire before it is used for the styling of trees.

Galvanized wire is a possible substitute and the advantages and disadvantages are the exact reverse to copper. It is very cheap to buy and, because of this, it can be simply cut off from the tree without feeling any twinges of guilt. This eliminates the problem of breakages of branches due to heavy-handed unwinding. It is also available in many thicknesses and has no chemical reaction that adversely affects the trees. Thus, it may be a good solution for trees that are "allergic" to copper. The defects of galvanized wire are, firstly, that it cannot be annealed, so that it is quite hard to handle with the heavier gauges and, secondly, it does not become weathered and dull, therefore, one must put up with the wire being quite noticeable on the tree, or, artificially try to colour it by painting, for instance. Galvanized wire is quite acceptable to use in the backyard for training purposes, but it would not really be suitable for exhibition.

In Japan, the present trend is toward the use of aluminium wire — usually copper-coloured (anodised), to give a more unobtrusive appearance. It isn't as strong as copper, so that for a particular job, the necessary gauge of aluminium wire would be heavier than the gauge of copper. The main advantage however, is that it is very light and easy to bend — even with very heavy gauges. There is also the idea that there is more capability for "stretch" with aluminium, so that as the tree grows, there is less chance of cutting in and scarring of the bark. A disadvantage is that, as well as copper, aluminium may be toxic to some tree varieties, however this is less of a problem if the wire is anodised.

Avoid the use of iron wire, as it rusts and disfigures the bark, and, if using copper wire that is coated with plastic, shellac or enamel, burn the coatings off first as they stop the wire weathering to a dull shade.

What Gauge of Wire to Use: There is no set rule on what gauge of wire should be used for a particular branch or trunk thickness. Suggestions vary from wire being about one third of the diameter of the section to be wired, to about one sixth, and, largely, the decision will be made by the degree of change required and the resistance of the particular variety. If very dramatic shaping is intended, a heavier gauge of wire will probably be necessary, while a thinner gauge will be sufficient for minor changes of branch and trunk direction.

Making the correct choice of the gauge of wire necessary for the job is a skill that comes with practice, however, it is not so critical. If you choose a slightly heavier gauge than necessary, it will not make much difference, in fact, it will make your job a little easier. If you grossly overestimate the gauge of wire you need, there may be a risk of breaking branches, particularly if you are wiring very thin branchlets and twigs — but this mistake is rarely made.

If, on the other hand, you underestimate the gauge of wire, again there is not much of a problem. Simply get another length of wire of the same gauge and wire it parallel and as close as possible to the first wire, without crossing wires at any point. If this is still not strong enough, a third wire can be added. The important thing to watch is that the wires are very close together. Two or three strands of wire may, in fact, be better than one strand of heavy wire, as the pressure of the wire on the branch is more evenly distributed and the wire will not cut into the bark as quickly.

One note of caution, however, never be tempted to twist wires together, prior to wiring, in order to get the effect of a heavier gauge of wire. Wires twisted together touch the trunk or branch unevenly and the points of contact will cut into the bark very quickly.

SOME GENERAL CONSIDERATIONS:

Some soft-barked trees may be difficult to wire without damaging the bark. This problem may be particularly evident in spring when there is an excess of sap in the tree. To alleviate this problem, the wire may be covered with ricepaper or some substitute such as crepe paper. A strip of paper is cut 10 mm to 13 mm (⅜" to ½") wide and it is wound spirally around the wire, each turn overlapping the preceding one. The ends may be secured with a dab of glue.

Covering the wire in this way is also a good idea if the variety doesn't like copper wire or if you find that the copper gets too hot in the sun. However, the advantage of the dull colour of copper is lost by covering it, so that it doesn't look good except maybe for trees with light coloured bark. Unless you wish to use copper for its ease of handling when annealed, a cheaper wire, such as galvanized, can just as well be used.

When wiring, consider the tree's individual characteristics. First of all, some trees are easier to wire at certain times of the year. Secondly, different trees and different parts of a tree will vary in the lengths of time necessary for the branch or trunk to set in place and thirdly, some varieties will tolerate drastic wiring and others will not.

Best Time to Wire: Wiring may be done at any time, but each season has its particular advantages and disadvantages. Generally, though, wiring is done at the time of pruning, for easier access.

Spring: Shoots are very soft and delicate and easy to break when wiring. The tree is full of sap and it is easy to damage the bark. Trunk and branches are thickening quickly and wire will cut in too soon, particularly if wiring is a little tight. The advantage of spring wiring is that new cells are growing around the trunk and limbs, while they are held in their new positions, thus helping the process considerably.

Summer: The cambium is still full of sap and this makes it easy to bruise bark and for the bark to separate from the wood (and perhaps ringbark the section) if drastic changes of angle are attempted (this can occur in late winter to spring as well). Small branchlets that were too soft in spring are now in a semi-hardened condition, however, and may be wired easily. One of the main disadvantages of this time, though, is the abundance of foliage that gets in the way and makes wiring difficult. At any time, avoid catching leaves and needles under the wire. If some do get caught, remove them immediately, as the rotting vegetable matter will mar the bark and attract insects. It also looks messy and unattractive.

Late Summer to Early Autumn: The wood is again thickening rapidly at this time, so don't wire too tightly.

Winter: It is easier to wire deciduous trees in winter, after leaf-fall. Remember, though, that buds should be treated with as much respect as leaves. Even though they may be insignificant in the winter season, they represent next spring's crop of new leaves. Another problem with winter is that if you live in an extremely cold climate, wood may become brittle and bending will have to be done with caution. An advantage of wiring in early winter is that the tree does not thicken through the dormant season and so the wire may be left on for quite a while without the risk of scarring the wood. Also, as the sap drains down for dormancy, the setting of the limb or trunk is aided somewhat.

How Long will it Take to Set in Place: There are a few things that affect the time a trunk or branch will take to set in place.

1. One variable is the thickness of the section being wired. If it is about 13 mm (½") in thickness, or less, it may only take about sixteen weeks. If it is over 13 mm (½") it may be twelve months to two years.

2. Another variable is the type of wood. A pliable tree takes longer to set in place than a brittle one. N.B. Tropicals are usually more pliable than trees that go through a dormant period.

3. The age of the section being wired is also a factor. The older it is, the more "dead wood" there is and the slower the tree will be to produce new cells to hold the branch in the new position.

When wiring, leave the wire on a little longer than you think necessary, providing the wire is not too tight. As soon as the wire looks tight, remove it and then watch the tree critically for the next few weeks. Sometimes, if a tree is not yet set properly, it will revert back towards its original position very slowly and over a period of a few weeks. If this is seen to be occurring, rewire.

Brittle and Pliable Varieties: Some trees, e.g. Junipers, cedars and pines, are pliable. Others, e.g. azaleas and maples, are brittle, and it will not be possible to bend them so drastically. A couple of points, however, may be of help here. Brittle varieties may be "undercut" to produce a more drastic change of angle (see: Thick, Awkward branches, in Pruning & Trimming section in this chapter). Also, brittle varieties may become more pliable in late winter, as the sap begins to rise in the tree. Another point that is an extremely important consideration when wiring any tree, is that more extreme bending and less breakages will occur if the trees are in a dryish condition just prior to wiring. This doesn't mean "bone dry" so that the tree will be dead, but it should be in the state where it is just about ready for its next watering. If a tree has just been watered, the cells are in a "turgid" state (i.e. full of water) and, like fresh fruit and vegetables, they "snap" rather than bend. When a stick of celery has been cut for some time, the water content in the cells decreases and it can be bent right over without it breaking. The same process occurs in a tree, so for drastic changes of angle or just for safety's sake, check that the soil is in a dryish condition. After a prolonged rainy period, it may be a little easier to break branches as the tree has most likely accumulated a lot of moisture in its cells.

Avoid twisting the branch or trunk in many directions before finding the desired position, as this will kill or weaken that part of the tree. When bending a branch in one direction, the cells are stretched on one side and compressed on the other. If the branch is then bent back in the opposite direction, the cells are subjected to too much stress on both sides and the cells may be damaged badly right around. A ring-barking effect then occurs and the branch dies, even though there is no visible break.

To help prevent breaking, gently limber the trunk or branch in the direction in which it is to be wired. Keep your thumbs on the underside of the bend for support against cracking. It is also sometimes helpful to bend the branch or trunk in the desired direction while the wire is being put on.

If the plant is weak, do not wire. It is also bad to wire a week or two after rootpruning and repotting. At this time, the new roots are just beginning to grow and any movement would quite possibly break or damage them, as the tree has not yet got a firm grip in the pot. Wait at least a month before wiring a newly repotted tree.

Wire the trunk and heavy branches first and then the finer branches. With upright styles, this will mean working from the bottom upwards and with cascades, the reverse.

Artistically, this is the best procedure, as you are "blocking-in" the main outline of the design and then "filling-in" the finer details. Also, the finer branches will be the first to set so that if wired last, they will be accessible for easy removal at the appropriate time.

Shape the tree by wiring and pruning simultaneously. This is easier than doing all the pruning first and then wiring what is left.

If a tree has both good branches on the one side of the trunk or if a branch has all the branchlets, for example, on the underside, a slight twist may be made in the direction of the turns of wire, when shaping the tree (see Figure 59).

Figure 59: *Twisting trunk or branch when wiring to produce better disposition of branches or foliage*

Turns up to about 180 degrees may be achieved. However, care must be taken when applying the technique — particularly with conifers and especially with spruces. With these, the cambium separates very easily from the wood and ring-barking will result. This "twisting" has a slight dwarfing effect — particularly if it is done in late winter to early spring, when it limits the flow of sap and thereby checks excessive growth

TECHNIQUES INVOLVED WITH WIRE USE:

The "rules" for correct wiring are simple but, as with all things, practice is important for them to become second-nature to you. You will find that when you learn to wire properly, you will be able to achieve, with ease, all the designs your imagination can conceive.

The best wiring is unobtrusive, evenly spaced, has no crossing wires and has the end of each wire before or at the end of each branch. The most important thing to remember is that the start should be secure. All the techniques outlined below, make sure of this. Wiring should be **slightly** tight. If it is too tight, there is no room for the tree to grow and the wiring will have to be removed long before it has done the job. If, on the other hand, it is too loose, there will be no strength and the branch will not be held in place. The ideal angle is 45 degrees when viewed from all sides (see Figure 60).

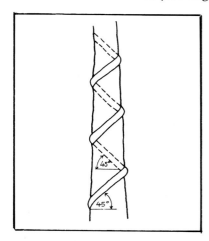

Figure 60: *Angle of wiring*

Figure 61: *How to wire the main trunk*

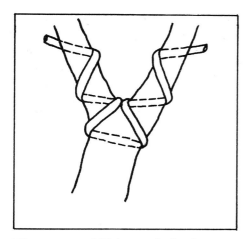

Figure 62: *Wiring a forked tree*

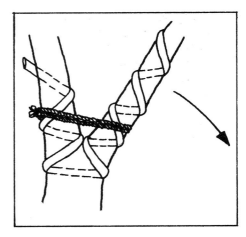

Figure 63: *Tying above crotch to prevent fork splitting if it is to be widened*

If the spirals are too close (say 20 degrees), the wire acts as a spring and will not hold the tree in place. Similarly, if too widespread (say 60 degrees) strength will be lost. Wiring at 45 degrees makes use of all the strength available in the wire. To determine how much wire will be necessary to complete the job, measure the length plus one third. It is better, however, to have more than what is needed, rather than less.

How to Wire the Main Trunk: The wire is "anchored" by sticking it into the ground at the back of the tree — preferably behind a strong surface root for extra stability. The trunk is then simply wired at 45 degree angle spirals (see Figure 61).

How to Wire the Branches on the Tree: There is not really much variation in the way branches grow on trees. In fact, there are basically four different modes of growth:

Forked Branches: By wiring two branches of the fork with one wire, each branch holds the other secure. The important point here is that wiring at the crotch of the fork should be secure and firm (see Figure 62).

The procedure is to begin at the fork, holding the wire at the back of the fork with one hand and then bringing the wires around and through the fork from the front, to form an upside-down "V". Wire a couple of turns on one branch and then after wiring the other completely, return to complete the first one. If only one branch of the fork is to be wired, a couple of turns on the branch that doesn't need wiring is usually sufficient to hold the other. If you wish to widen the fork, it is a good precaution to tie above the junction after wiring and before shaping. This will help prevent splitting as forks are reasonably weak points in trees (see Figure 63).

Alternate or Staggered Branches: Most of the wiring you will be doing will be on alternate branches. As you are shaping a tree, try to wire two branches at a time as this acts to secure the

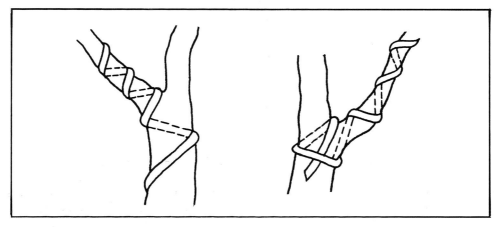

Figure 64: *Two incorrect methods of wiring a single branch*

beginning of the wiring on each branch. Start by treating the lower branch and the main trunk as a fork. After doing a couple of turns up the main trunk, wire the lower branch. Note that if you want to wire one branch, this would be the procedure, unless it was an extremely heavy branch, in which case you would probably "anchor" the wire in the ground, wire up the trunk and out onto the branch. These methods of wiring one branch are much stronger than wiring up the trunk a short distance and out onto the branch (see Figure 64) or merely anchoring the wire around the trunk (see Figure 64). After wiring the bottom branch, continue up the trunk to the higher branch. As is illustrated in Figure 65, make sure that the first half turn, on each branch, is parallel to the main trunk line.

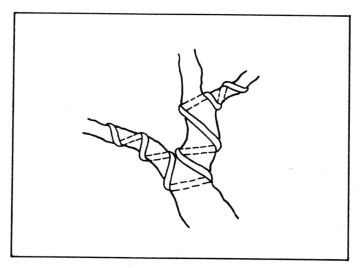

Figure 65: *Wiring alternate or staggered branches*

Whorled Branches: This pattern of branching is seen on pines and azaleas. It is the sign of an immature tree, so, generally, only one branch is left at each whorl. Thus, normal alternate branching is the result.

Figure 66: *Whorled branches*

If branching is sparse on the tree, sometimes two branches may be left at one layer: one on the side and one at the back.

Opposite Branches: Among other varieties, this type of branching is characteristic of maples. Opposite, or so-called, "bar" branches impart the feeling that the tree is immature. Artistically, it makes the tree too symmetrical in form. Therefore, one branch is usually removed so that, again, alternate branching is the result.

OTHER TECHNIQUES INVOLVED WITH WIRE USE:

There is a special technique for wiring two opposite twigs on a branch (N.B. In this case, where the result is a horizontal layer — opposite twigs are acceptable). If you wire them as a fork, disregarding the fact that there is a branch in the middle, the twigs will have no stability and it will be impossible to set them firmly in place. An extra turn is needed around the branch in the middle, as is indicated in Figure 67.

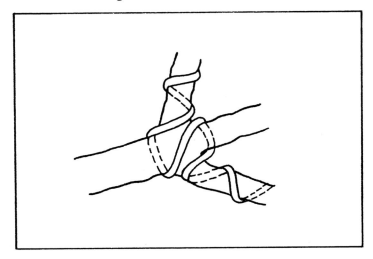

Figure 67: *Wiring two opposite twigs on a branch*

The procedure is to treat one of the twigs and the main branch as a fork. Then the wire on the main branch side does half a turn around the branch before going out onto the other twig. Again, remember to make the first half turn on each twig firm and running parallel with the main branch.

Technique for wiring a forked branch with one wire: By anchoring the wire around the main trunk, doing double wiring along the branch and then dividing onto the separate forks of the branch, a more continuous shape is achieved along the entire branch, as well as more security.

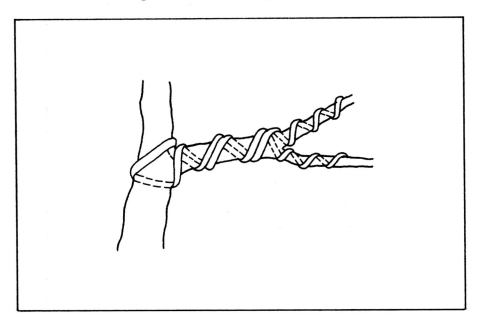

Figure 68: *Wiring a forked branch with one wire*

Where a branch or trunk is being bent or straightened sharply, the wire should be wound so that the turn is on the outside of the curve (see Figure 69).

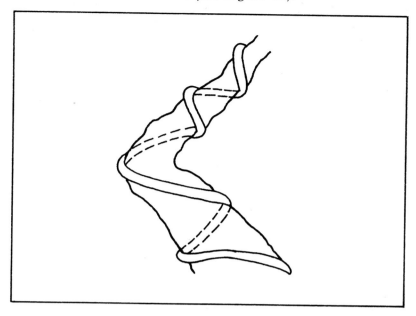

Figure 69: *Turn of wire on outside of curve*

Where the turn of wire is, is where the strength is to hold the particular curve. Also, this technique helps to prevent splitting or cracking of the branch or trunk. When a limb is bent, there is compression on the inside of the curve and tension on the outside. Thus, having the wire on the outside of the curve, provides a compressive force that counteracts the tensile force and the result is that cracking of the branch is less likely to occur.

The following couple of points are helpful when dealing with heavy or difficult branches to wire. When bending a branch downwards, the first half turn of wire should come over, then under the branch (as is illustrated in Figure 70 below). When bending a branch upwards, the reverse is practiced, that is, the wire approaches the branch from below (see Figure 71).

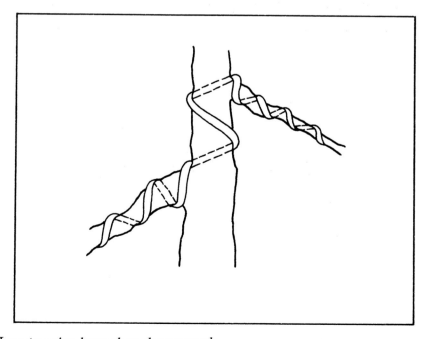

Figure 70: *How to wire branches downwards*

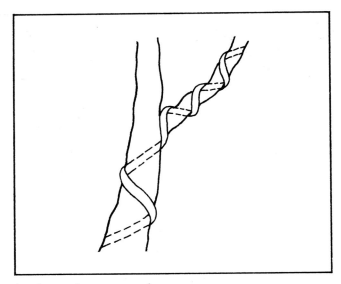

Figure 71: *How to wire branches upwards*

When working on branches on the right-hand side as you look at the tree, anti-clockwise wiring will help in bringing branches forward and clockwise wiring for pushing branches away. If wiring on left-hand branches, as you look at the tree, the reverse holds true — clockwise wiring for branches brought forward and anti-clockwise for branches pushed back. N.B. To tell if you are wiring clockwise or anti-clockwise, look from the end of a branch towards its base and see which way the wire is turning.

If you are right-handed you will probably find it easier to hold the tree with your left hand and do your wiring with your right hand and, therefore, turning the tree around so that you are always working on the right side. If this is the case, you need only remember the directions for wiring on the right-hand side.

Alternatively, for left-handed people, you will be turning the tree so that you are working on the left side, so the directions for this side are the only ones that apply.

Note, however, that the "forward" and "backward" directions refer to the current position of the tree and not the front and back of the styled bonsai.

It is better if thin branches and tips are not wired with thick wire, so, as these sections grow, wire with thin wire parallel to the existing wire for a few turns and then out onto the new part. The wire can be bent back on itself at the end, so that it does not unwind. For pines and cedars, the ends of the wire can be formed into loops to cradle the needle tufts and flick them into a vertical position. The tufts would naturally grow upwards toward the light, but this technique creates the effect instantaneously. It gives a neat and classical effect.

When a young shoot develops on the trunk in a place where a branch is desired, wiring should not be done too early, as the shoot may snap off while still tender. However, most buds will begin to grow vertically and the angle so formed at the base of the branch will be unattractive and difficult to rectify later on.
Solutions to this problem are:
1. To wire, carefully, in summer when the shoot is semi-hard.
2. To pull it down, with the use of string, in summer.
3. A suggestion that seems logical[5], is that a piece of rigid or semi-rigid clear plastic is attached to the tree so that it sits horizontally over the bud or young shoot. As the shoot grows, it is forced out horizontally and growth is not stopped, as light is able to reach it through the plastic. It is suggested that the plastic is best positioned before the bud opens, so that it grows out, horizontally, right from the base. Note that the tree should not be kept in full sun, as the suns rays would burn the bud through the plastic.

A spreader or brace may be made from thick wire as illustrated in the diagram;

Figure 72: *Spreader or brace made of thick wire*

This can be used to separate parts of the tree that are growing too closely together and is often far more effective than conventional wiring — particularly in the initial stages of shaping.

How to remove wire scars: If you have missed the correct time for removing the wire, and wire scars do result, probably the best course of action would be to put the tree in a slightly larger pot and let it grow vigorously for a while without trimming the effected parts. This rapid growth causes the cambium to swell, and if scarring has not been too severe, the depressions may even out.

Another method that may be used by itself, or in conjunction with the one mentioned above, is to make longitudinal cuts on the branch or trunk, to the beginning of hard wood. Again, the cambium layer swells as scar tissue is formed. Occasionally, a gnarled effect is created that is not objectionable.

If wire has cut in badly, make a cut in the wire at a point where it hasn't cut in, if possible, and then unwind it. More damage will be done to the bark if you try to cut it off with wire-cutters. N.B. If the branch or trunk needs to be rewired, make sure wiring is coiled in the opposite direction.

Trees may also be shaped by attaching them, as they grow, to a piece of heavy wire or a strip of metal approximately 3 mm (⅛″) thick and 7 mm (⅓″) wide which was previously bent into the required shape.

For very thick or very rigid branches and trunks, specialized aids may be necessary for achieving the desired design. Below are illustrated some of the tools and techniques involved:
1. The Lever — A simple lever to help limber a branch, or bend it down to the desired angle, after wiring.

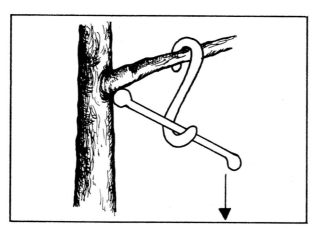

Figure 73: *Simple lever*

Another type of lever to be used in the limbering and/or bending or straightening of very stiff branches and trunks. One or two may be used, as is necessary. A piece of rubber between points of contact with the tree will stop the bark being damaged.

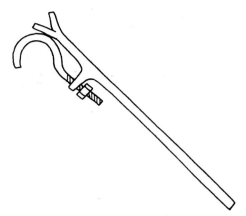

Figure 74: *Another lever*

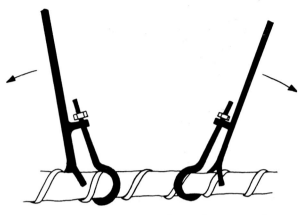

Figure 75: *To bend a branch or trunk*

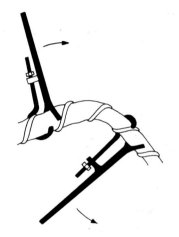

Figure 76: *To straighten a branch or trunk*

2. Clamps or Jacks — This is used with branches or trunks that are extremely rigid, and where bending or straightening is achieved gradually, over a considerable period of time[6].
Type 1:

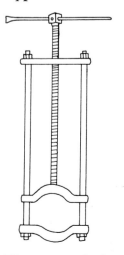

Figure 77: *Jack*

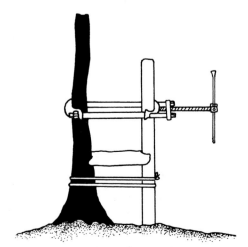

Figure 78: *To bend a branch or trunk*

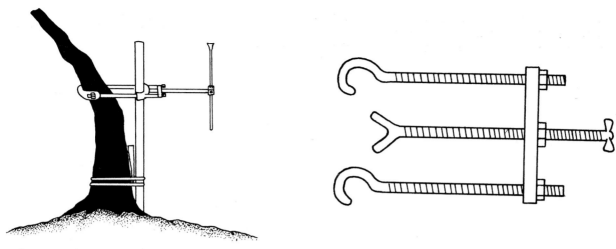

Figure 79: *To straighten a branch or trunk*   **Figure 80:** *Another jack working on same principle*

U-Bolt Vice: To straighten a curved trunk or with the use of wedges, to curve a trunk[7]. This type of clamp was invented by T. Tokuhara and is discussed and described fully in *Bonsai-Saikei: The Japanese Miniature Trees, Gardens and Landscapes.* by Toshio Kawamoto and J.Y. Kurihara.

Figure 81: *U-bolt vice used to curve trunk*   **Figure 82:** *U-bolt vice used to straighten trunk*

REFERENCES

Chapter Two
1. Koreshoff, V.A., Unpublished article.
2. Koreshoff, V.A., Unpublished article.
3. DeGroot, D., "Undercut Carving for Creating a New Apex" in *Florida Bonsai*, 10.1.19.
4. Kabata, Akitoshi, "How to make Shari and Jin" in *Bonsai Sekai*, 1.1.9–18.
5. Knobloch, F.W. "Bud Training on Trunks" in *Bonsai International Magazine*, 16.240.
6. Masakuni, Kawasumi, *Introductory Bonsai and the Care and Use of Bonsai Tools*, Tokyo & San Francisco: Japan Publications, Inc., 1971, p. 80.
7. Kawamoto, T. & Kurihara, J.Y., *Bonsai-Saikei: The Art of Japanese Miniature Trees, Gardens and Landscapes*, Tokyo, Japan: Nippon Saikei Co. (printers) 1963, pp. 141–143.

CHAPTER THREE

"A Symposium on Soil"

Preamble

We can start, of course, by saying: "From dust
we are created and to dust we return". A little morbid,
but truly representing the COMPLETE cycle of Life.
V.A. KORESHOFF.

The topic of "soil" is one that can be considered as dreary by those who are not specifically interested in the subject. If we begin to read books on "soil science" we are amazed at the complexity of all there is to know about soil and what is yet to be discovered and, at the same time, we marvel at the apparent ease with which Mother Nature takes control of the situation and, without booklearning, succeeds in producing a perfect soil mix for a particular variety of plant life.

"Soil Science" is, indeed, an interesting subject, however, no matter how far we progress in our knowledge of Nature's workings, we still find that unanswered questions exist and that the intimate relationship between plants and soil still remains, at least partially, a mystery.

In some respects we are going forward with our knowledge of Nature, yet, as with most things nowadays, this knowledge is divided into various specialist's fields. In our Modern World, the almost instinctive feeling for the "whole" has given way to a piecemeal knowledge that seems difficult to apply when we begin our work in the garden or farm.

Obviously the specialist's work has its place, but, in the process of gaining knowledge, we should not lose the special feeling and love for Nature that allows us to pick up a handful of soil and "know" whether or not our trees will grow well in it. With this approach foremost in our thoughts, soil will no longer seem alien to us, or dreary to discuss. Rather, it will seem close to us — truly the Mother of all Life on Earth and the final resting place to which all things return.

In this chapter, a number of different approaches to soil will be discussed, starting off with a Romantic story told to me by someone very special a long, long time ago . . . . . .

Romance of the Soil

Once upon a time, in the far and mysterious Middle Kingdom, a Chinese gardener tilled his little block of land, as his father did before him. He used his muscles and sweat and worked from sunrise to sunset everyday except for those which were set aside for bringing gifts to the Gods who provided and protected them from Demons.

On winter days, when other chores finished, he would watch the snow covered fields and think about the winter wheat which he had planted for the next spring.

Plate XIV: *Japanese black pine,* Pinus thunbergii, *informal upright style, height: 79 cm, Japanese pot, grown from seed in 1951, trained since 1968, photograph taken in 1982*

Plate XV: *Atlas cedar*, Cedrus atlantica, *informal upright style, height: 65 cm, Japanese pot, grown from seed in 1909, trained since 1970, photograph taken in 1981*

He was watching his small son who was now five. Next spring he will be able to start helping him in the field. He will play and work at first, then there will be more and more work and very little play.

Spring came and work started. His young son was always with him, and now that he was growing up, he was asking questions. Why do you do this or that to the soil? Why do you look at the swelling buds on the trees before you start sowing corn? Why the wind and clouds tell you about tomorrow's weather? The answer was always the same! — My father did so. He told me that the Sun and the Earth are the two most bountiful deities! They are the givers of Life!

Earth being a mother of all — gives us as much as we deserve. If we do things right, and learn her language and observe the way she guides things around us in different seasons, we are rewarded for our labours by a good harvest in autumn.

She is a kind mother then, but she is stern too with those who do not learn what she teaches. She demands love and diligence from men. The soil is not only the means of livelihood, it is the Way of Life.

The son listened to his father. He saw demons lurking in the forest, and dragons in a shady pool. The soil was alive and held in its bosom good things for his dinner, but he had to help father to obtain them. There was much mystery around. Life was very interesting. There was so much to learn.

The son asked why father did not have workers to help him? Why others did? . . . . . . "It was all arranged from the beginning of time! It was all written in the Book of Life. To each man there is the Tao (road) to walk. All roads lead to the great mountain . . . If you walk on your Tao without turning into smaller roads and tracks, you will reach the top of the mountain . . . It does not matter by which road you arrived.

"The Mother Earth and the Sun God are the best Gods. They teach you all there is to know. You can be rich in this knowledge even if you have to wear rags . . . But enough of talk; do your chores; the garden bed you prepared does not have enough manure to give your melons food. Mix the soil well and deep. When the appointed time comes, you will eat them in the heat of a summer day. It will be the reward for your diligence today".

The son worked, he did not begrudge the lost day which he had planned to spend fishing in the lake. He told his father that it would be good to catch some carp for tomorrow's dinner . . . But was told that it will wait . . . When the rain comes, the carp will be better. The dinner can consist of rice and pickled vegetables as yesterday . . .

Years passed, the son was grown up. His father was now old. The son was tilling the earth and reading the signs with more proficiency than his father did before. The land was giving a more bountiful return. The father was now telling stories to his son's son. The stories of old . . . About the dragon, about the Tao. About the world that has balance which men should not disturb too much, or they will pay for their temerity.

He was telling about the Earth that fed them, and how to make it grow things. In life you cannot take all the time . . . you should give back too. If you don't . . . you will end with nothing.

The grandchildren were listening to his tales . . . And they were growing wise. They knew the penalties of laziness and the rewards of diligence. The world seemed in the flickering light of the oil lamp, so big and mysterious . . . They listened, then dreamed until the Sun God rose again and the song of a bird woke them up to the new day.

Soil for the Cultivation of Bonsai

1. PROBLEMS TO BE CONSIDERED WITH CONTAINER GROWING

Trees react differently when grown in the ground and when grown in containers. Without the confines of a pot the roots of a tree can grow, relatively unhindered, according to the characteristics of the variety and the type of soil it is in. Usually, if the soil is moist and rich in nutriments, the rootspread will be small, as the tree's needs are to be found at close range. If, on the other hand, the soil is arid and dry, the roots are usually spindly and long as they search far afield for moisture and fossick for nutriments.

In a container, though, the roots are restricted and therefore react in a slightly different way to the type of soil in the pot. If the soil is poor, the roots tend to lose vigour and consequently their growth rate is slowed dramatically. In a very rich soil, vigour is too great and the roots grow out to the sides of the pot and then down so rapidly that the centre portion is unused and a great deal of space in the pot is wasted. This is quite a problem with growing trees successfully in containers. One must somehow strike a middle path between the two extremes, so that healthy but evenly distributed growth may be attained.

Another problem stemming from the fact that the tree is confined by the boundaries of a pot, is that the roots are growing both in length and volume. This means that if the soil is not being used at the same rate as the roots are increasing in size, considerable pressure will be built up as the soil is compacted more and more. In severe cases, the effect of this compacting can be such that the soil becomes impervious to air and water and rootgrowth may be stopped as the soil becomes impenetrable.

This latter problem exists to some degree with all container growing — yet different types of soil mixtures may alleviate or accentuate the effects.

If you use soil straight from the garden, without modification, the problems discussed above, will be accentuated — even if your garden is the best in the world. Soil in the ground and soil in a container have entirely different effects on trees.

Knowing that these problems exist, let us now also look at the functions of soil and the specific needs of trees, to see how matters may be improved.

2. A LITTLE BIT OF SOIL SCIENCE

The following discussion is partly scientific — explaining some of the "whys". Those who wish, may skip this section and turn to the "Practical Notes on Soil for Bonsai".

First of all, soil is the bed that covers and protects the roots from the sun and wind. It is also the medium to which the roots hang onto in order to gain stability. Finally, it is the repository of nutrient elements from which the trees' roots collect their nourishment.

When we look at a handful of soil, it seems to us to consist only of dry solid matter, but, in actual fact, only about half is solid matter, while the other half is made up of pore spaces. These pore spaces consist of soil air and soil water; the latter existing as a fine film around the particles of solid matter.

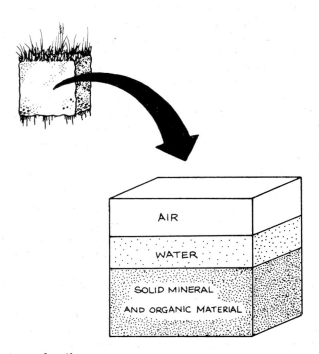

Figure 83: *Cross-section of soil*

It is in these pore spaces that the roots grow, seeking oxygen and nutriments in solution. Adequate amounts of both of these are necessary to keep the roots in a rigid condition and able to work their way through the soil.

The optimum moisture level for growing plants seems to be 25% of the volume of the soil mixture. When the plant is watered well, water fills the pore spaces entirely and at that moment, water occupies about 50% of the total volume. In a good soil, the water quickly drains away till about half of the pore spaces are filled, from which time the drying process is slower, and the trees begin to take full benefit of the moisture. At this stage, the smaller pores are usually completely filled with water and the larger pores are mostly filled with fresh soil air but with a fine and loosely held film of water around the surrounding larger particles. Gradually, the moisture from the smaller pore spaces seeps out to the larger ones and, as the film of water around the particles gets thinner, the water becomes more difficult to obtain and the stage is reached where the tree is ready to be watered again.

The tree's roots obtain some of the raw materials for their nourishment from salts and gases dissolved in the soil water (The usual concentration of soluble salts is between 100 to 1000 parts of the salts per million parts of water. If the concentration becomes very much stronger than this, toxic conditions may result).

Apart from needing salts and gases in solution, the tree's roots take in oxygen and release carbon dioxide, so that the soil air often contains up to ten or twenty times as much carbon dioxide as atmospheric air. If too much carbon dioxide is present, again toxic conditions may result. As was mentioned above, when the soil in the pot is saturated, the pore spaces are completely filled with water. This is the best way to water the plants because as the water is filling all the spaces, the old air is being pushed out and as the excess water drains away, fresh air is drawn into the container. If the soil mixture is one that takes a long time to drain or if drainage is slow due to the tree being rootbound, too much carbon dioxide may be building up and the health of the tree usually deteriorates.

The clay portion of a soil has many unique and important functions. One of these is that it is rich in available nutriments for plants. Clay is made up of extremely small, flattish particles of mineral matter, called colloids (in fact, 500 billion colloids equal the weight of one grain of sand and there are 160 million grains in a pound of sand). These colloids are derived from different potassium, aluminum silicates and are able to react chemically — being in a state of slow but active weathering (unlike sand which is made from minerals that have resisted weathering). This weathering process means that the granular structure of the clay particles is difficult to maintain but it also means that the particles are slowly parting with nutrient elements that may be used by the plant.

Also, because the colloids or small clay particles are of such a minute size, there is more surface area in a given volume of soil to react with the surrounding solution. (N.B. The rate of reaction with surrounding solution increases as the surface area increases) . . . *the activity for a given weight of clay particles would be between 10,000 and one million times that of a coarse sand, even if the sand particles were of the same chemical composition*[1].

However, as the particles become smaller there will be less pore space and these spaces will be smaller. Also, because the colloids are of a flattish shape, they easily settle to form "shingles". These characteristics make clay soils slow to drain when wet and almost water repellent when dry. When the clay is in a granular state, drainage is not too bad and, the good effect is that in clay soils that are well-drained, the rootsystem tends to be compact and healthy but does not encourage rank growth. As the clay begins to weather, the granules break down and pore spaces begin to be clogged. If this state is present for a prolonged period, drainage will be poor and the health of the tree will be in jeopardy.

Getting back to the question of the nutritional advantages of using clay, the following paragraphs may explain how the clay particles actually make these elements available to plants[2]:

The most important chemical property of the clay particles is that of Base Exchange (its ability to part with the nutriments required by the plants).

A clay particle may be considered as having hydrogen, sodium, potassium, magnesium and ammonium ions and these elements are important in the nutrition of plants. When the surface of such a particle is covered with water some of these ions are released and equilibrium becomes established. If these ions are removed from the solution by plant roots, or by

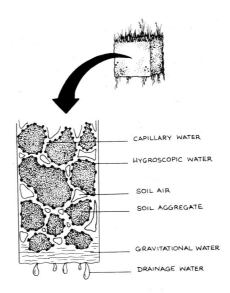

CAPILLARY WATER

HYGROSCOPIC WATER

SOIL AIR

SOIL AGGREGATE

GRAVITATIONAL WATER

DRAINAGE WATER

Figure 84: *Different types of soil water*

leaching, the equilibrium can be restored by the movement of more ions from the surface of the clay particle into the water.

Conversely, if nutrient cations are added to the soil in the form of fertilizers, these can be stored on the clay particles to be released later when the soil solution becomes depleted.

Clay soils, therefore, have considerable reserves of nutrients, including trace elements. They hold added fertilizer nutrients (except nitrate) against leaching by rain and they resist rapid changes in pH value.

Another interesting property of clay is that the particles exhibit a strong attraction to water as well as the ability to absorb water. Some of the water — capillary water — is held loosely around the particles and is available for plant use. Some, however, is chemically combined — hygroscopic water — and this is not available for plant use.

Other chemical aspects of clay are of interest. Following is a paragraph written by a "Practical Horticulturalist" in 1818 (taken from *Treatise on Soil and Manures*)[3]:

There is besides, in particular earths, an agency subservient to plants, which depends on chemical affinities, in those earths, for elementary substances floating in the air, or deposited in the soil. Thus both pure clay and carbonate of lime (chalk) have an attraction for volatile oils and solutions of oil and saponaceous matters, and for much of the pulpy stuff first disengaged from organic remains. Hence, a limited proportion of these earths contributes to form a **rich** and **generous** soil; because they long preserve in their pores the prepared nourishment of plants, parting with it gradually.

As well as clay, the humus portion of a soil has many desirable characteristics. Firstly, humus turns the earth into a "living" soil — inhabited by organisms varying from one-cell bacteria to earthworms (it has been calculated that as many as 500 biilion living organisms may inhabit a pound of soil). It is the beneficial bacteria, formed through the death and decay of living organisms in the soil that transform the humus, mineral and chemical compounds into nutriments available to plants. Another reason why good drainage and aeration is necessary in the soil mix is that the beneficial bacteria need Oxygen to stay alive. It is, primarily, the bacteria in the soil that transform nitrogen — essential for plant growth — into an acceptable form for the tree's roots. Seventy per cent of the air is made up of nitrogen — but this is not in an acceptable form for trees. The job of the bacteria is to transform organic matter into acceptable nitrogen (only a very small proportion of air nitrogen is used by the Bacteria). Nitrogen, being one of the essential elements needed for plant growth, is not available from rocks or inorganic matter — thus the importance of humus is quite considerable (the reason why rocks do not contain nitrogen is that when they are in a molten state, nitrogen is not stable and escapes into the atmosphere). Apart from its nutritional value to plants when broken down by bacteria, humus itself has some nutrient elements in the form of "exchangeable bases", that are acceptable to plants.

Another advantage of humus in the soil is that as the bacteria break it down and as the roots take up the nutriments thus produced — its volume gradually becomes smaller. Thus, the process of disintegration makes way for the roots as they are growing and the problem of compacting is minimized. The effect of compacting is also alleviated by the fact that humus has a spongey and resilient texture which will give under pressure. It also has the effect of keeping the soil temperature at a fairly uniform level — a helpful point, since the rootsystem can tolerate a narrower range of temperature than the top part of the tree (Roots grow and absorb nutriments only when moisture and temperature are adequate — about 20 degrees C (68°F) — a temperature lower than the ideal temperature for top growth).

Another good reason for having humus in the soil is that the byproducts of the bacteria, along with the humus itself, causes the smaller particles in the mix to form larger granules. This creates larger pore spaces and thus improves the circulation of air and water. Humus is, also, porous, which allows the tree's roots to penetrate the soil easily, and, while not keeping the soil soggy wet, it will usually condition the soil so that the optimum moisture level is maintained for a longer period of time.

Finally, since clay is in a process of active weathering and since humus will deteriorate as time goes on, some material is needed in the soil mixture that will be impervious to water and retain its shape, in order to separate the particles in the soil mix and create passages for water and air to circulate freely. Usually sharp sand is used for this purpose.

3. PRACTICAL NOTES ON SOIL FOR BONSAI

The above discussion has given us some clues on what plants need from soil and also of some of the characteristics of different parts of soil. Now we will look at the actual ingredients needed to mix a good bonsai soil and consider the proportions and the preparation of the components.

The best type of soil, obviously, would be one that combines all the best points of the ingredients discussed in the previous section and, in so doing, alleviate the problems associated with any single type of soil component.

Basically, three ingredients are necessary to mix a good bonsai soil.

Clay or Clay Loam (or a good, heavy garden soil):

Firstly, before going on to the preparation of the clay element of the soil, a short discussion on "loams" may be in order. The word "loam" has many varied meanings. A loam is basically a mixture of different ingredients and of particles of various sizes. A clay loam, or a heavy garden soil usually has the clay portion predominating over the humus or sandy section, while a sandy loam is mainly made up of sand. A clay loam, however, may have 95% clay or perhaps only 50%. If pure clay is desired, it is usually necessary to dig down to the subsoil, below the layer of loam. Because there is less humus, the nitrogen content will also be less and the clay will be less granular than the clay loam of the topsoil. It may, however, be rich in phosphates, potash and necessary micro-nutrients.

Following is an interesting quote discussing loams and different soil ingredients[4]:

Thus as clay is a substance of which a comparative small quantity will give a cold and stubborn character to the soil, the name clayey is often properly bestowed, where the quantity of pure clay to be collected from a given piece of land is but 8 to 42, compared with the quantity of sand which another field may contain, and yet barely deserve denomination of sandy. The term clayey should not be given to a soil which contains less than 1/6 of aluminous matter, because less than that will not be attended with the common effects which govern the culture and limit the crops, for a clayey soil.

The epithet "sandy" is not an appropriate distinction for any soil that does not contain at least 7/8 parts of sand; the sandy soils are to be distinguished into siliceous sandy, or flinty sand and calcareous sandy, or chalky sand.

The combination of animal or vegetable matter in an inferior proportion with earthy matter, but not lower than 1/6, makes a loam; the word "loam" should be limited to soils containing at least 1/3 of impalpable earthy matter (distinguished by the touch from sand, chalk or clay), combined with decayed animal or vegetable substances not exceeding 1/2 the weight of the mere earth; the earthy matter may comprehend aluminous, siliceous, or calcareous ingredients, and in some cases be mixed with mineral oxides. According to proportions of which, the soil may be red loam, brown loam or black loam, and, in regard to the basis, a clayey loam, a sandy or a chalky loam.

A superior proportion of vegetable matter, that is to say, an excess of this above half of the bulk of the earthy basis, makes a peat.

Clay or clay loam has many advantages, as were discussed in the previous section, but it also has a problem associated with its use. Because it is weathering slowly, its granular structure is breaking down and when in a fine state, it becomes sticky, like potter's clay and, with watering, the pores of the soil mixture will become clogged.

For this reason it is essential that the clay or clay loam portion of the soil mix be sieved to get rid of the fine silty part. Of course the granules will be gradually breaking down, as time passes, but at least a good start has been made and the bonsai can be repotted before lack of drainage and aeration becomes a problem.

For bonsai under 15 cm (6"), use the granules that pass through ⅛" sieve but are retained on 1/16" sieve. For bonsai 15 cm (6") to large, use the granules that pass through ¼" sieve and are retained on 1/16" sieve.

To easily and inexpensively sieve your soil, the coarse plastic sieves sold in hardware and garden shops for a few dollars can be used first to remove the larger particles. Then, by cutting to size a piece of fibreglass insect screening (which is approx. 1/16" size) and placing it in the sieve, the finer particles that fall through are discarded and what is retained is the correct size for your soil mix.

If you wish, you may grade the particle sizes when potting bonsai (although with the soil mix described in this chapter, it is not essential). In this case, the coarsest granules will be in the bottom third of the container, medium size in the middle third and the finest on the top. Finally, a very fine topsoil can be sprinkled on the surface on which moss may be planted. There are basically two reasons for this procedure. Firstly, when watering, usually the top surface of the soil will dry out first, while the bottom section of the pot — particularly if deep — may be waterlogged. Coarse particles of soil encourage quicker drainage while finer particles tend to hang on to the moisture content for a longer period of time. Thus a more even moisture content through the entire pot can be attained. Also, with watering, finer particles will tend to move down toward the bottom of the pot, so by putting these on the top sections, it will take longer for this effect to occur.

Sand:

The sand for use in the bonsai mix may be river sand or sand from crushed or weathered rocks, such as granite or basalt. Volcanic or mountain sand, made primarily from pumice or lava have also been used in bonsai soil mixes and growers have found that their rough surface holds capillary water better than other types of sand but that it still keeps the soil mix well aerated by quickly draining off the excess water in the container. Sand from weathered rocks also would have more nutritional value than predominantly siliceous or inert sand (N.B. Never use sand from the sea or beach, as the salt content is too high for most plant life).

If you wish, you may sieve the sand — particularly if the sand contains any foreign matter such as twigs or rocks. Use what passes through a ¼" sieve and what is retained on 1/16" sieve. Finer sand tends to encourage a finer branching of roots and slower growth than coarse sand, so the smaller grained sand may be used for older or smaller bonsai. It is important to wash the sand before use, however, as the grains have a strong attraction to dust. When unwashed sand is incorporated in the mix, the dust or silt is washed off the grains by watering and clogs the soil pores.

It is also important to use sharp sand, if possible. This is sand that has not undergone much weathering. Most newly crushed or weathered rock sand is sharp and if collecting sand from a river the sand at the head of the river is more likely to be sharp. Sharp sand is angular in shape, whereas after it has been weathered or carried downstream for some time, it is round and smooth. If smooth sand is used, the roots of the tree tend to go around the grain if one happens to be in the way. Sharp sand, however, produces a finer branching of the rootsystem and encourages the roots to change directions many times — thus making good use of the full container of soil, rather than simply growing out and down the sides of the pot. The reason for this is that when the roots strike the angular surface they are usually inclined to branch rather than simply grow around it.

Humus:

Leaf mould of deciduous tree varieties (e.g. beech, liquidambar, poplar) produces a very good humus (however, avoid leaves of trees that will greatly affect the pH level of the soil. Most Australian Natives produce a leaf mould far too acidy for the majority of trees).

Well-rotted cow or horse manure is another type of humus that is very good. Whatever you use, though, make sure that it is really rotted thoroughly. Materials used, that decompose rapidly in the soil mix — such as pine chips — have been found to induce Nitrogen depletion.

One humus product that should be avoided, if possible, is peat. There are a couple of disadvantages with its use. Firstly, it is sterile and lacks in nutrient value for the tree. Well-rotted manure or leaf-mould take up the same volume in the pot and similarly give the soil a friable texture but also have the added benefit of supplying food to the tree.

The other disadvantage of peat is that when wet, it tends to hang on to the moisture too long and when dry, it becomes water-repellent — having to be actually submerged for quite a while to rewet it. This can be very dangerous if used in a bonsai soil mix, due to the fact that if a tree does manage to become quite dry, the speed at which it is watered becomes all-important. Also, the fact that it remains wet longer than well-rotted manure means that aeration will be poor and the tree may suffer. The peats that are older geologically tend to exhibit these problems more, so that Irish or German would be the worse to use, in this respect; Polish a little better and Australian probably the best (rewetting a little easier than the others). Well-rotted manure, however, rewets straight away when in a dry state.

When preparing manure for use, it should be allowed to rot for three to six months. The pile may be interlayered with soil or lime if you wish, but the most essential thing is to turn over the pile regularly — particularly with large amounts — so that all parts are being exposed to the air. It is the bacteria that need Oxygen that are responsible for breaking the manure down into a good, clean, sweet compost for trees. The anaerobic bacteria (i.e. those that can live without oxygen) make the manure sour and unfit for trees to grow in. When the manure is a dark brown or blackish colour and looks more like soil than manure, it is ready for use. It can then be sieved through about a ¼″ mesh to break up the larger pieces and make the particles a more even size. (N.B. Chicken manure is not a good substitute, as it is so strong that only a small amount can be added to the mix as compared with the amount of horse or cow manure that would be used. Thus, one of the advantages of creating a spongy texture by addition of humus, would be lost. Chicken manure is also quite alkaline and if a certain variety likes more alkaline conditions — a little may be added to the mix).

Thus we see that a mixture of clay loam, sand and humus provides a good, well-rounded soil for growing bonsai. The necessary proportions of each ingredient is best calculated by weight: 45% of clay loam, 45% of sand and about 5 to 10% of humus. After the components have been weighed once, marks may be made on the container and subsequent mixings may be made by volume. When a new batch of an ingredient is used, amounts should again be weighed initially, as variations do occur.

One need not be so particular though, as small variations will not spoil the soil mixture. In fact, you will most probably find that the amounts, by weight, of each of the three ingredients work out to be roughly equal by volume.

This is a basic soil mixture that is suitable for most varieties. It has adequate food for one year without it being necessary to fertilize. The problem of "compacting" is minimized by the addition of humus and aeration and good drainage is achieved with the use of sand in the mix. There is no need to include extra drainage material at the bottom as it is already a very open mix. Trees grow better in a soil mix that is uniform. Water is often blocked at the interface formed by two different mixtures or materials, thus slowing down the drainage process considerably.

Remember though, if you are using a different soil mix and your trees are growing well and look healthy — do not change. If, on the other hand, your trees are not looking so well and you think the problem may be with your soil mix, you may find the above discussion helpful.

While the mix just outlined is a good, basic soil, some varieties will benefit by some variations in the proportions. Some of these are listed below:

Most flowering and fruiting varieties: An extra 2% of humus (by weight)

Stone Fruits: these like a rich virgin soil so, ½ clay loam, ½ sand (by volume)

Wisteria & Pomegranites: These like a heavier soil mix, 1½ clay loam, ½ sand and 1 humus (by volume)

Pines — humus cut to ½% by weight, and sand increased by another measure.

Junipers: Basic mix or mix for flowering varieties, except for Sargent Juniper which prefers a leaner soil. Junipers also like slightly alkaline conditions so a little well-rotted chicken manure may be included and/or agricultural dolomite may be sprinkled on top of the soil occasionally (perhaps once every couple of months in the growing season) and watered in.

In most cases, the type of rootsystem a tree has, will reflect its preferences as far as soil texture is concerned. Trees that have very fine, fibrousy roots (e.g. azalea) tend to prefer a more fibrousy soil, whereas trees with thick roots (e.g. wisteria) often like a heavier soil.

4. STERILIZATION OF SOIL

In theory, sterilization of soil sounds good: disease micro-organisms will be eliminated and nearly all weed seeds will be destroyed. In practice, however, it is found that there are also many disadvantages in sterilizing soil and in the majority of cases these far outweigh the good points.

Firstly, overheating the soil (over 180 degrees F) or, by chemical sterilization, all the beneficial bacteria (the advantages of which are discussed above) will be killed as well as the disease micro-organisms. If the soil is steam sterilized — the physical structure and texture will be spoilt. With some soils, excessive salts and toxins are set free and a "rest" period is necessary before planting takes place. Furthermore, there may have been no disease present in the first place.

After all the trouble of sterilization, recontamination is extremely easy, so storage bins and all other articles should also be sterilized, but, even so, airborne diseases or contamination by seeds, is almost impossible to control. Also, if any old soil remains on the tree's rootsystem this may contaminate the fresh, sterilized soil.

Probably the worst problem of all, however, is the fact that the beneficial bacteria are destroyed. If a bad micro-organism happens to reach the sterilized soil first, there is no opposing force to combat it, and, usually, the disease then spreads rapidly.

5. MUCK

When making built-up styles of Saikei (see Chapter 8) or Rock settings (see Chapter 7), some additional type of soil that is stickier and firmer is necessary to keep the soil around the rootsystem of trees. This soil preparation, called "muck", is very much like plasticine in consistency and has the dual purpose of keeping the soil from falling away from the tree's roots and also of giving some nourishment to the tree.

The best way of making muck is to use 50% fresh cow manure and 50% clay (this may be the fine clay silt that has been discarded when sieving the clay for your ordinary soil mix). These ingredients are mixed together with enough water to make a loose consistency and it is then left for four to six months in a container, being stirred occasionally and allowing fermentation to take place. During this period, watch that the water does not evaporate completely away, by adding more water as is necessary. After fermentation is complete (N.B. the container should be open to the air during fermentation period), the muck should be allowed to reach the consistency of putty — if it sticks on a vertical rock section easily, the right consistency has been reached.

It can then be kneaded like potter's clay or bread and used immediately or stored for as long as you like in air-tight plastic bags. It is better to mix the muck this way, as fresh cow manure will combine with the clay and produce a consistent and homogenous mixture. Also, the longer it is stored in plastic bags afterwards, the more pliable and workable the muck will become. Watch, however, that it does not dry out.

If you do need muck immediately, already well-rotted manure may be used. Simply mix equal measures of well-rotted manure and clay, with enough water to reach plasticity and knead well. Cow manure is still the best to use and a more workable muck will be obtained if the manure has been put through a fine sieve beforehand.

Some Scientific Aspects of Plant Nutrition

A. MACRO & MICRO NUTRIENTS

The question of what it is that makes a plant grow, has haunted the minds of plant lovers and botanists for centuries. One of the earliest experiments with regard to this question was conducted about 300 years ago by the Flemish scientist Jan van Helmont. A willow was planted in a weighed quantity of dry soil and then watered, when necessary, for a period of five years. After this time, the tree and the soil were separated, the soil dried, and both weighed. The result was that the soil had dropped in weight by two ounces and the willow had gained 165 pounds. The conclusion was made that water was the element that made trees grow.

This is true; however, it is not the whole answer, and it is now known that the two ounces missing from the soil and certain elements from the air are just as essential to the growth process as is water. These are the Macro- and Micro-nutrients[5].

Some elements are needed by plants in reasonably large quantities — these are termed the MACRO-NUTRIENTS — while others, that are also important to plant health, are needed in smaller amounts — these are referred to as the MICRO-NUTRIENTS. These are listed below with some information on what their effects on plant growth are.

B. MACRO-NUTRIENTS

Carbon (C), Oxygen (O), Hydrogen (H), Nitrogen (N). Potassium (K), Phosphorus (P), Calcium (Ca), Sulphur (S), Magnesium (Mg).

Nitrogen: This element is used quickly by trees (whereas the use of potassium and phosphorus is slower) and is the main constituent of proteins both in the protoplasm and in the food stored in plant cells. One of its main functions is to promote healthy foliage growth. Trees must have some Nitrogen so that phosphates in the soil may be utilized. Thus if you wish to slow the growth of a tree and discourage the formation of large, lush leaves, Nitrogen may be limited but should not be eliminated entirely. Trees deficient in Nitrogen are stunted in all aspects of their growth and have a yellowish hue to their leaves — particularly in the older leaves (this latter symptom, however, may be caused by other reasons as well). Nitrogen deficiency may also make a plant more susceptible to winter die-back.

An excess of Nitrogen, on the other hand, will promote overly vigorous growth, less food storage and will inhibit the development of fruit and flowers. Also, too much soft growth may be produced that cannot be supported by the rootsystem and unless hardened, will not stand a harsh winter.

Most of the Nitrogen in soil is not readily available for plant use, being tied up in organic compounds. This organic form of Nitrogen is broken down by Ammonifying Bacteria into the Ammonia form of Nitrogen NH_3 or Nitrites. This form dissolves easily but is held by soil particles so that it is slower acting and remains longer in the soil. The Ammonia form of Nitrogen, however, is toxic if present in the soil in large quantities. In one to four weeks, though, Nitrifying Bacteria will convert this form into Nitrates NO_3. This form dissolves easily but is not held by the soil particles — therefore, it is both used quickly by the tree but also leaches out quickly. The nitrifying bacteria are thus essential for the availability of Nitrogen.

Organic Nitrogen is better for bonsai use, as it is slower acting and is less prone to leaching. Water insoluble Nitrogen may be obtained from natural organic sources such as tankages, seed meals, sewage and sludge projects. This must then be converted to Ammonical Nitrogen and then into Nitrates (takes about four weeks) before it is in an acceptable form for plant use. Water soluble organic Nitrogen or Urea (chemically made but the same as animal urine) is also used. This form changes to the Ammonical form in a few days and therefore can be considered as the Ammonical form when applied. It is interesting to note that some trees, e.g. Podocarpus, Locust and Alder, have nitrogen fixing nodules on their roots. These nodules are formed by bacteria and enable the tree to assimilate nitrogen from the air and convert it to Nitrates. Even though $4/5$ of the air is nitrogen, it is in a form unacceptable to most trees and less than 1% of Nitrogen used by the majority of plants comes from this source.

Phosphorus: This element is also found in plant protein, especially in areas of rapid growth such as the meristem, root-tips, buds and fruit. It is important for the health of the tree's metabolism and is necessary for good root-growth and development of characteristics of maturity. Phosphorus, however, is easily "locked-up" as it combines with other elements. Chelating, however, will stop this process.

Potassium: Acts as a catalyst for other elements to do their jobs, and acts as a check on Nitrogen — countering the formation of too much soft, lush growth. Potassium plays a part in cell division, helps in the manufacture and movement of sugars and starches, activates on enzyme in glycolysis, reduces Nitrates, aids in the development of chlorophyll and plays a part in good root development. Potassium is stored in the meristemic areas and can be moved from the older tissue to newer plant tissue areas at times of rapid growth.

A tree that is deficient in Potassium usually has a low production and poor quality of flowers and fruit, is more susceptible to disease and is not as able to endure low temperatures.

Calcium: plays a part in the tree's cell structure (helps construction of cell walls) and in the distribution of sugars , starches and amino acids. It is also a catalyst — making phosphorus and potassium more available to plants. This element also promotes good root growth and vigorous top growth. Plants preferring acidy soil, however, do not like large quantities of calcium. Small amounts though, will lighten clay soils.

Magnesium: This is one of the elements that make up the chlorophyll molecule. It is also a catalyst for the plant's use of other elements. Trees deficient in Magnesium have yellowish foliage and develop a condition known as chlorosis (a condition that may also stem from a deficiency of iron).

Sulphur: This element forms part of the molecules that make up plant proteins. A deficiency leads to weak root development and a paler foliage colouration. Roots are able to absorb sulphur when it is in an oxidized state.

C. MICRO-NUTRIENTS

These elements, while being necessary for plant growth, are required in extremely small amounts. It would hardly ever be necessary to add these to the soil as the amount necessary would either be in the soil already or added by dust, rain or tap water. Too much of most of these elements would be toxic to plants.

Iron: This is sometimes referred to as a MACRO-NUTRIENT, however, only 0.003% is necessary. This is absorbed as free iron or in its ferric state (iron oxide) but will reduce to the ferrous state unless an oxidizing agent is added. Iron is insoluble and needs the natural action of the soil to make it available. Iron is not part of chlorophyll but it must be present for the compound to form. If the tree is deficient in iron, chlorosis results. Because iron cannot be translocated to new tissue, iron chlorosis will show up in new leaves (they will be pale and small). Nitrogen chlorosis, on the other hand, shows up in the old leaves first, as the element can be translocated for use in production of healthy new growth. Iron is also used for plant respiration. In alkaline or neutral soils, iron may be "locked-up" — thus appearing as though it is deficient. This can happen if there is an excess of lime or phosphate or heavy metals (manganese, copper, zinc) in the soil or if drainage is bad or overwatering practiced.

Boron: Only 10 to 15 parts per million is necessary. A deficiency in Boron leads to growth abnormalities, but large quantities of it are highly toxic to plants. A Boron deficiency can be produced by an excess of limestone in the soil.

Zinc: This element is a catalyst in plant metabolism and aids in respiration. It is also essential for the production of certain enzymes, helps in the composition of some plant hormones and also cell elongation. Another beneficial effect is seen in its strengthening of plants against certain diseases.

Manganese: This is a very important catalyst in plant metabolism. It aids in CO_2 assimilation and in the action of various enzymes. Deficiency causes chlorosis, but the symptoms are different to iron chlorosis. Both forms have paler young leaves but, while in iron deficiency leaves are pale with darker veins, manganese deficiency produces mottled leaves.

Copper: This is also a catalyst in plant metabolism and respiration and is part of many enzymes systems. It has a very narrow range between beneficial effects and toxicity (0.2 per million parts).

Molybdomen: Again, only very small amounts necessary — 1 in 100,000,000. It is used in reduction of Nitrates and is a part of Nitrate reductase.

Cobalt: As yet, this seems to be essential only for lower plant forms such as algae and fungi.
Chlorine: Also seemingly necessary in very small quantities.

D. ACIDITY AND ALKALINITY OF BONSAI SOIL

The pH of the soil is measured on a scale from 1 to 14 — 7 being neutral, while 1 is strongly acid and 14 strongly alkaline. (Acidity is formed by a high concentration of hydrogen ions and usually occurs in areas were there is higher rainfall, while alkalinity has a higher concentration of hydroxyl ions and occurs usually in areas of lower rainfall).

Most trees tend to prefer a soil that is neutral or just slightly acid (around 4.5 to 6.5). Some acid loving trees (e.g. rhododendrons, azaleas, camellias) thrive on a pH of 4.5 to 5.5, but not many trees like an alkaline soil and almost no plant will tolerate a pH over 9.

If you wish to make your soil more alkaline, or to make it less acid, agricultural dolomite should be sprinkled on the surface of the soil and watered in. If, on the other hand, you wish to make the soil more acid or less alkaline, wettable sulphur, dilute vinegar (2 tablespoons to just over a litre (quart) of water) or a soil acidifier, may be applied. Be careful not to change the pH level drastically in one go. Change it by one unit at a time and, if more change is necessary, repeat the process in about 30 days.

Extremes of acidity or alkalinity can cause the effects of various nutrient deficiencies, as certain elements are "locked-up" and cannot be released to the plant. Also, mycorrhiza (see further on in this chapter) may be destroyed. In highly acid soils, bacterial action is inhibited, so that bacteria are not competing with the roots for oxygen and are not giving off much harmful Carbon dioxide, but, at the same time, they are not decomposing organic matter or fertilizers, so that even when fertilizer is applied, the trees cannot make use of it. In highly alkaline soils, bacterial action is stimulated so that a lot of food is produced but there may be a deficiency in Oxygen for the roots and a toxic amount of Carbon dioxide in the soil (If this CO_2 can escape, however, it may be used by the top portion of the tree for photosynthesis).

Practical Notes on Fertilizer for Bonsai

With the type of soil mixture discussed in this chapter, it will not be necessary to fertilize older bonsai for one year. However, if you do not rootprune and repot yearly, a fertilizing program should commence in the second year to keep your tree in good condition. If your tree is young, or still being developed it would be advisable to feed it in the first year, but wait at least 6 to 8 weeks after rootpruning, or else the recovery of the tree may be jeopardized.

Trees' roots are able to accept food (i.e. salts and nutriments in solution) only when moisture and temperature levels are right. The temperature should be around 20 degrees C (68°F), that is, spring and autumn temperatures (winter is too cold and summer, too hot) and when there is about 25% moisture in the volume of soil, so, water your trees prior to fertilizing (this also prevents the fertilizer from burning the roots and promotes quicker, more thorough and even dispersal of the fertilizer).

Another important point is that organic fertilizers are better than chemical fertilizers — partly because the former are slower acting and are not so inclined to produce rank and unnecessary growth and, also, because they encourage the beneficial bacteria in the soil, whereas chemical fertilizers can destroy these bacteria.

Fertilizer should never be mixed into the soil before potting. At potting time, however, Osmocote or Nutricote — slow release fertilizers that work by the process of osmosis — may be applied. These work so slowly that the tree's roots will not be damaged, and they can be used in conjunction with other types of fertilizer. It is possible to buy 3 to 4 month and 8 to 9 month types and there is also the choice of higher or lower levels of Nitrogen. A longer acting, low Nitrogen type would be suitable in most cases. Also, a pinch of superphosphate included when potting aids in the development of a strong root system. However, this should not be used with any Australian natives as they have a low tolerance to phosphate.

A good organic fertilizer that is easily obtainable is Fish Emulsion (use at half strength every two to three weeks in spring and autumn), however, if you want to make your own fertilizer, here is a recipe:— 3 parts soya bean meal, 1 part blood & bone, 1 part chicken manure, 1 part wood ash, 1 part fish emulsion.

Put all the ingredients into a container at least 4 times the volume and add water to reach a little over half-way up the container (don't fill the container completely while fermentation takes place, as the liquid may bubble over — also, it is a good idea to keep the lid on during this time). When fermentation has stopped (in about 3 months time) then top-up the bin with water and when the mixture settles, use one part of the liquid to five parts of water. Either dunk the trees in this solution or pour it over the soil (if you pour it over, make sure you pour enough to soak through). If you wish, you may add fish bones, fish heads or fish meal with the soya bean meal at the start of the procedure. Alternatively, you can add a tablespoon of fish emulsion to a bucket of the solution at the end of the process, just prior to fertilizing your trees.

An alternative to liquid fertilizing is to make fertilizer cakes. To do so, make the same mixture as above, but use less water, or allow the water to evaporate. When it reaches a thick consistency, add enough plain flour to make it sticky. Form this mixture into small biscuits or cakes and dry in the sun. The cakes are simply placed on the surface of the soil and a little fertilizer leaches out into the pot each time the bonsai is watered. Put four, one in each corner, in a large bonsai pot, two in a medium sized one and one in a small bonsai pot.

The advantage of fertilizing this way is that it is time-saving and is a very safe and slow method of feeding trees. The disadvantages are that it tends to encourage feeder roots to come to the surface of the soil and, occasionally, insects may lay eggs under the cakes and the larvae that hatch may damage the tree's roots.

Another point that may be useful is that if foliage is not looking a healthy, green colour, a solution made up of a heaped teaspoon of Epsom Salts to a small bucket of water, will promote a better colour if sprayed onto foliage.

Remember that with all fertilizing, it is better to underdo it than overdo it. Also, it is more beneficial to fertilize more frequently with a weaker solution (say every 2 to 3 weeks in spring and autumn), than less frequently with a stronger one (say once a month). (Another point that may be of interest is the fact that warm water is absorbed more quickly by a plant than cold — a fact that may be helpful when applying liquid fertilizer).

Mycorrhizae

Sad, melancholy, slow, dwelling at the base of trees between earth
and root, they embody the Wisdom of the Tree . . . .
BRIAN FROUD[6]

Mycorrhiza (pronounced: my-ko-rise-a, plural: mycorrhizae) is a symbiotic parasite (that is, where both host and parasite benefit from the union) that lives on and within the rootsystems of many trees.

On the tree varieties that have mycorrhiza attached to the outside of small roots, the fungus is visible and appears like a fine, usually white, webby substance surrounding the rootsystem. This is seen on the rootsystems of healthy trees such as pines, firs, cedars, spruces, beech, oaks, birches and hornbeams, and could easily be mistaken as being a disease, (N.B. for a long time it was, in fact, thought of as a disease or parasitic infection). On other trees, (e.g. junipers, maples and many Australian natives, to name a few), it is not so visible, being located mainly inside the tree's roots.

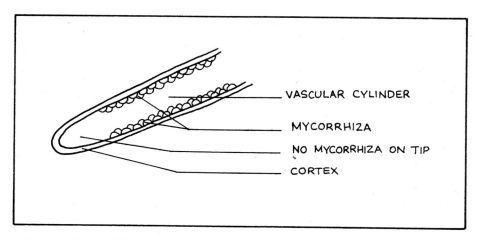

Figure 85: *Mycorrhiza inside tree root*

Each variety of tree that has mycorrhiza has its own characteristic type — the mycorrhiza of a pine, for example, would not live on the roots of a spruce tree and vice versa. Within the same variety, however, trees that have very little or no mycorrhiza may be inoculated with some from another tree at the time of repotting.

It is important to remember never to bareroot (that is, completely remove soil from the rootsystem) a tree that has mycorrhiza attached mainly to the outside of roots, as it is more likely that most of the mycorrhiza will be removed in the process. Many trees may take up to two years to die after such a procedure, since they are dependent upon their mycorrhiza for much of their nutrition and cannot reproduce more in time. The importance of mycorrhiza is illustrated in the experiment where some of the fungus from a particular tree variety was put in a blender and the resulting solution sprayed on small plants of the same variety. These sprayed trees showed a better growth rate and a higher proportion survived transplanting than those not sprayed.[7]

The mycorrhiza attaches itself to the tree's roots and actually becomes like the tree's own root hairs and, while the mycorrhiza obtains carbohydrates and vitamins from the tree, at the same time it makes the roots more efficient and gives increased access to soil nutrients. It does this by providing more absorbing surface on the rootsystem and breaking down soil into available nutriments by producing acids that dissolve silicates in soil. Mycorrhiza is also able to absorb released ions and transmit these directly to the tree.

It has also been suggested that mycorrhiza produces Nitrogen and plant growth hormones, protects the rootsystem against pathogens and, in forests, can move carbohydrates from one tree to another.

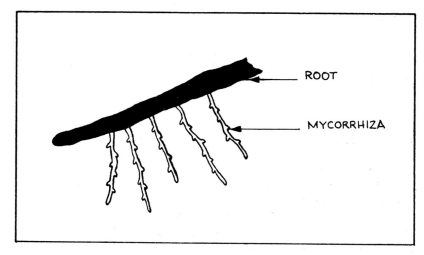

Figure 86: *Mycorrhiza on tree root*

It has already been mentioned that one tree can be inoculated with mycorrhiza from another tree of the same variety. To encourage the growth of the fungus, however, the pH range for the tree should be correct, drainage should be good and the tree should not be overwatered. It has also been suggested that mycorrhiza is more abundant in soils that contain reasonably low amounts of Nitrogen and Phosphorus.

Even though many questions remain unanswered about this mysterious fungus, there is no doubt that it is beneficial to many trees and should be encouraged.

REFERENCES
Chapter Three
1.   Custard, F. "Using Clay Soil" in *Bonsai in Australia*, January–February, 1972, pp. 25–28.
2.   As Above.
3.   "Treatise on Soils and Manures by a Practical Horticulturalist" in *Bonsai in Australia*, October 1970, p. 12.
4.   As Above, p. 12.
5.   Behme, R.L., *Bonsai, Saikei and Bonkei*, New York: William Morrow & Co., Inc., 1969, p. 93.
6.   Froud, B. *The Council in "The Sword of Thrac"*, Unpublished story, 1976.
7.   Koetsch, J., "Mycorrhiza: Why Plants live!" in *Bonsai Clubs International*, 19.138.

CHAPTER FOUR

"Rootpruning, Potting and Repotting Techniques"

The Roots of the Tree

There would not be a life on earth without soil and
no soil, or very little poor soil, without life. Sun and its
light is necessary too, although there are forms of
life that go on in darkness . . .
*   V.A. KORESHOFF.*

The roots of trees are very interesting forms of life. They are, in many respects, like a mirror image of the top portion of the tree (fine branching of roots usually produces fine top branching and the depth and spread of the rootsystem generally balances the height and spread of the trunk and branches). Yet, despite this, they exhibit characteristics totally opposite to what lies above ground.

The branches and leaves of a tree are totally dependent upon the sun for light to manufacture food through photosynthesis and they use carbon dioxide while releasing oxygen into the atmosphere. They also live in a bright and breezy world full of birds and insects that help in fertilizing their flowers and distributing their seeds. The roots, on the other hand, live in a world of darkness . . . and, as they secretly and silently push their way in the direction of the earth's centre, using available oxygen and giving off carbon dioxide, they form intimate relationships with the soil bacteria and often with the beneficial fungus known as Mycorrhiza.

The roots have two main functions. Firstly, they provide an anchor for the tree, to hold it steady in the ground and give it stability. The "tap-root" is specifically for this purpose. The other job is to inquisitively fossick through the soil for moisture and nutriments and to translocate these to the top portion of the tree in the form of salts and minerals in solution.

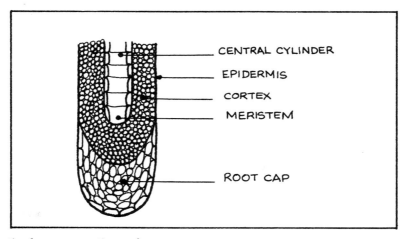

Figure 87: *Vertical cross-section of root*

Roots are growing fairly constantly. The function of the root tip is to push its way through the soil and to determine which way is down. It does this by a small, marble-like ball of starch that rattles in the hollow chamber at the very tip of the root. This indicates the pull of gravity and the root pursues that basic direction.

As the root tip pushes its way through the soil it is continually casting off old cells and these act as a lubricant for the root passage. The roots also give off a small amount of acid (mostly carbonic acid) that acts to dissolve the necessary elements for the tree. Thus we see that the intimate relationship between the roots and soil is chemical as well as physical.

Behind this root tip are the fine root-hairs and it is these that collect the nutrients in solution to feed the tree. It is an interesting fact that of all the tree's rootsystem, it is only these very young roots (usually not more than 2 weeks old) that are actively collecting food. All the others are merely forming the "go-between" channels and providing support by balancing the top part of the tree.

Why Rootpruning is Necessary

If a tree is planted in a container, the roots will continue to grow until they have used all the nourishment and space available. At this point, the tree must be either planted in a larger container or rootpruned, if the health of the tree is to be maintained. As we have just seen, it is only the very youngest roots that are acting to feed the tree and, like the top portion of a tree, cutting actually stimulates re-growth. A tree in a container doesn't need the heavy roots for stability that the tree in the ground requires and, when rootpruned, the tree reacts by sending out a mass of new, active feeder roots. The response is seen, above ground, by renewed vigour and health. Instead of having a pot full of old roots that are no longer functional, we are renewing them with those that will act to rejuvenate the tree.

Thus, we see that rootpruning is good for trees and while each passing year imparts more of the venerable characteristics of age to our trees, they can simultaneously have a perpetually young system of roots. Trees, in fact, can probably come closer to immortality than any other life form on Earth.

With rootpruning and repotting also comes the opportunity to study the rootsystem and check for any damage or the existence of any diseases or pests.

Also, as a tree becomes rootbound, porosity decreases and consequently, circulation of air and water is reduced. This is due to the fact that fewer soil pores exist as the granules in the soil mixture break down and the fine root-hairs have grown through the mix, clogging most of the remaining pores.

Times for Repotting

The best time for repotting is at the end of the dormant season, just prior to the main growth period for the tree. For most plants, this means late winter or early spring, when the new buds are swelling but have not yet opened up into new growth, (note that for sub-tropicals it may be late spring to early summer) (see Figure 88).

There is another time when many tree varieties may be rootpruned. This is late summer to early autumn, at the end of the summer dormancy, (N.B. when temperatures become too hot in summer, most trees cease growing. The temperature range for growth is approximately 5 to 40 degrees C (40°F–104°F), depending on the species, and growth is already slowing down at 30 degrees C (86°F) for most trees) and before the short period of active growth that usually takes place in early autumn. For the more touchy varieties, the late winter to early spring season is better, as the period of time for safe rootpruning is longer and the subsequent

Plate XVI: *Blue atlas cedar*, Cedrus atlantica *'Glauca', Informal upright style, height: 63 cm, Japanese pot, estimated age: from 1957 nursery stock, trained since 1975, photograph taken in 1981*

Plate XVII: *Alberta Spruce,* Picea abies *var.* albertiana *'Conica', free-form informal upright style, height: 57 cm, Japanese pot, estimated age: from 1950 nursery stock, trained since 1975, photograph taken in 1981.*

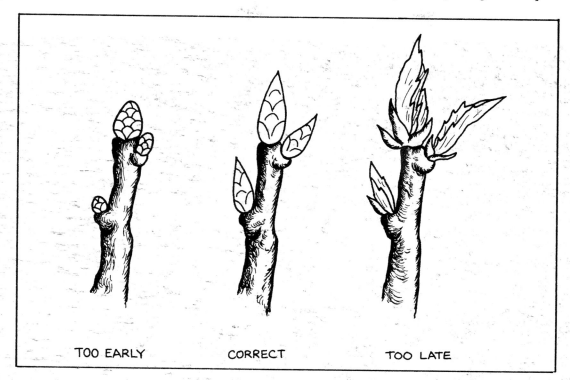

Figure 88: *Determining Time for Repotting by State of Buds*

regrowth is stronger than in autumn. The tree is, therefore, more likely to go through rootpruning without any setback.

Winter is not a good time for repotting most trees, as the roots are making little or no new growth to heal the cuts and supply more feeder roots. As a consequence, root-rot may often set-in. In spring to mid-summer, rootpruning and repotting is also risky as this is the tree's active growth period and while the tree is vigorously producing new, soft foliage any break in the supply of water may damage or kill the tree. If an emergency occurs where rootpruning and/or repotting is essential in summer, complete defoliation of trees that may be defoliated, and trimming back of other types, will act as a safety measure (as the tree will not lose so much water through transpiration).

With many trees that flower before leaves appear, repotting is generally done after flowering but before the leaves open. Those that flower in late spring, though, are repotted before flowering.

How Often to Rootprune and Repot Your Bonsai

Trees do not like being disturbed unduly, as, in nature, they live in the same spot of ground all their life. If the tree is in a good, healthy condition after last year's rootpruning and repotting, you may wish to leave it undisturbed for a further twelve months and perhaps fertilize during the growing season to maintain the tree's vigour.

Young trees, very vigorous varieties, trees that have very heavy crops of fruit or flowers, or trees in small or shallow containers, would benefit by being rootpruned yearly (and some — like privet or willow — twice a year!). Actually, for some varieties, where the winter temperatures are not severe, there is often no real dormancy. The top of the willow, for example, may be bare through winter, yet the roots can continue to grow at quite a fast rate.

Conversely in early spring, sometimes the top of the tree will start to grow — using stored nutriments — while the roots are still dormant. Thus while the top portion reflects the rootsystem and vice versa, occasionally they are out of step for a short period.

As trees become older, they begin to slow down their rate of growth and consequently, rootpruning need not be done so frequently — perhaps once every 3 to 4 years will be sufficient. True pines, Japanese Black Pines for instance, can even be left for 5 years without repotting, particularly when they are over 15 years old. When a tree does become older it is better not to rootprune too frequently as this will only encourage unnecessary growth and perhaps promote juvenile foliage (on appropriate varieties) or loss of bark.

It may be relevant to mention here the danger of suddenly improving the conditions of an old tree that is in a poor state of health. Such a tree often has branches that are so old and woody that they are no longer capable of sending out new growth. If conditions are suddenly improved in terms of fresh, rich soil and space for rootgrowth, the tree wants to grow on top as well and frequently reacts by sending up suckers. This is an attempt, made by the tree, to balance the above ground portion with the rejuvenated rootsystem, however, after the suckers grow, the old trunk and branches may die. If improvement of conditions is made more slowly, the tree is better able to cope with the changes.

Finally, do not think that roots coming through the bottom drainage hole is a sign that the tree needs repotting. Sometimes roots will appear through the hole very quickly if the area under the pot is moist or humid. There may still be adequate nutrition and space left in the container.

The Procedure for Rootpruning and Repotting Bonsai

The roots of trees don't like being exposed for too long, so the operation of rootpruning and repotting should be done quickly and performed in an area that is sheltered from the sun and wind. It is also a good idea to have everything that will be needed prepared and close by before you start. Basically, this should include:

The soil mixture

A pot. If you are potting the tree in a proper bonsai pot, rather than a training pot, it would be preferable to have more than one suitable pot handy, so that choice is available.

Plastic or fibreglass screen mesh to cover the drainage holes in the container.

The necessary tools: A sharp pair of scissors, a saw if heavy roots need to be removed, a rootpruning and repotting hook to make the job of removing soil from the rootball easier, and a potting stick to help work the soil in around the roots and eliminate air spaces. (The rootpruning and repotting hook may be made from a shortened and slightly pointed screwdriver that has been turned over or alternatively you may wish to use a horse's hoof-pick; the potting stick may be made from a dowel with the end pointed like a large knitting needle, see plates X & XI.

A trough, or sink where the tree can be watered after potting has been completed. It is better to soak the tree so that the entire volume of soil in the pot is saturated.

A water spray atomizer to damp down the roots if they are drying too rapidly during the rootpruning process, and a plastic bag large enough to cover them in case you get called away unexpectedly.

Now we come to the actual procedure of rootpruning and repotting:

If potting your tree for the first time, it is better to overpot (that is, choose a pot larger than the ideal size as far as the artistic appearance is concerned), partly because you will not have to be so drastic with the cutting of the rootsystem, and partly because the tree will develop more quickly if it has more soil and available room. Perhaps a pot ¾ of the size of the original rootmass would be a safe choice.

Preferably, the new soil should be bone dry. Thus, as it is being worked in with the potting stick, it falls into the large air spaces easily.

To prepare the container, simply cover the drainage holes with plastic or fibreglass screening (do not cover the entire bottom of the pot — only the actual holes. The former procedure encourages a layer of roots to grow under the mesh). If you think you will be moving the tree or trees as you are arranging them (usually for groups and saikei) you may wish to wire the mesh into the pot. The procedure for this is illustrated in Figure 89 below.

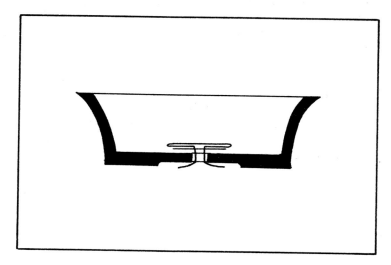

Figure 89: *How to wire the mesh into the pot*
N.B. The loop of wire can be on the inner side of the pot base, as shown in the diagram, or on the underside.

Actually tying the tree into the pot is sometimes practiced as well — the purpose being to keep the tree stationary in the period prior to new rootgrowth. Trees do need to be stationary for healthy root development to occur and before the new roots grow and become firm in the soil there is a possibility that there may be movement of the tree. Generally, though, unless there are specialized problems such as an extremely shallow pot, a top-heavy tree or rough weather, tying is unnecessary if the tree is placed on the bench after potting and not moved till new growth is established.

If you consider that tying the tree into the pot is necessary, uncoated natural fibre string is the best material to use. If bare copper wire is used, it may cut into the roots and the copper ions may negatively react with the damp soil and rootsystem and thus poison the plant. A couple of methods for tying the tree in are illustrated below.

Figures 90 & 91: *Tying a tree into the pot*

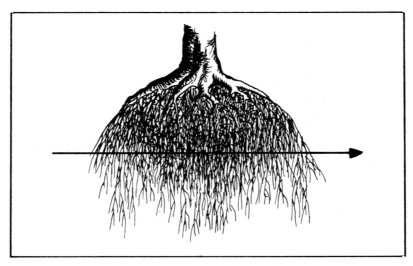

Figure 92: *How to rootprune fibrous rooted trees*

Different trees have vastly different types of roots. Some, like the Wisteria and Pine, have coarse, thick roots, while others, like junipers and azaleas have many fine fibrous roots. These differences should be considered when rootpruning is done. With the latter type that have a mass of fibrous feeder roots, the rootball can simply be sawn off at the appropriate point, while coarse, thicker roots are better rootpruned selectively (this means investigating the rootsystem and removing entirely the old, non-functional roots, while leaving, in full, as many of the new fresh roots as is required).

With all trees — and particularly those with thicker roots — the policy should be to remove as many of the older heavier roots as possible, in order to replace them with the young ones that are going to supply nourishment to the tree.

With rootbound trees, the method of sawing-off say the bottom third of the rootball, is often the best solution. Most times you will find that the mass of roots is on the outside portion of the rootball and that, once cut, there is easier access to tease out the remaining roots. Another advantage is that there is actually less damage done to the rootsystem by using this technique than by hacking and tearing slowly at the rootball with a hook and probably letting the roots dry out in the process.

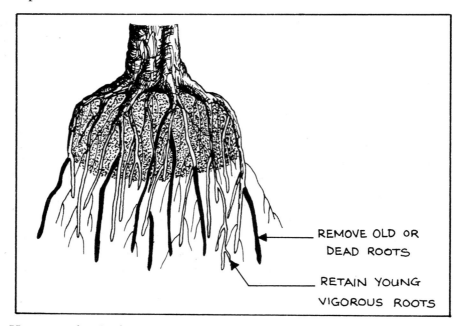

REMOVE OLD OR
DEAD ROOTS

RETAIN YOUNG
VIGOROUS ROOTS

Figure 93: *How to selectively rootprune trees with thicker roots*

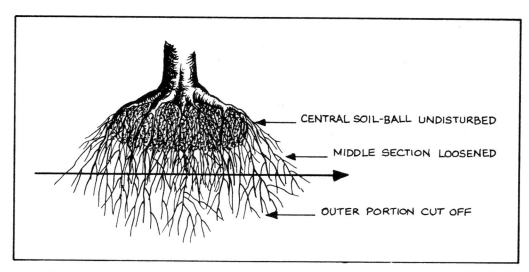

CENTRAL SOIL-BALL UNDISTURBED

MIDDLE SECTION LOOSENED

OUTER PORTION CUT OFF

Figure 94: *Normal rootpruning and repotting procedure*

If you are wary of this technique, however, start loosening the rootball from the bottom centre point and gradually work outwards, as this is often the area least crowded with roots. Another point is that heavy roots are better cut on a slant rather than straight across, as this exposes more of the cambium layer, thus facilitating the formation of new roots.

For normal rootpruning and repotting, the procedure is to remove approximately one third of the volume of roots from the outer section, to leave the centre third undisturbed and the middle third disturbed but not removed.

Most conifers and older trees, however, require more care and it would be advisable to leave the centre half of their rootball undisturbed.

Most deciduous trees and some vigorous evergreens (e.g. figs, privets, azaleas) can have more drastic treatment and may even be bare-rooted (i.e. all the soil removed from around their rootsystems) providing this procedure is done at the optimum time for rootpruning (note that varieties that have mycorrhiza on their rootsystems, for example, beeches, (see Chapter 3) should never be barerooted).

If you do not intend to rootprune, it is still essential to disturb the outer portion of the rootball before potting on. If you don't, the roots are not inclined to venture out into the new soil.

Before you cut the rootsystem of the tree, consider how you are going to plant it. Is it going to be set at a different angle? Or, is it going to be closer to one side of the container? When it is mentioned that one third of the volume of the rootball is usually cut-off, this does not necessarily mean evenly around the entire rootball. If more is removed from, say, the left-hand side, so that the tree can be planted to this side of the pot, more may be left on the right-hand side to compensate.

The basic positioning of a tree in a container is best determined by looking at the triangular mass of foliage and seeing that this is balanced over the mass of the pot. For oval or rectangular pots, the tree is planted off-centre and slightly to one side, as shown in the diagram below. The distance "A" should not be more than ¼ to ⅓ of the total length of the pot. For round pots or pots with sides of equal length such as square, hexagonal or octagonal, the tree should be planted centrally but slightly behind the centre point.

When potting the tree, firstly cover the bottom of the pot with a very thin layer of soil and then position the tree, making sure that there are no air spaces between the soil ball and the new soil. If there are some longish roots, never be tempted to simply tuck them under the soil ball as rotting will be likely to occur at any place where rootsurface touches rootsurface. Rather, work the roots into the soil during the potting procedure so that they are completely surrounded by soil.

Work the soil mix in with the potting stick until there are no air spaces and, if possible, leave a depression around the edge of the pot to make watering easier if you use a hose or watering can. If the soil is bone dry, you can press down on the soil fairly firmly and this will not affect

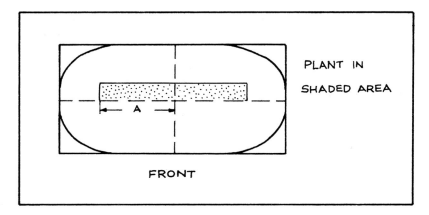

Figure 95: *Positioning in oval or rectangular pots*

the structure or porosity of the soil. Once the soil has been watered, however, you should avoid pressing down on it as this makes it compact too much and soil pores are eliminated.

There may be an advantage in watering your tree a little while before rootpruning is done, as moisture will be taken into the tree before pruning makes a temporary break in the water supply. One disadvantage of this practice, though, is that you will be working with a damp rootball and this will make it more difficult to work the soil in around the roots and to eliminate air pockets.

Watering — preferably by immersion — should be done immediately after potting as this settles the soil and brings it into intimate contact with the roots. If you wish, you may dissolve a Vitamin B tablet into the water you immerse your tree in, as it has been found that it helps root-growth considerably, (Vitamin B is a plant hormone, i.e. a substance that is produced in a particular part of the plant and transported to a place where it creates a certain effect or response. As mentioned above, it acts to increase rootgrowth and it has been found that slow growing trees are often those that don't produce much Vitamin B).

After rootpruning and potting has been completed, put the plant in a sheltered position, for about ten days, where it will receive about two to three hours of sun every morning. Gradually, it may then be exposed to more sun and in three weeks it may be put in a more sunny or windy position, if necessary. The main point to watch — immediately after potting — is that the tree is not placed in a position where it gets a direct draught (normal circulating air, however, is quite alright).

As far as temperature goes, 15°C–24°C (60 to 75 degrees F), is the optimum temperature for rootgrowth. At 13°C (55 degrees F) rootgrowth is slowed considerably and at 10 degrees C (50 degrees F) it usually stops altogether. Therefore, considering the season of repotting, choose a position that will come nearest to the ideal temperature.

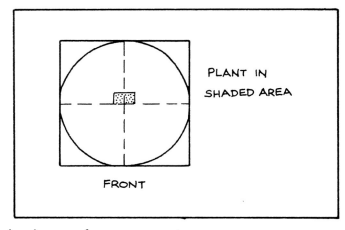

Figure 96: *Positioning in round or square pots*

Watering is probably the most important factor determining the success of your rootpruning and repotting. After the initial saturation of the soil you must then wait until the surface soil looks dryish (but when there is still a slight dampness below the surface) before you rewater the tree. (Remember that the soil should be saturated **every** time you water). If the soil is kept soggy after potting, the newly cut root ends may begin to rot and there is no available oxygen so that the rootsystem, in effect, suffocates. If there is a period of slightly dryish conditions, the roots are also stimulated to go out in search of water.

Another aspect of watering is the foliage watering. While it is possible to overwater the soil — the foliage or top portion of the tree can be sprayed as frequently as possible (make sure, though, that you don't keep rewetting the soil when you do this). Spraying of the top stimulates bud development and cuts down on the excess water loss through transpiration, by providing extra humidity. In humid climates, top watering is not **essential** for the tree to continue in good health after rootpruning but if the natural humidity in the atmosphere drops below 25%, it would be advisable to spray the tree as much as you can. Immediately after the roots are cut, the tree is unable to supply the same amount of moisture to the top and if transpiration is excessive, dehydration of the tree is the result.

CHAPTER FIVE

"The Care and Maintenance of Bonsai"

Preamble

The initial process of creating a bonsai — especially if it has been "sculptured" from a seemingly formless mass of branches and foliage — is charged with excitement! Ideas come to mind and our imagination is filled with visions of how our tree will develop and how it will look in fifty years time — or more . . . Yet, after this extremely stimulating period has passed, we must then turn to the perhaps more routine job of the day-to-day care of our tree — However, if our love for trees and for the bonsai hobby is real, we will find, in this task, a pleasure of another kind — perhaps less immediately exciting but nonetheless stimulating and rewarding.

As we check our trees daily to see if they need water, if they are troubled by pests or diseases, or, as we give them an occasional feeding and attend to trimming and repotting, we observe their individual characteristics and gradually, if we listen to the story each tree has to tell, we can answer them by giving each one the environment and conditions necessary for perfect growth. Our reward comes as much from the actual "doing" of the task as from the results, yet, as an added enjoyment, we see the slow but definite development of our trees as they move closer, each day, toward the vision held within our imagination.

The Position and Environment for Healthy Bonsai

Bonsai are, most definitely, outdoor trees; needing the natural elements of sunlight, fresh air, rain and dew, for healthy growth. They will, however, tolerate being brought indoors occasionally to be specially admired and enjoyed. Trees will live indoors for approximately a quarter of their life and two or three days indoors should be the maximum at any one time. Therefore, if you want to bring them in regularly, you can safely work on the basis of two days inside and six days out. Because they are not indoor plants, one must have enough trees so that, if so desired, they can be brought in on a rotational basis and thereby always have one inside. Another alternative is to make the outdoor display area as attractive as possible so that they may be enjoyed in a pleasant environment that is more conducive to the health of the trees.

The reason why the health of a bonsai cannot be maintained indoors for a long period of time is twofold. Firstly, trees need adequate light to produce enough food for growth through the process of photosynthesis and if light is inadequate, internodes become longer and growth becomes leggy and straggly as the tree stretches toward the strongest light source. This is not good for bonsai, since we are trying to attain healthy, compact growth. Most indoor positions would not have adequate light, however, this requirement may be provided either by artificial lighting or, if there is a light and airy room in the house.

The second requirement that is lacking in most indoor conditions is humidity. All trees have small openings on the underside of their leaves, called STOMATA and these automatically close if the air is dry so that the tree does not lose too much of its moisture. When the air has enough moisture in it (i.e. rainy days, when the air is laden with dew or humid weather) these stomata open and the exchange of gases allows the trees to "breathe". Indoor atmospheric conditions are usually very dry, as far as plants are concerned (particularly if there is air conditioning) and consequently, the stomata are perpetually closed and the tree suffocates.

If enough light and atmospheric humidity are provided (the latter through the tree being placed over but not standing in a tray of water so that the evaporation provides a humid "microclimate", or, by spraying the foliage with water as frequently as possible) it may be possible to grow some tree varieties indoors, but, the effort far outweighs the gain and it is a better and healthier proposition, for the tree, to keep it outdoors.

The position you choose should be sunny and well-aired but with no direct draught. Sunlight is essential for good plant growth and has many good effects on trees. Firstly, it helps keep growth compact, making stems thick and strong, and foliage close and small. It has been found that the very short waves in light — particularly the ultraviolet waves — are responsible for this more compact habit of growth by *inactivating growth hormones which cause stem elongation . . . This phenomenon in trees is frequently observed at high altitudes where light intensity is higher, specially in ultraviolet portion of the spectrum*[1].

If the position you choose has uneven light it is a good idea to turn your trees periodically so that uniform growth may be obtained on all sides. Another point is that the conifers that exhibit juvenile and mature foliage tend to develop the latter type when placed in more sun. Too much shade seems to inhibit the "cording" or "scaling" of the foliage. A more sunny position also has the advantage of helping the plant's resistance to pests and diseases.

One should realize, however, that along with all these advantages of having trees in more sun comes the need to water more frequently. For this reason, you may wish to keep your trees in the shade on summer afternoons. Also, be aware of the individual likes and dislikes of certain varieties. Many of the conifers — and especially Pines — would thrive on full sun all day, throughout the year and wisterias produce better flowers if kept in a sunny position. Generally speaking, a lot of light is necessary for good flowering. Trees grown in an open and sunny position usually produce more flowers and fruit than those planted in the shade. They also may begin to bear fruit and flowers earlier than shaded trees. A high amount of sunlight is particularly important at the time flower buds are being set and it increases the subsequent crop of seed or fruit.

Azaleas, variegated varieties of trees, maples, hornbeams and beeches, however, to name a few, would need protection from the afternoon sun in summer, otherwise they are prone to burning. Even some conifers — particularly Hinoki Cypress and spruces are prone to burning in very strong sunlight. Trees that have autumn colouring should be shaded in summer to prevent burning and scorched leaf margins but should be given more sun in late summer and autumn to develop good colour.

It has also been found that different trees have optimum photosynthesis at different light intensities. Maples and beeches, for example, are able to produce more food at a lower amount of light than the amount preferred by pines.

When choosing a protected spot for your trees, never be tempted to place them in the shade of an overhanging larger tree. Bird droppings and leaves may land on your bonsai as well as various insect pest and perhaps diseases. Another consideration is that all trees excrete a substance called "lye" and some types are incompatible with other tree varieties, causing die-back. Thus, if shade is necessary, choose a form other than overhanging trees.

Another precaution when choosing a suitable position for your tree is to watch that they are not placed close to a brick wall, glass, or concrete, in the full sun, between the hours of 12 noon and 3 pm — particularly in summer. The reflected heat will burn the tree very rapidly indeed.

It is also a good idea to keep your bonsai on some raised surface — partly to protect them from cats and dogs and, partly, to discourage ants, earthworms and other insects from choosing your bonsai as their home.

A well-aired position is also an important consideration, as it is in pokey, overprotected corners that pests and diseases lurk and spread. A good, sunny position with circulating air discourages such problems and helps develop compact, healthy growth on trees.

Figure 97: *A Cold Frame*

If you keep your plants in fairly "soft" conditions, i.e. in a reasonable amount of shade, never change the position to a more sunny one too rapidly, as the tree will not have the resistance to withstand the change to harsher conditions. If you consider that the tree needs more sun — expose it to a little more each day. The opposite change, however, from a more sunny to a less sunny position is not dangerous for trees.

Another consideration is the harshness of your climate and the tolerance of the particular varieties in your collection. In some areas it may be the summers that cause the greatest problem. If you live in an area that has very hot summers with, perhaps, dry, scorching winds, some sort of shade house would be an advantage to have, in order to prevent burning of your trees. Also, if your winters are extremely cold (i.e. below freezing point) protection will be needed as well. Some varieties are resistant to cold and, in nature, can withstand temperatures well below freezing. However, in bonsai culture it is the pot that is the problem. When the water in the pot freezes, the container may crack and the frozen soil may be difficult to water. For hardy and semi-hardy varieties, a cold-frame or a cool green house will provide the necessary protection.

On the warmer, sunny winter days, the top glass frame of a cold-frame may be opened, however, it must be closed again before sunset. Temperatures of about 4.5°C–10°C (40 degrees to 50 degrees F) are good for most trees during the dormant period and they should not fall below 2 degrees C (36 degrees F). Subtropical and tender tree varieties are sometimes brought indoors in climates where the winter temperatures fall below freezing. They should, however, be given as much light and humidity as possible and temperatures should not rise much more than 10°C (50 degrees F).

When looking for trees for your bonsai collection, it is a very good idea to choose varieties that grow well in your particular climate and environment. If it is an uphill battle just to keep your tree healthy, the styling aspect of the hobby will be neglected or made more difficult.

The Art of Watering Bonsai

Water is essential for the life and health of trees. Yet, just as it is possible to kill a tree through lack of water, it is also possible for it to die from overwatering. A discussion, therefore, of the action of water in relation to the tree should explain the method of watering that will produce a plant that grows well and is in the peak of health.

Firstly, on the extremities of the fine, fibrousy feeder roots of trees, there are small pumps that seek out water and dissolved nutriments and pump these to the top parts of trees where the chlorophyll takes the hydrogen from the water, combines it with the carbon from carbon dioxide in the air and through the process of photosynthesis, transforms these elements into starches and sugars for the tree to use. To pump the moisture and dissolved nutriments efficiently, however, there must be sufficient moisture in the soil (this is approximately 25% of the soil volume).

Thus we see that sufficient water in the soil is very important and is indirectly responsible for the growth of the tree. A more direct effect of water on the tree's growth is seen in the fact that growth of any part of the plant will not occur unless the cells are turgid (i.e. full of water) in that area. It is believed that "turgor pressure" is necessary as an energy supply for the elongation of cells.

However, while all this activity occurs when water is readily available, this condition cannot be constant. Roots need Oxygen as well and if the soil is constantly wet for several days, the rootsystem actually becomes weak and eventually suffocates. The root ends then begin to rot and, as more and more feeder roots are destroyed, fewer nutriments are being translocated to the tree and it eventually dies through starvation. Usually about six weeks of constant wetness will weaken or kill a tree.

The other extreme is more immediately dangerous. This is where the soil throughout the whole pot is allowed to become "bone-dry". In this case, the ends of the feeder roots shrivel up with dryness and are thus unable to continue pumping water into the tree. If a tree is brought to this state, some varieties will die straightaway, while others, if they are caught and watered in time, may be able to regenerate new feeder roots and begin pumping dissolved nutriments and moisture into the tree once more.

Mostly, it is the deciduous trees and the vigorous broadleaf evergreens that recover more easily from wilting and drought conditions. If we look at a cross-section of the trunk of one of these trees we will see many dots. These are vessels running up the sapwood, from the roots to the tip of the tree, and their job is to transport water and dissolved minerals from the ground to the leaves so that photosynthesis may occur (carbon dioxide, needed for photosynthesis, must be dissolved in water before it can pass through cell walls, therefore, the surface of cells containing chlorophyll must always be moist). As the water is absorbed by roots and pushed into sapwood it is then pulled to the leaves by suction as water evaporates through the transpiration process.

For trees of this type, recovery is generally fast as water can be pulled up quickly. In most conifers, however, there are no such vessels and water moves slowly up the trunk from one cell to another. Thus, once wilting is to be seen on these varieties, it is often too late to save the tree.

If a tree is found to be "bone-dry" and, perhaps wilting, put it into the shade if it is extremely hot and sunny, spray the foliage thoroughly with water and water the soil but do not completely saturate it at that time. Half an hour later, the soil can be watered again and soaked well. The reason for this is that because the cells in the tree have shrunk due to dehydration, immediate saturation of the soil can cause sudden swelling and bursting of cells which may kill the plant. Frequent and liberal spraying of the foliage, however, is very good.

An interesting point is that while trees may wilt due to lack of moisture in the soil, it may sometimes occur on very hot or windy days even while the soil is damp. In this case, the loss of water or "transpiration" through the leaves is greater than the rate at which the roots can pump it up from the soil. Consequently, temporary wilting occurs. The solution for this is to place the tree in a more protected position and to spray the foliage with water to provide extra humidity and cut down on the transpiration rate.

Similarly, on a sunny cool day, it may not be warm enough for roots to absorb moisture from the soil, or the soil may even be frozen, but transpiration (i.e. loss of water from leaves) may still be taking place at quite a rapid rate with broadleaf evergreens. *Low temperatures reduce water absorption on account of a decrease in protoplasm permeability and an increase in water viscosity, but water transport is impeded less than ion transport. The optimum temperature for root development and absorption of nutrients is 20 degrees C for many plants but may vary with stage of development, this is lower than for tops; moreover, roots tolerate a narrower range than tops. Precise knowledge of the factors will not be secured, however, until we have a better understanding of root function*[2]. Thus, wilting may occur even though the soil is moist. The situation may be remedied by giving extra humidity to the foliage and placing the bonsai in a more protected position.

Hot summer winds and/or low humidity are often blamed for causing marginal leaf burn — especially on maples. In some cases, if the plant is young, with few leaves, it could be the case. Well established bonsai, however, with an over abundance of leaves, make it practically impossible for the roots to supply all of the foliage with moisture, thus causing the drying of the edges of the leaves. The answer is to remove up to half the amount of leaves on the tree. This not only eases the rate at which roots need to supply moisture to the top but also allows more air space to surround the remaining leaves, thereby reducing the risk of summer problems such as powdery mildew developing on the foliage.

THUS, THE IDEAL METHOD OF WATERING TREES IS, FIRSTLY TO SATURATE THE SOIL AND THEN ALLOW IT TO BECOME JUST SLIGHTLY DRY ON THE SURFACE BEFORE SATURATING IT AGAIN. The best way to water is by immersion, either with the water above or below the rim of the pot, as this method ensures complete saturation of the soil. If the water is above the rim of the pot, air bubbles will rise to the surface and when they stop (usually in about 4 to 5 minutes) you will know the soil is completely wet. If the water is below the pot rim, the water will be drawn up through the drainage holes. This takes a little longer than the previous method but it is just as good. When the surface soil looks and feels wet, it is ready to take out of the water. You may also water overhead, with a hose or watering can. This is the usual method used if one has heavy trees or a large collection. If watering this way, though, make sure you do so thoroughly. Perhaps water the trees once, then proceed to water another bench of trees before returning to water the first bench again. This will more likely ensure that the water soaks through the soil. Remember to water the backs of the trees, as well.

For trees that are rootbound, watering by immersion is really the best method if you wish your bonsai to remain in good condition. Often, when rootpruning and repotting a tree that is rootbound, you will notice that the soil in the central part of the rootball is dry and hard. This occurs, generally, with overhead watering because the water tends to drain between the outside of the rootbound soil ball and the pot without actually soaking into the central soil ball. If this condition is continuous, feeder roots in the main portion of the rootsystem will die and the tree will not be able to supply as much moisture and nourishment to the top, as it did previously. Gradually, therefore, the tree will lose vigour. If a rootbound tree is immersed in water for about 15 minutes, the entire soil mass should be saturated and when removed from the water, the draining action will draw fresh oxygen into the soil around the rootsystem and, the central portion will tend to remain damp a little longer than the outside of the rootball.

If you water your trees thoroughly each time, there are many advantages as far as the health of your tree is concerned. The better aeration of the soil as the water drains out has already been mentioned, however, another advantage is that the trees actually become more drought resistant and make better use of the space, moisture and nutriments available in the container. If you use the method of giving frequent "light" waterings, the feeder roots of the tree turn upwards and congregate on the top surface of the soil as that is where the moisture is. Thus, the rest of the space in the pot is being wasted and when a hot day arrives and you are perhaps a little late in doing your watering, the top surface soil dries first, along with all the tree's feeder roots. Thorough watering encourages roots to spread evenly throughout the entire volume of the container and if the surface becomes a little dry, there are plenty of roots further down to continue nourishing the tree.

Unfortunately, it is impossible to say how frequently it will be necessary to water your tree, as so many variables are involved. The weather is probably the most important determinant — very hot, sunny or windy weather making more frequent watering necessary. The variety of the tree affects watering as well — some trees like drier conditions, others, wetter; while some, like liquidambars, use the water more quickly than other varieties. The size and shape of the container, the proportion of the tree size to the container size, and whether or not the tree is rootbound, affects the drying rate. Finally, the type of soil and the position where the bonsai is kept, plays a part. Check your trees daily, and if watering is not necessary in the morning and the day has been hot and windy, check them again in the afternoon.

Fruiting and flowering varieties and large leaved trees — when in leaf — use more water than other types, however, be cautious if you have any trees that have been defoliated, because they are suddenly using less water (since there is no water loss through transpiration) and if you water at the rate that you did **before** defoliation, root-rot may occur.

In springtime, with the rapid growth of trees, quicker drying usually takes place. Also, a young tree may dry out more rapidly than an old tree for similar reasons, i.e. they are usually growing and developing more rapidly and therefore using water at a greater rate.

While the basic method of watering, outlined above, applies in most cases, there are some variations worth mentioning:

Pines, cedars and corokias appreciate **slightly** dryer conditions before being rewatered (N.B. this does not mean **bone** dry conditions). With pines, this dryish period facilitates the growth of mycorrhiza around the roots (see Chapter 3).

Willows, liquidambars, wisterias, swamp cypress and cryptomerias prefer wetter conditions and their pots can even sit in a shallow tray of water in summertime. Below is a short article about such varieties:

*WATER AT THE ROOTS — Some trees like to grow with exceptional amount of moisture supplied at the roots. Willow tree if grown in dry situation will always present a heavy die-back of branches and even parts of the trunk. When grown in pots this becomes rather a problem. The fluctuation between dry and wet conditions of soil is too quick and die-back of branches is difficult to prevent especially on hot summer days. Contrary to the "sound horticultural practice" a tray of water is placed under the pot. The water level reaching just slightly higher than the **inside** surface of the pot's bottom. This gives sufficient moisture to the roots and at the same time does not sour the soil because the water is allowed to be absorbed and is replenished only when the level is below the outside surface of the bottom of the pot. Similar procedure is followed with Wisteria, Moreton Bay Fig, Sheoak, Bald Cypress (i.e. Swamp cypress or Taxodium) and all plants growing in soils with high water table. This procedure prevents die-back in the willow bonsai, burning of leaves in other plants and growth as well as the health of such trees remains good even through the dry and hot days of summer. The feeding is accomplished through adding liquid fertilizer to the water, leaving it for several hours or a day and then pouring the remainder out of the tray, replacing solution with pure water. If this is not done, algae will develop and beneficial effect nullified[3].*

Rock plantings pose a special problem as far as watering is concerned, since they dry out very rapidly. See Chapter 7 for some solutions.

There is a technique of watering that can be quite helpful to the bonsai enthusiast in terms of checking rank growth and producing more compact foliage. However, it must be used with caution as it can also be fatal to trees if taken too far. This technique involves the reduction of water (i.e. the frequency, not the amount of water — you still saturate the soil each time) at springtime as the new growth is elongating on trees. The technique is used on pines as the candles are developing and when the new needles open, they are of a much smaller size. Many of the fruit tree varieties (e.g. apples, pears, peaches, apricots, cherries) produce extremely vigorous growth in spring and if kept in check simply by trimming, flowers and fruit would probably be sacrificed in some cases. Reduction of the frequency of watering, aids the process by slowing down growth. Dryish conditions when buds are forming (usually the summer before the flowers open) can often stimulate the development of more flowers, however after the fruit has set, more water is needed to maintain them on the tree (N.B. More flowers usually form if the tree is dryish due to the fact that the tree thinks it is undergoing drought conditions and since it seems to the tree that death may be imminent it makes a last great effort to produce flowers in order to reproduce itself). Dry, warm weather is the best for setting of flower buds but the conditions during pollination and the development of pollen grains also contributes to successful development of seed or fruit.

Frequency of watering is also often reduced with older, more mature bonsai specimens in order to discourage unwanted, rank growth. It may also be mentioned here that excess water, fertilizer, space in the pot and trimming, promote juvenile foliage on the varieties that exhibit juvenile and mature foliar formations.

In autumn, the frequency of watering deciduous varieties should be cut to improve autumn colouring. Also, watering should be done in the mornings as much as possible (this is discussed in more detail in Chapter 6).

As mentioned above, this technique of water reduction, must be used with great care. If allowed to become too dry before rewatering, the tree may die. Another point of caution is that while many leafy varieties wilt, and in this way tell you that they need moisture, the conifers and some of the firm-leaved trees (e.g. Box, Figs, Gardenias, Fukien Teas) don't or, at least, not until it is too late.

While reduction of frequency of watering at bud development time and as young growth is expanding, produces smaller sized foliage and shorter internodes, be aware that more frequent watering produces greater cambial development, i.e. thicker trunks. Consider your priorities then, when deciding how frequently you water.

The best water for trees is rain water. After a rainy spell — providing your soil drains well — trees look better than ever. Some of the reasons suggested for this is that rain water enters the soil at air temperature thus making it easier for the roots to absorb the moisture and also, in its journey through the atmosphere it has picked up certain nutrient elements that are used by trees. Less than 1% of Nitrogen used by trees, is obtained from the air, as it is not in a form available for plant use (it must be in the form of Ammonia or Nitrates). Small amounts of Ammonia, however, exist in the atmosphere and some nitrogen oxide is formed in the air, particularly after a thunderstorm. These nutritional substances are carried into the soil by rain. Even though the proportion of nutritional elements is small, it gives us another reason why trees show extra vigour and health after rain.

Tap water, however, is quite suitable, providing it is "soft" water. If the water is "hard", i.e. it has too high a mineral content — it is possible that the tree may not be able to use it at all; below is an interesting paragraph explaining how "wet soil" can actually be "dry soil" to a tree:

When we talk about watering plants we often forget an important aspect of nutriment in the soil or water (liquid fertilizer).

*When we use any kind of fertilizer, the plant accepts it **in solution only**. Since the salts influence the osmotic process and consequently the absorption of water — the concentration of salts in the water is very important.*

Roots take up more water when it is offered in a chemically pure state (without any salts dissolved in it) than they do when water contains dissolved nutrients.

For every species of plant there is a fixed optimum limit of such concentration, rarely exceeding 5%. Beyond this concentration roots no longer absorb water. A soil that is rich in soluble salts, even when thoroughly soaked with water is therefore TO A PLANT A COMPLETELY DRY SOIL. That is why a weak solution applied often does more good to a plant. And that is why every gardener avoids using liquid fertilizer on a hot day, as the absorption of solution by the roots slows down, whereas the evaporation by the leaves is increased by the high temperatures. The difference between loss of water by evaporation and absorption by the roots becomes so great that the plant wilts as if the soil is dry.[4]

Indications of high salt content in the water is the whitish deposit around the base of the tree's trunk or the inner rim of the pot. Often, though, these deposits are caused not so much by excess salts in the water but inadequate drainage or too sheltered an area, creating the need for less frequent watering. Soil mixtures should always be made to allow for good drainage, not only for the necessity of oxygen around the rootsystem but to allow excess salts to leach out at a reasonable rate.

Another interesting fact concerning water was discovered by two Russian scientists: Igor and Vadim Zelepukhin of the Institute of Fruit-growing and Vine-growing of Kazakhstan[5]. These two scientists found that "degassed" water improved the growth rate in plants and animals. Degassed water is produced by boiling it rapidly for about five minutes and then quickly cooling it in airless conditions before gases can redissolve into it. The thoughts concerning this are that "degassing" "restructures" the water molecules into a pattern that can pass more easily through cell walls. It is thereby used immediately for important cell functions in plants and animals.

Now we come to the question of when is the best time of the day to water trees. Basically, water when the bonsai show signs of needing water, however, below are a few ideas concerning the effects of watering at different times:

If possible, it is better to water trees in the early morning — before the heat of the day — as leaves can be watered at this time with assurance that burning will not result. Also, some varieties that are prone to mildew (e.g. Maples, roses, oaks, crepe myrtles) should only have their foliage watered in the mornings, as it will soon dry with the heat of the day. If foliage is watered on a summer evening, perfect conditions exist for the formation of mildew spores — i.e. dampness and warmth.

Spraying of the foliage with water is extremely good for trees. In city areas it cleans the foliage from pollution (Japanese Red Pine and Cryptomeria are particularly susceptible to the effects of pollution), it washes off dust and helps the tree breathe. It does the latter by increasing the humidity around the tree and cutting down the transpiration rate (i.e. the loss of water through the tree's leaves) and, consequently, the stomata open and the tree breathes. The openings in the leaf also have the effect of lowering the internal temperature of the tree and helps to keep the tree healthy in hot weather. Spraying of the top part of the tree more than the soil, stimulates bud and stem development and also acts as a preventative or deterrent for some pests (e.g. Red Spider).

If you live in an area that has very cold winters (i.e. temperatures close to freezing point at nights), don't water your trees in the evening as the freezing of the water in the soil can crack pots and damage the rootsystem of the tree. The best time to water trees in this kind of weather is about 10 or 11 o'clock in the morning.

Pines are always better watered in the morning as the moist conditions of frequent evening watering inhibits the growth of mycorrhiza.

Finally, a point relating to the watering of bonsai. It is a good practice to check the drainage holes occasionally, as roots, mud or slugs can sometimes block the openings and produce water-logged conditions in the pot.

Fertilizing Bonsai

The type of fertilizer suitable for bonsai was discussed above in Chapter 3. Here, a few more of the effects of fertilizing will be discussed. Fertilizing is usually attended to in spring and/or autumn, giving most trees a dose every two to three weeks at ¼ to ½ of the recommended strength. Here are some variations:

Never fertilize newly rootpruned and repotted trees — wait at least eight weeks.

Don't fertilize a sick or diseased tree and, if you think the tree is unwell specifically due to lack of nutrition — start by giving extremely weak doses of fertilizer and gradually strengthen the dose as the tree's condition improves.

Fertilizing with liquid fertilizer in rainy weather or in extreme heat is wasted effort. In the first case, it is leached out before the tree can use it, and in the second case the tree's roots are not absorbing nutriments and again it will most likely be leached out by watering the bonsai before it has been used.

With many fruiting varieties, moderate fertilizing is carried out during the flowering period and shortly afterwards to help the tree regain strength and to improve the fruit development but is then withheld until the fruit has begun to swell. A fertilizer low in Nitrogen and high in Potassium and Phosphorous, such as one indicated by the ratio 0.10.10, is essential for flowering and fruiting varieties. Mid to late summer fertilizing with a low nitrogen fertilizer is good for development of next year's flower buds. It is true that trees often produce the best crops of flowers and fruit when their lives are threatened by lack of moisture and nutrition or old age. But we should not jeopardize the health of our trees just to get some better blooms. As long as we do not over-fertilize and do not use a high nitrogen fertilizer, enough flowers will form and our trees will be in good health. Below is an interesting paragraph concerning this topic:

In a tree there is a delicate balance between vegetative growth and reproduction. If a tree grows too fast, it will not produce much seed or fruit. The reproductive stage is generally reached when a tree begins to slow down its most vigorous height growth.

The accumulation of carbohydrates is conducive to flowering, while the abundance of minerals, especially Nitrogen, promotes growth at the expense of reproduction. The proper balance between organic and mineral nutrition and the possible formation of flowering hormones occurs in the tree only after a certain stage of maturity has been reached[6].

Older bonsai and many conifers are fertilized less frequently and with weaker strength than other bonsai. In the first case, so that not so much rank growth will be produced and, secondly, because these trees do not use so much as young trees or deciduous trees that are in leaf. Also autumn, rather than spring fertilizing is practiced by some growers (particularly with fertilizer higher in Potassium and Phosphorus than in Nitrogen), so that the fertilizer may be used more for thickening of trunks than in producing excess foliar growth. However trees do **store** food in autumn and those that have a good store in autumn tend to produce strong growth in spring. Spring and early summer flowering varieties will do better if fertilized with a high Potassium and Phosphorous fertilizer the previous autumn.

Trees in small pots (e.g. Shohin bonsai) or pot-bound trees should be fertilized regularly to maintain health. Again, weak fertilizer more frequently is better than infrequent strong doses.

Emergency Treatment for Sick Bonsai

If a tree is unwell, do not, straight away, reach for the fertilizer bottle. Very few trees are sick from underfeeding and in the majority of cases, other factors are responsible, so check first to see if your care and the environmental conditions are suitable for that particular tree.

Probably the best thing to do if the tree is unwell, is to transfer it — with as little disturbance to the roots as possible — to the ground or in a larger but shallow box of sandy soil. Initially, try to provide similar light conditions that the tree experienced on the bonsai shelf, then, if more light is required, it can be increased gradually.

This kind of treatment (i.e. growing trees in the ground or in larger containers) has uses other than for trees that are unwell. It is often used to rejuvenate old bonsai, as a midway step between collecting trees from the ground (i.e. from the wild or digging out and cutting down large garden trees) and transferring them to their proper sized bonsai pot, and where a tree is critically root-bound and may not be rootpruned safely at that time of the year.

If the tree is specifically unwell because of too severe rootpruning, the top should be pruned back to maintain a balanced condition in the tree.

Another problem may be a badly draining soil mix and a rootsystem that is suffocating. If it is the right time of year and it is safe to do so with the particular variety, it would be best to remove all of the soil and plant it in a better draining, sandy mix to encourage the formation of new roots.

As a last resort, trees that appear to be almost dead should have all of the old soil washed away from their rootsystem, even if it is not a good time for root disturbance, and be treated as a cutting by planting in pure sand. These measures often revive at least the trunk, if not the entire tree.

Trees that are unwell benefit greatly from having their foliage sprayed frequently with water. The soil, however, should not be kept constantly wet, but, at the same time, should not be allowed to dry out completely.

Finally, if the worst happens, and your tree does die, don't give up in disgust — try and work out why the problem occurred, in order to avoid the same thing happening again.

The Prevention and Eradication of Pests and Diseases

Bonsai trees are as susceptible to pests and diseases as normal sized garden trees. However, being a more manageable size and with the daily care that is involved with their maintenance, any problem with pests and diseases is normally noticed before it becomes widespread.

Plate XVIII: *Beech tree in Autumn, Fagus sylvatica, free-form informal upright style, height: 53 cm, Japanese pot, grown from seed in 1960, trained since 1966, photograph taken in 1982*

Plate XIX: *Japanese juniper,* Juniperus procumbens, *full-cascade style, length of cascade: 83 cm, Japanese pot, estimated age: from 1969 nursery stock, trained since 1972, photograph taken in 1982*

Some growers find it helpful to spray the bonsai area (i.e. shelves and ground) once a year, with an insecticide to ward off problems even before they start. Do, however, be extremely careful when using any chemical spray or insecticide, and investigate first whether the problem can be eradicated by, say, hand removal and squashing of certain pests, or by using water or soap and water to wash them off. Below, some of the pests and diseases that may affect bonsai are discussed, along with ways of eliminating them. Always work from the simplest and safest method to the stronger solutions, as a lot of problems actually arise because of mankind's interference with the balance of nature.

Apart from harming the environment and the balance of Nature, sprays may also damage the tree being sprayed (liquidambars are particularly susceptible to all kinds of chemicals, while other varieties are harmed by particular types of sprays, e.g. figs and apricots with "Rogor 40"). Below is an extract that discusses some of the harmful effects of sprays on trees:

Injurious effects of sprays may appear as spotting, shot-holing, burning or scorching, and yellowing of the leaves.

Complete defoliation may occur. Injured twigs are spotted, generally discoloured, or cankered; die-back may develop.

Incompatibility of spray materials, plant susceptibility, lack of plant vigour, solutions that are too strong and high temperatures that cause chemical changes in spray material — are among factors that favour spray injury.

Furthermore, a heavy dripping spray causes more damage than a finely divided mist that covers the leaves with a thin film.

Certain combinations of fungicide and insecticide may cause damage. **Spray materials should be applied as soon as possible after they are mixed**. *Oil sprays are especially likely to cause damage to maples, beech, walnut and other deciduous trees, as well as conifers*[7].

It is good to realize that there are a lot of insects and creatures in the garden that act as preditors on the pests and diseases that harm our bonsai. These should be encouraged and in this natural way the problems will be held in check without the harmful side effects of more stronger solutions. A few of these creatures are: The Praying Mantis (eats aphids, mealy bugs and soft bodied insects), Ladybirds (eat aphids, mealy bugs and some soft scale insects), Icheumon Fly (a small wasp that lays eggs in caterpillars), Trichogramma (a small wasp that lays eggs in eggs of moths), Dragon Flies, Tachinid Flies, Puff or Bombardier Beetles, **Some** ants (Soldier Ant, Bull Ant, Common Red Ant, Jumping Jack), spiders, lizards, birds.

Below is a list of some of the more common Pests and Diseases and some methods for control and eradication. If sprays are suggested, use at the full recommended strength as the pests are "full size" pests.

Adelgid or Wooly Pine Aphid: This pest looks somewhat like mealy bug or a white webby substance at the bases of needles and candles. It is, in fact, a microscopic insect that excretes the web as a roof to protect it from outside predators and because it is a slightly waxy substance it also protects them from many insecticides as well. The pest seems to develop more often on trees that are kept in shaded conditions. A temporary measure is to spray the pest off the tree with a sharp jet of water from the hose. However, if the problem persists, malathion and white oil, 3 mls (or a small teaspoon) of each to 4 litres (about a gallon) of water, may be sprayed onto the tree. A substitute to white oil would be to use the same quantity of washing-up detergent.

Ants: These are mainly a problem spring through to autumn. They can disturb rootsystems and spoil the texture of the soil by their tunnelling, and they can transmit diseases as they travel from tree to tree. They are usually found with Aphids as they like the honeydew excreted by the aphids and consequently, they protect them. Any diseases carried by the ants often develops and spreads quickly as the honeydew is a good medium for fungal cultures. Because the ants protect the aphids, the problems associated with the latter are magnified. Ants on the top of the tree can be eradicated with an insecticide, while those below ground would have to be destroyed by soaking the soil in a systemic insecticide. (N.B. Don't use Clordane for Bonsai as it burns the roots).

Aphids: These green, brown or black insects attack the young leaves and growing tips of many tree varieties — sucking the sap and producing curled and malformed foliage. They can infect trees with any virus or disease they might be carrying or aid entry of bad organisms into the tree through the small punctures they make in the epidermis of the plant in the process of sucking the sap. Lady birds and Praying Mantises eat aphids but, if this dosen't work spray every 4 days (about 4 or 5 times) with an insecticide (the reason being that the insecticide doesn't affect the aphid's eggs). Aphids may also affect the roots of a tree, in which case soaking in a systemic insecticide would be necessary. Spraying the tree with a sharp jet of water is sometimes enough to remove them and some growers like to use a soapy water solution or spray made of Nicotine, soft soap and water (washed off with plain water after 10 minutes).

Borers: These are the larvae of certain moths and beetles and hatch from eggs laid under the bark, in any bark crevices or in holes in the tree. When they hatch, they start to eat their way through the wood, often leaving a covering of sawdust over the hole of entry. Firstly, try to kill the grub by poking some wire down the hole. To make doubly sure that you have killed it, some insecticide or mixture of Kerosene and soapy water (568 ml (1 pint) soapy water to one tablespoon of Kerosene — it separates so shake well every two minutes or so) may be sprayed or applied with an eyedropper into the hole and then plugged (with clay or gum) so that the fumes stay within the tree.

Caterpillars and other Leaf Eaters (e.g. Beetles, weevils): These are best removed by hand. However, if they cannot be detected, or if the problem is extensive, an insecticide may be used. Very few insecticides will kill caterpillars but the stomach poison types are effective, as are the many aerosol insecticides now on the market. Note: When using aerosols, be sure to hold the can well away from the foliage to avoid the damage caused by the coolant used to propel the spray.

Cockshafer Beetle Larvae: These white earth larvae live in the soil and can completely eat through a tree's rootsystem. Apart from manually removing them at repotting time, soaking the pot in a systemic insecticide is the only solution.

Die-Back or Stem Canker: This is caused by various types of fungi and bacteria. Cut the affected section off well below the damaged area, if possible, and put a fungicide such as Bordeaux Mixture on the cut surface. Burn the affected piece.

Earthworms: These do no direct damage, but they do spoil the texture and structure of the soil. Soaking the pot in a weak solution of Condy's Crystals (i.e. solution is a light pink colour) will bring them to the surface of the soil where they can be picked out. Another solution is to soak in a systemic insecticide solution.

Jassids: These are small, fluffy insects that fly. They are eradicated by the same methods as for aphids.

Lace Bugs: Same eradication methods as for aphids, but take care to spray insecticides on undersides of leaves as well — unless systemic sprays are used (i.e. those that go throughout the whole system of the tree). A strong jet of water in the affected parts may help control the problem.

Mealy Bugs: These are fluffy scale-like pests that increase rapidly, taking shelter in inaccessible parts of the tree, and sucking juices from the plant. If the infestation is bad enough the tree may die. They are difficult to eradicate, as most insecticides will not penetrate through their fluffy, waxy covering. If there are only a few on the tree, a cotton-tipped stick dipped in alcohol, such as Methylated spirits, may be dabbed onto each Mealy Bug, (however be careful not to get any alcohol on the tree). Some success may be gained by washing the tree with a soft soap and water solution (while protecting the soil), leaving it on for about 10 minutes and then washing off with plain water. If this doesn't work, a mixture of white oil and a compatible insecticide may be used. Mealy Bugs can also infest the rootsystem. For eradication, water the soil with a systemic insecticide.

Mildew: There are many kinds of mildew that may affect trees. Some are white powdery types while others are black and look like soot, or grey. Humid weather with temperatures around 21°C (70 degrees F) encourage their development and growth. The sooty mould type is believed to be a fungus that grows on the honeydew secreted by aphids and some scale insects, so spraying to eradicate these is the first step. Afterwards, the mould itself can be washed off with soft soap and water. Other types of mildew are best eradicated by wetting the foliage and sprinkling with Bordeaux Mixture or Flour of Sulphur. A winter spray of Lime Sulphur solution or Benlate is important to kill spores that overwinter in bark, buds and fallen leaves

(N.B. Trees that are susceptible to mildew should be sprayed with lime sulphur two or three times in winter, as a matter of course).

Phoma: This is a fungus that affects some juniper varieties, notably Juniperus procumbens. Affected trees have deformed buds which often do not open and elongate properly, knobbly growths on the small twigs and branchlets and more than normal browning back of the foliage. The problem is worse with trees kept in shady or humid conditions as this facilitates the fungal growth and trimming the trees allows the fungus to enter the actual system of the tree through the cut ends. The effects of this pest are extremely bad but luckily it can be eradicated completely and kept from the trees by spraying with a Benlate solution once a month in the warm months of the year, i.e. spring, summer and early autumn.

Red Spider: This is an extremely small spider-mite that affects many trees, particularly in hot, dry conditions. Some of the more commonly affected trees are: junipers, cryptomerias, pines, spruces, cedars and azaleas. The foliage affected by Red Spider loses its proper healthy colour and turns a greyish colour with a powdery texture and later becomes brown. If you think your tree may have Red Spider, hold some white paper under a branch and then shake the foliage. After a while, if you hold the paper stationary, you will see small dark spots begin to move on the paper — these are Red Spider. To prevent the occurrence of Red Spider, daily spraying of the foliage with water is important. However if they are already on the tree, only spraying with "Kelthane" will effectively eradicate them. On leafy varieties don't forget to spray on the underside of leaves as well.

Rust: Rust appears as discoloured spots on the foliage of affected trees. These spots are the spore bodies of fungus and, unfortunately, there is no really effective cure. A fungicide will kill the spores and prevent reinfection but the damaged foliage cannot be cleaned. Don't forget to spray the underside of the foliage and also the soil.

Scale: Scale is found in many forms. If the problem is not too widespread, it may be removed by brushing them off the leaves and stems with a mixture of 568 ml (one pint) of soapy water and a tablespoon of Kerosene. If this is too difficult or if the problem is extensive, spray with a mixture of White Oil and a compatible insecticide. However, in summertime when the young scale are without their protective waxy covering, an insecticide alone may be used.

Slugs, Snails, Slaters: These can eat foliage and/or block drainage holes. Remove by hand or use slug and snail pellets. These usually contain metaldehyde but develop mould very quickly and become unattractive to slugs and snails. To deter these pests, keep the area clean, as they hide, mate and oviposit under rubbish and debris.

Thrips: These small pests are mainly found on the underside of leaves and cause the malformation of leaves as well as causing blotching and often giving a silvery appearance to the leaf. They can also transmit disease as they travel from tree to tree. Eradicate by spraying with insecticide (same type as for caterpillars), taking care to spray the undersides of the leaves as well.

Bonsai Calendar

As we go through the bonsai year — moving from season to season till the cycle is complete — we notice many changes in our trees and also in the countryside and gardens around us. These changes provide our only true calendar, for the trees and plants around us are extremely sensitive indicators of the changing seasons. From year to year the advent of "spring", as far as plants are concerned, may vary as much as five weeks either side of the "calendar spring", and, after all, it is plants rather than the calendar that we are working with.

The following "calendar" is set out month by month (note that for the Northern Hemisphere countries there is a six month's difference, so that calendar spring begins in September in the Southern Hemisphere and March in the Northern Hemisphere). This monthly arrangement is only for the sake of convenience and it would probably be a good idea to be acquainted with the month before and after in order to be prepared for an early or late season. Also, this calendar has been calculated according to bud-burst of maples occurring in August in my area. If you watch when maples in your district begin to come into leaf you will be able to adjust the months to suit. Even though the information is set out this way, the changes and signs in the trees themselves have been described thoroughly and if these cues are followed, each job will be done at the ideal time.

SPRING

SEPTEMBER (March in Northern Hemisphere)

We are now right in the middle of the potting season for most varieties and if you have planned your potting and repotting program ahead of time, things should be progressing smoothly (see calendar for August).

It is a very exciting time in the bonsai year. For established bonsai, this is the time for giving them renewed vigour and we watch eagerly as the dull growth of winter changes to the fresh colour of spring. Some trees may have been in training containers for the past year or so and after patient training and waiting this may finally be the year for the transferral into an attractive bonsai container. Also, this is the best time for the creation of new bonsai and for beginners there is the thrill of seeing, for perhaps the first time, the transformation of nursery-stock into an "instant bonsai" — or, rather, an "instant bonsai-in-training".

Newly potted trees need a certain amount of special aftercare. For the first two to three weeks place them in a warm, sheltered position. There can be circulating air but it is important that there is no direct draught or strong wind. Newly potted trees will also benefit from having their foliage sprayed with water as many times during the day as possible — particularly if the weather is not very humid. Remember, however, that the foliage spraying must not constantly rewet the soil in the pot. After the initial saturation of the soil immediately after potting, the soil should then not be rewatered until it reaches a condition where it is just beginning to show dryness. Don't think that because the roots have been cut the tree should be treated like a cutting and kept damp. This is one of the surest ways of killing a tree after rootpruning. About two to three weeks after potting, the tree can be moved to a more sunny, open position and treated normally.

A tree that has just been rootpruned should not be fertilized for about three months if it has been potted into a soil mix with adequate nutriment. Also, sick trees — unless suffering specifically from malnutrition — should not be fertilized until they have fully recovered. If malnutrition is the problem, the tree should be given small, regular and very weak doses of fertilizer until it has recovered. The dosage can then be increased to the normal amount.

For trees not repotted this season, your fertilizing program can commence. It is better to fertilize regularly and fairly frequently in small, weak doses than to give a strong dose every now and then, so fertilize at half-strength every three weeks or once a month. For fruiting and berrying varieties, fertilizer should be withheld after flowering has finished and resumed again after the fruit has set. Remember, however, that if fruit or seed is not desired, the blooms should be cut off as soon as they pass their peak. Leaving dying flowers on the plant weakens it considerably. Even if you do intend to let the plant develop fruit, thinning-out may be necessary for trees with large fruit — particularly to make sure that one side or branch isn't overloaded.

It is best to use organic rather than chemical fertilizers for bonsai. The reason for this is that chemical fertilizers, in most cases, destroy the beneficial bacteria in the soil, the job of which is to transform fertilizer into an acceptable form for the roots to absorb. Fish Emulsion is a good fertilizer and easily obtainable, however, if you want to make your own, a recipe has been given in chapter three.

Always remember to water your trees with plain water just before you fertilize. Another point to remember is that at the time of repotting a slow-release fertilizer such as Osmocote, or Nutricote can be added to the soil mix.

Remember to start pinching back the growth of trees as early as shoots start to grow and elongate (unless you are varying your trimming technique to encourage certain parts of the tree over others, or trimming pines and older trees later in the season to encourage smaller-sized foliage). More frequent pinching will promote the development of fine branching and help your trees look fresh and attractive throughout the growing season.

As you repot your trees, look at each one critically. Some trees may need to be completely restyled; others may have small faults that you have detected now that your experience is growing and these can also be corrected at this time. Also, if we lose interest in a certain tree in our collection, sometimes a different pot will give it a "new look". Such a simple change can often turn a mediocre bonsai into an outstanding one.

Even trees not being repotted this year should be checked closely. They should be trimmed if necessary, restyled perhaps and if any wire is on the tree, it should be checked to see if it is getting too tight. Trunks and branches expand in diameter very rapidly in spring and if the wire is a little tight, it would be safer to remove it and rewire if the tree has not yet set in position.

As the season advances and the trees waken, so too do the pests and bugs. Aphids can be particularly troublesome on the new buds and young growth. If you check your collection regularly, say at least once each day, the problem of pests becomes negligible. When problems are detected early, eradication is usually quite easy with little or no ill-effect on the tree.

OCTOBER (April in Northern Hemisphere)

By October, most of our repotting will have been completed. Cryptomerias, many juniper varieties, serissas, chinese elms, gardenias and azaleas may still be done, and trees such as figs, pomegranites, cotoneasters and pyracanthas prefer to be done at this time or even a little later.

If pines are repotted later in the spring (about October) it is possible to reduce the size of needles. However, do not wait too long or the tree will not recover from rootpruning.

As the weather gets warmer, some trees will benefit from more shade and protection from wind. Sun and wind are good for trees as they make leaves smaller, internodes shorter, and help resistance to pests and diseases. However, the soil in the pot should not be allowed to dry out as burnt and scorched leaves occur only when the balance between supply and demand of water is broken. This is very easily disrupted in hot weather as the tree is not able to supply water to the leaves as quickly as it is being lost through transpiration. Such trees as maples will thereby benefit from shade on hot afternoons. Other trees that benefit by more shade in warmer months are: azaleas, camellias, pieris japonica, hornbeams, beeches, ume (Japanese plum-apricot) and zelkovas (the last two can get unattractive, leathery leaves if left in full sun in summer). It is mostly bushes and small tree varieties that in nature would grow under the shade of another tree, that benefit from a semi-shaded position in summer.

The pines and cedars can stand more sun. Spruces, however, should be protected from the burning rays of early afternoon. Variegated trees also need more protection from summer sun and wind. Fruiting and flowering trees are generally better in more sun, particularly when buds are forming.

Another point concerning position. When finding a shady place to put your trees, avoid the protection of overhanging trees. All trees excrete lye and some types are incompatible with certain trees. Apart from this, there is the problem of insects dropping out of the tree, bird-droppings and falling leaves.

It is particularly important at this time of the year to check each tree individually when watering. The varieties that are already in leaf may be using water quite quickly, while those that are still dormant will be using it less rapidly. As well as this, there will be marked variations in frequency of watering due to the fact that some trees will be newly rootpruned and some still fairly rootbound. The ones that have just had their roots cut will not be drying out so rapidly. Also, the weather is very changeable at the moment — one day being like early summer and the very next day changing to cold weather again. Once more, this means checking trees daily, but not necessarily watering daily, and, when watering, not necessarily watering every tree.

At springtime, there is a variation in watering technique that may be used to reduce the size of leaves and needles of some tree varieties. However, it must be used with care or else loss of the tree might be the result. As the candles of pines are developing, watering can be less frequent as this helps the needles to be smaller when they emerge (N.B. This does not mean LESS water. You still saturate the soil when you water — but you wait till the soil is beginning to get dryish before you rewater).

This technique of watering can also be applied to apples, pears, apricots, peaches and cherries. If these varieties are watered too frequently in spring, more leaves than flowers may be the result. They should also be watered less when the buds are forming, for example, if they flower on last year's wood, then reduce watering during the end of the last growing season. After the fruit is set, however, watering should be more liberal.

Some bonsai growers reduce the frequency of watering for most varieties at this time — when the growth is still soft — even to the point of allowing deciduous trees to begin to wilt a little before rewatering. The intended result is to shorten internodes and reduce leaf-size. It is, however, a dangerous technique if not carefully controlled and the result, in practice, may be dead trees.

Pests and diseases can be quite troublesome at the moment — particularly aphids on the young growing tips of deciduous trees and junipers. Sometimes a strong jet of water will remove them, or else an insecticide may be used with a second application about four days later to catch those that are newly hatched.

As mentioned last month, pinching and trimming should be attended to as soon as leaves develop and shoots elongate. Buds that develop on the wrong positions should be rubbed out immediately, while other shoots are cut back to one or two leaves. If a bud or shoot develops in a place where a branch is required do not cut it back. Leave it to grow until it reaches the required thickness — then trim. The girth of trunks or branches increases faster if the terminal bud is left.

Remember that some trees such as taiwan maples and pomegranites look beautiful when flowering, but if they are allowed to develop seeds and fruit, the trees themselves are seriously weakened and their shapes may be destroyed through loss of branches.

Trees that will flower next year on this season's wood should not be trimmed too late into the season or else the buds will be lost. So, for these varieties, make the most of the early months.

NOVEMBER (May in Northern Hemisphere)

The month of November is largely dominated by the activities of watering and trimming of bonsai. With most trees the new spring growth would be elongating fast and beginning to harden. This indicates that the time for trimming has arrived. With broadleaf varieties and deciduous trees, cut back to one or two leaves for vigorous trees and back to three or four leaves for those that are less vigorous.

Excessive growth also indicates a healthy plant and such a tree will produce a better bonsai in a shorter time than a tree that grows slowly. The reason for this is that a healthy, vigorous tree may require trimming say three times in a particular growing season. Every time most deciduous varieties are cut, two sub-branches develop from the single branch. This means that if your tree requires trimming three times per growing season, a single branch will be replaced, at the end of the season, by eight sub-branches. Subsequently, by wintertime, the tree will have a much finer tracery of twigs that will be pleasing to view.

Many conifers require "Finger-tip pruning", which means that as the new buds develop, they are removed by pulling them out with the fingertips. A few weeks later, smaller buds develop further back along the branch. This is how junipers and some other conifer varieties can gradually build up dense layers of growth that catch the eye and give weight and substance to the tree. Also, the more frequently the trees are trimmed, the smaller the leaves and needles become and the internodes become shorter.

Wiring may be done at this time if necessary, however care must be taken not to wire too tightly. The trees are thickening quickly at this time of the year and consequently, if the wire is put on too tightly it will have to be removed before the branch or trunk has set into place. New growth is also reasonably soft at this time and heavy-handed wiring may cause damage.

The other main bonsai job at this time is watering. Maples, camellias, azaleas, willows, liquidambars, wisterias, alders and swamp cypress (taxodium) will require watering more often to prevent scorching of the leaf margins. The pines, cedars, corokias and celtus varieties, on the other hand, prefer dryer conditions, so they should be dry on the surface of the soil before they are rewatered. Also, pines and cedars will develop mycorrhiza on their roots if allowed to be slightly dry before rewatering. Another point about mycorrhiza is that it is encouraged by watering mostly in the mornings rather than the evenings (mycorrhiza is a beneficial parasite found on the roots of some trees).

If possible, it is better to water in the early morning — before the heat of the day — because at this time, the entire tree can be showered (personally, I have not experienced burning when the tree's foliage is wet in the heat of the day, but local conditions may be different and it is probably better not to take the risk).

If you must water in the evenings, it is best to avoid showering the foliage of trees that are susceptible to mildew, for example, maples, roses, oaks, crepe myrtles and olives. If your trees are showing signs of mildew already, either spray the tree with lime sulphur at summer strength solution, or Benlate or wet the tree's foliage and dust with bordeaux mixture or flour of sulphur.

All trees like to have their foliage showered with water — particularly in late spring and summer — so even though watering may occasionally be necessary at other times, try to make a habit of watering in the mornings. Spraying the foliage cleans the tree from dust and pollution and helps the tree to breathe. It also discourages certain pests such as Red Spider and stimulates bud and stem growth.

If a tree is suffering from dryness in the middle of the day and is on the point of wilting, take the tree to a shady position, soak the soil well and spray the foliage. Leave it in the shade until it has fully recovered.

One of the advantages of watering correctly (i.e. saturating the soil completely when watering) is that the container plant will be more tolerant of dryer conditions. If a tree is sprinkled lightly when watered, so that only the top surface of the soil is wet, the roots are encouraged to grow towards the surface. The result of this is that if the tree experiences dryness, it usually dies since all the tree's roots have dried out. If the tree has been saturated each time it was watered, roots will have developed evenly throughout the pot and if for some reason it becomes a little dry, the surface roots may dry out, but there are many more underneath that will continue to sustain the tree.

If you have missed the repotting time for some of your deciduous varieties and if it is important to replenish their food supply this year, there is a brief time for safe repotting in between spring and summer, just as the new leaves harden. Do not be too drastic with the rootpruning, however, and defoliate the tree to compensate for the removed roots. If you feel unsure about repotting at that time, then either leave the tree in the rootbound state till autumn and in the meantime fertilize, or repot the tree into a larger container without disturbing the roots.

November can be a slightly quieter month in the bonsai year, as most of our repotting has been completed. It is the time of the year for enjoying your trees and watching them grow as you go about the tasks of watering and pruning.

SUMMER

DECEMBER TO JANUARY (June – July in Northern Hemisphere)

These hot months of the year are reasonably quiet as far as bonsai work is concerned. Watering should be attended to carefully and the procedure for this is the same as was outlined last month. If the weather is reasonably dry, don't forget to wet the foliage daily of trees that are prone to Red Spider. This is an easy and particularly effective preventative.

Spring and summer months are the times when pests and diseases are troublesome so it is a good idea to look closely at your trees each day as early detection means very little ill-effect on your tree. Caterpillars can be eradicated by hand or with insecticides. An insecticide may also be necessary to get rid of aphids that are particularly fond of juniper varieties and the new growing tips of broadleaf trees. Check also for any sign of borers in trunks and branches.

As was mentioned last month, many varieties will benefit from being more shaded from the afternoon sun in summer. Trees that are appreciated for their autumn colouring will also have more chance of reaching autumn with fresh, healthy leaves if they are not exposed to the extreme summer sun.

If you intend to defoliate some of your trees, especially ficus varieties, December to mid-January is the time for this process (see section on "Defoliation" in Chapter 2). Note that after defoliation has been done, the tree will not be using water at the same rate as before, so don't fall into the trap of constantly wetting the tree as you go about your normal "summer" watering — root-rot may be the result.

Much of your trimming may have been completed by now, but for trees that send out shoots all growing season, continue pinching back new growth as it elongates or finger-tip prune varieties such as junipers as the buds develop. Some conifers that missed being trimmed in spring may be pruned now but scissors rather than the finger-tips may be necessary as the growth has hardened. As trimming is attended to, the pots should also be weeded. Weeds in pots look unsightly but also have vigorous roots that use the valuable food in the small container.

Wiring can be done at this time, however, two things must be watched. Firstly, unhardened or semi-hardened growth can be easily damaged and the bark and cambium can be easily scraped off in these months, so extra care must be taken. Secondly, from now till the beginning of dormancy, is the time for the trees to thicken and build wood. Consequently, wire can cut in and form scars very quickly. This means any wire put on now will have to be a little less tight than usual and wires previously put on will have to be watched carefully.

As far as fertilizing is concerned, most trees slow down their rate of growth in the very hot months and therefore fertilizing is not necessary. Also, there is the theory that better autumn colouring may be achieved if feeding is ceased in the summer months. If, however, a particular tree shows signs of needing more food, fertilize at less than half strength. Toward the end of January, if the weather is a little cooler, slight feeding can begin again, i.e. feeding at half stength every two to three weeks with an organic fertilizer that is high in potassium and phosphorus rather than nitrogen.

FEBRUARY (August in Northern Hemisphere)

The basic care of bonsai in February is very much the same as was outlined for the December to January period. If we continue to have hot, scorching days occasionally, it would be wise to keep your trees in a position where they receive morning sun but where it is shaded in the afternoon. If the weather begins to show signs of coolness, however, start to give your trees progressively more sun — this will promote better autumn colouring in your deciduous trees. It is also a good idea to turn your trees occasionally if they are in a position where they receive uneven light. This will ensure that buds develop with equal strength over the entire tree.

It is now too late to prune trees that will flower early in the following spring, such as azaleas, camellias, apples and prunus varieties. However, new, vigorous shoots on Rosaceous varieties (i.e. apples, prunus etc.) that would not produce flowers can be pruned if desired. Most trees will not be needing trimming at this time, except perhaps for healthy vigorous conifers such as junipers which may still need some pinching back of buds.

In late summer and early autumn there is a short burst of growth before trees go into winter dormancy. This means wiring is likely to cut in if it is getting a little tight after the spring to summer growing season. If wire has already marked the tree remove the wire immediately and leave the tree to grow without top pruning. This will stimulate more rapid expansion and growth of cells in the cambium layer of the trunk and branches and if the cutting in of the wire has not been too severe, it will swell out thus making scarring less noticeable.

If you are at the stage of refining the shape of your bonsai you can now wire the newly hardened growth that developed last spring.

Just prior to the short period of growth in late summer to autumn, we are given a second chance for repotting our bonsai. It is not as safe as the late winter to early spring period since it is of much shorter duration and is a little harder to detect due to the fact that deciduous trees are already covered in leaves. This makes the emergence of new growth less noticeable. Watch your trees closely, however, and if the tree is still in "midsummer dormancy" and it is late summer, you can repot, but don't be as drastic with the rootsystem as you may be in the late winter to early spring period. If you live in an area that experiences very cold winters, make sure you keep the trees repotted now in a protected area that receives as much sun as possible in the autumn to winter months.

As the weather is beginning to cool down, fertilizing with an organic fertilizer every two to three weeks at half strength is a good idea. Fertilizer that is high in potassium and phosphorus will help build wood and discourage winter die-back in trees such as maples, elms and flowering trees. If foliage is not looking the best at the moment, feeding now will not do a great deal to improve it, but it will be stored by the tree and used for the production of healthy growth next season.

AUTUMN

MARCH (September in Northern Hemisphere)

As we move quietly into the autumn months, many of our trees may be displaying a blaze of colour with the autumn hues, fruit and berries gradually deepening every day. For many trees, this time of the year brings a special beauty that is hard to surpass.

A couple of points, however, need to be kept in mind concerning the autumn fruit and berries. Many trees are seriously weakened and next year's crop lessened if the fruit is left on for a long time. The pomegranite seems to be the most touchy in this regard and I would suggest removing the fruit entirely in this case or leaving them on for only a very short time. If the crop is lightened somewhat, it may be possible to leave them for a longer period.

Another point associated with the subject of fruit and berries is that if you radically change the conditions and position of a plant that is bearing fruit, they may fall due to "physiological dropping".

As far as top-pruning of trees is concerned, at the moment there is little work to be done. Prune only the very essential and unruly parts.

It is also unwise to rootprune at this time unless you are working with nursery stock up to semi-advanced size. With older or better stock, it would be advisable to wait till the late winter to early spring period, as by now most of the trees have already put out their so-called "autumn" spurt of growth, (usually late summer). Prior to this growth, it is reasonably safe to rootprune. However, if your trees have already started shooting, wait till the growth has hardened before repotting. Some writers suggest that it is safe to rootprune after leaf-fall but in many areas and seasons there is less than six weeks after leaf-fall for the trees to establish themselves before the winter cold hits.

If you do pot at this time, don't cut the roots back as drastically as you would in spring. Try to cut only one third of the volume and leave at least a half of the rootball undisturbed. The soil mixture should not be quite so rich as your normal potting mix, for if the roots don't develop sufficiently after cutting, the extra richness of soil may promote rotting of the roots. Another point to watch is that newly repotted trees should not be overwatered. They should be allowed to become dryish on the surface before rewatering occurs.

The position of the newly rootpruned tree should be sheltered and sunny, for it is around the temperature of 18 degrees Celsius (64°F) that feeder roots develop. In cool, open shade (the kind of position you would put your newly potted tree in spring) the temperatures may drop below 10 degrees Celsius (50°F) at this time of the year and so root growth would be inhibited. If the nights are cold, you can give your newly potted tree an added chance for growth by keeping it indoors at night for ten to fourteen days after potting.

Many writers suggest that autumn is, in fact, the best time for repotting flowering quinces, persimmons, apples, pears and other fruiting trees and shrubs, jasmine and very early varieties of flowering cherries and apricots.

With fast growing varieties, such as willow and privet, it is found that even while the top portion of the tree is dormant, the rootsystem continues to grow. In autumn, a good practice would be to repot into a slightly larger container without disturbing the rootsystem and then rootpruning and replacing it in the smaller pot prior to growth in spring. This promotes more attractive and healthy foliage in the following growing season.

Most varieties are drying out more slowly in autumn, so you will probably find that watering is less frequent. Check the trees daily, however, and "spot water" if one or two trees are dry. Trees that are moving into autumn colouring need less watering and if you had carefully reduced the frequency of watering of your deciduous trees from late summer on, the colouring will probably be more brilliant.

After fruit has set, such varieties can be watered more and you will probably find that rock-plantings, miniatures, large healthy trees in shallow containers and evergreens, still will need frequent watering if the weather is warm.

Continue fertilizing your trees with a low nitrogen organic fertilizer at half-strength, every two to three weeks. This helps build dormant buds and stores food, mainly in the form of starches, that will be used to produce healthy growth next spring as well as spring and early summer flowers. With fruiting varieties, however, withhold fertilizer till the fruit sets and it begins to swell. At that time a light fertilizer can be given and continued right up to fruit-fall.

Autumn fertilizing is suggested for pines and conifers whose needles are too large if fed in spring. If you have just repotted, though, don't fertilize.

Keep your trees in more sun from autumn onwards and spray your trees with an insecticide if pests strike. These can be particularly troublesome at this time as they are feeding prior to their movement into the pupal stage. Slugs and snails are also quite hungry at this time and snail bait can be used to counteract the problem. Birds (particularly Bower Birds and Magpies) may also pose a problem at the moment, as they pull up moss from trees. Unfortunately, the only solution is to put some sort of protective covering over your moss (such as stockings) or put your trees in a protected area.

All in all, it is a very pleasant season, in which there is much time to enjoy our trees at leisure.

APRIL (October in Northern Hemisphere)

The month of April usually brings the autumn season to a dramatic and beautiful climax. Throughout many gardens and the countryside, as well as in our deciduous bonsai, colours deepen to a rich, warm hue that tells us winter is near.

There are relatively few bonsai jobs that are pressing in autumn, so that much time may be spent simply enjoying our trees and the mellow beauty of the season. The notes on care mentioned last month should continue to be observed in April. A few additional points, however, may also be kept in mind.

If the weather continues to have frequent warm days, check the wiring on your trees. The wood thickens rapidly in the autumn season as the tree stores food in the stems and roots in the form of starches. Consequently, wire can easily cut in and scar the bark.

Pruning and trimming is not a major job at this time. Every two years or so, however, it's a good idea to trim back pines reasonably hard in autumn. The current year's growth can be cut off, leaving, perhaps, a few needles at the base. Buds will develop below the cut and subsequent growth will be more compact and the needles will be smaller. Deciduous trees can also be trimmed back to their minimum proportions after leaf-fall.

While evergreens do not completely drop their leaves or needles at the end of autumn, they still shed some of their older foliage at this time. Occasionally cleaning your trees and removing dead needles and leaves will greatly improve your tree's appearance in these autumn months and allow for more circulation of air and light. Dieback of foliage from the inside of the tree is a natural process. More, however, will result if the tree is crowded with foliage and kept in a dark, shady position. Also, lack of trimming through the growing season tends to produce more dieback in old needles and leaves.

Fertilizing may be continued this month, in weak doses, every two to three weeks. It is preferable to use an organic fertilizer that is high in potassium and phosphorus, as this helps to discourage winter dieback in flowering trees, elms and maples and also promotes healthy growth in spring as well as better flowers for spring flowering varieties.

The trees are quite active in these autumn months — particularly in preparing food that will be used in the next growing season. Starches are stored in stems and roots and energy is used to ripen seeds and fruit while nourishment is deposited in the seed for the plant embryo to use in the process of germination in the spring. Flower and leaf buds for the following growing season are being formed and as the cold weather advances they will noticeably swell and appear plump and healthy, suggesting life and regrowth in an otherwise quiet season.

MAY (November in Northern Hemisphere)

As autumn draws to a close the weather gradually becomes cooler. The leaves of the deciduous trees clothe the countryside in shades of brown and beige, prior to their falling, and herald the advent of winter. The trees have just about completed their year's growth and are now ready for a well-earned rest.

If you have not already done so, lighten or remove completely the load of fruit, berries or seed on your tree. If the load is too heavy, or left on too long, the tree's energy will be depleted — perhaps promoting some winter dieback — and the flowering and fruiting will not be so good next season.

Later in the month, after all the leaves have fallen, the bonsai area should be cleaned up and prepared for the winter months. Old, rotting leaves should be removed from benches and soil surfaces, as they encourage pests and diseases. Also, after the deciduous trees have lost their leaves, the varieties prone to mildew may be sprayed with a winter-strength solution of lime-sulphur (take care with the apricot family, including Ume, as these varieties may burn from the use of lime-sulphur).

In mild climates, any shading that may be over the bonsai collection in the summer months should be removed by now and trees may be repositioned in your area so that each one obtains as much sunlight as it needs. Trees that like similar conditions as far as watering is concerned may be grouped together and this will make winter-care easier. Be careful not to overwater by keeping the soil constantly damp or soggy and if the soil of a particular plant is found to be not draining well in the autumn to winter months, make a note of it and repot just prior to the next growing season into a better draining soil-mix.

If you are in an area where temperatures drop below freezing point, your trees that need more protection should be moved to a sheltered position.

The late autumn to winter months are a very good time to improve the styling and designs of your trees. After the leaves have fallen from deciduous trees, faults are more easily noticed and improvements should be made if possible. If you live in an area that has very cool autumns and cold winters, you will notice that the wood of the trees does become more brittle during dormancy. Wiring may still be attempted with care, however, and if you live in an area that has mild winters, the wood will still be reasonably pliable. Wiring at any time should, nevertheless, be practiced with care and remember that if your tree has been watered just prior to wiring, it will be much easier to snap branches.

Fertilizer should not be given to the trees at this time of the year. As mentioned above, most trees have, by now, completed their cycle of growth and are moving into dormancy. From now till late winter is a quiet time for bonsai growers, but it is a time that can be spent well through general reading and the improvement of our styling, which is, after all, the most important factor in our hobby and determines whether we are growers of potted trees or bonsai.

WINTER

JUNE (December in Northern Hemisphere)
Now that winter has arrived, the time for autumn potting and repotting has finished. The reason for this is that new feeder roots need warmth to develop and so with the onset of cold weather the possibility of root-rot occurs. Some bonsai growers do, in fact, repot during the winter months. For some, this may be possible due to the provision of an artificial climate (i.e. temperature, light and humidity artificially controlled) for the first six weeks after rootpruning. However, without this set-up, it would be advisable to confine any repotting to hardy trees up to semi-advanced nursery stock size — the older trees being less inclined to recover from a disturbance at this time.

What then CAN be done in these cooler months? Most of us, I think, have many bonsai jobs that we have had to put aside due to pressures in the busier seasons. Now is the time to catch up on these.

Firstly, autumn to winter is an excellent time to shape your trees. Deciduous trees, in particular, are best shaped at this time as we can observe their structure and form without any leaves to obscure it. It is a very good time for wiring also. Again, for deciduous trees, access is easier. In books, you may read that winter makes the wood more brittle and thus easier to break. This is true — if you live in a very cold area. If winters are mild, the problem is not so great, but to be on the safe side, let your trees be in a dryish condition at the time of wiring. The cells of the tree are thus not so "turgid" and breakages are not so easy.

In the cooler months, because of the absence of more pressing jobs, one can go rock-collecting (for use in rock-settings, saikei or as viewing stones), spend more time in making the outdoor display more attractive and perhaps in rearranging trees. From the horticultural point of view, it is advisable to place tender trees in a more sunny position. However, most trees would benefit by having more sun during the winter months (this promotes better bud development and healthier growth in spring).

Frequently, problems associated with watering arise in the winter months. Often, people get into a habit of watering at a particular time during the summer months and do not vary this even when the cooler period begins. The result is that trees are being rewatered while still damp — thus giving the chance for root-rot to set in. Deciduous trees that use water so quickly in summer are now using far less due to the absence of leaves, but all trees are using less and one must be sure that the surface of the soil is, in fact, dry before rewatering (Note that trees should be saturated when you water — do not think that the fact that trees are slower to use water in winter means that they should only be sprinkled). If your trees have developed a thick coating of moss over the soil surface, remove some to allow for better air circulation and drainage in the container. The parts you have removed can be placed in shallow trays of damp soil to be kept for use in spring.

Also, try to make a habit of watering in the morning or warm part of the day — especially if you are in a very cold area. This gives a chance for excess water to drain off before the colder night temperatures (in extremely cold areas, excess water may freeze in the pot. This damages the root system and in some cases even cracks the pot).

Another job that can be done in the winter months is to check your trees for insects and pests. The trees that are prone to mildew (e.g. maples, crepe myrtles, oaks, roses and olives) should be sprayed with lime-sulphur solution, about two or three times during winter months. This kills the mildew spores and gives the chance for an unmarred crop of fresh leaves in the following spring.

JULY (January in Northern Hemisphere)

Early to mid-winter are the quietest months of the bonsai year and the suggestions made last month of what may be done in the cooler weather apply also in July. As mentioned before, winter is a good time to think about the styling of trees. Try taking some photographs of your trees. It will be interesting later as a record of how your bonsai have developed but it also serves the immediate purpose of showing more clearly any faults of styling. It is a good time to browse through books on the Art of Bonsai. Many new points may be gleaned and the photographs of bonsai masterpieces can be studied to improve our own style and give us inspiration to put into practice new ideas.

As you probably know, late winter to early spring (before the new buds open) is our main season for rootpruning, potting and repotting. As such, it is one of the busiest times in the bonsai calendar. In warmer years, buds often begin to swell early in August, in other seasons it is late August or perhaps early September. As yet, most trees are still in a dormant condition and it is too early to attempt serious (i.e. heavy) rootpruning — particularly on older stock. The warm weather, however, may arrive without much warning and all of a sudden we may be faced with more work than we can easily handle. To ease the pressure to a certain extent, there is at least one job that can be done in preparation for the coming busy season — this is soil preparation, (see Chapter 3). Whatever kind of soil mix you intend to use this potting season it will certainly lighten the workload for spring, if you start getting it ready now.

AUGUST (February in Northern Hemisphere)

As the winter season draws to a close, trees are beginning to waken and so commence another cycle of growth. This is a busy and very critical time for bonsai growers. If one has a reasonably large collection, or if time available for caring of bonsai is limited, we may find that there are too many trees to repot in too short a period of time. Consequently, some trees may miss repotting, or we may be tempted to repot them after the ideal time has passed and, in so doing, stand the risk of them dying. With some varieties we have considerable latitude in the space of time for safe rootpruning and repotting, but with others it is more critical and we must watch them carefully from late winter onwards.

To a certain extent, we can delay or speed up the emergence of spring growth in trees by placing them in cooler or warmer positions. Such a process may give us a short period of ''breathing space'' and help spread out the repotting workload.

In most cases it is the deciduous trees that will give you the first indication that spring is approaching and here it must be stressed that spring repotting does not mean ''calendar spring'' but the ''spring'' for each individual tree (this, incidentally, can vary considerably depending on variety, district where grown or even position in the yard). For most deciduous trees the ideal time for repotting is when the leaf buds start swelling but are not yet opened into new leaves. If they are tight and hard it is too early and if you can see the green of unfolding leaves it is too late and in most cases, extremely dangerous to disturb the roots. Because the majority of deciduous varieties are so critical in the timing of their potting, these will probably be the first trees you attend to in the season. Mulberries and liquidambars are usually very early in their sending out of new shoots, while in Sydney (Australia), Zelkovas (Japanese Grey-bark elms) fagus varieties (beeches) and are generally the last of the deciduous trees to show signs of spring and so can be left toward the end of your repotting schedule.

With conifers, the cedars, spruces and pines tend to be the earlier and more critical ones, so watch them carefully. Cryptomerias, like the zelkovas with deciduous trees, tend to send out new shoots later and so again, this can be a tree placed toward the end of your schedule.

Most blossoming and fruiting trees are best potted after flowering, but in many seasons leaves emerge with flowers or during the flowering period. Consequently, one must watch these trees carefully and make sure they are repotted BEFORE leaves emerge — even if this means potting during flowering.

As mentioned above, use the swelling of the new buds as a guide to ideal potting times. There are some variations, however, and being aware of these can effectively lighten your springtime repotting workload. Listed below are some of the more common variations:

Cotoneaster — late spring to summer (i.e. during the growing season).

Flowering Quince — best in autumn.

Pomegranite — later in spring, AFTER new leaves open.

Chinese Elm — may be rootpruned later.

Figs — late spring (October to late February).

Azalea — spring, after flowering.

Gardenia — late spring.

Camellia — autumn potting or after flowering.

Eucalypts and Leptospermums — summer (during summer dormancy).

Serissas — these are not so critical and can be potted later in spring.

Chamaecyparis — anytime except mid-winter and mid-summer.

Juniper procumbens — anytime but more care if done in mid-winter or mid-summer.

Cryptomeria — can be rootpruned later in spring.

Remember that, if repotted at the correct time, most deciduous trees can withstand quite drastic cutting of the roots and if necessary, bare-rooting (or washing all the soil away from the rootsystem). Variations are the beech, hornbeam and oak. These should never be bare-rooted as they have mycorrhiza — a symbiotic or beneficial parasite — on their rootsystems. Conifers should never be bare-rooted and also less drastic cutting of their rootsystem is advisable (remove approximately ⅓ of the rootsystem).

Most trees are top-pruned in conjunction with rootpruning and some trees (particularly elms and birches) must be checked at this time for winter die-back and pruned if necessary. Often, dieback of one or more branches during the winter months or early spring as the buds burst, is caused by a poor rootsystem due to rootrot and a badly draining soil-mix. If this is the case, now is the time to remedy the situation at the time of repotting.

Usually there is some confusion concerning the pruning of flowering and fruiting varieties. These are pruned depending on the season of flowering and also with attention as to whether flowers are borne on old or new wood (see Chapter 2 for more detail of trimming and pruning of flowering trees).

Finally, a couple of points concerning things NOT to do at this time. Firstly, directly after rootpruning and potting, trees should not be fertilized as this may burn the roots. If your soil mixture is good, the tree will not need fertilizing for the first year. However, if you want to give your tree an extra "boost" you can start fertilizing trees repotted this spring from late summer. Trees that have not been rootpruned though, can be fertilized with a weak solution as soon as the new buds burst and the leaves begin to unfold.

The second point concerns the shaping of trees by wiring, after repotting. It is important to wait for a few weeks before attempting to wire your tree, the reason being that if you attempt to wire too soon, the tree's rootsystem will not yet be established and the fine roots just emerging, will be easily damaged.

REFERENCES
Chapter Five
1. "Briefs" in *Bonsai in Australia*, September, 1970, p. 28.
2. Koreshoff, V.A., "Root Temperature and Plant Growth" in *Bonsai in Australia*, July-August, 1972, p. 16.
3. Koreshoff, V.A., unpublished article.
4. Koreshoff, V.A., "When Wet Soil is Dry Soil to a Tree", in *Western Suburbs Bonsai Journal*, April, 1969, pp. 8–9.
5. "Super Water" in *Bonsai International Magazine*, 18.299.
6. Mirov, N.T., "Trees and Men — A Tree is a Living Thing", in *Yearbook of Agriculture*, U.S.A., 1949.
7. Koreshoff, V.A., "Beginner's Section" in *Bonsai in Australia*, March 1971, p. 13.

CHAPTER SIX

"Seasonal Colour Changes in Trees"

Preamble

In many ways, the Art of Bonsai emphasizes the appreciation of monochrome. The accent on "style" develops a highly refined awareness of the effects of line and mass in space and our eyes often take "black and white photographs" of the images we see. These highly styled yet subtle Works of Art — mostly found in containers of an earthy, non-obtrusive hue, have the power to call forth visions of the past, our deepest emotions as well as our imaginations.

It is true that too much colour would tend to stop our journey through the imagination, even before it begins. It would also dull our appreciation of the abstract beauty of line and form. Nevertheless, if this emphasis and point of view is regarded almost as a rule in Bonsai Art, much pleasure will be lost.

Bonsai should suggest the beautiful aspects of Nature, and part of this is the way the four seasons are distinguished by the sometimes subtle, sometimes flamboyantly bright colour changes in the various seasonal cloaks worn by trees.

The Colour of Flowers and Fruit

All the sweetness of Nature was buried in black Winter's
  grave
and the Wind sings a sad lament with its cold plaintive
  cry . . .
But the Spring will come, bringing Life in its arms,
and will strew bright flowers on the face of hill and dale.

In lovely harmony the wood has put on its green mantle
and Summer is on its Throne, playing its string-music;
The willow, whose harp hung silent when it was withered in
  the Winter,
now gives forth its melody — Hush! Listen!
  The World is Alive!

THOMAS TELYNOG EVANS 1840–1865

Figure 98: *Flowering bonsai*

The seasons for growing — spring through summer and autumn — are particularly exciting times for the bonsai grower. Trees are growing quickly and changes or improvements in design may be attained in a reasonably short period of time. For trees that are still at the beginning stages of styling, it is often best to sacrifice flowering and fruiting in order to take advantage of this period of rapid growth. Initially, it is more important to develop the basic lines of the style and to build up a network of fine branching that eventually will display the flowers and fruit to best advantage. A tree that is producing flower buds will not regain its ability for sending out vegetative growth and elongation of its stems until the flower has been fertilized or removed. Even then, vegetative growth is held back, as most of the plant's energy is transferred from the vegetative shoot apex and the roots to the embryo within the seed, for the development of the new young plant (i.e. if the flower was not removed).

Flowers and fruit use a very high proportion of the starches and sugars produced by a tree — particularly if the fruit is sweet and fleshy. Consequently a weak tree is weakened even more by bearing fruit and flowers, and, if the styling is not yet developed satisfactorily, this energy can be better used for vegetative growth — after all, the shape of the tree is of primary importance. Most trees can adequately support flowers and fruit — providing they are in reasonable health — however the Pomegranite is a notable exception. This tree is greatly weakened by the effort and sometimes branches are lost as a consequence.

Figure 99: *Pomegranite*

Plate XX: *Broom style in leaf. Japanese grey-bark Elm (as in Plate XIII), photograph taken in 1980*

Plate XXI: *Washington Hawthorn in Autumn,* Crataegus phaenopyrum, *plaited-trunk style, height: 45 cm, Japanese pot, grown from seed in 1966, plaited in 1967 as one year old saplings, photograph taken in 1982*

Figure 100: *Tree with berries*

If your bonsai has reached the stage where the basic styling lines have developed, however, and if it is an appropriate variety, the occurrence of flowers and fruit can give great pleasure. Our awareness and appreciation of seasonal change is heightened, our senses are excited with displays of beautiful colour and, often, delicate scents and poignant contrasts are drawn between the characteristic roughness and heaviness of an aged trunk and the fragile lightness of a newly borne flower. Old age and rebirth are brought together, suggesting eternity and the beauty of life.

As was mentioned in previous chapters, leaf size and shape may be modified by age, light, water and nutrition and we find that the longer a tree has been kept as a bonsai and, providing it is trimmed consistently, most leaves or needles gradually become smaller in size. With flowers and fruit, however, their form and size is not affected by environmental and conditional changes, or by trimming and, therefore, simple and small flowers and smallish fruit would be a wise choice. If you have your heart set on a miniature orange, for example, choose a cumquat and, if you have always wanted a small apple tree, a crab-apple would be a good choice. Don't forget with flowering varieties that some trees, e.g. wisteria and prunus mume, produce flowers early on bare wood. This enables us to appreciate the blooms without the distraction of leaves and imparts a feeling of the beauty of simplicity (see Plate XII).

To produce a tree that flowers and fruits well, the basic elements of care should be attended to with, perhaps, slight modifications. The complete reproductive process requires the setting of flower buds, the development of male and female flowers (on some), pollination and the subsequent formation and development of fruit. Each step in the process depends on internal (i.e. mainly nutritional) and external conditions. The slight variations of care and maintenance, pertaining specifically to flowering and fruiting varieties, have already been covered in previous chapters and the relevant sections will be listed here for your reference:
1. Methods of Pruning and Trimming Flowering and Fruiting Varieties Chapter 2
2. Variations in Soil Mix for Flowering and Fruiting Trees Chapter 3
3. Rootpruning, Potting and Repotting Flowering and Fruiting Varieties Chapter 4
4. Fertilizing for better Flowers and Fruit Chapter 3 and Chapter 5
5. Methods for Watering Chapter 5
6. Positions most suitable for Flowering and Fruiting Trees Chapter 5

SOME INTERESTING SCIENTIFIC DISCOVERIES CONCERNING FLOWERING AND FRUITING
1. The following article[1] discusses some interesting experiments done with flowering and fruiting trees:

Some interesting physiological facts about plants can be gleaned from experimental work of scientists, even as far back as 1820. For instance, Andrew Knight writes: "The true sap of trees is wholly generated in leaves from which it descends through the bark to the extremities of the roots, depositing in its course the matter which is successively added to the tree, whilst whatever portion of such sap which is not thus expended sinks into the alburnum (xylem), and joins the ascending current, to which it communicates powers not possessed by the recently absorbed fluid. When the course of the descending sap is intercepted, that necessarily stagnates, and accumulates above the decorticated space; whence it is repulsed and carried upward, to be expended in an increased production of blossoms, and of fruit . . ."

These statements were recently proven correct by further experiment on an apple tree which was not due to flower and bear for 2 or 3 years.

One branch was carefully RING-BARKED by making parallel incisions to the wood around the branch. The band thus formed between the cuts was cut vertically and the bark carefully lifted, turned upside down and replaced in its place. The joints thus made were covered with grafting compound. Next season the branch flowered and produced fruit, while the control branches which were not operated upon, produced only vegetative growth.

The inverted bark band slowed down the downward movement of sap and it accumulated above the ring, depositing food and probably some hormones, thus influencing the flowering and fruiting. This inversion should, of course, be made early in the season, before flower primordia are formed.

Similarly, this technique slows down the growth of trees which are planted in parks. To retard rapid growth of large trees, the inversion is made and dwarfing effect is produced which lasts 3 to 4 years. After some years the normal rate of growth returns.

These techniques might be of some interest to Bonsai growers. For instance, the difficulty in making Wisteria bloom may be overcome by trying this method. Also an incision below a dormant bud usually starts it into growth quicker, provided the cut is separated by a film of grafting compound or other means which stops the healing of the cut before the bud is forced to grow.

2. The next article concerns the Discovery of Gibberellins[2]:

The terms "Gibberellin" and "Gibberellic Acid" reached the horticultural public only recently. However, they have a lengthy history, going back over 30 years.

It all started with an investigation of plant disease. All cereal crops are prone to fungal diseases and in particular to invasion of roots and basal parts of the stem by some soil fungi.

Like others, rice is subject to foot rots, one of them is quite unique because its symptoms of infection are shown in a seedling by abnormally rapid growth.

This feature of the "bakannae" disease as it is called in Japan, attracted the attention of several investigators in the first two decades of this century. Very soon, the fungus which caused the disease was isolated, described and named by K. Sawada. The fungus is now known as "Gibberella fujikuroi".

Eventually in 1926, a Japanese plant pathologist, E. Kurosawa, made the discovery which is basic to all that follows.

He grew the pathogenic fungus, G. fujikoroi, on a nutrient solution containing sugar and some mineral salts. He found that after the fungus had grown on the solution, and had been removed by filtration, the solution itself was capable of making rice seedlings grow faster if applied to roots or leaves. He concluded that the rapid growth of rice seedlings infected by the fungus was caused by some chemical substance secreted by it in the plant tissues, and that this same growth-promoting substance was also secreted into his nutrient growing medium.

This discovery triggered off a lot more work in Japan, though remarkably little elsewhere.

In 1939, two Japanese chemists — T. Yabuta and T. Hayashi, isolated a crystaline material which appeared to be the chemical responsible for the growth promotion.

It was active in very low concentrations, of the order of one part per million. They considered it to be a pure substance and called it "Gibberellin A".

Today we know that in fact it was not pure and that probably explains why their chemical investigations of the compound over the next 15 years were inconclusive.

In the early years of the present decade (50's), the importance of this Japanese work became fully appreciated in other countries, notably in the U.S.

In 1954 P.J. Curtis and B.E. Cross, described discovery of a substance similar to Japanese "Gibberellin A", yet chemically distinct. This they called "Gibberellic Acid". It was the first truly pure Gibberellin.

Now in Japan, U.S. and U.K. it was found that there are four closely related gibberellins formed by the fungus Gibberella fujikaroi. These are called A_1, A_2, and A_4 and Gibberellic Acid A_3.

Of these, A_3 is the easiest to prepare in commercial quantities and is usually most active.

What effect, if any, can this discovery have on cultivation of bonsai?

Its effect on plants is evidenced in a. vegetative growth, b. flowering, c. fruiting, d. leaf fall, e. germination.

a. is not of any interest for bonsai culture, with one exception. Some dwarf varieties of rare trees if sprayed with A_3 begin to grow as the normal plants of their varieties.

One might want to experiment with a naturally dwarf conifer to produce a quicker and larger growing plant.

However, the elongation is concentrated in the main stem only and side branches do not increase in number.

The familiar winter dormancy of our deciduous trees and shrubs is also a photoperiodic phenomenom induced by the short days of winter.

New growth only recommences after exposure to low temperature, or to increasing day length in spring, or both.

In several species, notably beech and ash, treatment of dormant twigs with gibberellic acid induces resumption of growth without exposure to low temperature or long day.

Or again, seedlings produced from seeds of some Rosaceous plants, e.g. species of Malus, remain dwarfed and stunted unless seeds have been after ripened, or stratified by exposure to low temperatures while moist. Such "physiological dwarfs" will resume normal growth after treatment with gibberellic acid.

Thus a further characteristic effect of gibberellins on shoot structures is breaking of dormancy, especially those kinds of dormancy which normally respond to vernalization or exposure to long-day photoperiodism.

The development of autumn colour in the leaves of deciduous trees and leaf-fall are responses to the shortening length of day in autumn and can be prevented (experimentally) by giving supplementary artificial light.

Trees near street lamps often show delayed leaf-fall. If the leaves of such trees are sprayed with gibberellic acid, this treatment too, causes a delay of several weeks in colouring and leaf-fall. It can be particularly well demonstrated in cherry and ash.

This is mentioned not because it has any great practical significance, but because it is yet another example of the way in which gibberellins simulate the effects of long-day photoperiods.

We have already seen that gibberellic acid speeds up many growth processes.

The germination of seed is a form of growth, and germination is frequently accelerated by gibberellic acid. In seeds which germinate easily, the effect may be slight. But it is on some dormant seeds that gibberellic acid has its most striking effects.

It is astonishing that a group of related chemicals synthesized by a single species of parasitic fungus should induce such diverse, yet essentially natural effects.

This discovery greatly increases the significance of the way in which gibberellic acid stimulates the effects of long-day photoperiods, or vernalization at various stages of plant development.

Gibberellic acid does not have much effect on roots. There is a strong suspicion that gibberellins inhibit rooting of cuttings, but very few woody plants have been used in rooting experiments.

In his recent Master's lectures, Professor J.P. Hudson expressed a view that the responses of plants to photoperiod or vernalization were probably based on induced synthesis of active chemicals or hormones.

It now appears likely that the gibberellins are among the hormones involved.

It is instructive to reflect that this, our first major clue to the nature of the long-suspected chemical basis to responses to photoperiod should have arisen directly from the observations of a Japanese plant pathologist on a disease of rice, made as long ago as 1926.

3. Photoperiod, or Daylength as was discovered in 1920 by W.W. Garner and H.A. Allard of U.S. Dept. of Agriculture, can greatly affect flowering of trees. Some varieties bloom when

days are short and others when days are long. A change in environment and climate, therefore, can either encourage or discourage flowering of a particular plant.

4. Certain chemical substances are known to break the dormancy of flower buds. Ethylene is one such substance and because a high proportion is found in smoke, the effect of "burning-off" near a flowering tree in bud, is often the cause of premature opening of buds.

Autumn Colour

A pathway — lonely and dark
But for a single golden leaf,
Dancing to the song of an autumn wind.

Autumn is a season that, throughout history, has impressed the poet and the artist with its mellow beauty. On a superficial level, many colours harmonize and contrast to excite the eye. There are spectacular colours of red, gold and purple and the more quiet, earthy tones of beige and brown. On another level, the season of autumn reminds the contemplative or sensitive soul of the ephemeral, but none-the-less cherished beauty of life . . .

The scientist and the artist may often be thought to be working at cross-purposes. One dissects and analyzes, the other sees the total or overall effect, the impression that is left in the mind. A truer view, though, sees the scientist and the artist working perhaps at different parts of the spectrum but with the work of each one complementing and broadening the perspective of the other.

The bonsai grower is a good example of the latter approach. He must be both scientist and artist — understanding the needs of his tree and often learning through experiment, as well as stepping back to appreciate a beautiful form or colour. In a discussion on autumn colour then, specific knowledge on how and why the autumn hues are produced, should not hinder your artistic appreciation of the end product but rather, should improve it. Information on why such effects occur, can lead to knowledge on how to improve the situation so that autumn colours may be encouraged to be richer and more beautiful. Also, if your autumn colours are not so good, such a discussion could lead you to the reasons why, so that a remedy may be found.

Firstly then, let us consider what actually occurs when the tree dons its autumnal cloak. In temperate climates, as the cool weather of autumn approaches, certain changes occur in the pigmentation of deciduous trees and shrubs as well as in a few selected evergreen trees. The green colour of the foliage in the growing season is the result of a group of chemicals that we call chlorophyll. This chlorophyll is situated in chloroplasts — small structures within the leaf that are like minute factories producing sugars from the sun's energy as well as carbon dioxide, water and minerals, in order to feed the plant. Chlorophyll, being an unstable chemical is continually breaking down. However, in the active growing season, providing the plant receives sufficient light, the chlorophyll is being produced by the plant in adequate quantities to replace that which has broken down to colourless compounds. The plant, therefore, retains its green colouring.

With the cooler weather of autumn, this production of green chlorophyll is retarded in some trees and finally the stage is reached where it is being destroyed at a faster rate than it is being produced. When this occurs, the pigments formed by the chemicals known as carotenoids (carotene) and anthoxanthins (xantophyll) become apparent and the leaves take on a yellow to orange hue. These colours have been present right through the growing season but the production of the chlorophylls in the warmer seasons masks these weaker pigments. In autumn, yellow to orange pigments are seen in elms, birches, ginkgos, larches, tulip trees, beeches, hornbeams, the golden ash, the golden variety of zelkova and some maples e.g. the english maple.

The reason why evergreens such as pines, retain their green colouring throughout winter is that their biological processes slow down at a much lower temperature. In cold winters, however, a slight colour change is noticeable, even in these varieties (pines, for example, taking on a more yellow tinge in winter).

In some types of trees a slightly different process occurs. With the onset of cooler weather, pigments known as flavinoids: flavones and anthocyanins, are produced through the action of sunlight on excess sugar and waste products that are trapped within the leaf. In the growing season, the leaves produce the sugars during the day and these sugars are transported during the night to be stored in stems and roots. When autumn comes, the day temperatures are usually warm and the weather is sunny so that sugar production continues. The night temperatures, however, are usually cool and particularly when the temperatures fall below 9°C (49 degrees F), the biological processes of the tree are slowed down and, as a consequence, the tree is not able to move out all the sugars and waste products produced by the leaf during the day. 7°C (45 degrees F) seems to be the temperature where this movement ceases altogether. If these sugars were left in the leaves, the pressure in the cells would become so great that the cells would be destroyed. As a solution to this problem, the plant converts these sugars into quite harmless pigments, that is, flavones and anthocyanins. These pigments produce the spectacular reds and purples, and are a result of pigments specifically produced in autumn, rather than having been masked by chlorophyll in the growing season. Examples of varieties producing these red and purple hues are: some maples, nyssas, rhus, liquidambar, virginia creeper, some oaks, the claret ash and the red variety of zelkova, (see Plate XIII).

To produce the best pigments, just when the leaf reaches the proper maturity, five consecutive nights of cool or frosty weather are necessary, while the days are warm, sunny and dry. If the plants are overwatered at this stage, or if continued rain occurs, the more rapid movement of sap within the tree counteracts the entrapment of sugars in the leaf. Consequently less colouration occurs.

The tannins that are present in yellow leaves produce a golden to brown colour, while the effect of tannin on trees that produce flavones and anthocyanins results in a purplish hue. Eventually, when all the pigments are decomposed, the tannins alone remain, clothing the trees in earthy brown garments prior to the stark bareness of winter.

The reason why leaves of deciduous trees fall in winter is that cells in the "abscission layer" where the leaf stalk joins the tree, begin to break down. The leaf eventually falls and cells grow across to seal the break and form a "leaf scar". It is interesting to note that while this break down of cells is the usual procedure, it doesn't always occur. The beech is an example where the brown dry leaves remain throughout winter only to be pushed off in spring with the new growth.

Another slightly more unusual occurrence is where certain evergreen trees produce "autumn colouring" throughout the autumn to winter months with the leaves regaining their green colouring in spring (examples of these are the boxwood, cryptomeria japonica, chamaecyparis squarrosa). With these varieties, full sunshine in the autumn to winter months is essential as well as frosty nights.

Before we leave the more scientific vein of this discussion, a few extra points may be of interest. Following is an extract from an article[3] that goes into a little more detail about the pigments themselves:

A BIT OF SCIENCE —
Pigments of the chlorophyll-bearing plants may be classified by their solubility and by the manner in which they occur in plants.
Ether soluble pigments: Chlorophyll (Green colour)
Carotenoids (Orange colour)
Water soluble: Anthocyanins (Red, blue, purple colours)
Anthoxanthins (yellow colour)
An interesting connection between chlorophyll and certain animal pigments lies in a certain similarity between chlorophyll of plants and hemoglobin of the blood of animals.
It has now been established that the pigment contained in the nodules of legumes, when infected with nitrogen-fixing bacteria, almost definitely contains some hemoglobin. Thus far, hemoglobin has not been found in uninfected legumes, or in pure cultures of bacteria.

As mentioned previously, carotenoids — the yellow pigment — are present in all green plants and has about 60 different chemical variations. Three of these are called Vitamin A precursors because they are converted to this vitamin in the animal body when consumed.

The role of carotenoid pigments in plants is not completely understood. The fact that chloroplasts contain both green and yellow pigments suggest that carotenoids play some part in photosynthesis. Water soluble pigments are found in the sap of the plant cells.

Anthocyanins account for red, blue and purple colours in flowers and leaves. Anthoxanthins produce only pale yellow. Often the anthoxanthins occur in colourless form, as in white flowers. This colourless pigment can be converted to a yellow by treatment with alkalies.

Anthocyanins may serve as pH indicators in the presence of acids or alkalies. Anthocyanins will appear bluish red in acid, violet in neutral solution, and blue in alkaline solution.

Although it is often possible to change the colour of a flower petal from blue to red, or red to blue by dipping it in acid or alkali solution, the great variety of colour in nature is doubtless the result of other factors than differences in pH.

WANT TO EXPERIMENT? —

We all enjoy autumnal colouring of trees. Now we realise that different shades of colour are due to different proportions of certain pigments in the tissues of the plant. We also know that alkalies or acids change the colour of these pigments.

How about an experiment with some young bonsai?

Say, if at the beginning of autumn we spray some young trees with a solution of citric acid (say 10%) and with solution of potassium or other alkalies. Some with combination of both in different proportions.

If seedlings are small, put them in a refrigerator (4°C or 40 degrees F) for several nights and take out during the day.

The results may be of some interest! Keep some control plants too, because otherwise one would not have the measuring stick to compare the results.

Now that we know a little about the processes involved in the production of autumn colour, as well as having observed the natural effects of climate that seem to produce the best colour, we can compile a checklist of things to do in view of producing better colouring.

First of all, choose a tree that does produce a good natural colour. Cuttings have the same genetic characteristics as the parent plant, whereas seedlings exhibit quite marked variations. In zelkovas, for example, a tree that turns an orange-red in autumn will produce some seedlings with scarlet autumn colour, some the same as the parent and some with a golden yellow hue. Therefore, if it is possible, choose your autumn colouring trees in autumn — particularly if you are collecting trees for a group setting, where harmony of colour is important.

Your next consideration should be summer care. In nature, the best autumn colouring seems to occur after good summer rainfall and when autumn days are dry and sunny with cool nights. It is important that leaves shouldn't burn, so make sure your trees are watered before they become too dry and keep them in a cool, shady and protected place, particularly in the hot, scorching afternoons of summer.

Another point is to spray your trees occasionally for insects and caterpillars, or remove the larger pests by hand. Tree varieties that are likely to get mildew or other fungal diseases (e.g. maples, crepe myrtles, oaks and roses) should be watered in the mornings and if watered in the evenings should not have their leaves wet. Also, if these varieties were sprayed with a lime-sulphur solution three or four times during the previous dormancy, it would reduce the chance of mildew forming.

If your leaves have come through summer without damage, the autumn colour has the chance to be quite spectacular. However, midway through summer, if the leaves have been damaged, the tree can be completely defoliated and a second chance is obtained with the growth of new leaves. Also, this second crop of leaves often produces better autumn colouring. The reason for this is as follows:

When compared on a fresh weight basis, it is found that young leaves have more rapid rates of respiration, more synthesis of R.N.A. (Ribonucleic Acid) and protein, a higher content of growth hormones, starches and chlorophyll and less transport of solutes through the phloem, than older leaves. It is also known that the photosynthetic capacity of a leaf reaches its maximum level when it has *just* reached maturity (i.e. it must be fully expanded, but not too old).

Since there is a higher chlorophyll content, there is also more carotenoids and anthoxanthins present, thus producing better yellow and orange colours in autumn.

For red and purple colours, it is known that the production of anthocyanin pigments requires soluble sugars which are produced by photosynthesis (cool temperatures converting the starch to sugars). Thus, since there is more starch and chlorophyll in younger leaves, more sugars will be present to be converted to anthocyanins. As well as this, the sugar build-up in the leaf is better maintained in younger leaves because of their lower rate of solute transport through the phloem.

The above factors would help produce deeper and richer colours in the leaves, but it is conceivable that autumn colouring would also *last longer* on younger leaves. Senescence of the leaf and the breakdown of cells in the abscission layer takes place, mainly, due to reduced levels of R.N.A., protein synthesis and growth hormones. Because young leaves have more of these substances present, they are more likely to maintain themselves for a longer period of time after production of these ceases.

Finally, younger leaves have had less of a chance to be damaged by wind, heat, dryness, insects or diseases — therefore making autumn colouring more effective.

The next stage in helping the production of autumn pigments is that when the leaf is at the right stage of maturity, and when the intense heat of summer has subsided, the tree is moved out to a more exposed position. Bright autumn sunlight is an essential part of the colouration process, as we have seen, and if you are lucky, there will be five consecutive nights of frosty weather followed by sunny, warm days.

The weather should also be dry and watering should be done only when necessary. Don't rewater when the soil is still moist and water preferably in the morning so that it drains through during the day. Watering in the evening leaves the soil soggy through the night and increases the sap flow in the evening so that sugars are more easily transported from leaves to the roots and stems.

Yet another interesting point is that production of anthocyanin pigments seems to be more effective if there is a deficiency of Nitrogen and Phosphate.

Following are a couple of extra thoughts that may be of interest. It has been found that a bonsai often produces better autumn colour than a tree in the open ground — particularly a bonsai that is slightly rootbound — the theory being that the restriction of the roots also slows down the movement of sugars from the leaves. An older tree also seems to colour more easily. As with all living things of reasonable age, the biological processes begin to slow down. Younger trees would be more likely to use the available sugar so that there would not be an excess left. They would also have more rapid sap movement and remove the sugars from the leaves before the weather becomes too cold.

One final point is that after autumn colour has been achieved, it has been found that leaves tend to remain longer and their colour enhanced, if the tree is sprayed with a weak solution of white oil and water.

The preceding points, if followed, will definitely enhance your autumn colouring. It is an interesting process and it is fascinating to follow the seasonal changes of trees and see why they occur. Such knowledge, however, should not affect our appreciation of the sheer beauty of trees or our sense of wonder at the pattern and order inherent in Nature.

REFERENCES
Chapter Six
1. Koreshoff, V.A., "Did You Know?" in *Western Suburbs Bonsai Journal*, June, 1969, p. 22.
2. Koreshoff, V.A., "Discovery of Gibberellins" in *Bonsai in Australia*, September, 1971, pp. 34–36.
3. Koreshoff, V.A., "Autumn Colouring" in *Bonsai in Australia*, October 1970, pp. 8–9.

CHAPTER SEVEN

"The Art of Bonsai Styling"

Introduction

No illusion — no enlightenment
JAPANESE PROVERB

In this chapter, the styles and guidelines for shaping will be discussed in some detail. It is the intention of this book, however, to not only mention the "rules" but to explain why they exist and suggest ways of making artistic compromises in order to work with the particular tree in front of you. As was mentioned in chapter one, the guidelines for shaping represent the "distillation of the collective subjective thoughts of past artists — which, being generalized, become more objective".

The different styles and the guidelines for shaping them have been formulated for various reasons. Firstly, they reflect the observations that many bonsai artists have made of the characteristics of trees in nature. Yet, because trees cannot be portrayed in full detail as an exact reproduction of Nature, a process of simplification is used to determine the essence of a scene that is either real or imagined. Bonsai, like all art forms, is a suggestion of reality rather than a mirror image of reality itself.

Some of the guidelines are directed toward giving trees an aged appearance. Young trees are marked by similarity and symmetry while an old tree is asymmetrical in form and has individuality. Time and the influence of environment develops the character lines of a particular tree. Also, as time goes on, smaller leaves develop, twiggier growth is formed and the apex becomes more rounded.

Another point to realize is that it is not every old tree in nature that provides a suitable model for Bonsai — it is the tree with beauty and character that tells us the story of its life as well as perhaps being a symbolic representation of human qualities and emotions.

Even though the guidelines for shaping are constant, no two bonsai will ever be the same, even if shaped by the same person, due to the fact that no two trees are the same and each stylist will make the compromise between tree and guidelines in his own individual way. This process can be likened to a person learning to write. At first, one must learn the recognized forms for the letters — even if this means copying the accepted shapes without much thought. As time goes on, though, and the forms are thoroughly learned, variations arise due to individual characteristics. Handwriting, in fact, becomes so personalized that it is possible to recognize who wrote certain pieces — it becomes like a signature. Some who are artistic will produce beautiful calligraphy while the writing of others may be ordinary or sloppy. Thus we see that there is a great amount of room for variation, however, this must be within the framework of an accepted and recognized form. If the overall guidelines are not adhered to, one would not recognize the letters and while the result may be interesting, it could not be called "writing". In the Art of Bonsai, then, it is important to learn the guidelines first and then begin to make compromises and variations within the generalized forms.

As far as styling of trees is concerned, another argument that is frequently heard concerns the question of why we should follow the oriental methods and guidelines. As was mentioned in chapter one, bonsai originated in China, and when the Art spread to Japan, styling was modified to fit in with Japanese culture. Broadly speaking, there are distinctive differences between Chinese and Japanese bonsai and these will be discussed in more detail further on.

When bonsai spread to the Western world, however, the cultural changes were not acting in quite the same way as they did when the Chinese Art of Bonsai was modified by the Japanese. The results produced by Westerners seemed to be something different to bonsai — the "oriental feeling" was not being transmitted.

One opinion is that each country has a right to its individual characteristics as far as styling is concerned. With bonsai, though, each country will have a distinctive "feeling" due to differences in tree species and differences in climate but, nevertheless, the oriental feeling of style should be retained. By this I mean the features that the Oriental tends to highlight from his environment and all forms of art are the products of a human response to the environment. It is reality seen through human eyes — not a camera lens.

There are trees in every country that can be an inspiration for us. The exceptional tree with beauty and character has a common link with the admirable tree of any country, whether it is a Eucalypt from Australia or a pine from China or Japan. Superficial qualities such as leaf shape or colour, are unimportant. What has attracted you is the FORM and STYLE — the characteristics that the Chinese call the "bones of the design". The Oriental artist looks at these elements and they are there to be seen in all countries. Also, the fact that we like bonsai as it is made in the Orient, means that we are responding to their emphasis on style — it is not something alien to us.

The Five Basic Styles

In the Art of Bonsai there are many styles in which trees may be designed and each one describes a particular situation or type of tree that may be found in nature. For single trees, however, even though there are many variations, such as "Windswept Style" or "Broom Style", Five Basic Styles have been classified to cover all possible angles of the tree's trunk line.

When thinking about a suitable style for a tree, therefore, it is usually the case that one of these five designs will be appropriate. Don't automatically settle for the most obvious choice, though. If, on first glance, slanting style seems fitting, check if a slight tilt to produce less slant might make it into a more artistic bonsai as an informal upright. On the other hand, there may be more design possibilities if the tree is shaped as a semi-cascade, so tilt the tree over more

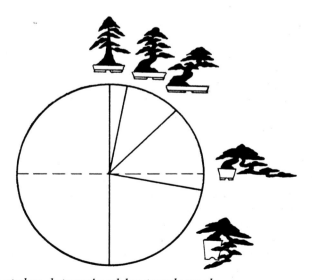

Figure 101: *Five basic styles determined by trunk angle*

and see what the effect is if the slant is accentuated. Sometimes a design is chosen that seems totally in opposition to the pattern of growth of a tree. An upright tree, for example, may be shaped into a full-cascade or a prostrate variety may be shaped into a formal or informal upright (see ''Vertical Horizontalis and Vice Versa'' Chapter 2). In short, keep an open mind and check as many possibilities as you can before you begin your shaping. This way, the full potential of a tree may be realised and there is more chance of producing an artistic and beautiful bonsai. Don't forget, though, that there is rarely one ''correct'' choice of style for a particular tree. Often, there are many possibilities — each potentially giving a pleasing result — and the final decision lies with the individual preferences of the bonsai grower.

Let us now look at each of the Five Basic Styles in more detail, starting first with the classical Formal Upright Style . . .

FORMAL UPRIGHT STYLE

Formal Upright is, in some aspects, the easiest and, in others, the most difficult style to produce. Because of the strictness and formality of the design, one can fairly easily produce a balanced work of art providing the guidelines for styling are followed reasonably closely. Yet, because of this, it is necessary to find tree material that has the desired characteristics and this isn't an easy task.

Perhaps the most difficult feature to find is a straight trunk that tapers fairly evenly from base to apex. However, even if a tree with such a trunk is found, the position and distribution of branches is fairly critical in the production of a well-styled Formal Upright, as will be outlined below. Consequently, while not impossible, it is infrequent that one finds nursery stock suitable to make an ''instant'' Formal Upright, and it may not be a bad idea to start from a seedling or young nursery stock in view of training it, gradually, into this style. While the trunk is still young and pliable, for example, it can be tied to a stake to produce a perfectly straight trunk.

The Formal Upright Style is, in many ways, the best one for beginners to start learning about the guidelines for shaping as most of the aspects of this style follow through to the others. We will begin by discussing the trunk of the Formal Upright as, in numerous examples, this is the most striking characteristic of the design.

The feeling of dominance and strength that is imparted to us when we view many formal uprights is largely due to the perfectly straight and vertically upright trunk. Also, the trunk should taper from base to apex and the wider base should extend into surface roots that hug the earth and give visual as well as physical stability to the tree. Because there is no lean or curve in the trunk of a Formal Upright, the weight of the tree is reasonably well balanced and it is fairly equally affected by the pull of gravity on all sides. Consequently, one should strive for surface roots extending out from the trunk in an all-round spoke pattern — avoiding, of course, the direct front of the tree (see Figure 102).

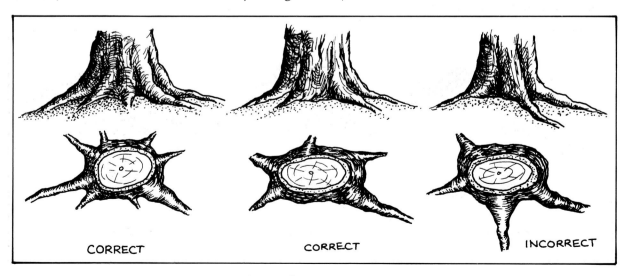

CORRECT   CORRECT   INCORRECT

Figure 102: *Surface roots of formal upright*

Often, however, heavy roots occur under a heavy branch, as the movement of sap tends to take a directly up-and-down route. The main branches on the tree, then, and their relative strength, can guide you in the positioning and direction of surface roots.

Since it is the wish for part, if not all of a tree to grow toward the light, the straight, upward direction of the Formal Upright trunk symbolizes strength and the defiance of adverse elements. Through the shaping of the branches, the story is told of how the tree reached its present stature. Some may have had an easy life and naturally assumed the upright direction, while others may show signs of past struggles. There may be some dead stubs where there were branches, a silvery patch where bark was ripped off in a violent wind storm and then polished smooth through years of subsequent battles — or, perhaps, branches pointing downward indicating extreme age or the weight of many snowfalls. Whether the tree had an easy or a hard life, though, Formal Upright can have a feeling of dignity that comes from balance and composure.

Before we move on to a more detailed discussion on the branching of a Formal Upright, one more point should be mentioned about the trunk line. If you are lucky enough to find nursery stock or an old tree that is suitable for this style, and, if it needs to be cut down and a new apex established, there are a couple of ways of achieving a good result.

One way is to cut to a frontward branch and wire it up into the same line as the trunk below, or, leave a bit of a stub and tie the branch to this in order to achieve a perfectly straight line from base to apex. After the branch is set in position the stub can be removed. The second way is to make a jin at the top which becomes the new apex of the tree. The latter method is good for trees with stark styling of branches and adds to the illusion of an aged tree that has lived in a rough environment.

Now we come to the arrangement of branches for Formal Upright. The distribution should be in groups of three branches or layers, that is, one to the side, one to the back and one to the opposite side. This is the best arrangement but if the back branch or layer doesn't fall between those on the side, another pleasing arrangement is to have the back layer situated in the third place, above the two side layers, (see Figure 103).
The only order that is not so attractive is if the back branch is the lowest, as this makes the style too heavy at the back and tends to lose the feeling of depth and perspective in the design.

The lowest two branches on the side should be the longest and the strongest on the tree and, generally, the first branch is the most dominant one. This first side branch is usually found at a point about ¼ to ⅓ of the distance up the trunk, however, this measurement applies more to the position of the layer of foliage rather than where the branch comes out of the trunk. Thus, the branch could be a little higher than ⅓, if it is gracefully shaped in a downward direction until the layer is in the right position. Usually, if layers start lower down, a feeling may be imparted of strength and massiveness, especially if the lower branches are long and heavy. It may even have the effect of making the tree appear shorter than it really is. Conversely, if the layers start higher up, a taller, lighter effect may be created.

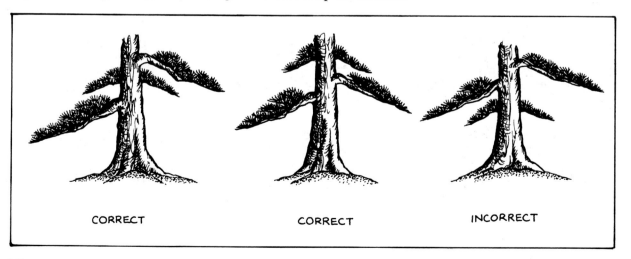

CORRECT   CORRECT   INCORRECT

Figure 103: *Patterns of branch placement*

The back branches on the tree are always shorter than the side branches, the reason being that if we look at a large tree in a field, even though the branches at one level are approximately the same length, the ones on the side are seen at their full extent, while those going out to the back and to the front appear shorter due to a phenomenon known as foreshortening. Thus, by making the back branches shorter, we are helping to create a feeling of perspective and depth.

The fact that back branches are shorter, points to the fact that all bonsai must have a definite front. Some may argue that this is artificial, however let us go back to the idea of viewing a large tree growing in a field. The tree, itself, has no concept of "front" or "back" but perhaps *we* have a favourite direction of viewing the tree. From a particular side, more of the trunk may be visible, thus allowing us to fully appreciate line and texture. This may then be our "chosen" front and, as we view it from there, front and back branches will not appear as long as they really are.

These groups of three branches or layers are repeated as we move up the trunk line, preferably in the same pattern or order that was established in the first set. Gradually, the branches become shorter, as do the distances between the branches. At about two thirds of the way up the trunk, you may begin to shape short branches directly out to the front and, finally, the top of the tree should be a soft conical shape with branches extending out in all directions.

For trees over 15 cm (six inches) high, the minimum amount of branching is usually two groups of three layers, plus a soft, conical top. For miniatures, under 15 cm (six inches), however, not much more scale can be achieved beyond one group of three and the top. The main determinant, though, as to how many branches there should be is not really the height of the tree but the heaviness of the layers of foliage on the branches. A cluttered effect should be avoided and it should be made sure that some empty space frames each layer.

Another important aspect of branch arrangement is that when we refer to side branches it is not meant that these branches extend directly out to the sides, as this would give a very flat and uninteresting face to the front of the tree. Rather, they should extend out to the right or the left and a little to the front (see Figure 104).

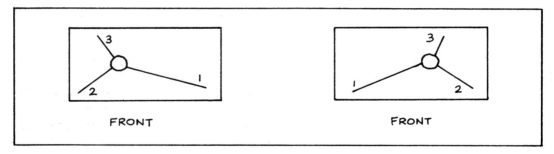

Figure 104: *Plan view of branch positions*

The second group of three should follow the same pattern, that is, if the lowest branch in the first group was on the left, the lowest in the second group should also be on that side. However, when we have a plan view of the tree, no branch should be directly over the top of another. A possible arrangement would be as illustrated below:

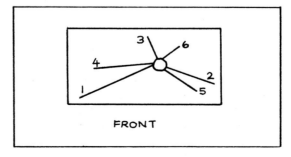

Figure 105: *Plan view of branch positions*

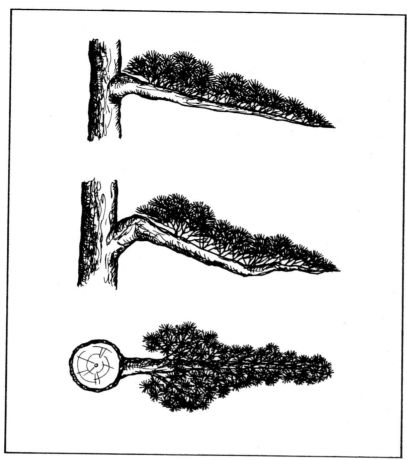

Figure 106: *Side and plan views of formal upright branch*

Each branch, in each group of three, is shorter as we go up the tree so that the final design is an asymmetrical triangle, though this should not be looked upon as a limiting factor to creativity. There are so many variations to the proportions and shapes of triangles. They can be extremely tall and narrow, or, on the other hand, wide, low and spreading.

In three dimensions, the shape could be described as a cone with an oval base, and, from the top the branches would extend out like spokes of a wheel, each one being visible and with a wider gap at the chosen front of the bonsai.

The actual shape of the branches and the foliage on the branches should be considered as it is these factors that largely contribute to the appearance of age. In the classical design of Formal Upright, foliage should not start right at the base of the branch and the underside of the branch should be completely clear of foliage as well. From the side, the shape of the branch can be straight or, very slightly curved. If the curve is too great, though, it would not fit with the straightness of the trunk. If branches are slightly curved, the formal upright can be termed "feminine" — if straight, "masculine". Foliage, when viewed from the side should be like a long, asymmetrical triangle, with the long sides tapering away from the trunk. From above, the layer of foliage can be in an oval, egg, pear or triangular shape, again, with the heavy, wider side closer to the trunk. The branch line, however, *must* be straight when viewed from above.

The angle of the branches can tell us a lot about the age of a tree. Usually, when a tree is young, the branches tend toward an upward direction due to their vigorous, active growth. In middle age, lower branches begin to grow downward, middle branches are horizontal, while young branches at the top still tend upward. In old age, the tree has ceased vigorous growth and branches grow downward due to their own weight as well as environmental conditions, such as years of supporting heavy snowfalls. Also, the apex is usually not so pointed, in old age, as the vigorous growing tip has, likewise, ceased its active growth.

Figure 107: *Conventional pyramidal form of formal upright*

The choice of pot for Formal Upright can be round or square if the design tends toward symmetry, and rectangular or oval if it is more strongly asymmetrical. Round or oval would be chosen for the so-called "feminine" Formal Uprights, or, perhaps, those with thinner trunks or more delicate features. Many growers, however, prefer rectangular pots for Formal Upright — thus stressing an asymmetrical form and complementing the formal lines of the tree with the straight sides of the pot. The length of the pot should be approximately ⅔ of the length of the major dimension, that is, the height or the width, and the depth should be medium or shallow. A medium depth container would suit a tree with a massive, heavy appearance, while a shallow pot would suit a taller tree with a thinner trunk. The position in the pot is slightly behind the centre line when viewed from the side and, if viewed from the front, off-centre, if it is a rectangular or oval container.

The type of Formal Upright we have been discussing, is the conventional pyramidal form. It is the most commonly seen design in this style and the guidelines for shaping, if followed, can successfully make a tree look much older than it really is. However, there are some interesting variations to the basic Formal Upright style.

One variation is called the "Columnar Formal Upright" (see Figure 108).
In this design, branches are very short in proportion to the length of the trunk and layers of foliage may start at the base of the branch, yet they must be compact and well-trimmed. Also, because there are not a lot of branches, bushiness does not result. The basic group of three

Figure 108: *Columnar formal upright*

Figure 109: *Double cone formal upright*

layers or branches does not have to be adhered to, but still, no branches should be placed directly over another. If each branch is visible when viewed from above, depth and variety will be created in the design. The overall shape is somewhat like a column, for even though there is an apex, the tapering is very sudden — often with branches exhibiting a ragged outline — some shorter, some longer as your eye travels up the trunk. Due to its severe lines and its dramatic quality, the Columnar Formal Upright is a style that is more favoured by Chinese rather than Japanese Bonsai enthusiasts.

Another variation that is more of a Chinese Style of Formal Upright is the "Double Cone" design, (see Figure 109).

With this style, the widest point is found a little above or a little below the halfway point of the tree and on the bottom half, the branches form an inverted triangle. This design is suitable for both deciduous and evergreen varieties, however, if it becomes too bushy, it would no longer be considered as a Chinese design. Usually it is the conifer family that is used for Formal Upright style, as it is their habit to have a single trunk line, whereas deciduous varieties often have several stems or branches that are competing for light.

There is another design of Formal Upright that may be suitable for certain trees. This is known as the "Wide Conical Shape" or "Umbrella Shape". Branches from about midway up the trunk or from the top half of the trunk are brought down like a half-opened umbrella. This style is very good for trees that are lacking in lower branches (see Figure 110).

Figure 110: *Wide, conical shape formal upright*

As was mentioned earlier, a well-styled Formal Upright imparts a feeling of composure and balance. Because trees wish to grow in an upward direction, this style shows us a tree that has achieved its aim. For some trees that have grown in a calm and sheltered environment, there may have been little resistance, and these will be somewhat like the description of the classical Formal Upright. With other trees, however, a constant battle may have been fought against a rough environment and, with these, the upright trunk stands as a poignant symbol of a hard-won victory. Such trees typify the Chinese way of Styling. Texture is appreciated greatly so that rough bark, scars on the trunk and the smoothness of exposed, dead wood are often incorporated in the design. There is far less branching than in the Classical Formal Upright and the layers of foliage are more compact, emphasizing the elements of space and line.

Formal Upright Style, in many ways, represents the ideal tree. With the more lush designs it tells us of a land where perfect forms exist — a Garden of Eden — which, like a dream, is unattainable but forever in our minds. Others, shaped more in the Chinese style and showing the marks of earthly battles, give us hope. Perfection is suggested and through hardship and loss, beauty and an air of dignity and composure is gained.

INFORMAL UPRIGHT STYLE

The second of the five basic styles is Informal Upright (see Plates XIV, XV & XVI). It is seen fairly commonly in bonsai collections as it is far easier to find suitable trees to shape into this design than it is for, say, Formal Upright. The guidelines for shaping do not have to be followed rigidly and consequently this allows more scope for choice of tree and for the individual preferences of the person styling the bonsai. Concordant with this, though, is the fact that more imagination is needed and the ability to make compromises by knowing which rules may be ''bent'' or ''modified'', while still following the overall, general guidelines. Mostly, if the rules are to be relaxed, it is likely to be in the area of branch arrangement and some ideas that may be helpful will be discussed below.

Firstly, though, let us go through the characteristics that determine a tree as being an Informal Upright Style. If a line is drawn from the tip of the tree to the centre of the base, it will be vertical, or a few degrees off the vertical to either side. Usually about 15 degrees is the limit. Also, for any tree other than Formal Upright, the tip should lean slightly toward the viewer (about 5 degrees), (see Figure 111).

The reason for this latter practice is that the optical illusion is created that one is looking at a large tree from the position of ground level, rather than looking down on a small tree or shrub. Think, for example, of the effect of looking up at a very tall building. The top seems to lean forward, a little, as if overhanging — even though it is vertical. Thus, if we apply this styling technique to a container-grown tree, it will help to transport us into a world where the actual relationship between the dimension of the tree and ourselves, is forgotten.

Within this basically upright direction of the trunk, however, there may be curves or angles and these may be soft, sharp, exaggerated or slight — depending on the tree to be shaped and the preferences of the grower. Major bends, though, should go to the right or left and not toward or away from the viewer. There should still be a fairly even taper, however, from a nice wide base to a thinner tip.

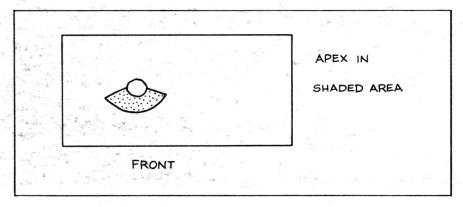

Figure 111: *Position of apex in plan view*

Plate XXII: *Japanese black pine,* Pinus thunbergii, literati style, height: 91 cm, Japanese pot, grown from seed in 1951, trained since 1976, photograph taken in 1982

Plate XXIII: *Hinoki cypress,* Chamaecyparis obtusa *'Juvenile', group setting, height of main tree: 79 cm, Japanese pot, estimated age: from 1969 nursery stock, group created in 1979, photograph taken in 1982*

The distribution of surface roots is much the same as was mentioned for Formal Upright. Because the distribution of weight is fairly even on all sides, the surface roots are also fairly evenly placed around the base of the tree for support. The major branches, though, as with Formal Upright, can still be a guide for the positioning of surface roots as they tend to develop in a similar vertical line due to the up-and-down movement of sap in the tree. The frontward position, though, should be clear of both heavy branches and heavy surface roots.

Now we come to the branching arrangement for the traditional Informal Upright style. The group of three branches or layers, that was discussed for the Formal Upright design, applies here as well. However, it is not so rigid, especially after the first set, so that if the same order cannot be continued right to the top, it doesn't matter so much. Still, the first branch should be on the side, preferably from the outside of a curve and is usually the longest and the strongest branch on the tree. Perhaps one of the most important guidelines is that branches should not come directly from the inside of a curve. Also, the basic overall shape of the tree should be triangular.

As was mentioned earlier, the way one makes compromises with the guidelines, is usually connected with the way the branches are shaped on the tree. If you are going to successfully "bend" the rules, the reasons for their existence should, first of all, be considered. Usually, branches or major layers of foliage tend to be situated on the outside of curves, firstly because the tree strives to balance itself by growing in the opposite direction of a heavy branch and, secondly, having done this, more light is available for the foliage of the heavy branch and it, consequently, grows stronger. If there is no branch situated at this point though, don't give up in despair, but use a branch that is either above or below the main curve. If it is above, sweep it down, gracefully, following the same general line of the trunk until it reaches the correct position and then shape it out into a horizontal layer (see Figure 112).

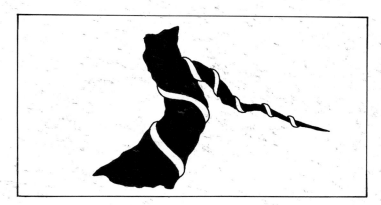

Figure 112: *Branch situated above ideal position*

If, on the other hand, it is situated below the curve, the reverse is practiced: the branch is shaped upward and then out, horizontally.

Figure 113: *Branch situated below ideal position*

Figure 114: *Branches up on one side and down on the other*

This idea is used, also, where a branch doesn't exist, say, one third of the way up the trunk, that is, the recommended position for the first branch or layer of the tree. The most important point, though, is that once a pattern of ''bending'' the rules has been established — stick to it. The only exception that may work is if branches on one side go up and out and those on the opposite side go down and out, horizontally.

An interesting situation may arise where a branch does exist at the position of one third of the way up the trunk but where the main curve exists, say, higher up. If we blindly follow the rules and shape the branch straight out at that point, the result is not so attractive (see Figure 115).

However, by ''feeling'' for the rules rather than merely following them without thought, a slight modification may be made that is more pleasing. If if is realized that layers look good at a point, one third of the way up the trunk and that the branch looks good if it thrusts away from the trunk on the outside of a curve, the branch may be shaped upward, initially, to the curve and then swept down to the best position for the layer, (see Figure 116).

Figure 115: *Conflicting guidelines for shaping*

Figure 116: *Making a compromise with the guidelines*

This, of course, is providing the curves in the trunk cannot be modified in the first place.

Another situation where modification of the rules may arise is that the lowest branch on the tree may not have to be the longest and the strongest if a major curve exists somewhere higher up on the tree. If the curve above is a major feature of the trunk line, then the branch or layer, at that point, may be the most dominant (see Figure 117).

Figure 117: *Longest branch at major curve in trunk*

Yet another example where rules may be "bent" is that it is possible to leave more than the basic group of three branches or layers if it is made certain that no branch lies directly over another when viewed from above and that there is a reasonably clear view of the trunk up to about two thirds of its height. This idea may be suitable in the styling of some younger trees that don't have such dominant branches or layers or for trees whose distribution of branches is such that the basic group of three would appear too scanty.

The shape of the branches and foliage layers of Informal Upright are similar to Formal Upright. From the side, though, the curves in the branches can be quite pronounced. The foliage is shaped in a long triangular shape with the thinner part tapering to the tip of the branch, however, the layer may be closer to the trunk than in the classical Formal Upright, if this suits the tree in question. The underside of the branch, though, must still be completely clear of foliage. When viewed from above, the branch can have curves and angles, as well, and the foliage layer is pear or oval shaped, again with the wider side closer to the trunk.

The usual type of pot for Informal Upright is rectangular or oval, as this complements its strongly asymmetrical character and the depth depends greatly on the diameter of the trunk — a thick, stocky tree for example, would look better in a deeper pot. Generally, the length of the pot should be a little less than the overhang of the branches, however, a reasonable guide is to choose a pot about two thirds of the length of the major dimension, that is, either the height or the width. The tree is, most commonly, planted off-centre and somewhere in the shaded area indicated in the diagram below.

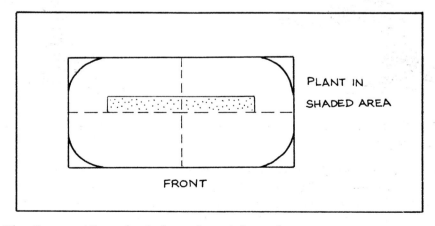

Figure 118: *Planting positions for informal upright style*

Figure 119: *Free-form informal upright*

One variation to the traditional Informal Upright discussed above is the so-called ''free-form'' Informal Upright (see Plates XVII & XVIII).

This style still has a basically upright trunk, with perhaps some curves, however there is far greater freedom in the distribution of branches. They are often longer than in the Traditional Informal Upright and are not usually in a definite group of three, while foliage layers are frequently massive and rounded, rather than defined and tapered. Also, the trunk may not always continue in one definite line right to the apex.

Still, the general rules are adhered to — basic triangular shape, though usually softened, some space framing layers or masses of foliage and a reasonably clear view of the trunk for at least half of the distance up the tree. It should also have asymmetrical balance.

This style is, perhaps, closer to the idea of the Western potted tree than any other in the Art of Bonsai, but if it is made with artistic feeling backed by the traditional guidelines for shaping, it can impart the illusion of age to a tree. It is a style that is most suitable for many deciduous trees and is close to ''Broom Style'' in feeling and character.

Finally, a few words about the Chinese version of Informal Upright. Like all Chinese Styling, the emphasis is on creating the feeling of a rugged, aged tree that has lived in a harsh environment. Consequently, angles in trunks and branches are chosen over soft curves, so that the Lingnan ''Grow and Clip'' method (see Chapter 2) or the Sculptural Method (see Chapter 2) are often used in the training procedure. There is also a definite line from base to apex, fewer branches and foliage layers are compact and not so lush as in most Japanese examples of the style. Like most Chinese styled trees, the effect is severe and dramatic.

Figure 120: *Chinese style informal upright*

The Informal Upright style is an excellent one for beginners to start on their practical shaping experience. Learn, first, the guidelines for shaping Formal Upright, look at the basic differences in Informal Upright and then think about the reasons for the existence of many of the guidelines. The next step is to choose a suitable tree to shape — here you won't have too much difficulty — and finally, begin your styling, taking into account the traditional ideas as well as the individual characteristics of the tree in front of you. Practice will improve your confidence and exercise your imagination — and, don't forget, the tree is always there to help and guide you along the way!

SLANTING STYLE

Slanting style — the third of the five basic styles — is transitional between Informal Upright and Semi-cascade. The main slant of the trunk may be to the right or left and if a line is drawn from the base of the trunk to the apex, the angle so-formed should be between 11 and 45 degrees from the vertical.

Environment and time leave their special marks on trees and it is through our styling of potential bonsai material that we allow our trees to tell us a story. We try to make our trees appear old, as it is through time that the characteristics of variety and the individual are made distinct. Note, however, that the tree need not be very old — it is through styling that the illusion of age is created.

A tree with a slanting trunk can be a very interesting style, for unlike the previous styles discussed (i.e. formal upright and informal upright) we are, in this case, showing definite marks left by the environment. Formal Upright and Informal Upright, while exhibiting age and character, are usually trees that have been growing in a reasonably gentle or protected environment. The trunks are growing in the ideal direction — vertical or near vertical and upwards — and branches and roots are distributed in a balanced fashion. The slanting style, on the other hand, has been changed from its preferred direction of growth and such a change describes the story of the tree's life in vivid and concise terms.

The first thing to consider is the position and shape of the surface roots. In any style, it is the pleasing arrangement of surface roots that gives us a feeling of stability and balance. In slanting style, however, the design of the surface roots is even more important as a leaning trunk could more easily appear unstable. In Formal Upright and Informal Upright, surface roots should be distributed fairly evenly around the trunk, with the provision that no heavy roots extend straight out at the front or back. This particular guideline to styling stems from the observation that on vertical or near-vertical trees, the pull of gravity is fairly equal on all sides and an all-round buttress provides the necessary support. (A heavier root, however, is best placed generally under the position of a heavy branch).

As the trunk angle changes and approaches the area of slanting style, the situation concerning the support necessary for the tree is also altered. The greater the angle and general weight of the trunk, the greater will be the effect of gravity trying to pull the tree down to ground-level. Consequently, the pattern and general profile of the rootsystem will be modified.

The position of the surface roots in this style is not so much determined by the location of heavy branches or foliage masses but by counterbalancing forces needed to support the trunk. Thus we find that the two main areas where surface roots are necessary are directly under the lean of the trunk and on the opposite side of the lean.

Another point to keep in mind is that the general shape of the surface rootage will be different in slanting style due to the special and usually more intense stresses that are functioning — especially with thick, heavy trunks and those on a sharp angle of lean. The roots under the trunk's lean are subjected to compressive forces and consequently the roots assume a "buttress" or "knee" formation (see Figure 121).
On the side opposite to the lean, there is a pulling or tensile force operating and the roots take on an "anchoring" function and have a smoother profile radiating gracefully from the trunk (see Figure 121).

When we come to the trunk design of a slanting style tree, there are many variations and possibilities for the designer to use his imagination. First of all, the actual slant may begin at ground level or a short distance above ground level (see Figures 122 & 123).

Figure 121: *Surface roots of slanting tree*

An interesting variation would be where the trunk begins by going in the opposite direction of the general slant for a short distance and then turns acutely into the other direction (see Figure 124).

There is also the possibility of shaping the tree with a curved trunk or straight trunk. If curved, it is far easier to impart the feeling of stability. Each time the trunk changes direction to grow in a more vertical manner, the tree tells us that it has spent quite some time in the slanted position, as it has attempted, in times of relatively calm or favourable conditions, to grow upwards toward the light. Remember that if the trunk is curved, the apex should lean slightly toward the viewer (i.e. about five degrees).

Figures 122, 123 & 124: *Slant at ground level, Slant above ground level, Slant beginning in opposite direction*

Figure 125: *Straight trunked slanting style*

A straight-trunked slanting style, on the other hand, may give the impression that it has just blown over recently. If you are attempting this variation, make sure that the tree has good surface roots, as described above, and that the branches have been shaped to a horizontal or slightly downward direction to suggest that the tree has been growing in that position for a reasonable length of time (see Figure 125).

The arrangement of branches is our next consideration. With this style, the rule of "group of three branches" or "group of three layers" should be considered and applied if possible. Often, however, improvisation is necessary, and it is the way this artistic compromise is made that may make the bonsai into a work of art.

The branches must be horizontal or shaped into a slightly downward direction and, generally, the branches on the opposite side to the slant grow out fairly straight and strongly or begin in a slightly upward direction before turning out horizontally (see Figure 126).

The branches on the side of the trunk's lean, on the other hand, are often firstly shaped downward and then out (see Figure 126 below). The reason for this is that in nature, when the tree begins to grow on a lean, for one reason or another, the branches on the opposite side of the slant generally receive more light and therefore grow out vigorously and straight. Also, if the initial direction of the branch is slightly upward, it indicates the original position of the branch when the tree was growing more vertically and the branch was horizontal. The branches on the side of the lean are now in a downward direction, also due to the change in trunk angle. What was initially a horizontal branch is now growing in a downward direction and being on the side that is generally more deprived of light, it takes longer than the other side to re-establish itself and grow in the new horizontal direction. This is why the initial curve is usually more noticeable on the side of trunk lean.

Figure 126: *Branches on slanting style*

Figure 127: *Slanting tree on sea-coast*

The branching on the tree tells the viewer many stories of the environment and life of the tree. Of particular importance is the first branch (the first branch usually being the strongest and longest in the design).

In most cases, the first heavy branch should be on the opposite side of the tree's slant. In nature, as mentioned above, this side would usually receive more light and the strongest and longest branch would thus be found in such a position. Having the heaviest branch on that side also visually and physically acts as an anchor that balances the weight of the tree.

A point to keep in mind, is the fact that branches tend to grow on the outside of curves. A tree naturally grows AWAY from a heavy branch in order to balance itself and gain equilibrium.

Another natural situation that tends to produce the heavier branches on the opposite side to the tree's slant is the tree growing on the sea-coast. Often trees are seen leaning into the wind toward the sea. This occurs because the drying effect of the wind retards the growth of cells on the windward side, while on the protected side the cells elongate at a more normal rate. The result of this is that the tree's trunk leans into the wind. The branching, however, is another situation — heavier branching tending to develop on the side opposite to the trunk's lean — where more protection is available (see Figure 127).

Occasionally, however, a slanting style tree may be seen with the first heavy branch occurring on the side of the tree's lean. When trees grow along the bank of a river or stream, the trunks tend to grow out over the river as the tree competes for light. The heavy, first branch also tends to grow out over the water due to the fact that there is more available light on that side and the humidity also facilitates growth.

Generally, if shaping a slanting style with the first branch on the side of the trunk's lean, the design discussed before for branches on this side would be used (i.e. initially downward and then out in a more horizontal direction). A branch growing out straight and horizontal is generally more forceful in appearance and may tend to unbalance the design if placed on the side of the slant. Such a branch, however, would be acceptable if the trunk changed direction radically at that point (see Figure 128).

If you decide to put the first and heaviest branch on the side of the slant, take care that it is not too heavy or long, otherwise the style will be closer to semi-cascade.

A couple of advantages with this style is that trees with one-sided branching or trees with very high branches and a trunk that is unsuitable for literati style, can be made into balanced and attractive slanting styles. By placing the trunk on a lean and perhaps curving it a little, the distance between the first branches and the ground level becomes shorter and more proportionate to the tree's height. Also, the lack of heavy branches on one side becomes less important when they are on the side of the trunk's lean.

Figure 128: *Straight branch at major curve on side of lean*

Slanting style poses many interesting design possibilities for the bonsai artist. It is definitely an asymmetrical form that requires thought on the artist's part in order to achieve the feeling of balance and stability. Stability, however, does not imply passivity. Slanting style designs are often very active in feeling due to the many tensions involved in their form, and movement may seem to be frozen in space with delicacy and balance.

SEMI-CASCADE STYLE

By definition, if a straight line is drawn from the base of the trunk to the tip of the tail of a semi-cascade, the angle should be between 45 degrees above and a few degrees below the horizontal. Usually, a semi-cascade does not fall far below the pot rim and sometimes one hears that a tree may be classified as a semi-cascade if the tail does not fall below the bottom of the pot. Such a definition works well, providing the pot is of medium depth or semi-deep. If the pot is quite deep, however, the tree may be a full-cascade even though the tail does not fall below the bottom of the container. For this reason, the distinction by angle is more accurate.

THE SURFACE ROOTS:

Of all the bonsai styles, semi-cascade is perhaps the most difficult one with which to achieve balance. With the upright styles and the full-cascade, it is generally easier to produce a well-balanced result due to the vertical nature of these forms in conjunction with the action of gravity. Because semi-cascade is basically a horizontal design, gravity is exerting a much greater pull and consequently the tree must have a sturdy, buttressed trunk and/or strong surface roots to anchor the tree in the ground and impart the feeling of stability. When it comes to the actual design of the rootsystem, we find that the ideal design and shape is similar to slanting style (discussed previously) but with a few slight modifications.

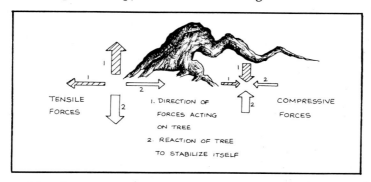

Figure 129: *Root profile of semi-cascade*

Under the curve or lean of the trunk, we still find the "knee" or "buttress" type of root design that has been formed due to compressive forces. On the side opposite to the lean, however, while there is still a horizontal pulling force as in slanting style, the strongest force seems to be a pulling force in an upward, vertical direction. As the weight of the cascade pushes down and horizontally out on the lean side, the opposite side is being pulled up and out of the soil in an upward, vertical direction and in a horizontal, outward direction. To counterbalance these forces, "anchor" roots probe downward with a sleek line but with a shorter root run than in slanting style (see Figure 129).

THE TRUNK LINE AND BRANCH STRUCTURE — A STARTING POINT:

As mentioned above, the basic angle of the trunk line, when viewed from the side, should fall between 45 degrees above and a little below the horizontal. When viewed from above, the tail of the semi-cascade can cross the pot rim anywhere between a complete profile view and about 45 degrees towards the front (see Figure 130).

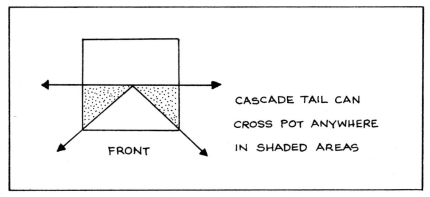

Figure 130: *Plan view of where tail of cascade can cross the pot*

Generally, the semi-cascade would be planted toward the centre of the pot or a short distance in the direction opposite to where the tail crosses the pot rim.

When considering the branch placement in a semi-cascade, it is not a bad starting point to think of the style as an upright bonsai that has been bent over to a horizontal position. What was the front of the upright bonsai, now becomes the underside of the semi-cascade (see Figure 131).

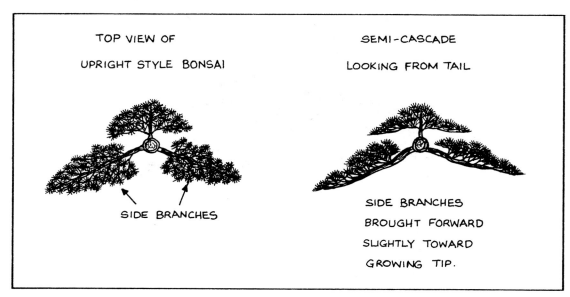

Figure 131: *Branch placement in semi-cascade style*

Figure 132: *Semi-cascade with counterbalancing head*

The cross-section should be a flattish ellipse — not round — and the tip of the tail — like the apex of an upright styled tree — should be triangular and bent slightly towards the front.

Such a preliminary description of semi-cascade may be helpful, however, if the above instructions of branch placement are followed exactly, the result will most probably be artificial and stiff as well as lacking balance and a unified design between pot and tree. If one has an awareness of the problems involved with the style, though, certain ideas may be thought of that can improve the end result.

Possibly the most difficult problem is the fact that the style is basically horizontal and consequently, the end result is often flat due to the difficulty in forming horizontal layers. To overcome this, curves should be shaped into the trunk line in both the side and plan views. Wherever a curve is made, a position is created for a horizontal layer but obviously, the distance of the vertical drop should not be long, or else the style will become a full-cascade. The mood of the semi-cascade can be changed considerably depending upon the type of curves that are made. They may be sharp and angular, imparting a rugged, weather-beaten appearance (see Figures 133 and 135) or they may be more moderate and soft, thus creating the feeling of informal elegance (see Figure 132). Once the design of the trunk line has been established, the branches must follow the same general design as well.

Figure 133: *Semi-cascade with sharp angles and rugged appearance*

Figure 134: *Counterbalancing head situated one-third of way along cascade*

Another problem that again stems from the basically horizontal structure, is the difficulty of forming an attractive apex or even in making an apex at all. Once again, if one is aware of the problem, solutions may be worked out. With semi-cascade, there are three different places where the apex may be positioned:
1. At a point approximately two thirds along the horizontal length (see Figure 135).
2. At a point one third of the distance along the horizontal length (see Figure 134).
3. To design the semi-cascade with a counterbalancing head (see Figure 132). This can be a very attractive design for semi-cascade, as the counterbalancing head helps to unify and balance the pot with the tree. One caution with this variation in style, however, is that the branch or trunk-line forming the cascade tail, should be reasonably strong, otherwise it will appear like the lower branch of an upright tree. Also, while the head can be reasonably full, it should not be too dominant or tall, as, once again, the style will be bordering on the upright forms.

Another problem that often crops up with semi-cascade is that frequently, depth is lost by forgetting to include back branches in the design. One position that seems to work well is to have the back branch incorporated in the first layer on the side opposite the lean. Shorter branches or layers on the tail should also extend toward the back to impart more of a three-dimensional feeling.

Figure 135: *Counterbalancing head situated two-thirds of way along cascade*

Semi-cascade style is very versatile as far as tree varieties are concerned. It can look good with conifers, deciduous or broad-leaf evergreens. Another advantage is that there is no significant loss of vigour in the tail of the cascade as is often a problem with full-cascades.

There is also a large variety of pot styles and types that look good with semi-cascade. Following are some of the pot types that may be used and their effects on the style:

1. Shallow to medium: oval, rectangular, free-form. Complements the horizontal nature of the style and imparts a light, almost windswept feeling (see Figure 134).

2. Semi-deep: oval, rectangular, round, square, hexagonal, octagonal, flower-shaped. This type of pot is generally used for softer or more moderate styling. Semi-deep round or square pots are probably the most frequently used style of container for semi-cascade (see Figure 132).

3. Deep: round, square, hexagonal, octagonal, flower-shaped. This pot type imparts a stark contrast between the vertical and horizontal planes. A very strong impact is created and is most suitable for a rugged and striking style of tree (see Figure 133).

The semi-cascade design — making the step between the upright forms of bonsai and the full-cascade — is a transitional style that is charged with problems . . . and possibilities.

At times it appears to float effortlessly and almost carelessly in space, while at other times it vigorously and roughly sculpts the air surrounding it. Whatever the design though, semi-cascade, with its strongly horizontal form, seems to skim between heaven and earth, defying gravity as does no other style.

FULL CASCADE STYLE

Of all the styles of Bonsai, full cascade is the one that asks the most of trees in terms of their ability for adaptation and their acceptance of hardship — yet, despite this, such trees may have grace and dramatic beauty as well as an air of impressive strength. It is a design born amongst sheer ravines and towering cliff-faces where icy winds carve the rock and sculpt the trees that cling tenaciously to small crevices. Solitary and shrouded by mist, they are pressured by the elements downward toward the abysmal depths — yet they still look upward and dream . . .

By definition, if a line is drawn from the base of the trunk of a full-cascade, to the tip of its tail, the angle so-formed should be somewhere between about 30 degrees and 90 degrees below the horizontal.

The style is more favoured by Chinese, rather than Japanese bonsai growers and it is the Chinese method of shaping a cascade that will be discussed here — partly because of its immense character and beauty and partly because this styling technique makes it possible to transform suitable nursery stock into an attractive cascade "bonsai-in-training" almost instantaneously. Japanese cascades tend to be softer in feeling than the Chinese type. Quite often they may have more than one tail, they may be more liberally covered with foliage and have fewer angle changes.

In many respects it may help the beginner to start thinking of full-cascade in terms of an upside-down informal upright. Imagine the upright tree with its front turned 45 degrees to 90 degrees around and then bent over. In this way we can see that the rule of three branches still can be applied, however the back branch is now on the side or slightly towards the front.

This may help as a starting point, but such a style would be fairly stiff and uninteresting without some kind of modification. Following is a step-by-step description of the process of making a full-cascade.

Firstly, the trunk should rise out of the pot for a short distance, but far enough so that when it is bent to form the cascade, it is able to clear the rim of the pot. If it is resting on the rim it makes the cascade look weak and unstable. It is also important that this first bend in the trunk be as sharp an angle as possible, as this adds greatly to the dramatic nature of the style.

When viewed from the top it is often a good idea to train the trunk in such a way that it sweeps slightly backwards in the area where the first bend is when viewed from the front (see Figure 136). This can give a great deal of depth to the design.

Next we come to the actual shaping of the trunk line. Angles are essential in the Chinese style cascade and these should be as definite and acute as possible. Again, this will add to the dramatic effect while soft curves are not in keeping with the rugged, mountainous type of landscape where this style would naturally grow. The angles can be put in the trunk wherever you like, but, remembering that major branches look better if placed on the outside of curves, you may wish to use the existing branches as a guide for where you make these angles.

Figure 136: *Side and plan views of bend in lower trunk region*

Another point to keep in mind is that a regular zig-zag pattern is not so interesting, so vary the distances between the angle changes and work basically toward the distances becoming shorter as you move down toward the tip of the tail. Another consideration is to avoid shaping the tail in one plane — such designs lack depth as well as variety.

The design elements of DOMINANCE and LINE are very important to the Chinese and the fact that there is a single line forming the cascade (rather than many tails dropping vertically as seen in some Japanese cascades) means that the viewer's eye is led along a very definite and carefully exaggerated path. Because of this dominance of a single basic direction and line, a feeling of strength and impact is created and the artistic linear movement can be appreciated to the full.

Now we come to the shaping of the branches. Firstly, consider whether you wish to shape your cascade with a head or not. When shaping the branches of a cascade, the usual procedure is to start with the top and work down (this is opposite to upright styles where you begin with the lowest branches and work up toward the apex), so, if you decide to have the counterbalancing head on the cascade, shape this part first.

The style of cascade with a "head" is called by the Chinese: "The Mist Rising from the Waterfall" — the "Head" suggesting the mist that rises from a rugged and spectacular cascading stream. The effect is heightened even more by the Chinese method of "cloud pruning". Layers of foliage are clipped to form compact and definite layers that highlight but do not hide the trunk line. These appear like clouds of mist that rise as the stream turns abruptly in the course of its mountainous fall.

Such romantic images impart much to our appreciation of the style, but, apart from this, the head of a cascade does help to create the effect of stability and balance. It should be in a low triangular shape when viewed from the front and may be made up of layers or a single dome of foliage. Watch, though, that it is not too tall or else it will compete with, rather than enhance the cascade.

The first branch of the actual cascade tail is usually a fairly dominant one and is most commonly the longest branch on the cascade. It should also be situated at the point of a major bend in the trunk. Sometimes the foliage layer of this branch can be trained to partially jut across the container to break its line and add more interest to the design.

As we move down the tail of the cascade, major layers should be located at the outside of each curve and short frontward branches (like the back branches of an upright tree) placed midway between these angle changes.

Finally, the tail should be a triangular layer trained slightly toward the viewer (like the apex of an Informal Upright). The whole effect should be of two triangles: the "head" forming a triangle with the apex pointing up and the cascading section forming a triangle pointing downwards.

The shaping of the layers of foliage is quite important. From the side they should look something like those described for the upright styles, making sure that there is no foliage on the underside of the branches. From above, the layers should appear triangular, oval, or pear-shaped, with the widest part closer to the trunk.

As mentioned above, the Chinese keep these layers meticulously clipped — creating the effect of clouds floating in the air. Also, if the layers are trimmed and compact, they will enhance rather than obscure the line (trunk and branch lines being considered more important than the volume or mass of foliage). In parts, the line will be broken by the foliage layers, but this adds an element of mystery to the design. It is like the dragon that flies through the clouds — our interest is aroused because we are not shown all . . .

To the Taoists, the Dragon was the Tao itself, an all-pervading force which momentarily reveals itself to us, only to vanish again and leave us wondering if we had actually seen it at all. "Hidden in the caverns of inaccessible mountains", wrote Okakura Kakuzo, "or coiled in the unfathomable depths of the sea, he awaits the time when he slowly rouses himself to activity. He unfolds himself in the storm clouds; he washes his mane in the blackness of the seething whirlpools. His claws are in the forks of the lightning, his scales begin to glisten in the bark of rain-swept pine trees. His voice is heard in the hurricane which, scattering the withered leaves of the forest, quicken the new spring. The dragon reveals himself only to vanish".[1]

Space is another prominent element in Chinese design and again, keeping the foliage layers in check, adds to the effects of spaciousness and depth.

Cascades are seldom shown full-face (i.e. with the tail facing the viewer) as much of the line would be hidden. Usually they are viewed either from a three-quarter face position (see Figure 137), or in profile (see Figure 138).

The surface roots of a full cascade should, ideally, act to visually balance and stabilize the tree. Due to the forces of gravity on the trunk, we find that compressive forces are acting on the roots on the side of the cascading trunk and that the weight of this trunk will be tending to pull the tree upwards on the side opposite the cascade. Thus on the opposite side, tensile stresses would produce surface roots with a sleek profile and a short root run as they quickly grow down deeply in the earth to anchor the tree. On the side of the cascade though, buttress roots would develop due to compressive forces acting there.

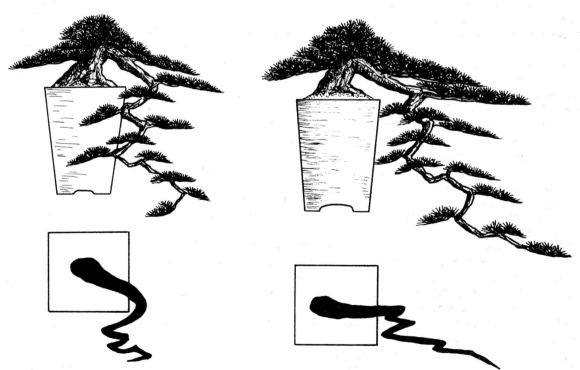

Figure 137: *Three-quarter face view of full-cascade*

Figure 138: *Profile view of full-cascade*

Figure 139: *Root profile of full-cascade*

There are, in fact, a few different styles of cascade. A cascade with a counterbalancing head and with the tip of the tail directly in line with the apex of the head is often termed a "Formal Full-Cascade" (see Figure 140 and Plate XIX) while a cascade with a head but with the tail going out to the side, may be referred to as an "Informal Full-Cascade" (see Figure 141).

Figure 140: *Formal full cascade*   **Figure 141:** *Informal full cascade*

There is another very interesting style of cascade called the "Cliff-hanging style". This design suggests a tree that has lived in a very harsh and rugged environment. There is no "head" of foliage, so that the quality of line and texture at the base of the trunk are all important. Often a good effect may be created if jins and shari (see Chapter 2) are incorporated in this style. There should be relatively few foliage layers and these should be compact, with foliage kept to a minimum. Also, the longer branches should be on the side that the cascade falls and the line of the cascade should gradually tend toward that side as well — the reason being that the tree would not grow back into the cliff, but outwards, toward the light. In its natural environment, this kind of style would be formed by landslides or the pressures of snows in winter pushing it down, as well as the resurgence of vigour in spring and the tendency to grow toward the light which shapes it out horizontally and perhaps slightly upward, for a short distance. Such trees — rugged and lean — can often capture the mood and feeling expressed in the poetic Literati Style (see Figure 142).

The pot type for a cascade is usually of medium depth to very tall and either round, square, hexagonal, octagonal (or any other shape with sides of equal length). For very long and severely styled cascades or the cliff-hanging style, often a very deep and narrow container has a pleasing effect. Deep pots are generally used for cascades, as they both physically and visually balance the tree. Also, in the mountainous areas where cascades would grow, the roots would grow deeply to help stabilize the trees. The tall containers suggest these aspects as well.

Plate XXIV: *Sargent Juniper,* Juniperus chinensis *'Sargentii', group setting, height of main tree: 45 cm, Japanese pot, trees grown from cuttings struck in 1966 & 1968, group created in 1976, photograph taken in 1981*

Plate XXV: *Meyer Juniper, Juniperus squamata 'Meyeri', group setting, height of main tree: 95 cm, Japanese pot, trees grown from cuttings struck in 1960, 1966 & 1968, group created in 1981, photograph taken in 1982*

Figure 142: *Cliff-hanging full cascade*

Usually, the tip of the cascade is below the bottom of the pot, however this is not imperative. The only point to be watched is that the cascade is not the same length as the pot and, when displaying, the stand should not be the same length as the pot or the cascade.

The positioning of the cascade in the pot is fairly critical. Never plant the tree on the side of the container closest to the fall, as it looks top-heavy and visually, if not physically, unstable. It should be either planted near the centre of the pot or slightly to the opposite side of the fall of the cascade. If the pot has three legs, one leg should be situated at the point under the cascade's tail.

On a horticultural note, cascades can often pose a problem with watering and drainage — particularly if the pot is very tall and/or narrow. Because there is little drying through the effects of evaporation, water loss is only occurring through drainage and the tree's use of moisture. Usually, the top will be dryish, while the bottom is still soggy. Also, if you don't water very thoroughly, the top may be moistened constantly, while the bottom remains dry. To counter these problems, firstly attend to the soil. Either put coarse sand or gravel on the bottom third to half of the pot and normal soil mix on the top, or use a more sandy mix for the entire pot. This will assist drainage so that the bottom of the pot does not become waterlogged. Once this has been done, make sure that you water thoroughly when you do water, so that the whole container of soil is saturated. To determine when watering is necessary again, feel the surface soil and also under the drainage hole. This will indicate the state of dryness fairly well. Another point that should be considered is the size or amount of drainage holes. Make sure that they are sufficient for the height and width of the pot (more drainage is needed for taller and thinner pot types).

When choosing suitable material for creating a full-cascade, there are a few points that should be considered:

1. If the tree has pliable wood, this will be an advantage, as the tree will more likely stand the sharp bending required to produce an attractively styled tree (N.B. Junipers are pliable and Juniper procumbens is usually prostrate growing, thus making it easier to shape into cascade style. Cotoneasters also give pleasing effects — particularly when the berries are on the tree. They take longer than Juniper procumbens, however, to produce dense layers of foliage).

2. If you wish to style a cascade with a "head", make sure there are enough branches or foliage low down on the tree.

3. It is better to choose a tree slightly longer than the intended cascade, because once styled, the tip usually doesn't develop further and, sometimes will even lose vigour. If the tree is initially longer and you cut it back to the desired place, there will often be more foliage and branches to work on than you would find on the new growing tip of the tree's extremity. (N.B. For methods to encourage growth on the tip, or at best, to even out the vigour over the whole tree, refer to Chapter 2 "Regulating the Vigour Distribution" — An additional method for

cascades that has been used by some growers is to place a tray of water beneath the tip of the cascade. This provides extra humidity and reflected light to encourage growth. It also may be an idea to display cascades on pedestals set in pools — a thought to keep in mind if landscaping your garden).

Since the beginning of plant life on earth, trees have lived patiently with their particular allotted environment — reacting and adapting themselves to it, in order to survive. The style and character of a tree is shaped by its intrinsic nature, to be sure, but as well as this, the type of environment and its degree of harshness, plays a large part in the ultimate design.

With Full Cascade, we see Nature pushing a tree to what seems the limits of its endurance. All trees, seeking the light, attempt to grow towards the heavens, yet here we see them pushed to the opposite extreme. Even so, the fresh green of their foliage and the very tip of the downthrust tail, turns optimistically toward the sky.

Such trees, because of the extreme nature of their style, may seem to come from wondrous and unchartered lands, and can tell us many strange and captivating stories. They can inspire the deepest chasms of man's imagination and, commanding the powers of illusion, they seem to point downwards to our earthbound nature while revealing — almost secretly — a feeling of ethereal beauty.

Other Single Trunk Styles:

WINDSWEPT STYLE

Figure 143: *Windswept style*

Windswept style can be one of the most fascinating of bonsai designs as in no other style do we see such a dramatic interplay between a tree and its environment. Practically speaking, one advantage of such a style is that use may be made of trees that are unbalanced by having most of their major branches on one side of the trunk. However, a tree that has one-sided branching is not necessarily suitable for windswept style and when choosing material, qualities such as trunk line and good sturdy surface roots that grip the earth should be taken into account.

When we think of a tree that is windswept, most of us imagine a tree with a slanting trunk style. This is probably the most common design but it is by no means the only possibility. If the majority of the branches are showing the effects of being exposed to wind, the tree will be classed as being windswept, no matter what the direction of the trunk is. In fact, each of the first four basic bonsai styles may be designed as windswept, simply by repositioning the branches (see Figures 144–147).

Even with the slanting and semi-cascade windswept styles there are interesting variations to the norm. Figures 146 & 147 below, show the more usual designs, where the branches are swept around in the direction of the trunk's lean. In certain environmental conditions, however, it is possible to see trees shaped as in Figure 148, with the branches tending in the opposite direction of the trunk's slant.

This interesting phenomenon occurs through the force of the drying wind in relation to the tree's growing period. If a seedling germinates on a windy shore, the cells on the windward side will be of smaller size due to the drying effects of the wind, while those on the protected side will be growing at the normal rate. The seedling will, therefore, bend into the wind. In the dormant period, however, the younger, more pliable parts of the trunk (i.e. the top part of the tree) will be swept back with the wind, along with all the branches. The characteristic shape, as seen in Figure 148, is thereby formed.

Figure 144: *Formal upright windswept*

Figures 145: *Informal upright windswept*

Figure 146: *Slanting windswept*

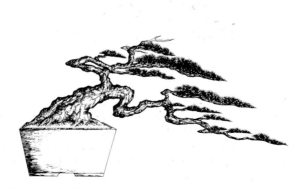

Figure 147: *Semi-cascade windswept*

Figure 148: *Branches in opposite direction to trunk's lean*

As well as single tree designs, it is possible to make a twin trunk or two-tree setting (see Figure 149), or a larger group of trees (see Figure 150).

Figure 149: *Two-tree windswept style*

Figure 150: *Group setting windswept style*

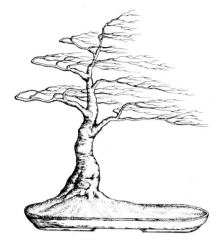

Figure 151: *Temporary effects of wind*

Even a connected root system, such as a clump or raft style, can be effective.

Thus we see that this style is very much determined by the arrangement of the branches and it is the relationship between trunk and branches that indicates the force of the particular wind acting on the tree. If all the major branches, as well as the smaller branchlets show the effects of wind, we feel as if the tree has been withstanding adverse conditions for most of its life and that it is growing in a perpetually windy area. If, on the other hand, only the smaller branches are showing the effects of wind and the trunk and main branches seem unaffected, the feeling is conveyed that the tree is in a fairly quiet environment and that the effects of wind are only temporary (see Figure 151).

STYLISTIC CONSIDERATIONS:

The basically triangular outline should still be observed and it is essential to have an apex in the design.

To guide you in the placement of branches, you may follow the usual "group of three" branches or layers that is used in other styles (i.e. side, back, opposite side). The procedure would be as is indicated in Figure 152.

However, as with most informal styles, it is not essential to follow this branch placement exactly. In this style, there is much scope for the individual artist's interpretation and the characteristics of the tree you are working with will determine how closely you can use this basic pattern.

Figure 152: *Branch placement*

One common error is that many trees styled as windswept lack depth. Because we think of all the branches going in one direction, it is easy to forget about back branches and a two-dimensional effect is the result. As we see in Figure 152, branches number 2 and 3 were originally on the windward side and by being swept around the back and the front of the trunk, depth is obtained as well as a very dramatic design. Windswept and literati styles are the two instances where it is acceptable to cross the trunk line with major branches. One of the main reasons for this is that both of these styles are fairly sparse and branches are few, so that confusion and messiness is less likely to result. However, it would still be better in most cases, not to cross the front of the trunk with a major branch until about half-way up the tree and if the crossing branch is lower, to make sure that the foliage doesn't begin until after the point where crossing occurs. This way, the view of the trunk and the main line will not be obscured too much.

Windswept style is perhaps one of the most difficult bonsai designs to create and while it is possible for the style to be extremely beautiful, it is quite easy to create a grotesque or pathetic effect. As we walk through the countryside, we often see trees that have been subjected to severe winds. Some of these are unbalanced and lead a very precarious existence. When we view such trees, we feel unsettled and imagine that the next strong wind will completely uproot the tree. The tree is passive and cannot offer much resistance to the harsh effects of nature.

Other windswept trees, however, display positive qualities of strength and endurance. When we view these trees we feel as though they have endured the hardships of wind and weather for many years and will continue to do so for many more years to come.

To create this effect of strength and beauty, we must first consider the surface roots of the tree. It is a great advantage to have strong surface roots radiating out from the sides of the windswept tree, as in the kind of environment that would foster such a style, roots would develop that grip the earth strongly and they would be exposed as the top-soil is gradually worn away by the wind. Never expose surface roots so that empty space may be seen between root and soil. This gives an unstable feeling and we imagine that the tree is in a precarious situation and may be uprooted at any time.

In all works of art, it is largely the elements of rhythm and repetition that impart the general mood and feeling of the work to the audience or viewer, and with a windswept styled bonsai, these elements are of especial importance. It is the repetition of branches tending in one direction that enables the viewer to feel the wind blowing through the tree. However, this aspect can be overdone and if there is no variety in the design, created by parts of the tree going against the wind, the result will be too artificial looking and also give the viewer a feeling of passivity. Much more interest and tension is created by a tree that fights the wind and makes an attempt to grow in the other direction as well.

Figure 153: *Small branches on windward side*

Figure 154: *Literati windswept*

Some windswept designs may be completely bare of branches on the windward side but such trees would look better if the trunk was curved or angular, rather than straight. This way, the trunk can provide the variety by growing into the wind at some points (see Figure 146).

Other ways of providing variety would be to have small stubborn branches that are still managing to grow on the windward side (see Figure 153), or to have jins where branches have been broken off and weathered by the wind (Figures 144 & 156), or to sweep branches around from the windward side (see Figure 152).

In windswept style, perhaps more than any other, the use of space is of extreme importance. It is almost used in the same way as we use masses of foliage in other styles. It balances the foliage that is there and suggests the wild, empty spaces and wind that sculpts these fascinating forms.

Associated with this idea of space, is the fact that the layers of foliage on the branches should be kept trimmed so that they do not become overly bushy and lush. Artistically, the streaming lines, that are the feature of the style, would be lost, and, practically speaking, it would be incongruent to have luxuriant growth in this kind of environment.

Many different moods may be created with this style. Some trees may be almost "literati" in feeling — being slender and delicate (see Figure 154), while others may be rough and rugged, with thick trunks and short heavy branches (see Figure 155). Others may be angular — having been trained by the Lingnan "grow and clip" method and simulating the way branches have been broken by the action of the wind and the line of the trunk or branch being re-established by a side-shoot.

Figure 155: *Rough and rugged with thick trunk and heavy branches*

Figure 156: *Smooth curves and driftwood*

On the other hand, some windswept styles may have smooth, soft curves that give one the impression of a tree with a more pliable wood that has been twirled and turned by the wind rather than being broken (see Figure 156). Often driftwood may be incorporated in this style, as the tree is weathered and polished by the rough winds and the abrasive particles of sand or grit. Driftwood effects, such as "jins" and "shari", are particularly suitable in windswept style.

THE CHOICE OF POT AND PROCEDURE FOR PLANTING AND POSITIONING:
Usually, a shallow container is chosen, unless the tree has a very thick trunk or the style is semi-cascade, and the pot may be of any shape. The use of a flattish rock, such as a slab of slate, is particularly effective, and if the tree is planted so that it is on a slight mound, this hints at the type of elevated areas where windswept trees would be seen. A strategically placed rock that is rough and rugged, but not overly large, can also add interest to the setting. Another point to watch is that a lush covering of moss is not planted over the entire soil surface as this would be out of character. A partial coverage of moss, interspersed with pebbles or sand is suitable, however, or, alternatively, a covering such as lichen, that grows in dryer, more rugged conditions may be a good choice.
The tree-to-pot relationship is very important, and it is here that we find two conventions in tree placement. The first way, which I tend to favour, is illustrated in the above diagrams. The basic triangular design is considered and the tree is placed so that this triangle is balanced over the pot. The second way, seen occasionally, is where the tree is planted in such a way that the greatest expanse of space is on the windward side. This, apparently, is to suggest the movement of wind, but personally, I find that such settings appear unbalanced. The balance in this style is always precarious, due, mainly, to its extreme nature, and, while balance is largely established by proper placement of space areas, it is, to my way of thinking, possible to impart the feeling of wind simply through the styling of the tree. Creating an unbalanced relationship between pot and tree can push this extreme style to the level of the grotesque.

TREE TYPE:
Two things should be considered when choosing a variety for windswept style. Firstly, the tree should have small leaves or short needles, or the capability to become smaller after being trained for a while. Secondly, the variety should be of the type that would possibly grow in that style. A soft, lush tree, for example, would not really be suitable, whereas most of the conifers would be a good choice.
As we have seen, it is difficult but not impossible to create a windswept style that has balance and beauty, and it is through the emphasis on strength, action and endurance — the positives — that this effect is achieved. All trees change as they grow older, largely through the effects of their particular environments. Symmetry turns to asymmetry — stereotyped form

turns to individuality. Not all achieve beauty, but each tells us its particular story. The windswept tree tells us its tale clearly and dramatically. We can almost feel the wind and hear its melancholy song, and, if there is balance and grace, we are left with the sense that there is much more to life than to merely survive.

BROOM STYLE

This bonsai style, as its name suggests, is somewhat like an upturned broom in its basic appearance and form. The trunk is vertically upright to about ⅓ to ½ of the overall height and it then divides into two or three main branches. These branches subsequently fork into sub-branches which, in turn, divide into even smaller branchlets and the distances between forks becomes progressively shorter as the twiglets become finer. The overall design, then, is of a multi-branched form with a soft, rounded top.

The Broom style is mostly suited to deciduous, broadleaf varieties such as Zelkovas (keyaki), Chinese Elms and Trident Maples and it is, in fact, the Zelkova that originally inspired this style (see Plate XX). It is, therefore, a favourite tree to use — particularly the "Maki" variety whose red young twigs are appreciated in winter as their density creates the effect of a soft, vermilion halo around the tree. One of the reasons why deciduous varieties are usually used for broom style is that they look so beautiful in winter when the gradual development of fine twigs on the tree can be fully enjoyed. When in leaf it is frequently only the trunk and the thicker branches that are visible, and this points to the importance of having an attractive trunk with a good, even taper and division into major branches as well as nice surface roots radiating out to the sides of the tree.

This design is a relatively new bonsai style in Japan, as it has only really been practiced since the turn of the century. At that time a certain bonsai grower in Japan who had, all his life, loved the natural "broom style" Zelkovas that were growing around him, decided that he would grow some as bonsai so that he could always have them nearby.

Due to the bushiness of this style, it is, perhaps, closer to the Western idea of potted tree than any other design in bonsai art — yet it is, nevertheless, one of the least tried of all styles, even in the West. The reason for this, I think, is because to produce a really first class broom style with a gradual taper and even distribution of branches, it does require some time and patience. This bonsai grower, at the turn of the century, decided that to produce broom style like the beautiful examples seen in Nature, one had to use the "Modelling Technique" — that is, to gradually build up the form over a period of time, starting off with young Zelkova seedlings. Following, is the procedure of how to develop broom style from young seedlings.

Firstly, when the seeds germinate, it is found that only about 5% of the total number of seedlings are perfect specimens suitable for this style, that is, with straight, even trunks rising from a good, radiating rootsystem — there must be no curves, kinks or knotted roots.

Figure 157: *Broom style*

Figure 158: *Development of broom style — leave top 3 buds*

When the seedlings are about three months old, they are taken out of the seed tray or seed box and potted up, singly, in containers to promote even development. At this time, tap roots are cut short and the surface roots are distributed evenly around the base of the young plant. When they reach the height of, say, 20.5–25.5 cm (8 to 10 inches) they can be tied to a bamboo stick or a small stake to develop a perfectly straight line in the trunk.

Next potting season the trees are rootpruned and repotted into shallow training containers. They are also top-trimmed or "headed" — leaving only the top three buds on the plant (see Figure 158).

These are preferably situated on different levels and are directed in different areas — e.g. one fairly vertical but tending to the left, one almost vertical but tending to the right and one more toward the back for depth. These three buds will develop into the major branches on the tree. In order to allow the surface roots to thicken more rapidly — cover them with soil for about five or six years, or, at least, while the basic training procedure of the plant is being undertaken.

The next pruning job comes when these three major branches are shortened. Their length should be from about a half to about the whole of the distance from the base of the tree to the first branches (see Figure 159), however, remember that untrimmed branches thicken more rapidly, so make the cut when thickness is adequate. From then on, continue nipping to create forks and work towards distances between forks gradually becoming smaller. As the style is developing, some branches may need wiring to refine the shape and some branchlets or buds will have to be removed or rubbed off to avoid overcrowding. The perfect broom style has no branches crossing or conflicting with any other.

Figure 159: *Next trimming stage in development of broom style*

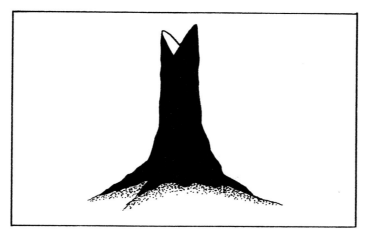

Figure 160: *"V"-shaped cut*

While the ideal method of producing a broom style is to start from seed, some growers may prefer to work from nursery stock or collected trees. It is not easy to find good material for this style — but it is not impossible — and, if the grower knows what features he is looking for, eventually a good specimen may be located.

There is a way, though, of creating Broom style from not-so-perfect nursery stock — providing the lower trunk and surface roots are attractive and the tree is a variety that will send out new shoots from old wood when cut back severely. It is a technique, however, that still requires some patience to develop a new head of branches to work with. In late-winter, early spring, before the new buds begin to open on the tree, it is cut down to a height, approximately three times the diameter of the trunk. This will give good proportions to the tree. The cut is usually made in an uneven "V" shape (see Figure 160), so that a more even gradation from trunk to new branches may be formed. If the trunk has an exceptionally wide diameter, some of the heartwood may be carved out to facilitate healing and to minimize the effect of a stub. This carving process is best done in the dormant period when sap is not flowing in the tree. Be careful, also, not to damage any of the cambium layer, as healing proceeds from there.

A helpful point is the idea of tying around the top of the cut trunk with string, tape or twine. This discourages the formation of heavy callus tissue in the form of bulges as the branches develop around the cut edge. Once the growth balance in the tree has been restored and shoots are not forming so rapidly, the binding may be removed without risk of bulges occurring. Another point to watch is that suckers or water sprouts don't form, and, if they do, to remove them immediately. These occur, frequently, when a tree has been heavily cut back and they are, basically, a safety valve for the tree. Since there should be a balance between above and below ground growth, these vigorous, quick growing suckers work to rapidly produce regrowth — though they seriously drain the main stem of nutriments — leading, usually, to its death. This fact also points to the importance of rootpruning the tree at the same time as the top is cut. Thus, the tree's balance is retained as much as possible.

The shoots that develop should be pinched often, so that they develop evenly and slowly, however, it may be decided that one, two or three branches should be left, initially, without trimming for a season or two so that they begin to thicken and thus develop a more even gradation from the base to these first major branches on the tree. The more rapid growth of these branches also has the effect of helping the wound to heal. The major one or two branches should be chosen at the front of the cut. If a third is used, it can extend from the back, to give depth. From this point on, the procedure for training is the same as for development from seed. Remember, though, that if cut scars are made to face inward, new growth will extend outward and fewer branches will conflict with the line of another.

Yet another point to remember, particularly with training from nursery stock, is that faster growth will be obtained if the tree is grown in a large container with a nutritious but well-draining soil. When the time comes for slower, more controlled growth, however, a smaller container would be a better choice.

Whichever way you decide to develop and train your broom style, it can be a most beautiful tree design. The diffuse nature of the branching arrangement, leading your eye upward and then out into a mass of radiating branches and twigs, imparts a feeling of softness and delicacy to the viewer — often interestingly counterpointed with the strength and dominance of a massive trunk.

The over-riding feeling, though, is one of tranquillity as the tree forms a gradual but definite link between earth and air. The surface roots, radiating from the base, lead us out of the ground to follow the main trunk line. We are then lead into a branching system that becomes ever finer until it almost disappears into the atmosphere with the soft halo of minute twigs, forming a hazy cloud and intimately uniting tree with air.

HORAI STYLE

Horai style is perhaps the most exaggerated of all bonsai designs and poor examples of it have resulted in quite a few people making up their minds that bonsai is a cruel and ugly art. Basically, Horai style is any tree that has very elaborate curves or angles and these can be made either artistically or almost by "formula", without much thought or feeling.

In all art forms, the commercial or popular art side is often responsible for mass produced products and bonsai is no exception so that in the past many examples were seen that had grotesque and overly exaggerated curves that were regularly spaced out on the tree like a zig-zag pattern and without any depth or perspective (see Figure 161).

Figure 161: *Unattractive horai style*

Because such designs could be made quickly and by people who were not particularly artistic, this style very much suited the commercial bonsai growers and the wide distribution of these trees helped to spread the idea that all bonsai were like that.

Another type of horai style that came into vogue, particularly at the end of the Ch'ing dynasty in China, was the shaping of the tree's trunks in the formation of characters (see Chapter 1 Figure 1). Such work requires time and dexterity, however, it is more gimmicky than artistic and because it no longer suggests a tree-like form, this style should be regarded more as an interesting potted tree than as a bonsai.

The fault here, though, is with the style as it is put into practice and not with the basic idea or techniques involved. In Nature, it is possible to find Horai style. On windy hills where there is hardly any life to break the line between sky and land, a few stunted trees are found that have managed to survive. Often there are some dead limbs and areas where bark has been ripped or worn away and these are polished smooth and silvery-grey by the wind-borne sand and grit. Sometimes the trees have a distinct windswept character — but this is not essential — and foliage may be dense or sparse — whichever best complements the curves and angles in the trunk. There is a feeling of dignity imparted as we view these strange but impressive trees silhouetted against the sky. Such trees found in Nature are superb, however, it is possible to produce similar effects artificially and the techniques involved will be discussed below.

The history of this style is quite interesting. Firstly, the design is much favoured in China, due to its rugged and dramatic character. Also, like all Chinese styling of trees, there are underlying stories or ideas involved. Particularly when this style is made from a pine with scaly bark, the design is seen as a dragon flying up through the clouds. The trunk twists and turns like the body of the dragon with some jins, perhaps, suggesting spines and claws, while the well-clipped but often dense foliage layers are like the clouds that mysteriously hide parts of the dragon from view (see Figure 162).

Figure 162: *Horai style pine*

The fact that the curves in horai style are often smooth and yet the environment from which the tree comes is harsh, also tells us something. In some cases trees are rigid and unyielding and when strong winds blow they are broken off. These trees ultimately have sharp angles if they continue to grow and in bonsai art we design such trees by the "clip and grow" method. Other trees, however, are more pliable and they bend without breaking. Smooth curves are the result and the Chinese liken this to other natural effects such as the process of a rough sea pounding on a cliff-face. Gradually, through actions that are harsh and rough, the rock is worn down to smooth sand.

In Japan, interestingly enough, the style was originated by commercial growers from a small village called Honai in Echigo Province, North-west Japan[2]. This village was developed on fertile ground near a castle town during the Tokugawa Period (1603–1867). The area for growing was divided into 150 acres of flat land where rice was cultivated and 130 acres of hillside land with red clay soil. This latter part was virtually unused for many years, as rice provided the main income for the village. This was not without problems, however, as the frequent floods that occured, continually destroyed many crops. Then, about 200 years ago, some of the farmers travelled to Edo (present day Tokyo) and learned bonsai techniques there. On returning home, the 130 acres on the hill was developed for cultivation of trees for bonsai and 75 acres was specifically for trees being shaped in the Honai or Horai style. By using the hill for bonsai cultivation an income was provided for the village that was unaffected by the floods. Incidentally, the style was sometimes called Horai as Mt. Horai is a legendary mountain island of Perpetual Youth and the name was similar to that of their village. These growers mainly used Japanese White Pine for this shaping technique.

The basic method for producing Horai Style is not difficult but it may be a little time consuming. First of all, conifers are generally used for these designs — particularly pines and junipers — as they are the varieties that would survive in an extremely harsh and windy environment. Also, practically speaking, they are reasonably pliable and thus more able to withstand severe bending. Leggy young pines about a foot or so in height are ideal and by bending the trunks so drastically, the height of these trees is effectively reduced and branches are brought lower down to the ground. This shaping technique is, therefore, very useful for pines that have been neglected in their very early stage of development and consequently haven't developed lower branching.

A couple more points need mentioning before the method for shaping is discussed. Firstly, it is advisable to train the trees in the ground. If you can't, then a large container will suffice, however, the process of trunk development will take considerably longer. The other point is that before shaping the tree, allow the soil around the roots to become dryish, as this will reduce the chances of cracking the tree when you are bending it.

The Chinese shaping technique of "string and stick" (see Chapter 2), is used to create Horai Style. In the first year, the major curves at the base of the trunk are established. The tree is wound around the sticks in whatever design you wish and attached with string at the necessary points (see also Figure 57 in Chapter 2). The main secret in creating an artistic Horai style is to achieve depth and variety in the design. Therefore, take special care to vary the distances between major curves or angles and to shape the trunk in three dimensions. In the second year the tree is lifted, rootpruned and replaced in the ground. Generally, at this time, the string and sticks from the previous year's training may be removed and the sticks repositioned to continue the process further. The next step is usually to bend down the top part that is growing vigorously and to begin the shaping of major branches. In the third year, the apex may be established and shaping is refined. Once more, the tree is rootpruned. Finally, a fourth year may be required if you want more height in your tree or if more refinement is needed. By this stage, the first year's shaping at the base of the trunk should be forming a knobbly and gnarled appearance.

Figure 163: *Procedure for shaping horai style*

Because most Horai style trees have elaborate curves and fairly thick trunks, medium to deep, massive containers are the most suitable. Rectangular, oval, square or round pots may be used but they are better unglazed and without fancy designs. If there are jins or shari on the tree, a pot with an inset may be chosen as this complements the peeled bark effects (it is almost as if some bark was peeled from the pot).

Horai style is definitely exaggerated and extreme in bonsai art. If made with artistry and an eye for design, though, it can be indeed impressive and particularly beautiful in its variety of forms and textures.

EXPOSED ROOT STYLE

This style can take many forms but in all cases what were once the roots of the tree are now forming part of the trunk and are exposed high into the air — usually up to half or two-thirds of the total tree height. The exposed roots may be left in their natural state, they may be trained into curves or they may be plaited, twisted or looped. Generally conifers are chosen as they would be more likely to be in the areas where this style may occur naturally. Apart from this, they have reasonably flexible roots that would be suitable if shaping was intended. This, however, doesn't rule out the use of other types of trees and good results have come from using Casuarinas (an Australian native) and Ficus varieties.

Firstly, let us consider the idea of plaiting or twisting the tree's roots. This type of exposed root style is perhaps the most acceptable due to the fact that the roots do become like part of the trunk. When the tree is at an early age, the major roots are braided or twisted as you wish, bound together with string or rags and then planted up to the original soil level for a year or two. The roots have to be covered if you wish them to thicken and graft together. Check the tree's progress each year at repotting time and when they have thickened enough and they have merged together, the soil level may be lowered so that the plaited roots may be exposed. These should now look like a continuation of the trunk line but should give added character to your tree because of their gnarled and knotted appearance. As time goes on, the original braiding design will be lost and an entirely natural effect will result. Bark will also grow on the exposed root area so that the junction between what was root and what was trunk will completely disappear.

Figure 164: *Plaited or twisted roots*

The other type of design that leaves the exposed roots in their natural formation, however, is more controversial. This overly exaggerated style is no longer so popular and indeed, many examples are quite bizarre. The style may be viewed in two ways. Firstly, it may be considered as natural, and illustrative of trees that come from areas with erosive soil conditions such as a tree growing near a waterfall or by the side of a river where torrential floods gradually expose the rootsystem. The second way of viewing the style is to say that it is a totally unnatural design and to develop it simply as an artistic expression using tree material. Here, the aim is to impart an almost "other-worldly" atmosphere — to produce a style that is fanciful and unnatural but none-the-less beautiful. My own view is that a combination of both ideas is best. I do believe that the style does occur in Nature, but that if we are going to portray it we should be careful to avoid the appearance of a pathetic or overly strange tree. At all times, the positive aspects of strength, endurance and beauty should be imparted to the viewer and much of this depends on the shaping of branches and foliage layers. They should balance and complement the arrangement of roots so that the top part never appears as if it was merely added to the exposed root system. The line of the trunk and the line of the roots should also blend together without a distinct junction point. Any style or direction of trunk may be used but generally slanting or semi-cascade designs are particularly suitable. Sometimes a windswept arrangement of the branches may be a good choice.

Figure 165: *Exposed root style*

As far as pots are concerned, deepish containers similar to the type for cascade styles are usually used. They are often more appropriate if unglazed and not too fancy as the tree itself is a particularly elaborate design.

The methods for producing Exposed Root style are not hard, but like "Root over Rock", it may take some time and patience before results are seen. There are a couple of different techniques but basically the procedure is similar for both.

The first method is as follows: Take a batch of year old seedlings, cut their taproots and replant them in a sandy soil mixture. As the mortality rate is fairly high at each stage of the procedure, it is a good idea to start off with quite a few plants. The following spring, the decision is made as to which of the roots you wish to train and all the others are removed. The roots that have remained are then stretched out and bound to a support. As the roots grow at different rates, however, each one may need to be staked separately so that sagging doesn't result. At this stage the tree is planted so that only the root tips are covered with soil. Each year the tree is raised up higher as the roots grow longer, and longer stakes are needed for support. When enough height is attained the procedure is stopped and as the exposed roots thicken and harden, the supports may be removed.

A second method is to use a long tube for the training procedure. The tube should be split lengthwise and after the tree has been planted in it with the base of the trunk at the top of the tube, it should be tied together and firmly planted in a pot or the ground. The soil used should be reasonably sandy to encourage more rapid root growth. If most of the tube is exposed, make sure it is anchored firmly as roots need stable conditions to develop. Generally the roots grow quite quickly down the tube to reach the greater amount of moisture and nourishment below. The advantages of this method over the first is that because the roots are protected, they develop in thickness and maturity more rapidly and, health-wise, there is less chance of losing the tree through it drying out too quickly. Also, the tube is easier to keep in an upright position than roots bound to stakes. Disadvantages, though, are firstly that the length of the tube determines the length of exposed root being developed and it may be difficult to obtain extremely long tubes and, secondly, that when the roots are suddenly exposed they will be in a tender condition and the tree may suffer some shock. This last disadvantage, though, could be overcome by periodically cutting sections from the top of the pipe, thus gradually exposing more of the rootsystem. Also, an alternative to the tube could be a tall narrow box made up of horizontal slats. This would make it easy to remove slats gradually from the top as the rootsystem grows longer. As the tube or box is shortened, extra support may be needed by the exposed roots, so they may have to be bound to stakes. Also, after the tube has been removed, support with stakes may still be necessary for a year or so.

Plate XXVI A & B: *Sargent Juniper group planted on slate,* Juniperus chinensis *'Sargentii' height of main tree: 27 cm, trees grown from cuttings struck in 1972 & 1976, group created in 1981.*
XXV1 A: photographed in 1981 **XXV1 B:** *photographed in 1983.*

Plate XXVII: *Dwarf Japanese Juniper, Juniperus procumbens 'Nana', clinging to the rock style, Gifu rock from Japan, height of main rock: 45 cm, Japanese ceramic suiban (i.e. ''Water Tray''), trees grown from cuttings struck in 1979, rock setting created in 1982, photograph taken in 1983*

Whichever method you use to develop your exposed root style, it is a good idea, while the tree is in the initial training period, to allow the top growth to elongate without trimming until the shoots are about two to three inches in length. After they have been trimmed, repeat the process. If the top growth is allowed to grow without too frequent trimming, the shoots thicken more rapidly and this growth spurt is reflected in the rootsystem. Results are, therefore, obtained more rapidly. These procedures do take time, however, and I would say three years would be the minimum training period.

PLAITED OR TWISTED TRUNK STYLE

The techniques for producing the Plaited trunk style — called Pien-tshu in China — can create beautiful gnarled and aged effects in the trunk designs of trees. The trunks of long-stemmed, pliable trees are twisted or plaited in much the same way as roots are braided in the plaited root style discussed above (see Plate XXI).

You may use two or more trees, plant them as close together as possible and then tie them at ground level with string to hold them firm. The plaiting or twisting process should then begin. If the trunks are twisted, the effect can be created of a tree whose trunk has been twirled and whipped about by the wind (see Figure 166).

Figure 166: *Twisted trunk style*

As the trunks graft together, one or two may be partially stripped of bark to increase the appearance of a tree found on a windswept hill. It will also highlight the twisting texture of the trunk. If you are working with three trees, the ordinary braiding procedure may be used and if there are four trees, two opposite trunks may be crossed over, followed by the other two. As branches are reached, these are carefully brought through as the trunks are plaited. There is no need to remove any bark where the trunks touch as they will graft together without much trouble. The twisting or braiding, however, should be done firmly and the trunks tied together with string at the top. If you plant the tree in the ground or a large container, the thickening and grafting processes will be hastened considerably and as time passes, the original braiding or twisting pattern will disappear leaving a gnarled, aged appearance.

By using the plaited or twisted trunk technique, long, leggy trees with few lower branches can be combined to make a single tree with a thick trunk and instantaneously there will be more branches to work with and they will be situated lower down on the trunk.

Figure 167: *Octopus style*

OCTOPUS STYLE

This is a style that is not often seen in bonsai collections and this is perhaps due to its highly elaborate appearance. Basically it is like a clump style at the end of a short trunk. The arrangement of the branches is the main feature of the style and these are long and often feature curves or loops as they reach out like tentacles of an octopus.

WEEPING STYLE

This is a style that is determined by the branch arrangement in the tree and not by the trunk design. This means that providing the branches are in a weeping form, the trunk may be in the design of any of the five basic styles. One important point as far as variety is concerned is that flowers or foliage that weep do not constitute weeping style. The formation of the branches must be the basis of the design (see Figures 168 & 169).

Another important point to consider is that branches curving downward usually impart a feeling of softness to the viewer and can also suggest weakness or depression. To counter this effect the trunk should appear strong and stable and the branches should form half circles with their bases initially growing in an upward direction before weeping downward.

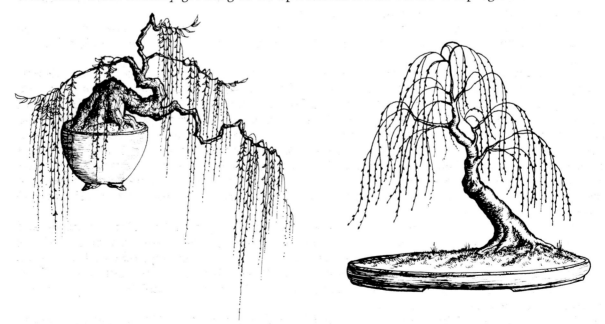

Figures 168 & 169: *Weeping style*

LITERATI STYLE

The stark beauty of some of the literati trees is hard to describe. Each has its peculiar appeal to the beholder. To a Chinese, each tree represents a symbolical story. In fact, many of us cannot create bonsai mainly because of this lack of the romantic. We do not have a story to tell while creating our bonsai. If you could tell one, your tree would repeat the story to those who look at it.
V. KORESHOFF.

Of all bonsai designs, literati style is the one that captures most succinctly and poetically, the Oriental view of Nature. It is purely Chinese and the original artists making bonsai in this style were from the so-called literati class.

What was this literati class of men? Firstly, in traditional China social advancement was by the law of succession so that the sons of wealthy merchants and landowners inherited their father's lot in life and positions of royalty were, likewise, passed down from father to son, unless the regime was overthrown. The peasants, similarly, had their predetermined lot in life, yet there existed two ways by which any person could attain a higher social position. One was to follow the road of Banditry. The leader of a band of robbers — if he was clever and strong enough and avoided being caught and executed — could progress to the position of general of an army. Such a life was exciting and romantic.

The other method of social advancement was suited to an entirely different sort of person. Annual Examinations were held by the Chinese Government and those who passed were given high positions in the Confucian Bureaucratic system, even if their origins were low in the social scale. Even in the days of the first Han Emperor (206 B.C. — A.D.220), the government asked provincial officers to find and send to the capital, men who had high intellectual and artistic ability, to work in the governmental system. Those who wished to sit for the Annual Examinations were men who were interested in Literature, History, Philosophy and the Arts, and were adept at intellectual gymnastics. If they passed they were called "Literati" (or "wen-jen") — "Men of Books".

These literati men led a frugal and ascetic life, spending their time studying, debating with other learned men, practicing calligraphy and painting landscapes. In time they turned their hands to sculpting and shaping the potted trees that grew in the courtyards of governmental buildings and monasteries. Because they were an elite and learned class their taste was extreme and their art forms not suited to the general masses. The trees — both in the paintings and the bonsai — were infused with the qualities of their makers. They had an ascetic appearance, were tall and thin and had the abstract beauty of calligraphy while still suggesting the rugged and spectacular tree designs seen in nature.

The landscape paintings of the literati are of particular interest and, in a sense, they are the best way of learning what literati style is and will provide a stimulus and a guide for our shaping of trees.

"Literati Painting" ("wen-jen hua") or, the so-called "Southern School of Landscape Painting" was developed in the T'ang dynasty (618–906) by the poet-painter Wang Wei (d. 759). This school of painting represented the ideal of the scholar-painter who sought to capture the spirit of Nature rather than mere outward representation or an immediately attractive and decorative surface beauty. With these paintings, the scene tells a story and the artist is revealed just as much as the landscape portrayed. As opposed to this artistic pursuit there was the "Northern School of Landscape Painting". Artists of this school were professional painters rather than amateur scholar-artists and their work was formulated and showy rather than the literati paintings that were made for personal satisfaction stemming from a private and intuitive creative feeling.

The Literati or Southern School of Landscape painting began in the T'ang dynasty and continued to develop as the centuries passed. Su Tung-po, the poet-calligrapher of the Northern Sung dynasty (960–1127) was a notable figure in the development of the Literati class of educated scholars and in the Ming dynasty (1368–1644) the critic and painter Tung Ch'i-ch'ang (d. 1636) codified the Southern School and Northern School to signify the two different trends of painting in China.

Finally, in the 17th and 18th centuries in the Ch'ing dynasty (1644–1911), interest in Literati painting grew even stronger and at this time literati paintings were becoming available in

Japan. There, they were known as "bunjin-ga" (literati painting) or "Nan-ga" (Southern Painting) and in the early 18th century, numerous Chinese paintings and Chinese block-printed books (e.g. "The Chieh-tzu yüan hua chuan" or "Mustard Seed Garden", a painting manual, published in 1679 in China and 1748 in Japan, that laid out the principles of Literati painting as well as providing illustrations of examples) were entering Japan through Nagasaki. It was also at this time that Japanese intellectuals were taking an eager interest in the culture and affairs of the outside world — particularly China — partly as a reaction against the Military Shogun's patronage of stereotyped and popular art forms and partly because, in the early Edo period, the Tokagawa Shogunate encouraged Confucian studies and the culturally privileged wealthy merchant class of the Kyōto-Osaka area had prepared the Japanese to understand the Chinese "Bunjin-ga".

Quite a difference existed in the reactions of the Japanese to Literati Art. Edo (present day Tokyo), being the domain of the military shoguns, who favoured more popular art forms, was not interested in the literati style. Kyōto, however, was the seat of the Emperor and many Ch'an Buddhist (Zen) priest-painters from China moved to Kyōto at that time. It was a city where learned men lived and artistic styles tended toward elegance and understatement.

Bonsai styling in the bunjin designs began around the nineteenth century and while the stimulus for Japanese bunjin bonsai and Chinese literati bonsai was the same (i.e. the Chinese literati landscape paintings) the Japanese shaped their trees with a slightly different flavour, stemming from their different cultural background.

As was mentioned at the start, literati style portrays and epitomizes the Oriental view of Nature and many beginners to the Art of Bonsai find it a style that is difficult to understand. Just when the basic styles and the guidelines to shaping have been learned, a tree is seen that seems to fall into no recognizable style and that appears to follow very few or none of the guidelines laid down. Branches don't begin ⅓ of the way up the trunk, but right up the top near the crown. Also, branches sometimes cross the trunk or other branches — something that is never done in other styles of bonsai.

Other beginners, perhaps, view literati style in a slightly different way. To them, the guidelines to shaping and the different styles seem artificial or too difficult to apply. Consequently, when a style is found with "no style" and, seemingly, no "rules", the enthusiast takes it as an excuse to "shape" without learning or paying attention to any guidelines at all. Because there are few branches, literati is thought to be a "simple" style, though it is soon found that simplicity with balance and beauty is one of the most difficult qualities to attain.

It is really only when one has learned the rules or guidelines, practiced them and realized WHY they are suggested, that one can successfully make literati style because if the reasons for their existence are understood, you can make compromises with the individual tree you are working with. Literati style doesn't so much "break" rules — but it "bends" them in a way that is a little more extreme and less "fussy" than other styles. Thus, once you have

Figure 170: *Traditional literati style*

progressed beyond basic knowledge of the guidelines, you are restricted only by the characteristics of the tree you are working with and your own imagination.

Literati style, however, does have certain characteristics that may be regarded as guidelines. Firstly, it is a single tree and the most important aspect of the style is the trunk — its quality and its line. Therefore, when looking for suitable trees for shaping into this style, regard the trunk line as the main feature and study this characteristic first. The trunk may be straight, curved or angular, but it must taper and if it is not straight, the line must move in three dimensions to give depth to the design. One half to three-quarters or more of the trunk should be bare of branches and the branches themselves should be few in number and usually short in proportion to the height of the tree. Furthermore, they should be sparsely greened, as an over abundance of foliage would not suit the stark beauty of this style. The branches may cross the trunk line or other branches, if necessary, and because of the simplicity of the style this does not become confusing and may create a point of interest and artistic tension in the design. Another important point is that Literati should be asymmetrical in form.

The effect of this style, then, is of a tall, elegant and slender tree, and consequently, the tree must be aged and have the texture of old bark to avoid the appearance of a sapling (see Plate XXII). If you are using an old tree to shape your literati style, then you have the advantage of aged characteristics immediately, however you will have to use the sculptural method of shaping and generally, you have to work with the line and angles already existing within the form of the tree. If, on the other hand, you start with a younger plant, you will have to wait for the tree to develop bark and maturity, however, the trunk is still pliable and you may then model it to the line and curves you desire.

The usual pot used for literati style is an understated shallow to medium depth container that is either round, square, hexagonal, octagonal (or any other pot with equal length sides). The reason for this choice is that our eye is not confused at the base of the tree, but moves straight from the centre of the small pot, up the trunk line. The main feature of the style is, in this way, emphasized and fully appreciated.

Varieties suitable for literati style are generally conifers e.g. pines, junipers, cedars, as they are more suited to a rugged, austere appearance. If broadleaf varieties are used, make sure they have small leaves, e.g. chinese elm, fukien tea or the ability to reduce in size through bonsai techniques e.g. some figs. A lush, opulent appearance would be incongruent with this style.

As time passed, the Art of Bonsai became a more widely practiced hobby, and, also, with the advent of printing, "learning" became more easily available to a greater proportion of the population. More people began to paint and to make bonsai in the literati style. From this, we find that variations resulted, due to differences in the character and style of the makers, and secondly, because some styles, created by the less artistic, were made, that somewhat degraded the literati ideal, and catered to the popular taste of the majority.

Some of the variations were quite beautiful and artistic. Some were made with very gnarled trunks and with many jins and, perhaps part of the trunk made up of silvery-grey driftwood.

Figure 171: *Literati with gnarled trunk, jins and driftwood*

Figure 172: *Angular literati style*

Others had exaggerated curves with strong lines and radical changes in direction that expressed the abstract beauty of calligraphy.

There was another style of literati that was quite beautiful. This was the style with the bowed head. A sharp angle at the top of the tree provides the "apex" point of the design and the foliage was below this point at the end of the trunk line. This design stemmed from the idea that man was not equal to God and the bowed head on the tree symbolized a feeling of humility.

Figure 173: *Literati with bowed head*

Another possibility with literati style is a design that involves two directions. This is suitable for windswept style as well. Here we see the trunk moving in a certain direction and then dramatically reversing its direction so that it looks back on itself. Either the "bowed head" design or the more usual situation where the apex is seen at the top of the tree, may be used.

Yet another variation was literati in cascade style, and, finally two-tree settings and even groups were made from trees with literati style designs.

Figures 174 & 175: *Cascade literati*

Figure 176: *Two tree setting — literati*

Other styles, however, were intermediate between the classical literati and other bonsai styles. Some were pseudo-literati, with branches starting about half the way up the trunk, with more branches and the branches themselves being longer and more profusely covered with foliage. Others made literati that were overly exaggerated — so-called "Horai style" — and made without artistic feeling and lacking in depth or variation of design.

The classical literati style, as practiced by the scholar-painters of China is definitely exaggerated but it is exaggerated with an eye for balance and beauty and within the bounds of suggesting a tree-like form. It expresses the Oriental view of the world in that the aim is to capture the spirit of the scene portrayed, using elements of line and space.

All bonsai styles are artificial in the sense that all styles of writing are. Yet literati, like poetry, seems more heightened, more stylized. It is these qualities though, that allow so much to be said with so little. Each tree has its story to tell and each awakens a different feeling within the viewer. The individuality of the artist is thus revealed as is the essential spirit and beauty of Nature.

Figure 177: *Group setting — literati*

Multiple Trunks from a Single Rootsystem

In these bonsai styles, where many trunks are joined to the one root-system, the basic guidelines to designing group settings of individual trees also apply. However, there are some definite advantages of these styles over groups. Firstly, they are easier to care for in terms of rootpruning and repotting and the "trees" grow at a uniform rate and they require the same conditions for growing. They also have the same characteristics such as autumn colour, bark texture etc., and they colour simultaneously in autumn and in spring they send out new buds at the same time. Their disadvantage, though, is that there is little choice of positioning of trunks and depth and clarity of design may be difficult to obtain in some cases. This will be discussed in more detail further on.

Another point to remember with all these styles — and it applies to group settings as well — is that it is the overall design that is of utmost importance. One should carefully consider the relationship that is formed between the "trees". No one tree should be perfectly balanced in itself — but should depend upon the others in such a way that the total design is balanced.

There are many variations to the style of "Multiple Trunks from a Single Rootsystem". These are:
1. Twin-trunk style
2. Clump style
3. Stump or Turtle-back style
4. Straight line or Raft style
5. Sinuous style.

These will now be discussed individually and in detail, beginning with the Twin-trunk style.

TWIN-TRUNK STYLE

When looking for material to shape into this style, either a natural twin-trunk tree may be chosen or else one with a very low branch that can be trained into the position of second trunk. The division between the two trunks, however, should be at ground level or very close to the base of the tree and the shape of this connection should be in an acute angle, somewhat like the form of a "V". Avoid rounded curves or "U" shapes between the two trunks as these look unnatural and tend to dissociate the two elements of the design. Another point to keep in mind when choosing your tree is that this style looks particularly good if surface roots spread out well from the base on either side as this, again, is a binding factor between the two trunks.

Another way of creating a twin-trunk style is to graft together at the base, two separate trees. This idea is good if two similar shaped trees of the same variety are obtained that have attractive features such as trunk and surface roots, but which have a one-sided branching arrangement.

Figure 178: *Twin trunk with same line*

As far as the actual trunks are concerned, it is important that the thickness and heights be different and that the tallest is the thickest. If you like, a rough guide to the ratio between the heights can be worked out according to the relative thickness of the trunks. This means that if the girth of one tree is 5 cm (two inches) and the girth of the other is 2.5 cm (one inch), then the thicker tree can be, say 50 cm (20 inches) high and the thinner one 25 cm (10 inches). The smaller tree is thus a scaled down version of the bigger one.

Usually, the shapes of the two trunks follow in the same general line (see Figure 178) however, if this guideline is varied either the bases or the apexes must have the same direction.

These latter variations, however, can lead to some very interesting tree designs as is illustrated below.

Figure 179: *Twin-trunk with bases in same direction*

Figure 180: *Twin-trunk with apexes in same direction*

Now we come to the branching arrangement for this style. Even though there are two trunks, each one should complement the other so that the overall design is a triangle — just as would be seen in a single-tree style. This is especially true when the two trunks are very close together.

When the trunks follow closely in the same direction and line, the guidelines for the positioning of branching is very much the same as for a single tree. Thus, a branch on one trunk should not be on the same level as a branch on the other trunk, and there should be no limbs crossing the trunk of the other tree, or growing directly towards it. When looking down on the bonsai then, branches should extend out like spokes of a wheel, as if the two trunks were one.

The front view, as with single trunk bonsai styles, shouldn't have any heavy branches extending out toward the viewer or greatly blocking the view of the trunk line. Small branches or tufts of foliage, however, may cross the front occasionally so that enough of the trunk is seen for us to be able to follow and appreciate its line but our imagination is consequently aroused as we are not shown all at once. Remember, though, that the first third of the total height is generally completely free of branches and the next third is mostly clear.

One guideline, however, that should be adhered to is that the lowest branch of the style should be on the smaller tree. Another critical branch in this style is the first branch on the larger trunk that faces in the direction of the smaller one. This one should not be situated immediately over the apex of the other tree, as in nature, the smaller tree would either grow outward so that it could obtain more light, or perish. Therefore, it is important to leave enough space between the lower apex and this branch and to make the length of the branch reasonably short. A good idea may be to position the first one on that side slightly forward or back, so that it is not situated immediately over the other tree.

When positioning your twin-trunk style bonsai in the pot make sure that the two trunks are slightly diagonally placed and not exactly in line when you view the setting from the side. It doesn't matter which trunk is in the forward position, as either way will create more depth in the design. The pot is usually oval or rectangular and from shallow to medium depth.

A twin-trunk bonsai, if well-designed, can be most beautiful and, in the oriental countries, it is often referred to in terms of relationships between people. If one tree is large and the other quite small, it is called "Mother and Son" style.

Figure 181: *Mother and son style*

If the difference between the tree sizes is not so great it is sometimes looked upon as a man and woman living side by side or, in some cases the two trees may be looked upon as the relationship that forms between an old and wise literati master and his scholar-apprentice. No matter what relationship you may see in this style, it definitely imparts to the viewer a feeling of warmth and companionship.

CLUMP STYLE

A clump style bonsai is characterized by having three or more odd numbers of trunks growing from a central point. In nature, this design may occur if a cone has fallen from a tree with most of the seeds still in it and if they subsequently germinate. As the trees grow they eventually graft together till they are completely joined at the base. Likewise, this style may be formed by suckers growing out from around the base of a larger tree. With some trees, suckers emerge after the original tree has undergone some injury or has been cut back severely. With others, though, such as Flowering Quince, it is their natural habit of growth.

Clump styles may be collected from Nature if you come across examples like those mentioned above or you may artificially produce one if you prune back a tree severely and, by disrupting the balance of supply and demand between the rootsystem and the top, thereby induce suckers to form. Care will have to be taken, though, that you do not kill the original tree as suckers are extremely vigorous and tend to drain the older tree of nutriments. It is best to undertake this procedure with the tree planted in a large container or box, or in the ground.

Another way of producing a clump style would be to take an air-layer of portion of a tree that has a whorled branch distribution.

It is also possible to form a clump style by planting some trees close together and binding them at the base. As they grow they will graft together.

As with the twin-trunk style, the division of the trunks should be close to the base and preferably with the joins between the trunks in acute angles. Each trunk should also be visible and not crossing the line of another trunk when viewed from the front and, if possible, from the side as well. Also, the distances between the trunks should be varied and, while the basal positions cannot be modified, the top parts of the trunks may be shaped to accentuate variation in distances.

Like group settings, the tallest trunk should be the thickest and the others graded down so that the thinnest trunk is also the shortest. It is important that the heights are different and that the overall outline is triangular or dome-like. Remember that if you are cutting down the trunks to produce good proportions, the cut scars should face inward. This way, new growth will tend to develop outward and won't be so inclined to cross another trunk. Another very important design aspect is that it shouldn't be symmetrical and fan-shaped, but asymmetrical and three-dimensional for depth. If you have only three trunks in the design, make sure that the middle trunk is either the tallest or the shortest, otherwise the design appears to be artificial.

Figure 182: *Clump style*

The type of pot for this style can be oval or rectangular and shallow, or else round, square, hexagonal, or any other shape with sides of equal length and shallow or medium in depth.

Almost any variety is suitable for clump style, however, it is particularly suited to trees like Japanese Flowering Quince, Azaleas and Maples. It creates the feeling of a quiet grove and has a soft, lyrical quality about it.

STUMP OR TURTLE-BACK STYLE
This style is similar to the clump design described above, but instead of having the trunks stem from a well-spread surface root system, and close to the ground, they stem from a dome shaped section, at the base of the trunks, that somewhat resembles a turtle shell. The Trident Maples in Japan, occasionally develop this effect naturally. Surface roots sometimes merge and bulge out as they grow, thus forming the turtle back shape. The style could also originate from a tree that has been broken away to a stump and that develops shoots which subsequently form into new trunks.

To create this style you will have to hunt for suitable nursery stock or collected stock. Many of the Australian Native varieties, such as Banksias and Gums, have a so-called ligno-tuber that is a bulbous form at ground level on the tree. This contains undifferentiated cells that can grow a new top or new rootsystem, as is required. This is a very good characteristic in the Australian climate where bushfires and drought can simultaneously destroy both parts and only the ligno-tuber is left to form regrowth. Trees with this ligno-tuber would form the turtle-back or stump style, however, in the Japanese version of the style, the stump is a hemisphere. This, unfortunately, cannot be done with the Australian native examples as the ligno-tuber is often reasonably spherical and does not survive being buried below its original soil level.

Sometimes you may find a tree with a good base for this style but with an unattractive or otherwise unsuitable top. Or, perhaps, it may not be a variety that will send up new shoots from the base to form additional trunks. If this is the case, consider that grafting new or extra limbs into the hemispherical base may create a good tree design with the added advantage of allowing you to "handpick" compatible trunk-lines.

One easy way of grafting the new "trunks" onto a flattish type of base is to drill holes right through the base at the appropriate places and then thread young plants of the same variety as the base through each hole. As they grow in diameter, the base and young plants will graft together.

Figure 183: *Stump or turtle back style*

RAFT AND SINUOUS STYLE

Most trees spend their entire life in one spot. The seed germinates and from then on the viewpoint on the World is unaltered, save for the changing apparel of the seasons.

The Raft or sinuous style of tree has a different character. Not being content to stay solely in the position of germination, he inquisitively wanders here and there, quietly exploring and observing the world.

The Raft and sinuous styles are characterized by a single trunk that is growing along the ground, with three or more odd number of trunks rising from it. In Raft style, the trunk along the ground is perfectly straight, and illustrates a tree in nature that has been blown over by the wind, taken root and had its branches on the new, upward side continue growth as new trunks. The style could also be formed in Nature, where a low side branch has been forced down to the ground by heavy snows, again has taken root, and the branchlets on it forming into trees on their own right.

Sinuous style is very similar, however the trunk going along the ground may be curved and this depicts the case where a travelling surface root has meandered along the ground and the suckers have developed into new trees.

One advantage of this style in bonsai training is that trees with one-sided branching may be used, by laying down the side, without branches, on the ground.

There are many ways of producing a raft or sinuous style. Perhaps you may be lucky enough to find an example in nature that has been produced in one of the above ways. If not, you will have to produce one artificially. One way is to force the subordinate trunk of a twin trunk tree down to the earth and then ground layer it. This creates a very impressive design as there will be one dominant tree giving weight and strength to the setting.

Figure 184: *Raft style with one dominant tree*

Figure 185: *Sinuous style*

The other way is to lay a single trunk tree down on its side and induce the formation of roots on the underside. Following is a description of the procedure. First of all, if there is a bow in the trunk, this should be placed so that it curves toward the back of the setting as this will add to the three-dimensional effect. Another idea that can create more depth in raft or sinuous style is to use branches going out horizontally from the laid down trunk, as well as those growing vertically upward from it. These horizontal branches may be ground layered for a certain distance and then trained upward to form trees. Some branches will be pliable enough to be bent, while others may need to be undercut with a wedge-shape wound (see Figure 187) in order to train them up vertically. This idea of undercutting is helpful also if you need another ''tree' to complete the design. In this case, the tip of the laid down tree could be raised up to form the additional tree.

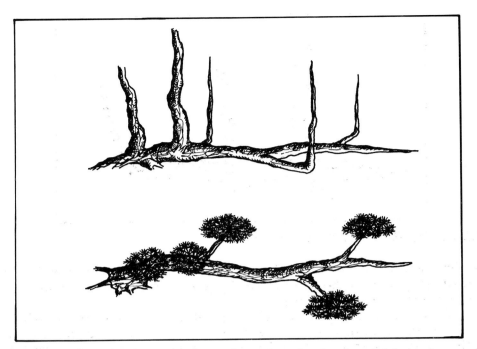

Figure 186: *Side and plan views of raft or sinuous, using horizontal branches*

Figure 187: *Undercutting to form extra "tree"*

To create a pleasing effect with these styles, at least five branches should exist on the tree, that can be subsequently trained into new trunks. These will probably need some wiring to place them in the desired positions but, if you wire two at a time, linking the wire with a few turns around the original trunk, you will conflict with the formation of the roots, the connecting trunk line may be strangled as it grows, and it will be difficult to remove the wire after the roots have developed. A better idea is to put a piece of heavy wire along the top side of the laid down trunk, attach it with string in a few places and then anchor the wires for each branch individually onto it. Another alternative would be to wire each branch individually with double wire looped once around the prostrate trunk — however, this would also interfere with root formation.

The technique for forming roots on the underside is reasonably easy. The bark is cut in the form of flaps on the underside of the trunk — especially under the position of strong branches. The actual cuts should be the width of about a third of the circumference of the trunk and be made in the direction from base to tip, as shown in Figure 188.

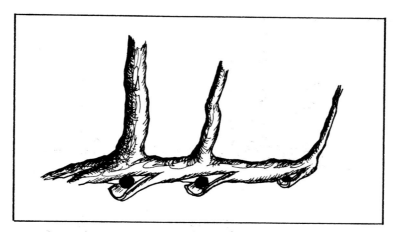

Figure 188: *Cutting flaps to induce root formation*

This means that the position where the flap of bark is joined is closer to the tip of the tree. A pebble or small piece of wood should be placed between the wood of the trunk and the flap of bark to stop the latter from healing over.

The raft or sinuous style-in-training should be planted in a training box in fairly sandy soil and the trunk should be buried but not so deeply otherwise roots will tend to form on the new trunks. Another point to keep in mind is that roots develop only on a stationary tree so tie the prostrate trunk firmly into the pot if it seems unstable. If the original rootsystem cannot be reduced more and if it is protruding out of the soil, it should be covered with soil that is reinforced on the sides with muck to stop it washing away.

It is better to choose quick-rooting varieties for creation of this style. However, if you want to develop a slower variety, such as pine, bottom heat would be advantageous. Normally, roots should form in one to one and a half years and at that time the bulk of the original rootsystem may be removed and the laid down trunk should be partially exposed. Also, rootgrafting may also be practiced with difficult to root varieties if it is well done.

Perspective is extremely important in this style. It will be easier to create the feeling of depth in sinuous rather than raft style, however strive to have trees on different lines when viewed from the front and side. The same rules apply as for group settings so that distances between trunks should vary and no trunk should cross in front of another.

Figure 189: *Raft or sinuous style growing over a rock*

There is a lot of variety that may be created with these styles. If large trunks are toward the front and smaller ones toward the back, the feeling of perspective is strongly imparted. Sometimes, if trees are more even in thickness and size, there will be the effect of a lyrical grove, and, if there is one dominant tree on one side, with the others smaller and graded down in size, a close-up view will result with the feeling of a small grove growing in the protection of the Mother tree. Raft or sinuous style may also be trained over a rock (as in root-over-rock style). However, the trunk must still be pliable at the time of designing the style, unless a tree is found in nature, already growing in this manner.

Even if the roots are not growing over a rock, it often looks good if the ground is landscaped and small rocks embedded in the soil. If the connecting trunk is growing over different ground levels, more interest and variation will be created in the setting.

The pot is usually a long rectangular or oval shape, or sometimes free-form and reasonably shallow.

Group Settings

I always feel that trees are alive, crouching, waiting to get up and do something. Often one can't see the giant for the wood, especially in Devon where trees seldom stand alone, but intertwine making a community of trees.
BRIAN FROUD.

Group Settings hold a special fascination in Bonsai Art. Throughout the history of storytelling the Forest or Woodland is a place where one can go when wanting to be alone, it is a place of refuge — not unlike the church, and, in the religious sense, it can make us feel humble and, in so doing, uplift the spirit. Magic and enchantment abounds there and, at every turn a new adventure is born. We are drawn into the mysterious depths as if entering another world and in the dark shadows dragons dream of long forgotten secrets . . .

Within the classification of group settings, there are three types:
1. Two tree settings, 2. Group settings and 3. Multiple Plantings. These will be discussed in more detail below.

The general guidelines for the styling of groups are the same as for single tree styles. It is almost as if all the trunks were part of the same trunk and the branches all belonged to a single tree. Therefore no one tree will be perfect on its own and depends upon its relationship with the others to achieve balance. It is for this reason that second grade trees or immature trees may be used with success in group settings. Perhaps you have a tree in your collection that has a beautiful trunk and surface root system but is lacking certain branches — this is probably a good tree to include in a group.

This point about groups being arranged and pruned as if a single tree, is an important one because what we are trying to portray is not just the appearance of one small section of a forest or wood but the whole atmosphere and mood of one entire wood and it is the guidelines for styling that help us condense and emphasize the main features.

With groups, there is an immense variety of different moods that may be conveyed to the viewer (see Plates XXIII, XXIV & XXV). Firstly, there are so many scenes that can be described. The forest may give a perspective view that makes you feel you can see far into the distance or it may depict a middle-distance scene or an intimate close-up view. The trees may be like those from an ancient forest, or a young, lyrical grove. Likewise, they may be densely grouped or sparse. A very dramatic setting could be formed if all the trees are clustered close

Plate XXVIII: *Dwarf Japanese Juniper and slate,* Juniperus procumbens *'Nana', Saikei, Japanese ceramic tray, height of main rock: 51 cm, trees grown from cuttings struck in 1974, Saikei created in 1976, photograph taken in 1982*

Plate XXIX: *What size do you think this bonsai is? When photographed, a well-proportioned bonsai could appear to be any size from miniature to large. In actual fact, this is a miniature, only 10 centimetres high. Hexe Azalea, informal upright style, Japanese pot, age: 1972 stock, trained since 1972, photograph taken in 1983*

together at one end of the container. The trees form a definite triangular design and this is emphasized by the abundant surrounding space. A more traditional setting, on the other hand, is often characterized by trees spread out more evenly in the container and the overall triangle being made up of two subsidiary triangles. Furthermore, some settings may have a fairly even balance between tree sizes, while others may exhibit a dramatic setting with one main tall tree and many smaller ones.

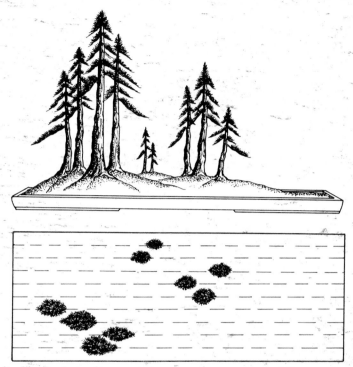

Figure 190: *Perspective view*

Figure 191: *Close-up view*

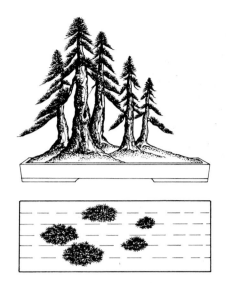

Figure 192: *Ancient forest*

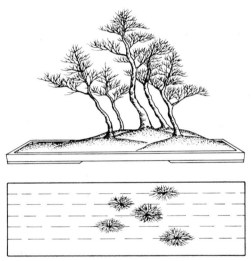

Figure 193: *Young grove*

Figure 194: *Clustered group*

Figure 195: *Traditional group*

We will now discuss some of the specific types of groups, starting with the Two-Tree Setting:

TWO TREE SETTING

This is the only group setting that may have an even number of trees in the same pot and because there are only two trees, there must be harmony between them so that the entire setting is unified and balanced. Therefore, artistically as well as horticulturally, it is better to have the same tree variety in the pot. Artistically there will be no "break" formed in the design as would occur if there were two different types of tree used and, horticulturally, both plants will require the same growing conditions, thus making care easier.

Another point to consider if one is going to create harmony and unity in the setting is that in most styles the lines of the trunk on both trees follow basically in the same direction from base to apex. However, if this guideline is to be varied, at least either the bases or the apexes must follow in the same line (see illustrations in twin-trunk style). They must never meet and separate.

As well as harmony, there must be some variety in the design. This is mainly achieved by having different heights and thicknesses of trunk. The taller tree must be thicker and sometimes it may help to work on the ratios between the thickness of the trunks in order to determine the best relationship between the heights for the trees, that is, if one tree is 5 cm (two inches) thick and the other 2.5 cm (one inch), then they could be, say 50 cm (20 inches) and 25 cm (10 inches) high respectively. If you are cutting the trees down, don't forget to make cut scars either face the same direction or both on the inside facing the other tree. That way new growth won't grow in toward the other tree.

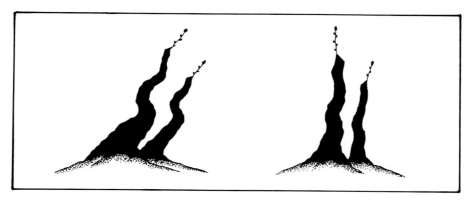

Figure 196: *Cutting down trees for two tree setting*

Again, there are many different moods that may be conveyed by two-tree settings. The two trees, for example, may either be close together or further apart. The Chinese have an interesting story about the order of planting the trees and their positions in a two-tree setting. If the large tree is placed first this is called FU LAO or "carrying the old on the back". On the other hand, if the small tree is planted first it is called HSIEH YU or "leading the young by the hand". When Westerners hear this they may think such a distinction is meaningless, however, if you try these different orders in planting you will probably find that they work. If you plant the small tree first, you will unconsciously tend to plant it further away from the intended place for the taller tree. Thus, the two trees will be quite separate — suggesting the old leading the young by the hand. If the large tree is planted first, though, it is more likely that you will place the smaller tree close and nestling into it — thus suggesting the young supporting the old on his back.

Figures 197–199: *Two-tree setting — trees close together*

Figure 200: *Two-tree setting — trees separate*

If the two trees are placed very close together, their branches are trained as if they were one single tree. So, no branches should be on the same level, no branches should directly cross the trunk of the other tree and the overall outline should be a triangle. As well as this, the trunk of one tree shouldn't cross the other at all, and heavy surface roots shouldn't cross.

Another point, that was also stressed in Twin trunk style is that the first branch on the larger tree that faces in toward the direction of the smaller tree must not be placed directly over the smaller tree's apex. This looks cramped and would not occur in Nature, as the smaller tree would strive to grow out toward the light.

Another point that applies with all two tree settings is that the lowest branch in the setting must be situated on the smaller tree.

Finally, as far as positioning in the pot is concerned, the two trees should not be in line when viewed either from the front or the side. They should be placed on a slightly diagonal line in the pot and it doesn't matter which of the two trees is closer to the front, as either way will create depth in the setting.

GROUP SETTINGS

The sub-classification of "group settings" consists of an odd number from three to nine trees. One question that is often asked is "why there has to be an odd number?" Firstly, along with the avoidance of equilateral triangles and the preference for planting trees off-centre and about one third of the way along the pot, odd numbers help to create the much desired effect of asymmetry. Even numbers tend to be complete and incline toward symmetry and static repose. Odd numbers, on the other hand, are dynamic and make it easier to create a striking focal point in the design.

As with two tree settings, it is better to use the same variety of tree for one setting — even though there is a style called the "Mixed Forest" that incorporates different tree types in the same pot. If the latter idea appeals to you, make sure you choose varieties that will tolerate the same growing conditions.

If you are going to make your group setting of the same variety, make sure that the characteristics of the trees are the same — such as autumn colouring. For deciduous trees, it is preferable to choose the trees in autumn so that the trees may be matched. Seedling variations do occur and in some varieties, such as Zelkovas, they are quite dramatic — changing from gold, through orange and red to scarlet. If you are propagating trees for a group setting, it would be better to grow them from cuttings from the same parent tree, if possible, as this will assure the same appearance in the trees.

I have heard people query the idea that the setting should be unified in its characteristics, saying that if a grove sprang up around an old tree in nature, seedling variations would occur. This is really a matter for personal taste, but my own views are these: We are attempting to convey the feeling and atmosphere of a wood or forest and thus we must concentrate on overall effects rather than individual effects. It is a matter of scale and stylization. Again, artistically speaking, if characteristics such as autumn colour is the same on all trees, this will create a "binding" effect holding the entire design together. The shape and outline will be more impressive and may be appreciated fully. A similar effect may be seen in the Art of silhouette cutting. If a silhouette is cut out on black paper or paper of one colour, every turn of the cutter's scissors can be clearly seen. However, if exactly the same shape is cut out on patterned paper, the effect is lost. Our eye is drawn first to the design on the paper, which, ultimately, spoils our appreciation of the overall shape.

When deciding on a suitable tree type, consider the size of leaves, needles, flowers or fruit. These should be small or, in the case of leaves and needles, have the ability to become fairly small through bonsai training. If these aspects of the tree's growth are too large, they will clutter the design too much.

Again, harmony and unity is important in group settings, so that the general shape of the trees should be similar and, if slanted, all the trees should slant in the same direction. One exception is the fanned out setting (see Figures 201 & 202), where the central tree is vertically placed and the trees on the left slant out in that direction while those on the right slant over that way.

Figures 201 & 202: *Fanned-out setting*

Direction is an important aspect of group settings, as it is in all bonsai art. This element is always determined by the movement from heavy aspects of the design to lighter ones, e.g. the direction of most trees is upward and the tree is heavier at the bottom and lighter at its tip. Thus, all settings, whether they are slanted or not, must have a direction. If the direction is to the right, the largest tree and the greatest number of trees should be planted on the left, while the smallest tree and a more spacious feeling should exist on the right. The overall plan shape should be somewhat like the plan view of the foliage on a branch in single tree styles.

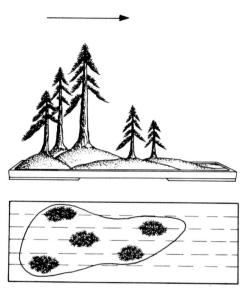

Figure 203: *Side and plan views of group setting*

In the plan view of the setting the distance from one side to the first tree on that side should be the same as the distance from the other side to the tree closest to that side. If this guideline is varied, though, it is acceptable to have more space on the side of the direction of the setting, and for slanted groups there **should** be more distance on the side in which the trees are leaning. Also, the distance from the back edge of the container to the tree closest to the back should be the same as the distance from the front to the front tree and if this guideline is varied more distance may be left in the front.

The heights of the trees should all be different, as this will make it easier to create depth and perspective. If possible, the thicknesses of the trunks should vary as well — the thickest being the tallest and then grading down to the shortest tree being the one with the thinnest trunk. Remember that heights can be adjusted by cutting and by lifting trees up with extra soil under the rootball. However, don't get a thick, short tree where it is impossible to acquire smaller trees for the rest of the setting.

One little trick that may be of some help is that if you are only able to acquire trees of even thickness, choose your most dominant tree — perhaps it is the best shaped tree — and make this the tallest in the setting. Next, grade the others down in height and finally, when planting, cluster the trees around the tallest one. This last point will create the optical illusion that the tallest tree is thicker than the others.

When viewing the setting from the front and from the side, no two trees should be in line and, if viewed diagonally, from the corners of the pot, there should not be three or more trees in line. These points also help to create depth and the feeling of variety in the design. Another important aspect of styling is that when viewed from the front, the distances between the trunks of the trees should vary. Forests grown by man have trees in line and equally spaced out. Nature tends more toward variety. Some closer, some further apart and definitely not in a straight line. It is found that the type of triangle made by the basic group of three trees is of some importance as well — if the triangle has an obtuse angle in it (i.e. over 90 degrees), the design will look natural and be appealing. This automatically stops us planting them in the plan of a right angle triangle or an equilateral triangle.

If the group is slanted or if there is any curvature in the trunks at all, the apex of the major tree in the design should lean slightly toward the viewer, as it does in single trunk informal styles. This guideline applies also to two tree settings and multiple plantings. The apex of number one tree does, in fact, take the place of the apex in single tree styles and, therefore, this tree is usually planted near the centreline when viewed from the side and off-centre (about one third of the way along the pot) when viewed from the front. The other apexes tend toward the basic direction of the group but grow out, slightly, from the other trees.

Another styling point, specifically concerned with three tree settings is that either the tallest or the shortest tree should be in the middle position when seen from the front. A straight out gradation from tallest to shortest is fairly uninteresting and looks artificial.

In group settings, as was hinted at the start, the trunks and their positions are of primary importance and the branches are secondary. Branches should not extend in toward the other trees so that the more trees there are in the setting the less branching there will be on any one tree. If you are cutting branches off the trees in order to fit them together, however, don't cut too many before you finalise the positions of the trees.

When starting out to make a group setting, the following procedure may help you. Firstly, work out the design that you are aiming for — at least roughly — before you start to work on your trees. You may have a design in your imagination, but it often helps, initially, to jot down a rough sketch of side and plan views to guide you.

Next, grade your trees from tallest and thickest trunk to shortest and thinnest trunk and then place them in the basic position shown in your diagram BEFORE you remove them from their containers. You may then begin to style the trees, always starting with the main tree. At this stage you will know, approximately, which sides of a tree will be closer to another and you can wire and cut accordingly, however, don't cut too much initially — final pruning and repositioning of branches comes after the trees have been planted. At the time of this first shaping, it is better to have more trees available than you intend to put in the setting because, like a tree that has more branches — there is more for you to pick and choose from.

Now comes the time for removing the trees from their containers, doing some rootpruning and placing them tentatively in their positions, always placing the tallest and thickest first. The rootpruning is usually a critical process. One of the reasons why we don't take the trees out of their containers until now is that the roots would become dry while the shaping was taking place. The other reason is that some trees will have to be placed very close together and consequently on the sides close to each other, practically all of the rootsystem will be removed and most will be left on the other sides to compensate for this loss. Thus, until we are pretty sure of the final positions for the trees in the setting, rootpruning should not be praticed. The actual loss of roots should balance the loss in foliage and branching in the sense that neither branches or roots should go in toward another tree.

If you are happy with the positioning, soil may be filled in around the roots and final trimming and positioning of branches may be done. Sometimes it may be good to tie the rootballs of trees together with an uncoated natural fibre string to stop the distances between the trees evening out as soil is added. After a couple of months when roots have grown into the soil, holding the setting firm, the string simply rots away.

MULTIPLE PLANTINGS

Multiple Plantings consist of more than nine trees in the same container. If there are a few over nine, the rule of odd numbers should be adhered to, however, if there are so many trees that you really have to stop and count them carefully, it doesn't matter whether there is an odd or an even number.

Sometimes a multiple planting may be successfully made from a group of "groups", but usually such a setting is large and becomes a garden or landscape feature rather than a moveable bonsai.

More commonly, though, multiple plantings consist of many thin-trunked trees clustered together in a grove or clump formation. These are often referred to as "fist-plantings" — the trees are not planted individually but a fist-full of young seedlings are grabbed and then placed in the container. Some may be weeded out that either cross the trunk of another tree or simply don't fit in the design, and, as time passes, they are trimmed to shape. These are often more successful than intentionally planned settings of this type and it is perhaps one of the only ways of obtaining a multiple planting in a manageable size.

Figure 204: *Multiple planting cluster or clump*

The same idea is used, but taken back a step, where seeds or a cone are planted in a cluster and the seedlings allowed to develop into a grove. The central ones naturally tend to grow taller as they compete for light — thus forming a dome-like profile.

CHINESE STYLE GROUP SETTINGS

To the Chinese, attitude or atmosphere is one of the most important elements in a good group setting. As was illustrated above in the story about two-tree settings, the trees are almost looked upon as people and the interaction between them can become the focal point of the setting.

One aspect of groups that wasn't mentioned above is that there is often a tendency to clutter the design — to put in as many trees as will fit into the container. This is the wrong approach. Space plays a very important part in any design and the Chinese use this element with great skill. Space accentuates the main feature of the setting, it shows up detail and balances areas of mass. Most of all, it can make the setting very dramatic as it emphasizes the closeness of the trees.

Some Chinese group settings are almost like groups of literati styled trees. With this type and with much skill on the part of the bonsai enthusiast, one of the major guidelines for group settings may be broken, that is, it becomes possible to cross trunks. This, however, must not be done on a whim. Much thought must lie behind the decision, much the same as when crossing a major branch across the trunk in literati style.

Figure 205: *Literati style of group*

CHOICE OF CONTAINER FOR GROUP SETTINGS

Generally, the pot is oval, rectangular or free-form and of shallow to medium depth. Medium may suit some settings consisting of thick, stocky trees, however, more often, a shallow container is chosen as it emphasizes the feeling of space.

Also, the tallest tree and the length of the container should never be the same. Usually the tallest tree is about two thirds of the length of the pot or vice-versa.

LANDSCAPING OF GROUPS

Unlike single tree bonsai styles, group settings depend a lot upon the shaping or landscaping of the soil to convey the feeling of depth and reality to the viewer. The soil should form mounds extending from the base of some or all of the tree trunks and out along the length of the container. These lengthwise mounds should be unevenly distributed over the area of the container and should taper off towards the sides. As soon as they are formed it is found that the whole setting opens up and displays depth and perspective.

Moss is an important element as well, for it not only binds the soil but adds to the realistic effect.

Avoid the temptation, however, of adding figurines to the setting — they always look artificial and put a break on the workings of our own imagination.

THE REPOTTING OF GROUP SETTINGS

The repotting of groups can pose some problems, however, with a little thought and care, it doesn't have to be such a difficult task. Below is an excellent article that may give you some assistance:[3]

One often hears of difficulties attached to repotting of group plantings. It is said to be too difficult to disentangle roots and replace everything in the same position after etc. etc. These difficulties are the price for enjoyment of a good setting, and the best way of repotting is, of course, the careful attention given to each individual tree. However, one can try the following two ways which may appeal to some.

1. Each year one can slice out a portion of soil and roots from the undisturbed setting in the same fashion as one cuts a cake. Avoiding main roots and cutting slices from the rim of the pot towards the trunks of the individual trees, one cuts smaller roots and through the soil similar to what you do with a slice of apple pie.

These slices are taken out at intervals, leaving approximately two-thirds of the soil untouched each year. Next year one cuts the other third, adjacent to the previous year's operation. On the third year cut out the remaining third. This operation can be repeated for several years without actually taking trees out of the pot.

The reasoning underlying the technique is this:— Soil under the trunks of the trees is seldom crowded with roots and hence this part can last longer undisturbed. Roots going out toward the edge of the pot will use nutriments and crowd themselves in this area. By cutting and removing slices of soil and portion of roots and refilling the space with new mixture, the new fibrous roots will develop and enjoy the new soil.

Occasionally the whole setting can be lifted up. Soil under the trunks scraped and renewed, without interfering with overall setting's placement.

DRAWBACKS to this technique lie in the following:— Root distribution of each tree is not even or regular. By cutting slices, one may remove too much of the roots belonging to one tree and not enough from another. Main roots may present a problem.

On the other hand, if this technique is followed right from the start, there is a logical thought which points out that roots from all trees will go to new soil in search of nourishment and that after a few years the methodical cutting of slices will become more balanced for each tree. We have tried this with large settings and so far found it workable and working well.

One may even consider this technique at the original setting and arrange direction of roots in such a way that they will be growing in required directions for this technique.

The plan of cut slice should be kept for future reference. Memory often plays tricks and one should not remove slices indiscriminantly.

2. The second technique is to put shallow partitions (strips of plastic for instance) at the time of planting, thus creating separate cells in the pot for each tree. This is not always easy or possible. But in the case of three to seven tree plantings it is not very hard.

The best way, of course, is the right way of separately attending to each tree, rootprune and replace them into pot as they were placed originally.

Rock Settings

(Rocks) have always been regarded by the Chinese as the most
magnificent symbols for the creative force of Nature,
fascinating in virtue of their grandeur and their wild
inaccessibility.
OSWALD SIREN

Rocks are greatly appreciated in the Orient. The beautiful, craggy mountains have been models for countless landscape paintings while artistically formed rocks on a smaller scale are used to landscape gardens, to use in bonsai art or, if very small and particularly beautiful, to appreciate on their own as viewing stones. Symbolically, rocks and water are significant to the Chinese as the Taoist philosophy of Nature describes water as the lifeblood of the Earth while mountains and rocks are the bones:

The Earth, like the other planets, was in their view a living organism built up of elements similar to those of which man is made . . . Water was thus, both figuratively and in fact, the life-giving source for the gardens, a circumstance that can perhaps be best observed when it has dried-up and the pulse-beat has stopped . . . They compare a clear lake to a rich piece of painting, upon which the circumambient objects are represented in the highest perfection; and say, it is like an aperture in the world, through which you see another world, another sun and other skies![4]

Rocks can be used in many ways in the Art of Bonsai, apart from simply being placed by the side of a tree. There are, in fact, quite a variety of Rock settings that can be made.

First of all, there is the type where the tree is planted on or in a flattish or slightly saucer-shaped rock instead of a ceramic bonsai pot.

This style really doesn't need much more explanation as there is very little difference between this and planting in a shallow bonsai pot. If the sides of the landscaped soil are a little steep, however, the reinforcement of a wall of muck (see Chapter 3) may be necessary to stop erosion — particularly if overhead watering is practiced.

Figure 206: *Tree planted in flattish saucer-shaped rock*

Figure 207: *Tree planted on flat rock built up with horizontal outcrops*

Usually, with this type of setting, there is no need to worry about drainage holes as the rock is shallow, allowing for easy run-off and/or evaporation and, often it is porous, allowing water to escape through the rock itself. If the rock you are planting in has a deep rock cavity though, and if the rock is not very porous, it may be necessary to drill a hole in the bottom to avoid waterlogged conditions.

When displaying this type of setting, it can either be exhibited as it is or it may be placed in a shallow tray of water or sand.

An interesting variation to this design is that of a group planting or a connected root style planted on a flattish rock, such as slate. Outcrops of flat rocks can be built up — following the same direction as the base piece and creating the appearance of a small community of trees growing on a rocky outcrop (see Figure 207).

The second type of rock setting is the "Root over Rock" or "Rock clasping" style. Here the tree is placed on the rock and the roots trained to grow over it as they travel down into the soil in the pot. As time passes, the roots grow in volume and they eventually tighten around the rock and become inseparable from it. These roots growing over the rock do, in fact, become like part of the trunk while the feeder roots are situated in the soil collecting the nourishment for the tree. Sometimes the rock for this style has a depression or shelf on one side where the tree can be placed and with this type, the rock may form the highest point of the setting (see Figure 208). Other times the rock is smaller and the tree is placed directly on top of it (see Figure 209).

Figure 208: *Root over rock with tall rock*

Figure 209: *Root over rock with small rock*

The third type of rock setting is called "clinging to a rock". Here the tree is dependent entirely upon the nourishment from the small amount of soil surrounding its rootsystem. No roots extend down into a container of soil. Even though crevices or hollows in the rock are sometimes used for planting in, muck is essential for this style, to keep the soil from eroding or falling away.

All of the types of rock settings discussed above, may have either one or more trees. If you choose to have more than one you should have an odd number of trees, except for two, and, if you choose to have a mixed setting of tree varieties, observe that in Nature conifers tend to grow on the higher, more rugged ground and deciduous varieties lower down.

Another consideration is the actual rock — what characteristics are desirable and what types of trees suit a particular type of rock. Generally, the craggier rocks with many crevices and fissures are the most prized as they impart the impression of the grandeur of a wild, harsh landscape. This type is also most suitable for conifers or starkly styled trees. Deciduous trees, though, because they generally grow at lower altitudes, may suit less rugged rocks while trees such as willows and alders that grow on very low ground, near water, would be suitable with smooth, rounder rocks.

As far as colour is concerned, darker colours or steel greys are chosen over very light rocks and any fresh breaks must not be visible from the front of the setting. Sometimes a rock may have a vein of quartz in it that may be placed vertically to represent a waterfall. The rock you choose need not be perfect in every aspect or from every angle. Artistry in the placement of the rock will conceal ugly or uninteresting parts and feature those that are appealing.

Finally, a couple of points to watch are, firstly, that the rock is not too heavy and secondly, that the type of rock is not brittle.

Now we will discuss some of the types of rock settings mentioned above, in more detail.

GROUP PLANTINGS ON ROCK

This type of setting can represent many different scenes, that can be either close-up or distant views. A distant view may represent an islet in the distance while a near-at-hand scene may be a rocky outcrop or a small section of the seacoast. Usually with group plantings on flattish slabs, the horizontal dimension is greater than the vertical (see Plates XXVI A & XXVI B). Be careful not to choose too small a piece of rock for the intended setting because it looks attractive to have portion of the rock bare and not to plant trees on all available surface area. Remember that space plays an important part in emphasizing the best qualities of your design.

The trick in producing a realistic effect is how you place the outcrops of rock and landscape the ground. Small rocks should follow in the same general direction as the main rock slab and they should be partially buried to impart the feeling that they are connected to a hidden bedrock or have been sitting there for centuries. An atmosphere of stability and permanence should always be aimed for. A slight mounding of soil around rock outcrops as well as around

Figure 210: *Small islet in distance*

the bases of trees, adds to this feeling as well. In Nature, sand and silt are blown onto the join between rock and ground and the effect is one of unity, as all elements of nature harmonize and blend together. Moss is also a helpful additive to further unify the setting. However, don't use too much, as the rocky areas we are depicting are never too lush.

ROOT OVER ROCK

The perspective of this setting is a near-at-hand view, so that the tree or trees may be relatively large in comparison with the rock size — usually the rock is not more than about a third of the size of the tree. Furthermore, the pot is usually quite shallow as the main feature of the entire setting should be the roots clasping the rock.

The actual procedure of training a root-over-rock style is not hard, but may take some time. If you decide to use a rock that is like a small boulder and not too large in comparison to the tree size, there is not much trouble. Usually the setting may be arranged immediately as some of the roots of the tree will most likely be long enough to reach the soil in the pot at the base of the rock. The art here, is placing the roots artistically over the rock and leading them along any crevices and depressions in the rock, as these are the areas where roots are likely to grow in Nature. The roots will be loose when first placed over the rock but after one or two growing seasons, they will begin to thicken and grasp the rock more tightly. With some trees such as Ficus varieties and the Trident Maple, the roots flatten as they grow, and mould themselves into the actual rock formation. They are vigorous varieties, as well, and this means attractive results are obtained sooner. Remember that roots thicken more rapidly when covered with earth, so you may choose to bind the roots to the rock with string or rags and plant this root and rock section below ground level for a year or two, or, alternatively, cover the roots with muck and moss, to keep them in a dark, moist atmosphere if they are left above ground level.

If your rock is reasonably large — perhaps it is quite tall with a ledge part of the way up, as was mentioned above — the tree's roots may not be long enough to reach the soil at the base. Therefore, some method will have to be used to gradually train the roots to grow over the rock as they grow longer. There are a few ways of obtaining this result.

One way is to train the tree in the open ground. Dig a narrow hole that is deep enough so that when the rock with tree is placed in it, the soil level will be at the base of the tree's trunk. The roots may be tied to the rock with string or rags to keep them growing in the correct position and direction. It is important that the hole is not much wider than the rock setting and it should be lined with some material such as wood, galvanized iron or heavy plastic so that the roots don't spread out but are forced to grow in the downward direction to follow the rock. After the setting has been placed in the hole, fill it with soil and leave it for one or two growing seasons.

Another method, which is similar to the first, may be more suitable for bonsai enthusiasts without available garden space. It may also be argued to be a little better controlled. Some handywork, however, needs to be attended to first of all. Make a deep box, with the dimensions that allow the rock and tree to be placed snuggly into it with the trunk's base at surface level. The procedure for preparing and planting the tree and rock are the same as if planting in the ground. The difference here, however, is that the box should be made up of horizontal slats, somewhat like a wooden fruit box, and gradually, every few months or so, a slat is removed from the top and the soil washed away to expose more of the rootsystem. At the same time the roots are growing longer and eventually will reach the bottom of the rock. A sandy soil and good growing conditions will speed up the process but, even so, it will take at least a year or two to achieve results.

Another way is to leave the rock and roots exposed, i.e. to plant the rock with soil up to the level it will be when ready to display. The roots of the tree are distributed over the rock in the desired directions and then completely covered with muck and moss down to the soil level. Roots follow the muck down to the soil but because the moisture level is less than if the setting were properly buried, the roots don't grow as rapidly and the whole process could take two to four years longer.

CLINGING TO THE ROCK STYLE

The objective of this style is to reproduce the feeling and impression of one of the many spectacular rock landscapes found in Nature (see Plate XXVII). It may be a mountain, a ravine, a sheer cliff or a rocky islet. While this is the aim, however, often, in practice, the effect is not so good. Usually, if the resultant setting looks artificial, the problem stems from an error in proportion. If we look at a towering mountain or cliff in Nature or even at some Chinese landscape paintings depicting mountains and ravines, the trees are very small in relationship to the rock. Perhaps the cliff is 60 to 90 metres (200 to 300 feet) high while the trees are around 3 to 4.5 metres (ten to fifteen feet). In our bonsai setting we often choose trees that are too large for our rock and this feeling of awesome grandeur is lost.

For a rock that is, say, 40 cm (15 inches) high we really only want trees that are about 5–7.5 cm (two to three inches) tall. This is where the problem lies. Most trees of that size are not more than sprouted seedlings. Being thin and immature, they don't really complement a good rock and definitely won't impart the feeling of old trees seen from a distance. A good source of trees for clinging to the rock style could be miniature bonsai that are imperfect in some way. If some branches are missing or if the surface roots are not so good — it doesn't matter so much as the rock will complement and balance the tree and perhaps hide some imperfections. On the other hand, if you are training trees for use in a rock setting, use the same methods as you would for creating miniature bonsai (see Chapter 9). The variety you choose should have small leaves or needles or the ability to develop smaller ones through bonsai techniques and, if they bear flowers and fruit, these should also be in scale. Low branching on the trees has an attractive effect as well, and in most cases slanting, semi-cascade or cascading styles are very effective with rocks. Horticulturally speaking, it will be easier to keep the trees alive and healthy if the variety has a compact and fibrous rootsystem as more feeder roots can exist in a smaller pocket of earth. They are also better able to penetrate the rock, if it is porous, thus obtaining a little more nourishment for the tree. As far as varieties go, you should realize that this style is more prone to dryness than most others, so don't choose varieties that are particularly moisture-loving.

This style usually depicts rugged landscapes so choose a rock that has as many crevices and craggy textures in it as possible. It should look very old and weathered. When choosing the best front, look at it from all sides and all angles and consider its shape, colour and texture.

When you have decided on the front and the angle at which you wish the rock to be viewed, check if it is stable. Any of these rock settings that we have discussed must be stable to encourage the growth of roots. If the rock is not completely steady, either make a flat base by cutting the rock or else use a plastic cement product to build up the base. Using the latter technique, it is sometimes necessary to build the rock up with small bits of the same type of rock as well as with the cement, to provide enough support.

When deciding where you want to place the tree or trees, a few points should be considered. Firstly, we don't want the effect to be of small bushes on the rock so make sure that enough of the trunk and surface roots are visible from the front of the setting. However we also don't want to hide too much of the rock, so plant the trees somewhere on the right or left hand sides. A couple of errors that are often made in this style are, firstly, that there is often too much branching and foliage on the trees and it is placed in such a way that the rock is hidden from view, and, secondly, if there is an interesting crevice or cavity in the rock, people are tempted to use this as a planting area. Choose the most uninteresting portion to plant the trees on and leave the crevices and cavities free to be viewed and admired.

Most commonly, the rock's top is higher than the trees. Artistically, it is fairly difficult to plant a tree directly on top of a rock. The only style that may work in such a position is windswept. Cascades are generally planted somewhere on the top half of the rock. In all styles, branches and the trunk-line should slant away from the rock with only small branches or tufts of foliage coming across the front of the rock-face as they would if the rock was the trunk of a tree and the trees were its branches. Finally, in all aspects of design, e.g. direction and mood, the trees and the rock should harmonize.

Figure 211: *Clinging to a rock style*

Before you make a final decision, test out all different positions. When you make up your mind, the next step is to firmly attach the tree or trees to the rock. This is the procedure:—

Firstly, around the circumference of the area where you wish to place a tree attach to the rock some small wire loops. These may be easily attached by some epoxy glue. In the past, the Japanese used to attach some lead to the wire loops and then push the lead into a small crevice in the rock. If there was no hole, a small one was made with, say, a drill. Nowadays, however, one of the many epoxy glues available, makes the job much easier.

After the glue has set and the wire loops are held firmly in place, dampen down the rock, as this will make it easier for the muck to adhere. Next, get some muck and cover the planting area with a generous layer. Some slow-release fertilizer such as Osmocote or Nutricote may be pressed into this layer, and the tree can then be placed in position, working the roots into the muck. To hold the tree firmly in place, tie the main roots to the wire loops with string or wire. If you like, a padding of rubber, cardboard or some other material may be placed between the root and the string or wire to stop it cutting in. Muck is filled in between the roots and around the rootsystem until there is about a 2 cm (½ inch) surrounding layer. The muck can then be shaped to blend in with the contours and texture of the rock. If you wish, small pieces of rock may be embedded in the muck, and the muck covered with moss. As well as looking attractive, the moss helps to hold the muck in place and stops it from cracking. At this stage, the setting must be watered, however, for the first week or so before the muck has set firmly, only a fine spray should be used, (N.B. remember to saturate whenever watering is necessary).

When displaying ''clinging to a rock'' style, the setting may be placed in a shallow tray of water, sand or gravel, and small rocks that echo the design of the major one may be planted at the base, slightly forward and to one side. This will stop the setting from appearing too stark and severe in design. Occasionally small bushes are planted at the base for the same purpose.

The maintenance of ''clinging to a rock'' style may be a little more trouble than the other types of rock setting. Repotting can be difficult and if the rock is porous, small rootlets do travel into the rock to obtain some nourishment so it is unwise to ever remove them from the

Plate XXX: *Display of miniature bonsai (photograph taken in 1982) (from left to right) Serissa ''snowleaves'',*
Serissa foetida 'Variegata', height: 11 cm, Japanese pot, estimated age: from 1976 nursery stock,
trained since 1978.

Golden Chinese Juniper, Juniperus chinensis 'Aurea', *height: 17 cm, Japanese pot, estimated age:*
from 1960 nursery stock, trained since 1967

Port Jackson fig, Ficus rubiginosa, *height: 17 cm, Japanese pot, grown from cutting struck in*
1966, trained since 1966

Dwarf honeysuckle, Lonicera nitida 'Aurea', *height: 13 cm, antique Chinese pot, estimated age: from 1960*
nursery stock, trained since 1967

Japanese Juniper, Juniperus procumbens, *height: 13 cm, Japanese pot, estimated age: from 1960 nursery stock,*
trained since 1967

(Bottom)
Japanese Juniper, Juniperus procumbens, *height: 17 cm, old Chinese pot, estimated age: from 1960 nursery*
stock, trained since 1967

Plate XXXI: *Macrantha Azalea, multiple trunk style, height: 15 cm, Japanese pot, age: from 1960 stock, trained since 1967*

setting. Some renewal of food besides fertilizing, however, is necessary and there are a couple of methods that may be used. One way is to use the "slice of cake" technique mentioned for group settings. Another method is to have a series of metal tubes of different diameters and to stick appropriate sized ones in various places over the soil area. When drawn out, a cylinder of earth has been removed and this empty cavity may be filled with fresh soil and then sealed with a daub of muck. Also, soil replenishment may be done by scraping and cutting away the outer layers of muck, soil and roots, and simply replacing and relandscaping with fresh muck.

Watering may also pose a problem in summer, as this style can dry out very rapidly. One way of cutting down on the frequency of watering is to cover the soil surface, firstly with damp sphagnum moss and then with an old stocking. Remember that if you sit the setting in a tray of water, the evaporation will create a more humid micro-climate which will also help to reduce the number of times watering will be necessary.

Elements of Chinese Design

Throughout the above discussion on different styles, the Chinese variations have been mentioned where applicable. However a more general summary of some of the elements that characterize Chinese style will be considered here.

DOMINANCE: A dominant element exists if there is a single sharp and outstanding feature in the design, for example, the effect created by the direction of a sheer, vertical rock landscape. The eye of the viewer is lead along a definite path and directed to one important point — usually from base to apex — and this imparts a feeling of strength and impact to the style. The Japanese do shape some bonsai with the elements of strength and dominance but they also favour soft designs. Compare the effect of a literati pine tree with a single trunk line (see Figure 212), with a Zelkova shaped in the broom style (see Figure 213). The former imparts a dominant, strong feeling, while in the latter, the diffuse design of the branches dissipates the tension in the style, resulting in a softer appearance.

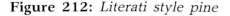

Figure 212: *Literati style pine*

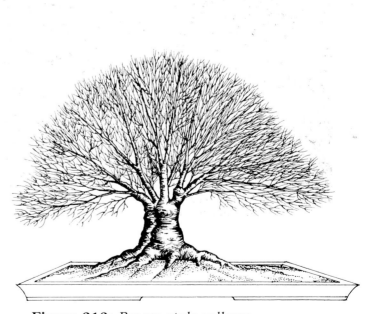

Figure 213: *Broom style zelkova*

Line: In Chinese Bonsai the trunk and branch lines are of utmost importance while the mass and volume of foliage is kept to a minimum and used only to highlight the basic lines or ''bones'' of the design. The Japanese consider the element of line to be of great importance as well, but they also make much more use of mass and volume of foliage than the Chinese bonsai artists.

Figure 214: *Chinese formal upright*   **Figure 215:** *Japanese formal upright*

Space: This element is used by the Chinese even more than the Japanese artists. Space has many purposes in the design. It can balance areas of mass, it highlights the ''line'' that frames the mass and it emphasizes the dominant feature of the style, perhaps a particular direction or an interesting line. Space is also essential in the creation of depth and perspective. Overlapping layers of foliage of diminishing size, when separated by space, can impart the feeling of depth and produce the effect that we are looking at a large tree in the distance.

Form and Texture: The Chinese have a very strong appreciation of these elements. Bark and driftwood are viewed as the bones of the tree. The aged trunk and the bark should show the scars of life and the grey lichen is seen as an old man's beard.

Abstract Beauty of Calligraphy: Basic beauty of design is also appreciated, however, this should always be in keeping with the depiction of a believable tree form. The Western Art of Topiary (see Chapter 1) or the Oriental art of shaping tree's trunks into the shape of a character may be seen to fall into this category, however, these latter examples are not growing in a manner that suggests a tree that may be found in Nature.

Symbolism: To the Chinese, a good tree is one that tells a story. It has an individual character and tells us the story of its life while symbolizing human thoughts and emotions. *They are like hermits, the immortals of legends, withdrawn from the world, whose purity shows in their appearance, lean and gnarled with age, their bones and tendons protruding. Such trees are marvellous!*[5] The hand of the artist is hidden from view, so that the tree looks as if it grew that way without the aid of man — ''The end of all method is to seem to have no method'' — yet, even so, the spirit and character of the artist is revealed.

As is seen in the art forms of many countries, there is a popular and often commercial version as opposed to the styles made by those with artistic gift and feeling. This is seen in Chinese Bonsai styles as well and it is the popular version that has been responsible for many people considering Chinese Bonsai as being overly exaggerated and grotesque. Also, some Japanese bonsai growers frequently condemn Chinese Styling saying that it goes against the true spirit of bonsai and does not impart the qualities of ''naturalism'' or ''beauty''.

If we look at the Chinese bonsai made by artists such as the ancient literati — or ''Men of Books'' — a different picture emerges. The designs are definitely more extreme but exaggeration is held within the bounds of beauty. Furthermore, the criticism of them being unnatural does not apply. As was mentioned above, even though these trees are made with an eye for design, they must always suggest Nature's forms.

Bonsai, though, is an Art and all art is stylized to some degree. In many ways, the difference between Chinese and Japanese bonsai can be likened to the difference between poetry and prose. The first seems more heightened, more stylized, while prose superficially imparts a feeling of "naturalness". However, if a writer is including a conversation in his novel, even though the exchanges seem natural, they will have been greatly changed from, say, a tape recording of the actual conversation that served as the model. The result is a suggestion of a potentially real situation.

Thus we see that bonsai must also be stylized and while many Japanese bonsai may seem more "natural" they still depend upon artistry for their effect. Chinese bonsai, in this analogy, is more like poetry. Stylization is extreme and the effect is heightened and dramatic. Also, like poetry, so much may be expressed in such a small space — we do, indeed, *see a world in a grain of sand* . . .

REFERENCES
Chapter Seven
1. Sullivan, M., *The Arts of China*, London, 1967, p. 168.
2. Yashiroda, K., *Bonsai — Japanese Miniature Trees*, London: Faber & Faber, 1960, p. 39.
3. Koreshoff, V.A., "Repotting of Group Plantings" in *Bonsai in Australia*, January 1971, pp. 32–33.
4. Siren, Oswald, "Gardens of China" in *Bonsai in Australia*, January 1972, pp. 33–34.
5. Chieh Tzŭ Yüan Hua Chuan (1679–1701), *The Mustard Seed Garden Manual of Painting*, A facsimile of the 1887–1888 Shanghai edition with the test translated from the Chinese and edited by Mai-Mai Sze, Princeton, New Jersey: Princeton University Press, Bollingen Foundation Inc., New York, 1956 & 1963.

CHAPTER EIGHT

"The Art of Saikei"

. . . thus may ten thousand miles be illustrated in a foot, and one is free to wander and roam in a landscape without having to wax one's sandals or take up a bamboo staff.
MUSTARD SEED GARDEN MANUAL

Saikei (pronounced Sigh-kay) — literally meaning "tree landscapes" or "living landscapes" — is a sister Art to bonsai. Like bonsai it uses the same principles of design and balance to achieve its effect, yet it is able to capture the feeling of an entire scene — whether it is a mountain range, a ravine or a seabeach (see Plate XXVIII).

The artform of saikei has a fairly short history. After World War 2 many of the bonsai collections and nurseries were destroyed and there wasn't much in the way of good, mature trees available to be shaped as bonsai and the few that were available were fairly costly. Young seedlings were available but they would take many years to develop into attractive trees and very few people had the patience to wait. Mr Toshio Kawamoto, a well-known bonsai artist, realized that if bonsai was going to continue as a practiced art form in Japan, then the general public had to begin to train trees and prepare them to become the future masterpieces. With this in view, Mr Kawamoto created the saikei art form where young plants and collected rocks could be put together in an attractive arrangement using bonsai techniques. Instantaneously the result is pleasing and as time goes on the trees will improve in maturity and style. The idea was that eventually the best tree may be removed from the setting and planted as a single bonsai while a smaller tree can be added to the saikei setting if necessary. Thus, in the original view, saikei was seen as a pleasurable stepping stone to bonsai. Nowadays, however, saikei has almost become like an extra bonsai style and most settings are made as permanent arrangements and appreciated for their own sake. As with group settings, one may use bonsai that are unbalanced on their own — perhaps due to the lack of important branches — but which have a well-developed trunk. It is an art form, then, that can be attractive for the beginner and the experienced grower alike.

In a way, saikei can be seen to have evolved from group settings and rock settings but the result is something quite new and different. Often the question is asked, "What are the differences between saikei and group settings?" or indeed, "saikei and bonsai?". In actual fact the settings exist at different points on a continuum and with some examples it would be very difficult to categorize them as one or the other. However, taking the extremes into account, let us firstly consider the differences between group settings and saikei:

Saikei can have one tree and one rock or it may consist of many trees and rocks, while groups must have more than one tree.

The relationship between tree and pot size is different. With saikei the trees are fairly small in relationship to the pot while groups generally have larger trees. The effect of this is that saikei indicates a larger area of land than groups.

The container that the saikei is planted in must be shallow and fairly unobtrusive. Mostly they are in quiet earthy tones and either oval or rectangular in shape. This type of container can also be suitable for group settings, however if a more striking colour or design is required for a group, this is acceptable and the pot may be medium in depth if this suits the type of trees planted in the arrangement (e.g. they may be short, stocky trees with thick trunks).

In a saikei, rocks are the "bones" of the setting. A saikei must involve rocks somewhere in the design and usually they are quite prominent, either equally if not more so than the trees. With groups, the use of rock is optional. Usually rocks are not used but if they are they should be small and far less prominent than the trees. When a group setting is viewed the trees should be the focal point and if rocks are present, these should be noticed later.

The trees in a saikei can be meticulously shaped and quite old if these are available, however, if not, young trees without much individual shaping may be used. For group settings, though, because the trees are the main feature they should be well-shaped and quite developed.

Speaking more generally, the differences between saikei and bonsai can, likewise, be discussed in terms of a continuum so that some saikei settings can have many characteristics of bonsai and some bonsai may approach the appearance of saikei. Again, discussing the extremes, saikei expresses a more obvious and literal view of nature. In many ways, it appears more "natural" than bonsai. Bonsai, on the other hand, is more subtle and suggestive in its view. It is stylized and dramatic.

A good analogy can be drawn between bonsai and saikei and the art forms of poetry and prose. Bonsai — like poetry — has more "rules" and the effect is more stylized and less "natural", yet it can be very dramatic and expressive. In this analogy, saikei tends toward prose. The effect is more "natural" and low key due to the relaxation of style and rules. However, even poetry and prose can be seen to lie on a continuum. Some poetry such as epic or narrative poetry may be "prosey" while some prose may be described as poetic and if studied it will be found that it is more stylized and adheres to more "rules". In this sense, saikei too may be made more like bonsai. The trees may have a lot of individual shaping done to them, they may be a little larger or more outstanding and they may be more mature. A dramatic scene may be portrayed with the rock — perhaps emphasizing a particular direction such as a vertical landscape with sheer rocks, or a windswept arrangement. The use of space to emphasize the main feature also adds to the dramatic nature of the scene.

As was mentioned before, when we make a bonsai, the main feature is the tree. With saikei, however, success depends greatly on the blending and balance of trees, rocks and soil. It is the clever placement of rocks that enhances the appearance of the trees which are often young and immature and it is the way the soil is shaped and landscaped that sets off the rocks and makes them appear natural. These three elements will now be discussed in more detail:

The Trees:

Most of the guidelines here are identical to those for group settings of trees. However, some of the major points will be mentioned again here. Either one, two or any odd number of trees over two may be used and, as in group settings, no trees should be in line when the setting is viewed from the front or the side.

For the creation of a harmonious design, it is best to choose trees of the same variety except, perhaps, if some trees are chosen to simulate low bushes on the edge of a forest. Also, for harmony, the trees should be of a similar shape and style.

It is important to have variety in the setting as well, so the trees should be of varying sizes and heights — the tallest being the one with the thickest trunk and the distances between the trees should vary.

For saikei, even more so than with groups, it is essential to choose varieties that have small leaves or short needles or the ability to develop smaller ones through bonsai training techniques. Some tree varieties that produce effective results are: Juniper varieties with small sized foliage, Pines (for larger saikei), Hinoki cypress, Cryptomeria, Azaleas, Serissas, Cotoneasters, Chinese Elms and Figs.

Finally, nearly all Saikei would be improved by some training, at least the wiring of the trunks, so that they conform in their basic direction and lines. Remember also, that it is far easier to shape them BEFORE planting them in the setting.

The Rock:

The rock plays an important part in saikei. It forms the framework of the setting just as bones form the framework of a man and much depends on the quality of the rock chosen and its placement.

Also, being the "skeleton" of the setting, the rocks should be positioned in the landscape before the trees. Considering the logic of this, we see that Nature plants her rocks before the trees, as well.

In estimating people, their quality of spirit (ch'i) is as basic as the way they are formed; and so it is with rocks, which are the framework of the heavens and of earth and also have ch'i. That is the reason rocks are sometimes spoken of as yün ken (roots of the clouds). Rocks without ch'i are dead rocks, just as bones without the same vivifying spirit are dry, bare bones[1].

When looking for rocks for your saikei you may collect them from any type of environment, however, if they are found by the sea shore they must be soaked well to leach out the salt before they are used. Volcanic rocks are good because they are porous and will hold moisture. Also, porous rocks will allow roots to penetrate the rock and grow in crevices, thus obtaining extra nourishment. It is also a good idea to choose lightweight rocks if possible, due to the fact that the settings can become very heavy with the combined weight of rocks, trees and soil. The Chinese often use soft stones, such as sandstone or stalectites that can be chiselled and shaped. Hard rocks such as LING PI and YING of the Anhouei Mountains of Canton are also used because they have interesting shapes and surfaces with veins suggesting the effect of a real mountain[2]. Generally, rough or jagged rocks give a better result than smooth rocks, however, it is important to realize that a fair proportion of the rocks will be buried so that they need not be beautiful from all angles. Learn to study the rock carefully beforehand and make use of its best parts while burying or covering the less attractive aspects.

Once more, harmony is important so that if more than one rock is used, they should all be of the same type. Also, the rock should harmonize with the type of tree used. Consider that when you are making a saikei, you are painting a landscape with rocks, trees and soil, rather than paint. Look at the roughness or smoothness of the rock, its size, colour and form and see if this suits the tree. For example, if the tree is a rugged and stark windswept style, the rock should add to the effect and appear to have come from the same environment. As far as colour is concerned, the colour of trees and rock should harmonize but there should be adequate contrast so that each element is distinct.

Another important point is how to determine the direction of a rock because all saikei arrangements must have a direction and in the one setting the general direction must be the same for trees and rocks. Direction in rocks is determined by such things as grooves, the vein, and exposed strata. If none of these are present then the overall shape and mass will be the indication. In this case, the movement from the heavier, larger side to the smaller, lighter side will determine direction.

The Soil:

As was mentioned above, the landscaping of the soil plays a very large part in making the setting appear natural. The area around trees and rocks should be slightly mounded and the surface of the soil should be uneven as this greatly adds to the effect of depth in the landscape. If a container is filled with soil that is scraped level, the effect is of a pot of soil, yet if the soil is shaped into a series of mounds running lengthwise in the container, depth is created instantaneously.

When positioning the rocks, they should never be simply placed on the soil surface. The bottom of the rock must be well buried and the soil shaped around it to flow in the general

Figure 216: *Rocks "planted" in the earth*

direction of the rock strata. This gives stability to the setting and creates the appearance that the rock is part of the bedrock below, or that it has been there for many years and the dust and soil has banked up around the junction between rock and earth. In short, the rocks should be "planted" and look as though they are "growing" out of the soil.

Muck is an important element in most saikei arrangements (see Chapter 3), particularly if they are built up or if rocks need extra stability to keep them upright or in the desired direction. If rocks are really unstable, consider trying to cut the bottom so that they sit on a flat base, or, try cementing them to the base of the container. Generally, though, muck is used to stabilize rocks and to form walls between rocks and around areas where soil is needed to be raised to a higher level.

It can also be used to simulate the effect of rock if you don't have enough or if you want to cut down on the weight in the container. Muck can be made in varying colours depending on the clay that you use, so that it may be made to match the rock colour fairly well. Pebbles, soil or small pieces of rock may also be mixed in or embedded on the surface of the muck to give a more realistic effect. Make sure you model and sculpt the muck to have the same general shape and texture as the rock already used.

Moss is fairly essential in saikei. Apart from making the setting appear natural, it aids in a practical sense by stopping erosion, holding the soil and muck together and preventing the muck from drying out and cracking. Grasses and small ground covers can be used in parts of the saikei as well, if you feel they are appropriate — however, don't choose overly vigorous or large foliaged types as they will look out of scale.

Saikei, very often, incorporates the suggestion of some water in the scene whether it is a lake, a river or the sea. Just as the rocks are viewed as the bones of the landscape, water is seen as the lifeblood of the earth. Usually sand or fine gravel is used to indicate a water course. Recently, an American Bonsai grower — Leon C. Snyder Jr., from the University of Missouri at Columbia has created another related art form or style that he has named "Microenvironments". These are similar to saikei but use extremely small trees with minute foliage and the effect is of a large expanse of a landscape in perfect detail. Bonsai and saikei principles are still used and mechanical pumps incorporated if a waterfall or running water is to be created.

Sometimes paths and roads form part of the setting. The "Mustard Seed Garden Manual" has some good advice on their design and this information applies to rivers as well: *In general they should be winding and sinuous, partly hidden, partly visible. They should never be straight like a dead snake, nor should they be jagged like the teeth of a saw.* If the effect of perspective is to be created, the path or river should gradually become narrower as it goes toward the back of the pot.

One final word about landscaping: avoid the use of figurines as they are too concrete and literal in expression. If this aspect is left to the imagination, the effect will be more impressive.

Points on How to Position One Rock

The main point here is that the rock must be placed near a tree and if there is more than one tree, the rock is usually placed near number one tree (i.e. the tallest and thickest). Direction of tree and rock should harmonize as well and in the design the tree usually leads our eye to the rock. The idea of using one rock can be helpful for bonsai as well as saikei. Sometimes, for instance, a bonsai may be a little unbalanced. It may, perhaps, be missing a certain branch that would complete the overall triangular design. In this case, a cleverly placed rock may take the place of that third point (see Figure 217).

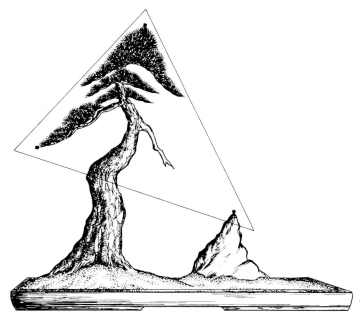

Figure 217: *Rock added to complete design of bonsai*

The larger and more dominant element (tree or rock) should be positioned first. If any compromises need to be made in choosing the front — these should be made with the less important element.

In most cases, the rock's centre of mass is placed on the same line as the tree when viewed from the side or in the same line as the tree's direction. Also, this is usually fairly close to the centre line of the container when it is viewed from the side. The rock should never block our view of the tree.

One variation to this guideline is if you are placing the rock lengthwise along the back edge of the container to create the effect of a distant mountain. In this case the tree is the main feature of the scene and the function of the rock is to add depth to the landscape. Remember also, to shape the soil as described above, if you are making this type of setting.

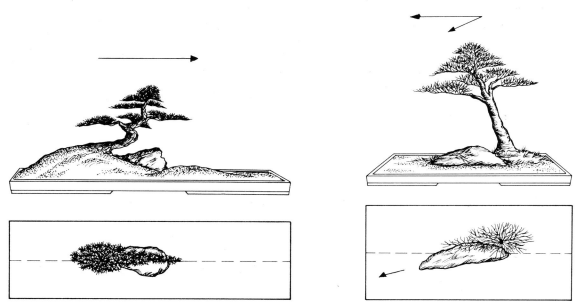

Figures 218 & 219: *Rock's centre of mass on line of tree's direction*

Finally, always try to leave more space on the side of the landscape's direction of flow.

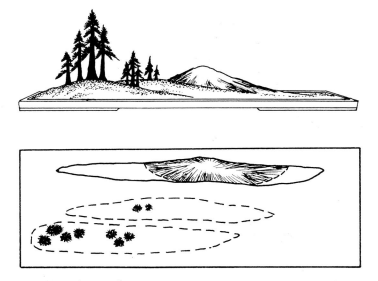

Figure 220: *Distant mountain setting*

Points on the Positioning of Groups of Rocks

The basic guidelines for positioning groups of rocks are the same as for positioning groups of trees, but the main points will be mentioned here as well. The Chinese view groups of rocks as people interacting with one another e.g. an emperor and his ministers, a host with his guests or a mother with children. The rocks should not be separate or isolated but at the same time, each should have its own individual character. To achieve this the elements of harmony, variety, stability and unity should be considered.

The number of prominent rock peaks may be 2, 3, 5, 7, or 9. After this number any amount may be featured in the landscape, odd or even. Often more than one rock may be used to give the appearance of a single rock by welding them with muck and moss that is modelled to follow the contours of the rocks. Similarly, one large rock can be used to give the impression of two or more rocks by burying certain areas and effectively landscaping the soil around the exposed parts.

As was mentioned before, rocks should be of the same kind, in order to create harmony in the setting and they should also be similar in basic shape. Sometimes, though, a rock is used that has a patch or a vein of quartz running through it. This can suggest a patch of snow, a snowcapped mountain or a waterfall in the scene.

Just as all of the trees conform with the shape and direction of the tallest and thickest tree, all of the rocks must conform to the largest and most dominant rock. This creates unity and harmony.

Generally, all trees and rocks in the setting should follow in the same direction. The only exception is the situation where there is a ravine or a river and the trees and rocks on the left hand side of the setting face to the right and those on the right lean over toward the left (see Figure 221).

Figure 221: *Example of opposing directions in a setting*

This occurs in nature as trees grow out over a cliff or a river to receive more light. Even in this sort of arrangement, though, there must be an overall direction in the setting so that one side has the largest trees and rocks and the greatest number of them. This will be on the opposite side of the direction of the landscape.

The most important rock is always positioned close to the major tree in the setting and usually they are on the centre line when the saikei is viewed from the side. This imparts a feeling of stability. The major rock and tree become like the trunk or pivot of the arrangement — giving it the basic character and line. The other trees and rocks are then seen to function as branches in a single tree, i.e. filling out and emphasizing the design. The overall shape of rocks and trees in every saikei should be a triangle and the major rock and tree form the apex point.

Variety is also important in saikei and this is achieved in a few different ways:

Rocks should be of varying sizes and different heights. This doesn't necessarily mean that a rock has to be very tall, as height can be adjusted to some degree by adding and taking away soil. Also trees and rocks should not be the same height. The spacings between rocks should be irregular when viewed from the front as this makes the setting appear natural and gives variety as well.

From the front and side views, no rocks should be directly in line and on a diagonal line there shouldn't be three or more rocks in line. If there are three rocks in the design, the centres should form an obtuse angle (i.e. one angle over 90 degrees). If there are more than three, this rule applies to the major three rocks.

The distance from the back of the container to the rock closest to the back should be the same as the distance from the front of the container to the rock closest to the front. This gives stability to the setting, however, if you are going to vary this, do so by leaving more distance in the front. This rule can apply from the front view as well but mostly more distance and space is left on the side of the setting's direction. Normally rocks are never positioned right on the edge of the container, however, if for some reason it is necessary to do so on one side, it is important that space be left on the other side. Rocks should never .overhang the container though.

Especially when you are arranging a large amount of rocks in the setting, be very careful that the setting is balanced, and check that you have followed most of the guidelines mentioned above. If a tree has many branches or if there are numerous trees in a group setting, mistakes in design are not detected so easily. With rocks, however, the reverse seems to hold true. If the setting is unbalanced, the more rocks you add, the more obvious it becomes.

Figure 222: *Saikei: Sheer cliffs*

Some Horticultural Notes

If there are insufficient drainage holes and if a large amount of muck is used to stabilize upright rocks, it is possible that some trees will be planted in pockets of earth with no access to drainage holes. In this case, some of the trees in the saikei will thrive (i.e. those planted over drainage holes) while some will suffer or die. If you anticipate using plenty of muck, stabilize your rocks first and then place a layer of pure, moist sand on the bottom of the container. Thus, no matter how much muck you use and how many individual planting pockets you make with it, the water will always drain through to the layer of sand at the bottom and travel out to the drainage holes. Perhaps a slightly sandier soil mix would also be advisable for saikei that may have a drainage problem, or which are greatly built up with muck.

Saikei need not be repotted for up to ten years, however they do need regular feeding in spring and autumn and/or the addition of slow release organic fertilizer in the soil. If you are happy with the design of your saikei and do not wish to pull it apart at repotting time, you may choose to use the "pie method" of renewing soil or the "cylinder method" (both are mentioned in Chapter 7 in the section on Group Settings).

REFERENCES
Chapter Eight
1. *Mustard Seed Garden Manual of Painting*, See Chapter Seven, no. 5. above.
2. "Paysages en Miniature (Landscapes in Miniature)" Translation from French by Mrs. F. Jossek in *Bonsai in Australia*, July, 1971, p. 4.

CHAPTER NINE

"Bonsai Classification by Size —

including a discussion on Miniature Bonsai".

Bonsai Classification by Size

When we talk of bonsai to people who do not make them or who are beginners in the Art, they generally think first of a small or miniature tree. It seems, to them, an impossible achievement to keep an aged tree in such a small container and, consequently, the measure of excellence in the Art is believed to be one of size. This is a misconception, as the beginner soon discovers. Size is relatively unimportant in bonsai — it is style that matters (see Plate XXIX). Thus, some people prefer large bonsai, some small and some medium, and, often, personal preferences are strongly argued to be the best. It is not bad to have favourite sizes but none are intrinsically better than another. The Japanese, themselves, have not got hard and fast rules on size classification, and as it will be noticed below, most of the names refer to a rough description of size according to how easy or difficult it is to carry the tree. Another point is that the cut-off point between size classifications and the names given to different sizes varies so much from one author to another. All in all, it is not such a critical issue, except perhaps in competitive situations and in this case one would be advised to check on any local variations.

Below is a general guide to size classifications and some of the names given to them. Usually the size is taken as a vertical measurement of the tree, excluding the pot. The Americans usually take the lip of the container as the bottom point, while in Australia the bottom point is

JAPANESE NAME	ENGLISH NAME	SIZE
1. shito or keshitsubu	"finger-tip bonsai", "tiny pea", "poppy seed size"	up to 5 cm or 7.5 cm (2" or 3") may be carried on fingertip
2. mame	"Baby Bonsai", "little bean"	5 cm–15 cm (2"–6") or 7.5 cm–15 cm (3"–6") may be carried on palm of hand
The above two size classifications are known as "shoohin" or "shohin" or, in English, "Miniature bonsai")		
3. kotate (or kotade) mochi or komono	small to medium	15 cm–30 cm (6"–12") can be carried in one hand
4. chiu or chu-mono	medium to large	30 cm–60 cm (12"–24") can be carried by one person
5. dai or ōmono	large to very large	60 cm–120 cm (24"–48") takes 2 or more people to carry it

236

the visible root system. The only problem that may arise with the vertical measurement system is with semi-cascades or full cascades. Because semi-cascades are fairly horizontal, quite a long cascade could conceivably be classed as miniature by the above method. Usually this problem doesn't arise due to the fact that, in competition, cascades are often placed in a class of their own. A solution, however, could be that size be measured, for all styles, from a straight line drawn from the base of the trunk to the apex (in cascades, the apex would be taken as the tip of the tail and if the tree had a crown of foliage, this would be disregarded.

The next question that arises is where the upper limit is? Many authorities consider it to be 120 cm (48″) but this is not accepted by all growers. Some say that there is no upper limit provided the tree and its container are designed together as a bonsai. Incidentally, some of the Japanese Emperor's bonsai are over 180 cm (six feet) in height.

Miniature Bonsai

The care and styling of miniature bonsai does require a little more discussion, not due to the fact that they are better or worse than bonsai of other sizes but because additional problems inevitably arise due to their small proportions.

To many growers, miniatures are the most fascinating trees in bonsai art, being almost like a bonsai of a bonsai. There is a special kind of magic about them though, as many examples display an achievement that seems impossible in horticultural terms e.g. a small tree bearing more fruit than it has soil in the pot.

Figure 223: Miniature bonsai crabapple

The interest in growing miniatures has existed for some time now. One of the most well known growers and collectors of miniature bonsai was Count Matsudaira', whose interest began after the 1923 earthquake in Japan. Today, Zeko Nakamura, a professional actor has done much to spread the interest in miniature bonsai both in and outside of Japan.

SUITABLE VARIETIES FOR MINIATURE BONSAI

With miniatures, scale is of extreme importance so that the size of flowers, fruit, leaves, needles, branches and internodes should be small. Some varieties with naturally large leaves or longish needles will reduce in size through bonsai techniques while some will not, however, some Japanese growers do use large leafed varieties for miniature bonsai by limiting the number of leaves and almost allowing leaves to do the job of layers of foliage. If the variety is deciduous, though, a tree shaped in this way will not look so attractive in winter without a fine tracery of branchlets. Some varieties that are natural dwarfs may seem good choices for miniature bonsai but this is not necessarily true. Many natural dwarfs are lacking in tree-like characteristics such as bark and a mature trunk. Other dwarf varieties though, are acceptable. Over the last fifty years or so the Japanese have been developing varieties with extremely dwarf growth patterns. These are called Yatsubusa and originate from selected clones from bud mutations and "sports", "witches brooms" and seedling variations.

Generally available trees that are suitable for miniatures, though, are maples, zelkovas, azaleas, miniature rhododendrons, berberis, figs, cotoneaster (microphylla and horizontalis), pyracantha, crabapples, cumquats, Buxus microphylla (Kingsville Box), junipers (particularly procumbens nana, hornibrooki), spruce, pines, cryptomerias. If the variety produces flowers or fruit, remember that these will not reduce in size due to bonsai training techniques, so choose varieties with these features that are naturally small. Appropriate varieties should bear fruit and flowers without any trouble. It would also help if the tree has a fine rather than a coarse rootsystem as this will allow the tree to obtain maximum nourishment from the tiny pot.

While the above is a guide for choosing varieties in order to produce an aged tree-like result, some growers prefer to use miniatures almost as "light-relief" or as companion plants for their main collection. Here, it is often the miniature pot that is the focal point and the planting may be little more than some grass, a flowering plant or a young seedling. The main concern is the horticultural feat of keeping a tree alive and healthy in a very small pot. In the very minute pots used for shito or poppy-seed sized bonsai, seed is sometimes sown directly into the container and displayed when germination takes place.

If you are interested in the type of miniatures mentioned first, i.e. those that impart the illusion of an aged tree with character, a great deal of skill is required both horticulturally and stylistically. The results can be rewarding though and if cared for properly, the length of life of these miniature bonsai will be normal for the variety being trained.

Apart from the disadvantages and difficulties involved, there are some advantages involved in growing bonsai of a small size. They develop and mature more quickly and more suitable stock is available in nurseries, as a tree of ordinary thickness and age can be cut down to produce an aged effect. Another advantage is that because they are of a small size, more trees may be kept in a certain area. This allows one to enjoy many different varieties and styles without needing a very large garden or bonsai area. However, willpower is necessary because the temptation to create new miniatures is strong and the number of trees in your collection is likely to grow rapidly if you are not careful. It is better to have a few trees and care for them properly rather than to have many that become mediocre due to lack of individual attention. Even though they are small, miniatures still need the same care of trimming, watering, fertilizing and repotting — and, sometimes more frequently than bonsai of a larger size.

METHODS OF PROPAGATION

All of the methods of propagation that were mentioned in Chapter 1 are suitable for producing miniature bonsai.

Growing from seed has some special advantages for the production of small bonsai. A very refined result may be obtained as the gradual shaping and trimming ensures a good development of fine branching and a well-tapering trunk with no large cuts on the tree. Usually, trees grown from seed have a nice buttress that develops at the base of the trunk and good surface roots. Scale and proportion can be gained, fairly easily, by developing miniatures from seed. Some growers even sow the seed in the intended bonsai container. The only drawback with growing miniatures from seed is that the trunk, while having a good taper, may not be very thick. To develop the trunk thickness some of the techniques mentioned in Chapter 2 may be used and the tree may be planted in a larger pot or the ground for a year or so to develop the required proportion or improve certain features on the tree more rapidly. Trimming, however, will have to be attended to carefully in order to retain the basic size and shape.

Producing miniature bonsai from thick cuttings or aerial layers has the advantage of gaining an "aged" appearance very quickly, and attractive characteristics can be literally "hand-picked".

Finally, small bonsai may be made from cutting down collected trees or nursery stock and very beautiful results may be obtained almost immediately, providing you have cut to a point where the trunk tapers from the base to its new apex (see Chapter 2 "The Sculptural Technique").

POTS FOR MINIATURE BONSAI

For many growers, the pots used for miniature bonsai are equally as important as the trees if not more so. The variety of colours and shapes is indeed outstanding and nowadays the choice of brightly coloured pots in exciting contemporary shapes is becoming the norm rather than the exception. This is partly due to the influence of Zeko Nakamura, whose well-known collection exhibits pots of all colours, shapes, textures and designs.

Many of the pots are ornamental in themselves — often being decorated in quite fine detail. There is more scope to choose unusual pots with miniature bonsai, however, if you prefer, you may still use small pots that are austere and classical in form and colour. Generally, if you are concerned with traditional styling of your miniature bonsai you would be more likely to choose a quieter toned container.

Remember that earthenware containers drain better than stoneware and that a glazed container will usually retain water the longest. Sometimes miniature pots are used that do not have drainage holes. This is not the best idea but if you have a nice little pot that you would like to use and if you are unsure of the safety of drilling a hole in the bottom, make sure that you turn it on its side for a while after watering, to let the excess moisture drain out. Another point to keep in mind is that if the drainage hole is very small, water may be unable to escape as the weight of moisture in the pot is not sufficient to push its way out of the opening.

CARE OF MINIATURE BONSAI

The disadvantage of growing miniature bonsai is the horticultural difficulty of keeping trees in such tiny pots, in good health. Often they are seen to be bordering on an unhealthy or weakened state. If the points of care discussed below are followed, however, most of the problems should disappear.

WATERING:

This is perhaps the most difficult aspect of care. Trees either die due to rapid drying out or because the owner is scared that they will dry out and consequently overwaters. Surprisingly enough, it is overwatering that is responsible for most fatalities. If you think this may be your problem, it would be better to plant the trees in a very sandy mix (up to 75% sand) and then, in summer, sit your miniatures in a larger tray that holds damp sphagnum moss, sand or gravel. When you water, the shallow tray will collect some water, allow the miniatures to soak up as much moisture into their pots as is possible and provide extra humidity as the water evaporates during the day. This will cut down on the frequency of watering in summer and the open, sandy soil mix ensures that waterlogging doesn't result. If you usually water overhead with a hose, it is a very good idea to occasionally water your trees by immersion. This way, you can be sure that there isn't a wasted section of your pot where soil and roots are constantly bone dry. In extremely hot weather it is a good idea to water the trees in the shade as it is possible that the water in the pot may boil and damage the rootsystem if left in the sun. On hot, windy days, Nakamura puts ice-cubes on the soil surface and as they melt, cool water slowly seeps into the pot.

In very cold weather, i.e. when temperatures fall below 0 degrees C (32°F), the opposite problem results and in order to avoid water freezing in the pot, make sure that you water at about 10 a.m. Another safeguard to avoid water turning to ice in the pot is to plant your miniature bonsai — pot and all — into a larger container or tray of soil. This will act as extra insulation. These points were mentioned in the discussion on watering in Chapter 5, however, the problems of boiling and freezing are more extreme with miniatures due to their small size.

SOIL MIXTURE:

As was mentioned above, good drainage is important so a higher proportion of sand than in the basic soil mix (see Chapter 3), would be a good idea. A finer grade of soil may be used for miniatures in order to encourage better branching of the rootsystem, however, it is still of utmost importance to sieve the clay loam or soil portion to remove fine silt as this would clog up the pores in the soil and stop good aeration and drainage.

ROOTPRUNING AND REPOTTING:

Repotting is best done annually. When rootpruning, try to remove as many of the old, heavy roots as possible. This will encourage more fine feeder roots that will make better use of the soil available in the pot. Remember, also that balance is important so if you are rootpruning, trim the top as well — even if only slightly. Every few years it may be necessary to plant your miniatures in a larger pot or in the ground for a year to boost their vigour. Trimming must be attended to at appropriate times so that shape and size is retained, however, some varieties do gradually become larger over the years and every ten years or so, a slightly larger pot may have to be chosen. With others, though, the original proportions can be kept indefinitely due to techniques such as renewal pruning (see Chapter 2).

POSITION:

Except for varieties that particularly prefer shade or semi-shade (e.g. azaleas), a sunny position is the best for your miniatures providing you watch that they don't become bone dry. If you prefer to shade your trees from the afternoon sun in summer, they should at least be exposed to winter sun and morning sun in summer. A sunny position has many advantages. It encourages finer, more compact growth, less pests and diseases, more flowers and better colour in flowers.

If it is extremely hot, though, protection will be necessary, just as extreme winter cold may be detrimental and consequently some shelter should be provided (see Chapter 5). If there is moderate cold and your tree is not frost tender, exposure will tend to encourage finer foliage growth in spring.

FERTILIZER:

It is generally better to underfertilize than overfertilize miniature bonsai — so, if you wish, give only weak doses of a low Nitrogen fertilizer in spring and autumn. If the soil you are using has adequate nutrition and if you are repotting annually, fertilizer is not really necessary. However, if you are using a very lean soil mix (i.e. high proportion of sand), fertilizing would be a good idea to keep your tree in good health. For fruiting and flowering varieties a fertilizer high in potassium and phosphorus would be a good choice.

TECHNIQUES FOR SHAPING MINIATURE BONSAI

PRUNING AND TRIMMING:

This method is fairly slow but it is often better for miniatures due to the difficulty in wiring them. The Lingnan "grow and clip" technique produces very attractive results and works particularly well for deciduous varieties. Frequent trimming is a major determinant of producing a miniature bonsai that looks in scale, as it is this aspect of the shaping process that is responsible for the development of fine branching and fresh coloured, smaller sized foliage. Defoliation — either partial or complete — on suitable varieties, is also a valuable technique in reduction of foliage size, while partial defoliation may be used to relieve overcrowding of leaves or needles in a small area. Remember also to use sharp tools and to seal cuts (see Chapter 2) when pruning miniature bonsai as their small size makes it imperative that there is no drastic moisture loss. If doing heavy pruning in a hot summer, then it is a good idea to keep the tree in full or partial shade for a week or so afterwards.

WIRING:

One of the main problems with wiring miniatures is the physical difficulty of manipulating the wire on such tiny trees. If you have large hands, it may help to use tweezers to apply the wire. Another caution is to watch that wire does not cut into the bark because again, due to the small scale, any scars or wire marks would be extremely obvious. String may be a good alternative to wire or may be used in conjunction with it. It usually rots before it cuts in and may be easier to apply than wire. Wire, however, does have a slightly stunting effect as was mentioned in Chapter 2 and this may be used to advantage, perhaps, with miniatures.

THE ART OF STYLING MINIATURE BONSAI

All of the styles mentioned in Chapter 7 may be made as miniatures, however, the illusion of a beautiful aged tree is more difficult to create with small sized bonsai. A more disciplined eye is needed that can discern the differences between young and old trees and learn what may be left out and what expressed. Because of the small scale in which we are working, economy of expression and the ability to capture the essence is the secret to success (see Plates XXX & XXXI).

To my way of thinking, the main elements are these:
1. A good taper from a thick base to a fine top in as short a distance as possible.
2. Good radiating surface root system gripping the earth.
3. Branches angled down slightly.
4. Fine sub-branches.
5. Foliage, fruit and flowers of small size.
6. For single tree styles, one group of three layers plus a crown of foliage is sufficient.

DISPLAYING MINIATURE BONSAI

To enhance the beauty of miniature bonsai, they should be viewed at eye-level, so that the trunk and branches may be properly appreciated. Positioning for exhibition is thus more critical than for larger sized bonsai.

Usually, miniatures are not exhibited singly but in groups, on stands that will hold many trees.

On these multiple stands the general observance is that conifers are placed on the top shelves, deciduous lower down and grasses at the bottom. This is to simulate the way different varieties grow at fairly separate elevations in Nature, due to their individual environmental preferences.

REFERENCES
Chapter Nine
1. Blogg, J., "Miniature or Mame Bonsai" in *The Journal of the American Bonsai Society*, 11.3.62.

CHAPTER TEN

''Exhibiting, Display and the Judging of Quality in Bonsai''

Exhibition and Display

Perfection is the measure of Heaven
and the wish to be perfect is the measure of man.

When a bonsai is properly displayed, we are able to fully appreciate every aspect of its beauty. Many elements are responsible for our reaction when we view a tree and, indeed, if the best bonsai was planted in an old tin and placed on the ground, it would most likely be passed by without a second glance. Throughout this book many of the aspects of styling, training and horticultural care have been discussed and the beauty of the tree, itself, depends on these. A bonsai, however, is not simply a beautiful tree — it is a beautiful tree in a pot and the correct choice of container is also responsible for our opinion of a bonsai. Still, this is not where it ends. Up to this point our tree is like the actor who has been trained in techniques and styles of acting, has learned his lines and has prepared himself physically and mentally for his work. Much enjoyment and satisfaction may have been gained up to this point but the final step is the important one of appearing on stage to present his art to the public. Bonsai is like this in many ways, as the proper displaying of our trees puts the final touch on our work and highlights the tree's inherent beauty. One difference with bonsai, though, is that display can be in the intimate surroundings of your own home, with — if you wish — only one viewer — yourself — or it can be at a public exhibition in the company of other trees and viewed by many people.

Before discussing in detail the techniques involved in the displaying of trees, let us briefly look at the history of bonsai display. Before the Taishō Era (1912–1926), bonsai were not often brought indoors and were not displayed in the tokonoma or alcove (the tokonoma is a small recess in the wall of a Japanese room where objects of spiritual significance are displayed). However, in the Taishō Era this trend changed and the tokonoma in formal rooms and tearooms became the main place of bonsai display. This shows a change in attitude toward bonsai but it still shared the space with other items such as scrolls, incense burners, buddhist statues and tea-ceremony implements. Bonsai was now attaining a spiritual significance but was not considered to have a special attraction over and above these other spiritual objects.

As time went on, though, there were many changes in daily life, including changes in architectural styles. Attitudes of people changed and bonsai were being made by many more people than in previous times. Consequently, from about 1935, principles of display altered. When bonsai were displayed now, it was not just for the spiritual significance but for the tree's individual beauty. The tree was now the main feature of the alcove and only a subdued scroll and a subsidiary plant or object was added. These, however, should only be used to emphasize the beauty of the bonsai and should never compete with the main tree in any way. Scrolls with pictures of trees are avoided as they would take away from the effect of the bonsai. Rather, pictures of mountains or rivers are chosen or calligraphy. The latter is probably the best choice as its abstract nature in no way conflicts with the bonsai on display and yet adds another dimension to the scene. In the spiritual sense this arrangement in the tokonoma has a special meaning. The bonsai represents man, the subsidiary tree or rock represents earth and the scroll, heaven. These three points should form an asymmetrical triangle in the display. Sometimes the scroll is used in such a way that it represents the flow of time, for example, if the bonsai represents a particular month due to some feature such as flowers or fruit, a scroll may be chosen that describes the month following.

Another change in ideas concerning display, was that bonsai no longer had to be displayed in the tokonoma. People were displaying them any place where they could be appreciated.

The setting up of a bonsai display — whether it is one tree with a companion or subsidiary plant or rock, or whether it is an exhibition of many trees — requires thought and the application of a few guidelines or principles that will help produce an artistic result. Firstly, consider the intended theme or mood of the scene as this will help to unify and harmonize the elements you choose for display. The theme may be a particular season (e.g. a winter display of a deciduous tree with a viewing stone depicting a snow-capped mountain) or it may be a certain type of landscape (e.g. a mountain setting depicted by a cascade and a rugged viewing stone). Pick out your main tree that typifies this theme (remembering that some trees look better in certain seasons and worse in others) and then make sure that the other elements harmonize, complement and enhance this tree, but do not compete with it. Be careful that all elements of the display harmonize with the chosen theme or mood.

One writer[1], has put forward an interesting idea on bonsai display. He says that there are three different styles or moods: ''shin'', ''gyō'' and ''sō'' and that these correspond to three different styles in calligraphy: the square style, the running style, and the grass style. The first, ''shin'', is characterized by decorum and imparts a grand impression to the viewer. A typical tree of this type would be a formal upright pine tree. The ''gyō'' style is the opposite in the sense that softness and mildness are stressed — often deciduous trees such as maples and zelkovas are suitable for this kind of display. The ''sō'' style is in some ways more casual but very refined in its simplicity. Bunjin or literati style would be a suitable tree design here.

A good display is not one that has all the best trees lined up in a row but one where the effect of the entire design is greater than the individual strengths and weaknesses of the trees involved. In order to achieve this effect, some principles of placement and design need to be considered.

A good way of thinking about a display is to visualize it as a group setting of trees. Most of the guidelines are applicable and the most important ones will be considered here:

The overall design should be of an asymmetrical triangle — the main tree or focal point providing the top-most point or apex of the triangle. Also, this point should be off-centre in the arrangement. As with bonsai, though, the triangle need not be very obvious and there are many variations of shape and proportion available to the display artist. The overall shape of this triangle may be influenced by the shape and size of the space available.

If two trees are chosen for the display that are the same or similar heights, the tree chosen to be the major tree of display, should be placed on a taller stand. Differences between heights of trees chosen for display is fairly important. If the trees are all of similar heights, the effect will be dull and boring, yet if there is too much of a drop in size, the display may become disjointed and the effect of balance and of a believable scale may be lost.

If there are more than two trees, the distances between the bonsai should be varied when the display is viewed from the front and when viewed from the side no bonsai should be in line with another. Furthermore, if there are three or more trees in the display, the triangle formed by any three trees should have an obtuse angle in it.

Also, if possible, choose trees in pots that harmonize but try to avoid having trees that are all planted in containers of the same colour and/or shape.

Just as with group settings, consider space as an important element of design. Don't clutter the arrangement or else the focal point and the theme will be lost.

Another point to consider is the background and the surface on which the trees stand. The background should be plain and of a neutral shade. White, off-white, grey, tan, ochre or beige are neutral tones that do not distract from the tree and help show up the details clearly. Make sure that the finish is mat or semi-mat, rather than glossy. Traditionally, gold is used for the display of pines or apricots on formal occasions. It can also look good as a backing for a red-berried tree. Silver is sometimes used for deciduous or fruiting and flowering varieties. A light blue is another possibility for a background if one wishes to simulate the effect of a tree silhouetted against the sky. Apart from an occasional use of a dull gold background, or perhaps a black background for a tree with light coloured bark, I personally prefer the neutral shades mentioned first. For outdoor displays, bamboo or wood screens provide an attractive background in keeping with the natural beauty of bonsai.

The tables or benches on which the bonsai stand should also be covered if they are not specially designed props for the exhibition. Usually, tatami mats are used for this purpose. Finally, the trees should be viewed at eye-level from a distance about double the height of the tree.

These points, just discussed, are concerned with the actual mechanics of the setting up of a display and the placement of trees. However the individual trees need to be groomed as well in preparation for display.

The soil surface should be cleaned of weeds and debris and the moss, groundcover or soil surface should be tidied or redone if necessary. The pot should be cleaned and an appropriate display stand chosen. Any die-back, dead leaves or needles should also be removed from the top part of the tree as part of the grooming process. By taking a tree away from the rest of the collection and preparing it for show, many faults in style may become noticeable to you. Seeing a tree against a plain background and away from the distraction of other trees, often has this effect. Another good way of having an objective eye as far as your tree is concerned, is to take a photograph of it or view it through a camera viewfinder. This change of dimension usually shows up faults in styling such as an unattractive angle or line or parts of the tree that are out of proportion or scale. If it is seen to be necessary some wiring may be done, though, trees exhibited with wire on the trunks, apart from looking too obvious, indicated very recent styling and should be avoided. However, neat & correct wiring on branches is preferable to poor styling. You can regard this preparation time as the "dress-rehearsal". Some of the procedures involved here and some guidelines that may be of help will be mentioned here:

MOSS, LICHENS, GROUND COVERS AND SOIL SURFACES:

Mosses are, perhaps, the most popular of all ground covers for bonsai, and, indeed, some of the varieties are very beautiful.

The advantages of moss are these:

1. It helps prevent soil erosion. Moss has no roots so it is not this that holds the soil together but the fact that it lets water enter the soil gradually, thus avoiding a heavy rush of water washing away the top soil. In saikei, moss is essential, firstly in order to stop the soil washing away from built-up areas and to prevent cracking of the muck and secondly, to impart a feeling of realism to the setting.

2. Moss helps to cut down on rapid drying out of the soil — a fact that may be helpful in summer — and it also helps to direct water into the soil, thus making watering easier.

3. Moss, by resembling grass in miniature, heightens the illusion that our tree is indeed a miniaturized version of a venerable old giant.

4. The appearance of moss also has a feeling of age and this is imparted to the tree as well.

There are, however, some disadvantages as well with the use of moss. If there is a complete coverage of moss, it is harder to tell when the tree is ready for watering. It may also reduce air circulation and keep the soil too soggy. If you really want the entire soil surface to be covered with moss, remove it when it is becoming too thick, roll it out with a dowel or rolling pin and replant it. It will soon green up and bush out but the covereage won't be so thick and you will probably have enough moss left over to cover the soil surface of another tree. An alternative to this would be to consider a soil surface design partly covered with moss and partly surfaced with sand or pebbles. This type of finish is artistically more suitable for trees that are not so lush or full in foliage cover.

For styles that simulate trees from a rough and rugged environment a lush coverage of green moss would be out of character. For these, just pebbles or sand may be a better choice. Make sure the pebbles are dull rather than glossy and avoid bright colours or tones such as stark white. Another soil covering for trees coming from dryer or rougher areas would be lichen. Lichen is a plant made up of a symbiotic (i.e. mutual benefit) relationship between two different plant groups: fungi and algae. They grow in such close relationship to one another that an entirely "new plant" is created by their union. Like moss, lichen grows on the soil, on stone or on tree trunks, but, usually, in dryer areas than where moss is found. It is a grey-blue colour and imparts the illusion of age to the tree or setting. Sometimes it grows up the trunk a little. This is not harmful to the tree and makes the tree appear very aged. The Chinese describe the lichen on a tree as the grey beard on an old, wise man.

Mosses are just about the most primitive and simply structured plants alive today, yet the variety of types is immense. There are over 14,000 species known in the world but not all are suitable for bonsai use. The most important characteristic of the moss is that it should be short and fine. This type looks more in scale and exposes all of the undulations in the soil surface. Perhaps the favourite variety of moss is the fine, bright green one that has the texture of velvet. One may decide to plant the same variety of moss over the entire soil surface, however, sometimes variety of colour and texture has a pleasing effect as well. Also, choose a moss that has been growing in sunny or semi-shade conditions as this will be a hardier type. Those that grow on soggy, damp soil and in deep shade may not stand the change to sunnier, dryer conditions that are necessary for the healthy growth of bonsai. The types of moss that grow in the bush are usually too long and coarse for bonsai. They may, however, be suitable for some saikei settings or large bonsai.

Generally, groundcovers are not so popular for bonsai use as they rarely look in scale, they have vigorous roots that rob the tree of nourishment and moisture, and they seem to detract from the effect of the bonsai. They may, however, occasionally be used in saikei, if they are low growing and kept in check. Some, for example "Babies Tears", appear to be very compact and low growing in dry, sunny positions but when put in a bonsai pot with regular watering, they often produce rank and vigorous growth. A ground cover that should be particularly avoided is "liverwort". This grows in pots that are overwatered and have poor aeration — and it is often encouraged by bonsai growers because it is extremely low growing, and spreads rapidly, providing a thick, even coverage. It appears like flat, green leaves, overlapping each other over the soil surface and when it covers over the soil it has the effect of repelling water like a "duck's back". Aeration in the soil is also stopped by the creation of an almost plastic-like covering over the soil. The advice here is to remove signs of liverwort as soon as they appear and if there are some persistent spots in "hard to get at areas", these can be eradicated by dabbing the liverwort with some vinegar.

Mosses are usually found when the weather is humid or after a period of rain and they are normally located in shady or semi-shade positions that are reasonably damp. In the southern hemisphere, they are often found on the southern side of houses, rocks, walls etc., as these are the most protected and shaded areas. In the northern hemisphere, it is reversed and they are found on the northern side. In areas where there is no snow, the growing period for most mosses is from autumn through to spring.

When moss is growing, it is a good time to collect it, either for planting straight onto your bonsai or onto seed flats where it can grow and spread until you wish to use it. A knife or a spatula is a good tool for collecting moss. Simply lift up the carpet of moss, in as large a piece as you can, taking a little of the soil with it. It is not a good idea to take a lot of soil, as insects often live under moss and you may transplant these pests into your bonsai soil. Always check the moss thoroughly before replanting and remove any insects that may be there.

If you are planting your moss straight onto your bonsai soil, there are a couple of procedures that may be helpful. Firstly, if you are not so impatient for results, the moss will go further and regrow more easily if you water the moss and then roll it out with a rolling pin or piece of dowel. This forms a thinner covering which is then pressed onto the dampened soil. The procedure just explained is a must if the moss you are using is very thick. If you want attractive results instantaneously though (perhaps you are going to display your tree in a show) plant irregularly shaped pieces directly onto the damp bonsai soil without rolling it out beforehand. Remember to press down firmly around the edges of the moss as these are the parts that will dry out first and begin to curl. By doing this the moss will bulge a little in the centre but these small mounds of moss look more natural and interesting than a flat coverage. If you are planting moss on a steep, built-up section, small hairpins of wire can be used to help attach the moss. These will not show up but will hold the moss in place until it has taken hold on its own.

The reproduction and growth patterns of moss is an interesting subject. Mosses reproduce by spores — not seeds — and when these spores germinate they form algae-like threads called "protonemata" that spread out over the ground. It is from "buds" in these algae threads that the moss plant, as we recognize it, emerges. The moss plant has no roots but anchors itself to the ground with the aid of Rhizoids which are like very minute threads. Because there are no roots, as such, the plant is able to absorb moisture through any part and consequently when humidity is present, dry, seemingly dead moss can quickly spring back to life. Reproductive cells are located along different parts of the stem and after fertilization has taken place, a capsule of spores appears on a specially extended stalk. Some mosses also have the ability to reproduce vegetatively. In this case, broken parts of stems and leaves or special sections called "propagules", detach themselves from the parent to become new moss plants.

Some mosses can be propagated from a dry, powdered state while others cannot. Test some out, if you wish, and if you don't have success, keep excess moss planted in seed flats where it will spread and reproduce itself until you need it. The procedure for making and planting powdered moss is as follows: Firstly, the collected moss should be completely dry, if it isn't, it may be dried artificially. Drying of the moss should be a reasonably fast process otherwise algae or mildew may develop and consequently cause the moss to rot. A position in open shade where there is movement of air is ideal. When it is completely dry, crumble the moss and rub it through a sieve. At this stage, the moss is stored in a container that is open to the air, or in a closed paper bag and in a cool, dry position until it is needed. Generally autumn is the best time for planting moss as the onset of cooler weather spurs on growth. The soil on which the moss is planted should be of a reasonably fine texture and damp. The powdered moss should then be sprinkled evenly over the soil surface. Position is probably one of the most important considerations. If the position is too sunny, the moss will dry out and fail to grow, while, on the other hand, if the soil is kept too moist without much sun, mould and algae may form. A position where there is open shade is ideal and the soil surface should be kept moist but not soggy-wet. Until the moss has started to grow it is best to water by allowing moisture to soak up through the drainage holes, as overhead watering with a sprinkler or hose would disturb the moss too much. An occasional application (say every two to three weeks) of a liquid made up of one part skim milk and seven parts water would also help the moss to develop.

ORNAMENTS AND FIGURINES:

My advice here would be to avoid the use of ornaments and figurines as they tend to stop the workings of the viewer's imagination, and to cheapen the overall appearance of the bonsai or saikei. A beautifully shaped tree or setting has the ability to tell us so many stories, if we will only listen. A winding path, leading into a forest may hint of a hermit's retreat and from the clear, strong lines of the trees, the sound of a solitary flute may be heard. There is a great power in understatement and if you feel your setting needs a figurine, look first to the trees to see if more attention needs to be given to their shaping.

HOW TO CLEAN BONSAI POTS:

Any clean oil such as baby oil or white oil may be used for this purpose. Rub over the pot with some oil on a rag and then buff it back to a semi-mat finish with a clean and dry piece of cloth. This brings out the colour of the pot (particularly unglazed pots), leaves a nice soft finish if you buff it back, and removes any dirty marks made from soil etc.

When preparing trees for display, some bonsai growers spray the foliage with a mixture of white oil and water to give it a slight sheen. One must be very careful here, not to spray the underside of leaves as this would suffocate the tree. My opinion is to avoid this practice. Your trees should not be on display unless they are healthy and if this is the case, they will already have a healthy, natural sheen on the foliage.

STANDS FOR DISPLAY OF BONSAI:

When exhibiting and displaying bonsai, they should be placed on some kind of base or stand. This is for a few different reasons. Firstly, it enhances the appearance of a bonsai in much the same way as a frame on a painting does. It lifts up and calls forth attention to the bonsai — setting it up as a thing to be admired and appreciated.

As far as a display of more than one tree is concerned, the stand's function is to govern the heights of the tree's apexes — to accentuate some and minimize the heights of others. Each tree in a display must have its own individual stand. If you are displaying one main tree and one subsidiary, make sure that the subsidiary is placed on a smaller stand with either very low legs or, preferably, none at all. Usually the main tree is placed on a stand with legs while the subsidiary is placed on a flat stand or a mat. Bonsai are always placed in the centre of the stand. Following are a few guidelines for choice of stands.

Stands should never be the same size or smaller than the pot. A good proportion would be to have the stand longer than the pot by about ⅓ of the pot's length. Also, try to avoid the height of the stand being the same as the depth of the pot.

Colour-wise, it is better not to choose a stand that is exactly the same colour as the pot, however, they should harmonize. Generally, stands are chosen that are fairly dark in colour, e.g. dark brown or black. Some very beautiful stands are made from rosewood — having a colour that is rich in depth of tone but not garish or overpowering in its effect on the viewer. Remember that the stand should not be dominant in the display. The bonsai is still the main feature and the stand should harmonize with it. A stand that is too elaborate will detract from the tree if it is not very good, old and beautiful. For a reasonably good tree a stand neatly made of timber, with simple lines will be the most suitable.

For cascade styles, stands are generally chosen that are round, square or any shape with equal sides, and which have long legs. The tail of the cascade should not touch the table or floor on which the display is set up.

For trees planted in shallow, oval or rectangular pots, a low rectangular stand is usually chosen.

A solid, more elaborate rectangular stand is suitable for deep rectangular pots.

Bamboo mats or slices of wood are used for very shallow containers or saikei settings. This type is also often a good choice for literati style.

Miniature bonsai are mostly displayed in a group on a stand consisting of staggered shelves. When arranging this display, consider the stand as a mountain setting. Conifers would be placed on the top shelves as these varieties usually come from high elevations in nature. Deciduous varieties, grasses and herbs would be placed lower down. Consider the styles as well. The top shelves would be reserved for cascades, windswept and the more rugged styles, while straight trunk, upright, broom and other styles that come from gentler environments would be placed lower down.

There is so much variety in stands suitable for bonsai and prices can range from medium priced ones to the extremely costly antique ones. The Ming Style stand (1368–1644) generally emphasizes the "lines" of the design, while the Ching Style (1644–1911) is more concerned with the carving. The best stands, supposedly, come from Peking, the next best from Shanghai and the third choice is from Kwangtung[2]. If you are a carpenter with an eye for artistic design, quite beautiful stands can be made for little cost.

The Judging of Quality in Bonsai

Chuang Tzu said:— What he must be freed from are his own prejudices,
his own partial view of things, his tendency to JUDGE all else in terms of HIMSELF . . .

The subject of judging bonsai is a controversial one and one where the inherent problems will never really be solved. With the judging of any aritistic effort, objective results are impossible to obtain. If we measure, for example, how far someone has thrown a discus, it is easy to award 1st prize. Likewise, if horticultural perfection is the goal, it is relatively easy to award first prize for, say, the best chrysanthemum. However, when Art is involved, the subjective element is always present. This, by the way, is also its attraction and to cut out this element in the judgement would be to destroy the thing being judged. Is judging necessary at all then? Many arguments for and against are heard.

In America and England, judging of bonsai was introduced early, almost as soon as the bonsai clubs were formed. The opinions were of a mixed quality and the results were not always appreciated. But judging, once introduced, continues in some exhibitions and does not in others. However, so far no one has come up with a reasonably OBJECTIVE measuring "stick" which would give "reasonably impartial judgements". Japan, the country of excellent masterpieces of bonsai apparently does not judge. This may be deduced indirectly from their albums of bonsai which contain almost a 100% of first class trees and a sprinkling of mediocre to bad bonsai[3].

One idea supporting the idea of judging, claims that judging helps to raise the overall standard of quality in our work. However, to counter this opinion, we can say that the guidelines and principles for quality in bonsai are readily available to the bonsai enthusiast and if he is interested enough in raising the quality of his work, he can refer to these and apply the ideas to his trees. It is often true, though, that people often overlook faults in their trees or have not developed their perception to the extent where faults can be pin-pointed. In this sense, a judge or critic may serve the function of improving quality by critically examining and discussing trees on display.

Another opinion claims that the public, in general, is interested in achievement in a competitive sense and that quality will be raised due to the fact that competition provides an incentive for people to improve their trees. Following from this it is believed that comparative measures are educational in the development of the viewer's ability to determine what makes up a quality bonsai. Furthermore, if he doesn't agree with the judge's choice, the questioning process will define his own views more clearly. Comparative measures in the sense of trees being awarded 1st, 2nd and 3rd prizes, however, are not really such good guides as they depend on the other trees on show at that time. Thus, the tree that gets first prize may not be an excellent bonsai if the other trees on show are of poor quality. In this case, a standardized points system would, perhaps, be more indicative. A first prize would still be given, but the score would tell us what the quality was like regardless of the other trees on display.

However, apart from all these arguments for and against the judging of bonsai, it is a fact that we all judge trees, whether they are our own or whether they belong to others. It is a normal human trait to compare things and to perhaps favour one item over another, whether or not we consciously relate this personal judgement to a kind of formal ribbon award system. Usually this judgement that we make is based on a vague, intuitive feeling and when we consider our own trees it is usually a biased opinion as we are either under or over critical.

Thus, if we are going to judge either formally or informally, it would be helpful to have some framework to guide us and while it would be impossible and undesirable to entirely exclude the subjective element, some kind of objective measure is necessary as well.

There are, in fact, two parts to the Art of Bonsai. There is the area of horticultural perfection and the area of artistic quality. Yoshimura in his book "Miniature Trees and Landscapes", states that some people are more proficient in growing bonsai and others in shaping. Seldom is a person adept in both of these aspects to a similar degree. Both are important in the creation of beautiful bonsai, however, the latter provides difficulties for objective measure.

Horticultural perfection, e.g. the health of the tree, freedom from disease, cleanliness of soil surface and good proportion and condition of foliage can easily be determined on a point-score basis. When determining artistic quality, though, some characteristics are measurable, while others are not so easy to define or explain. The characteristics of a well-styled tree as described by the basic guidelines to shaping are able to be analyzed and, to a degree, measured. But any successful work of art is far more than the sum of a measurable checklist of characteristics. One bonsai, for example, may follow all of the so-called rules of styling and may be in perfect horticultural condition and yet not achieve that indescribable quality that a less "perfect" tree might have. How can we measure such a characteristic? Surely not objectively. Judging or criticism of any kind fails if it is based on either the extreme of expressing only vague, intuitive and totally subjective opinions or the other extreme of being bound down by rules and theory. Thus, the fairest and most reasonably objective judging method must include points for analysis of those aspects that may be measured with a certain number of points set aside for the judge's own subjective opinion.

Below is an example of a guideline for judging, devised by my father some years ago. It exemplifies the ideas just discussed and is, I think, one of the most objective measures I have seen while at the same time respecting the fact that we are judging an Art Form.

GUIDELINE FOR JUDGING

JUDGE'S INITIALS:	STYLE:		EXHIBITOR'S No.		
	Not according to schedule .... Accepted for Judging....................				
Date	Remarks:		Max. Marks	Marks given	Sub-Totals
TRUNK Total Marks 15	Shape	Shape according to Style	5.....................		
	Bark	Well developed or not...........	3.....................		
	Marks..........	Wire marks (no points) other ..	2.....................		
	Blemishes......	Unsightly cuts (no points)	2		
	Tapering	Natural or artificial..............	3		
BRANCHES Total Marks 25	Distribution...	Groups of three	5		
	Development .	of main branches..................	2		
	Doubling	Branch directly over another.....	0–1		
	Whorled	Branches on the same level	0–1		
	Bark	of main branches (cuts etc.).......	2		
	Marks..........	Left by wiring	0–1		
	Shape	According to style	4		
	Wiring	Quality and correctness of........	3		
	Reticulation...	Branchlets & sub branchlets......	5		
	Lack of retic ..	Too few branchlets	0–1		
FOLIAGE Total Marks 15	Leaves	Horticultural perfection	4		
	Blemishes......	Insect or dry margins...............	0–4		
	Size	Proportionate to tree..............	4		
	Distribution...	Not hanging below branch	3		
ROOTS Total Marks 10	Visible	Well or badly distributed	1–4		
	Not Visible ...	Soil Condition (recent Pot).......	3		
	Butt.............	Shape of butt at soil level	3		
SOIL Total Marks 5	Well finished .	Clean of weeds etc..................	1		
	Moss	Quality...............................	2		
	Other Cover ..	Appropriate to tree.................	1		
	Figurines	DEDUCT TWO POINTS.......	....		
POT Total Marks 5	Pot.............	Cleanliness	1		
	Size	Overpotted: **Deduct 2 marks**....	....		
	Size	Good proportion to tree..........	2		
	Size	Underpotted (effect good).........	1		
	Placement	Tree well positioned..............	1		
AESTHETIC QUALITY (Subjective Judgement) Maximum Value 25 marks...			25..................		
		GRAND TOTAL...			

INSTRUCTIONS FOR JUDGING.

The Point Score overleaf is intended for the fairest judging possible.

If for instance, 15 points are allocated to trunk, one might quite easily miss the defects such as wire marks, etc.

More detailed subdivision makes judging a little easier.

* * *

Trunk.   Start to allocate marks after scrutinising all trees first. This will give you some idea which tree possesses the best trunk and it will be easier to allocate marks according to quality. If this preliminary scrutiny is omitted one might start allocation of points at too high a level, thus finding difficulty when coming to the best trunk or other main subdivisions.

Branches.   Similar procedure to be applied to branches and the rest of the subdivisions. When coming to marks like 0-1 you simply omit the mark if for instance one branch is placed directly above the other.

Foliage.   Size of leaves is partly subjective, but one can reasonably estimate the mark.

Roots.   When roots are not visible, points are allocated to the immediate portion of the trunk closest to soil level. If the junction is as a telegraph pole, no points should be given. If the butt is evident maximum points allocated to the best of the competitive trees.

Soil.   If "figurines" are placed on soil the marks are withheld and 2 points are deducted. (Exception may be in the case of landscape arrangements). Soil should be neatly finished, regardless of type of finish, e.g. moss etc.

Pot.   Clean pot is imperative. The size is also important in relation to the tree.

This is the first attempt at organising Bonsai Judging in Australia. Faults and improvements can be reached only after actual application of the above Point Score at the meetings or Exhibitions. Suggestions and criticisms are cordially invited in writing.

You will notice that "age" does not come into the judging of a quality bonsai. Below is an article discussing age and its effects on the value of a bonsai[4]:

When we talk about the age of a particular bonsai it can be considered from two points of view. Firstly, the actual age of the tree and secondly, how old it appears to the person looking at it. Also there is another point to consider: Does the age make Bonsai more valuable?

The general public, when looking at bonsai, always asks about its age. Unless you planted the seed yourself and watched the tree growing, its age cannot be determined with accuracy. After 20 to 25 years it is hard to assess. Some trees look old sooner than others and the tree grown from a large diameter cutting will look older than the tree from seed of the same age. If the tree was not grown from seed by the owner the age is hard to determine without cutting the tree down and counting its annual rings. Recently, in America, scientists investigating the age of almost prehistoric trees, developed a special hollow drill which is similar in principle to drills used in mining for sampling underlying strata. Such a drill, on a very small scale can determine the actual age of a bonsai, without destroying it.

The appearance of age, obtained by clever and artistic simulation of the branch and foliage distribution in old trees, can easily add five to ten years to the tree's APPARENT age and especially to non-gardeners. The gardener who knows his trees well will be able to estimate age within reasonable limits. He will consider the appearance of bark, its colour and texture, and he will consider the amount of branch sub-divisions, and within 5–15 years can be reasonably certain in estimating the age.

The third point: Does age make bonsai more valuable? Yes, with reservations. Age adds impressiveness to the bonsai, but if the overall shape of the tree is not aesthetically perfect, the value of age is of small consequence. On the other hand, if the tree is shaped artistically, the age of the tree certainly adds to its value.

If we have a guideline to judging, the next logical question is who is going to be the judge? and, to what extent is the judge different to other people? Firstly, as was mentioned above, we are all judges, both of our own trees and of the trees of others, and indeed, the checklist printed above, may be used by the grower himself, simply to improve the quality of his trees without the intention of preparing a tree specifically for competitive exhibition or display.

However, if it is used by a judge, as such, his opinion should not be regarded in terms of a final judgement on your tree, but rather, as a critical opinion that has been offered for your consideration.

The "man off the street" who walks into a bonsai show and looks at a certain tree, is dealing with exactly the same material as the bonsai judge. Each may have his own individual "aesthetic response" and each is entitled to it. But is this where it should end?

The individual's reaction, I believe, is highly important, particularly in terms of the person who styled the tree in question. Yet the individual's reaction is really only the beginning and by intelligently discussing one's ideas with others, each one will widen his perception while considering the other's viewpoint. Thus, everyone can and should participate in bonsai "judging".

Perception of any kind, however, has degrees. Some can perceive more than others and it is unlikely that any one person will be able to see all there is to see in a particular bonsai. This suggests that the critic or judge, being a person who should have a keen sensitivity and perception of bonsai, can greatly aid bonsai enthusiasts by presenting his insights to them for consideration. And, because no one can ever perceive the TOTAL picture, further discussion and consideration should be encouraged.

One engages in exhibition and judging, I believe, for the sake of what one might see and learn on the way and not for the sake of arriving at a conclusion or final "verdict". Thus, the essential function of criticism and judging should be to educate our perception of quality bonsai and to improve our work. It is true that some individuals already have a sensitivity to bonsai as an art form, and in these cases, criticism can perform the function of expanding and widening an individual's experience even further.

Never forget, though, that you are creating bonsai for your own pleasure and, because we are all different, we will not all like the same styles or the same kinds of trees. Even our own opinions about a particular tree are constantly changing, because bonsai is an art form where the medium is alive and growing — consequently the work is never completed.

Time changes trees as it changes us and as we watch our trees grow and develop with age, the beauty of character that they achieve teaches us humility and draws us ever closer to Nature.

Now that you have read this book on Bonsai, I hope your enthusiasm for the Art has grown and that you will begin to create your own miniature trees and landscapes. You will find that a beautiful bonsai can entice your imagination to wander and roam without any bounds and very soon you will be drawn away and given rest from the troubles and concerns of the everyday world.

As I have tried to show and explain throughout the book, it is not a difficult hobby, yet just as there is no such thing as a finished or completed bonsai, you will find that this is an Art where you will forever be learning new approaches and new techniques as your interest develops. I have included in the text as much information as I could concerning the historical, technical, horticultural and artistic aspects, while attempting to impart some idea of the philosophies involved as well as some of my own personal feelings about bonsai. Hopefully, from this approach, a fairly well-rounded knowledge will have been gained.

What has been included in this book, I have learned from my parents, from reading and from my own observations of trees. Ultimately though, after having read and studied horticultural techniques and the principles for shaping and styling, your own imagination, your love and respect for trees and the tree itself, will be your best guides.

An old, wise man once said that "Perfection just precedes a change and signifies the approaching end of an epoch . . . and, that if one attains perfection in his lifetime — the purpose of living vanishes". We all have so much yet to learn and trees, the silent race with whom we share this world, can teach us so much — if we will only listen . . .

A lonely leaf flutters and falls as the petals of a flower bud open — trembling in the wind . . .

REFERENCES
Chapter Ten
1. Masakuni, Kawasumi, "How to Display Bonsai" in *Bonsai International Magazine*, 18.229.
2. Wu Yee-sun, *Man Lung Garden Artistic Pot Plants*, Hong Kong: Wing Lung Bank Ltd., 1969, p. 66.
3. Koreshoff, V.A., Unpublished Article.
4. Koreshoff, V.A., Unpublished Article.

Index